Honor,
Status,
and Law
in
Modern
Latin
America

HONOR, STATUS, AND LAW IN MODERN LATIN AMERICA

Edited by
Sueann Caulfield,
Sarah C. Chambers,
& Lara Putnam

DUKE UNIVERSITY PRESS   DURHAM & LONDON 2005

© 2005
Duke University Press
All rights reserved
Printed in the United
States of America on
acid-free paper ∞
Typeset in Galliard
by Tseng Information
Systems, Inc.
Library of Congress
Cataloging-in-Publication
Data appear on the last
printed page of this book.

CONTENTS

ACKNOWLEDGMENTS

This volume had its inception in a conference organized by Sueann Caulfield at the University of Michigan in 1998. We are grateful to the institutions within the University of Michigan whose support made that initial conference possible, including the University of Michigan Law School; the Department of History; the Institute for Research on Women and Gender; the Humanities Institute; the International Institute; the Program in Latin American and Caribbean Studies; the Office of the Vice President for Academic and Multicultural Affairs; the Office of the Vice President for Research; the College of Letters, Science, and Arts; and the Rackham School for Graduate Studies. The editors are also grateful to the other institutions that have supported them as the joint project evolved in the following years, including the Department of History of the University of North Carolina, Chapel Hill; the Department of History of the University of Minnesota; the Escuela de Historia, the Centro de Investigaciones Históricas, and the Posgrado en Historia, all of the Universidad de Costa Rica; and the Department of History of the University of Pittsburgh.

Critical insights offered by participants at that first conference helped set the agenda for our subsequent work. For this we are grateful to Katherine Bliss, Jane Burbank, Arlene Díaz, John French, Donna Guy, Michael Heller, Aims McGuinness, Deborah Malamud, Richard Pildes, Karin Rosemblatt, Kristin Ruggiero, Rebecca J. Scott, and Heidi Tinsman as well as the authors whose chapters follow. The contributors to this volume showed flexibility, creativity, and patience as we worked to craft a collective work that would offer more than the sum of its parts.

Incisive comments from two anonymous reviewers for Duke University Press pushed us further toward that goal.

We are also grateful to our families, especially our long-suffering spouses Elizabeth Martins, Gene Ozasky, and Mario Pérez. Seven children—Miriam (10), Alex (10), Gabriel (8), Alonso (6), Easton (4), Joshua (4), and Benicio (1)—have grown up around this project. We might have finished this book more quickly without their arrivals, but it surely would have been poorer without the insights they have given us into the complexities of gender and the consequences of love.

Finally, each of the editors would like to thank the other two. When we began this project we had no idea how far it would take us. Honing this volume together has been a fabulous intellectual challenge and a real pleasure throughout.

Honor,
Status,
and Law
in
Modern
Latin
America

Introduction: Transformations in Honor, Status, and Law over the Long Nineteenth Century

Lara Putnam, Sarah C. Chambers, & Sueann Caulfield

This collection of essays examines relations between the law and concepts of honor, status, and modernity in Latin America from the shaky triumph of political independence and liberal ideologies in the early nineteenth century through the rise of nationalist challenges to liberalism in the 1930s. Colonial Latin Americans had been all but obsessed with honor and status, and the Crown passed many laws to regulate these attributes through the final decades of the eighteenth century. Modernity was the obsession of the professional and political elites who eventually came to power in postindependence republics and enacted legal reforms they hoped would shake off the weight of their colonial heritage. In theory, liberals sought to abolish what they considered the outmoded concept of birthright as the legitimate foundation of authority, replacing it with notions of representative forms of government and judicial equality. In practice, most of them were equally or more concerned with establishing modern, generally capitalist, forms of social control without destroying existing social hierarchies. By connecting these liberal projects with popular understandings of honor, status, law, and modernity, this volume sheds new light on broad changes and continuities in the region as a whole over the course of what historians often call the "long nineteenth century."

Although each essay presented here focuses on a particular historical setting, a remarkably coherent set of themes emerges when the essays are read together: the rise of liberal ideologies, shifting ideas about public and private spheres, the growing intervention of the state in defining and arbitrating individual reputations, and the enduring role of patriarchy—and its corollary, paternalism—in apportioning both honor and legal rights. Although the parameters of patriarchal authority were gradually narrowed, male control over women and women's sexual propriety remained at the core of modern definitions of honor, and dependent status remained a mark of dishonor for men. At the same time, honor played a crucial new role after independence, mediating liberalism's competing commitments to individual equality and social order. It is clear, for instance, that Latin American liberals were successful in establishing acquired rather than ascribed social standing and equality before the law as basic legal tenets by the dawn of the twentieth century. Yet they did not erase social hierarchies based on perceived biological differences, nor did they end social or legal practices of discrimination. Those who were not able to display the markings of honor—for men, economic independence and patriarchal authority; for women, sexual propriety and a dependent position in a patriarchal family—found it exceedingly difficult to defend their rights before the police or the courts. The state also played a newly enhanced role in distributing honor as it sought to check private authority in various forms. Officials stopped short, however, of stripping honorable men of their authority over their wives, children, servants, or other dependents.

The strength of the individual essays is in their rigorous local analysis, informed by rich ethnographic detail. Each essay focuses on specific struggles over status or honor: stubborn efforts by elites to retain a seigniorial worldview as slavery was drawing to an end; the drafting of legal codes that would reconcile a theoretical commitment to equality with the practice of discrimination; court battles over lost virginity or personal insults; conflicts between police and prostitutes, vagrants, or other poor workers over the maintenance of public decorum; debates over how best to represent national culture and defend national honor. Together, these studies show that class struggle was not the only dialectic at play in the formation of "modern" notions of honor and status. In none of the cases did elites or humble citizens form a coherent ideological block. Moreover, as was true in colonial times, individual struggles to restore injured honor or maintain status were most often between equals or almost-equals. Some of the specific ways people defiled or defended honor—especially that of women—also survived the upheavals of the nineteenth century. The significance of equality and citizenship, however, changed dramatically over the course of that century, allowing many common people—especially men—to defend their honor in new ways.

A brief discussion of the rich literature on honor in colonial Latin America will help place these broad changes and continuities into historical perspective. Although recent works have emphasized that the function and meaning of honor varied over time and space, it is nonetheless possible to describe common features for the Portuguese and Spanish colonies as a whole. At a conceptual level, honor tied together the various components of power and hierarchy in colonial society: authority over subordinates, landholding, racial purity, legitimate birth, and the regulation of female sexuality. Officially, honor was an attribute of elite, male heads of extended households, inherited from well-born parents. Elite women held honor so long as they maintained reputations as chaste and retiring daughters and wives; indeed their sexual purity was the key to maintaining familial honor based upon legitimate birth, clean (Christian and European) lineage, and the accumulation of property through advantageous marriage.[1] Although honor was seen as an attribute inherited at birth, it had to be publicly recognized and, therefore, defended throughout one's life.[2] One's public reputation, however, did not necessarily accord with private realities. Someone of illegitimate birth or racially mixed ancestry could enter the ranks of the honorable elite so long as such defects were not openly acknowledged, and women who had given birth in secret could still be considered virgins as long as such children remained anonymous.[3]

Although one's reputation depended heavily upon the recognition of one's peers, honor was also a matter of governance and law.[4] The king was the ultimate font of honor, dispensing titles, military and bureaucratic positions, and other honorifics in exchange for faithful service to the monarchy. Honor was the key to political authority: one had to prove legitimate birth and purity of blood to enter universities, professions, or bureaucratic offices. Further, in a few cases in which colonial elites refused to overlook the defects of someone's birth status, the king could legally repair honor, declaring someone to be legitimate or white.[5] Aspirants did not highlight their acquisition of honor; rather, the king's grace erased ignoble origins and retroactively acknowledged status. Those who officially enjoyed honor could defend their reputations in court. Medieval laws compiled in the Spanish *Siete partidas* and the Portuguese *Ordenações filipinas* stated that criminal dishonor to another could be committed either by word (insults uttered in public) or by deed (physical injuries). Neither code set standard sentences because, reflecting the hierarchical notion of honor, "persons and the acts committed by them are not counted as equal."[6] The paternalistic model of royal governance mirrored the rule of patriarchs within the household. Specific laws established the privileges of the patriarch and the regulation of female sexuality, both of which were directly related to honor.[7] The crime of abducting honest women from their homes in order to force or seduce them into sexual relations (*rapto*) was identified as particularly serious, because in addition to harming the women, "they do great dishonor to the relatives" of the victims.[8] In practice, *rapto* in Latin America often resembled elopement in which the woman agreed to run away with her suitor and consummate their relationship sexually, often in the hopes of pressuring their families to repair her honor by approving of their marriage.[9]

Although neither colonial elites nor (for the most part) officials acknowledged the honor of commoners, recent studies have demonstrated that small farmers, petty retailers, artisans, and even slaves claimed honor on their own terms. Middling and plebeian men asserted that their honest conduct of work, their control of female subordinates, and their strength and courage earned them honorable reputations. Ritualized challenges to honor, which often resulted in real injuries, were part of masculine sociability; although sexual and racial slurs were hurled at both men and women, the epithet "thief" was unique to men, implying that they were not economically independent.[10] Women of the lower classes challenged elite stereotypes of their immorality, taking pride in fidelity to a husband or committed partner, modesty, and a well-ordered household. They went to court to defend their reputations against slander, as well as to request compensation for stolen virginity.[11] It is important to note that both masculine and feminine understandings of honor in popular society emphasized individual conduct and merit rather than the status one acquired at birth.

Elites did not recognize this alternate system of honor, and colonial authorities made little effort to control the behavior of the lower classes. Rather, it was the church that took on the charge of regulating popular morality, convinced that poor people's errant ways had consequences for salvation even if not for honor. Even so, in contrast to their reaction to sins of heresy, ecclesiastical authorities treated lapses in morality with a certain degree of lenience, with the objective of bringing sinners back into the fold rather than excommunicating them.[12]

Responding to Enlightenment currents and the threat of financial ruin in the second half of the eighteenth century, both the Spanish and Portuguese Crowns tried to make the state bureaucracy more efficient and increase economic productivity. In order to encourage productive labor in the artisan trades, a Spanish royal decree in 1783 proclaimed manual crafts "honest and honorable" and declared that their exercise would not prevent an otherwise qualified person from holding municipal office or enjoying the privileges of nobility. A 1794 decree similarly declared that foundlings (*expósitos*) should be assumed to be of legitimate birth and, therefore, honorable.[13] Likewise in Brazil, the Crown enacted policies that aimed to transform those seen as living outside of state control into more productive subjects: it took control over Indians from the Jesuit missionaries; encouraged formal marriage; forced single men into military service or other labors; and bolstered the honor of merchants, permitting them to serve on legislative councils. In general, royal authorities granted higher honors to few who had not been recognized as peers by other elites.[14] Nonetheless, colonial elites in most parts of the empire reacted to the new measures by trying to maintain a greater exclusivity for the ranks of honor. Venezuelan aristocrats, for example, protested what they perceived as an increasing trend toward granting certificates of whiteness to upwardly mobile mulattoes.[15]

Apparently responding to pressures from all over the empire, both the Spanish and Portuguese Crowns passed a series of laws in the late eighteenth century that enhanced parents' power to oppose their children's marriages if bride and groom were deemed "unequal." In addition to appeasing an increasingly insecure aristocracy, these laws were among many measures that curtailed church authority. Previously, church policy had favored "free will" in marriage choices, and clergy were empowered to perform marriages against parents' wishes. In practice, clergy had often done so as a means of salvaging the bride's honor after a couple had eloped but not in cases in which the prospective bride and groom were socially unequal. New laws stipulated that state officials would replace clergy as mediators when parents opposed their child's marriage choice, opening investigations to compare the prospective bride and groom's honor and status.[16] Meanwhile, in some of the larger Spanish American cities Bourbon authorities began efforts to regulate the morals of the lower classes and to police public spaces, an early sign of state intervention that would increase in the modern period.[17] In slaveholding societies, notably Brazil, officials left the responsibility for discipline primarily in the hands of elites.

Bourbon

As Spanish American nations declared independence and established republican forms of government beginning in 1810, the formal abolition of privileges based upon birth and the declaration of juridical equality for all citizens marked, in theory if not always in practice, a dramatic change. Holding a government post could still confer honor, but appointees no longer had to prove their nobility, legitimacy, and racial purity to qualify.[18] In practice patronage and nepotism continued to influence bureaucratic appointments, but by law all government employees were to be judged upon their merits. Brazil followed similar trends, although more ambiguously and on a somewhat different timetable. Independence in 1822 marked the establishment of an empire—headed by the former Portuguese prince—which did not become a republic until 1889. Political continuity helped to keep radical movements in check and to ensure the survival of slavery. As Grinberg shows in this volume, this made it impossible for jurists to draft a coherent civil code based on liberal principles. Yet liberals did manage to influence the 1824 Constitution and 1830 Criminal Code and to pass a number of civil laws that created the principle of juridical equality.

The essays in part 1 examine legal transformations in honor and status as Latin America moved away from more corporatist forms of political and social organization under colonial rule toward republicanism and liberal institutions after independence. In their attempts to build strong and stable states, national elites in the postindependence period continued the trend begun during the Enlightenment, making laws more uniform and increasing the degree to which they regulated the lives of citizens. Wishing to break with the colonial past and cleave instead to contemporary ideals of progress, modernity, and civilization, legislators and jurists looked to European models for constitutions and legal codes. Nonetheless, such models were adapted to local conditions, and the process of codification itself varied according to the specific historical circumstances in each country, as shown by Rossana Barragán and Keila Grinberg in their essays on Bolivia and Brazil respectively.

Although the formal abolition of privileges based upon birth marked a dramatic change, liberal law did not abolish all social hierarchies. In addition to excluding minors and women from full citizenship, for example, most constitutions set minimum income or property requirements and in some cases literacy requirements as well. The objective of such restrictions was to exclude persons dependent upon others, on the grounds that they could not freely express or act upon their political opinions. In Brazil, this objective was made explicit in laws denying political rights to *agregados* (retainers), or those employed by or otherwise dependent on the household of another.[19] The condition of dependency continued to be closely linked to notions of honor and now also formally excluded certain people from the community of individuals endowed with liberal rights.[20]

Each of the essays in part I illuminates some of the ways that different nineteenth-century societies maintained or even heightened distinctions that were directly tied to honor, either in law (such as slave or free status, gender, and age) or in practice (such as race and class). Patriarchy and paternalism wove these different social relationships together, and they form a unifying thread through these essays. Even as national states increasingly intruded into the lives of citizens, laws generally affirmed the authority and privileges of patriarchs at various levels. Civil codes of the nineteenth century did not improve the position of women within the family. Male heads of households continued to exercise control over the property and labor of wives, children, servants, and slaves.[21]

Sarah Chambers's account of the uses of the law in early republican Arequipa, Peru, shows that when hereditary status distinctions were abolished, domestic patriarchy and dependency came to the fore in regulating access to the privileges of citizenship. Chambers demonstrates that for early republican jurists the very definition of the private sphere rested on the presence of a patriarch. This proved advantageous for many plebeian men, who won recognition as honorable citizens by maneuvering the liberal language of patriarchal responsibility. A house where no man ruled, however, was part of the public sphere, open to state intervention, with contradictory results for poor women. The state took on the role of protector for young women vulnerable to rapists outside their homes. In contrast, women under the authority of particular patriarchs were hard-pressed to win judicial intervention, particularly when the aggressors were their own household heads.

Peter Guardino's essay focuses on relationships within indigenous communities, offering the clearest example in this section of the implications of the liberal abolition of status as a birthright. Strikingly, Guardino asserts that the egalitarian elements of the Mexican village "*cargo* system," by which men rose in rank through the performance of successive services to the community, emerged from the conjunction of in-

patriarchy
paternalism

digenous commoners' struggles and liberal law. In the colonial period, descendants of the indigenous nobility had claimed exemptions from serving in lower offices as a birthright. Guardino highlights the abolition of "hereditary distinctions of authority and power" by the Oaxaca state constitution of 1825 as a "momentous change for these villages" because nobles could no longer claim service exemptions. Nonetheless, other bases of hierarchy and status continued under the broad aegis of patriarchal authority. As they had in the colonial period, women provided labor and payments to the community that went unrecognized and were not linked, as they were for men, to citizenship rights. The exclusion of women was consistent with liberal law, but indigenous villagers also continued to favor the generational authority within patriarchy that was contrary to laws of universal male suffrage.

The essay by Rossana Barragán offers the most explicit articulation in this section of the intersection of honor, patriarchy, and the law. Although the legal codes adopted in Bolivia after independence abolished noble privileges and explicit caste distinctions, they continued to distinguish among residents by their reputations. Presumably honor in the new context was earned through merit rather than birth, but the majority indigenous peoples were more likely to find themselves in positions of dependency that deprived them of both honor and civil rights. In liberal theory, dependent laborers and family members lacked the credibility, competence, and judgment to exercise independently the rights of citizenship. Moreover, they were more likely to commit the types of crimes (theft, assault) that resulted in the penalty of infamy, suspension of civil rights, and dishonoring corporal punishments, whereas crimes committed by government and military officials were punished with fines. Further, liberal laws left patriarchal domination intact, sanctioning violence within the domestic sphere, whether directed against wives, children, or servants. Female criminals were punished in distinct ways depending upon their reputations as either honest or dishonest, and female honor was to some degree inheritable as illegitimate birth continued to carry social stigma and affect one's civil status.

The final two essays in this section address the legal status of people of African descent within the Brazilian empire. Both authors note a paradoxical absence of explicit discussions about slavery in two key realms: the lengthy attempts at drafting a civil code, in the essay by Keila Grinberg, and the literature of Machado de Assis, in the essay by Sidney Chalhoub. These case studies spotlight the inability of bureaucrats and jurists to impose categorical divisions on a system in which social and economic power was built around nested dependencies. As we have seen, the possession of honor as status correlates well with hierarchies of race and class, but at its root is the control over dependents. Honor in this sense is reproduced not by generational inheritance but by the daily public display of authority. Chalhoub colorfully evokes this system of paternalism, as depicted with irony by Machado, as well as the attempts by subordinates to subvert the system from within. In his short story "The Canary," Machado parodies the seigniorial posture of the provincial elite, who clung tenaciously to the belief that they ruled the world despite mounting evidence to the contrary. The self-obsessed myopia of the members of this class blinded them to the arts of subterfuge and dissimulation perfected by their dependents. In his literature, Machado explicitly addresses these social symptoms of slavery rather than the system itself. In his position as a high-ranking official in the Agricultural Ministry, however, Machado was among those liberals who worked to curtail seigniorial power and subject masters to the authority of the law, particularly laws that favored freedom for slaves.

Grinberg's essay shows how difficult and lengthy this process proved to be. The crucial dilemma for drafters of a civil code was that slaves occupied in practice an ambivalent status, both the property of their masters and legal subjects who, like other dependents, could rent out their own labor. "Liberty is indivisible," declared one of the first jurists to surrender in the face of the legal contradiction of a uniform civil code in a slave society. Only well after the final demise of slavery in 1888 would jurists produce a comprehensive civil code.

For liberals, slavery was the last bastion of juridical inequality and ascribed status, which had been fundamental components of honor in colonial Latin America. The disintegration of slavery and other formal hereditary privileges certainly had important consequences for the terms under which power could be negotiated, as the essays by Chambers, Guardino, and Chalhoub vividly demonstrate. Yet honor continued to mark social differences in ways that affected both the codification and practice of liberal law. In some cases, such as the Bolivian legal codes and Peruvian courts, distinctions among citizens were explicitly based upon their reputations, as were their resulting rights and punishments. Elsewhere the connection between honor and legal standing was informal yet no less pervasive. In societies that continued to be shaped by relations of paternalism and dependency, members of indigenous communities, jurists, and even novelists implicitly linked honor to both social and legal status.

Thus, across Latin America the nineteenth century saw a shift from late colonial corporatist legal systems to fundamentally liberal ones in which legal rights and obligations inhered in individuals. The new systems created both stark exclusions—such as the categorical exclusion from citizenship of women, minors, and slaves—and many shades of gray: degrees of dependency that might be juridical, economic, or both. Meanwhile, and even more rapidly, the church lost its institutional role as arbiter of the private sphere.

Legislation instituting civil marriage and divorce was one unmistakable manifestation of the shift to state oversight of kinship. Such epochal changes in code were usually long preceded by a shift of the responsibility for policing minor domestic transgressions from church to state. Some scholars have argued that this shift from church to state authority brought a reinforcement of patriarchal privilege and a marked decline in women's relative status within marriage.[22] Ironically, by the time northern Protestant observers arrived to enshrine "Catholic backwardness" as the standard outside explanation of Latin American gender inequality, the onus of arbitrating and enforcing female honor and duty had already shifted from the Catholic Church to the secular state.[23] By the late nineteenth century the primary arena for the mediation of kinship conflict had moved from the priest's quarters and ecclesiastical tribunal to the courthouse and police station.

Conversations in Court: Judicial Practice and Popular Legal Cultures

The essays in part 2, "Popular Uses of the Law," offer a window onto heated debates over sexual virtue, personal reputation, and family obligation in precisely these settings, through the close analysis of a variety of court cases in which the (mostly female) plaintiffs' honor was at stake. Without question, the most enduring aspect of honor from the eighteenth century to the twentieth was its articulation with gender and sexuality. Liberal law uniformly accepted as natural the gender relations of the patriarchal family as well as the notion that family honor depended on women's sexual fidelity and propriety. Because they assumed women were dependents, lawmakers and jurists denied them citizenship rights (such as the right to vote or hold public office) and granted husbands authority over their sexual, professional, and public lives. Finally, civil and criminal law distinguished between "honest" and "dishonest" women in a variety of ways.

The cases covered in these essays make it very clear that poor women's lives rarely conformed to the supposed rules of patriarchal propriety. Laundresses, *chicheras*, and fruit sellers walked through the streets and did business with men and women alike as a matter of course. A large minority of women raised their children in homes with no resident men, while other women handed their children into service. Many mothers never married. Yet sexual morality mattered to these women, for their personal and familial status might depend on it.

Insults and deflowering cases are particularly revealing because, defined by code as private crimes, such suits could only be pursued at the initiative of the injured party. The frequency of such lawsuits shows state intervention in the realm of intimate relations expanding at the initiative of plaintiffs rather than merely at the dictates of legislators. People *used* the judicial system because it provided institutional space for the airing of grievances and held out the possibility of material redress. Through these interactions, laws and legal practice shaped the arguments regular people chose to put forth. At the same time, participants in legal disputes brought ideas of other origin into the courts as well. Some of their claims, like the accounts of the rape victims that Eileen Findlay studies, were roundly ignored by those in charge. Other claims slowly shaped the face of jurisprudence itself, as judges and jurists adapted their aims and means in light of the stories, dilemmas, and challenges plaintiffs so insistently presented.

The essays in this section allow us to observe the concrete social interactions through which popular culture and legal culture influenced each other.[24] Judicial procedures made their way into the repertory of street-corner insults in Port Limón, as when women called on onlookers to testify on their behalf in future lawsuits or boasted to their neighbors about having lawyers on retainer to protect them from prosecution. Meanwhile in Brazil jurists puzzled over the urban pleasures pursued by Rio's "modern girls," struggling to assess just how hard men had to work to awaken young women's sexual desire and whether it was an affront to the moral order for them to do so. Essays by Laura Gotkowitz, Lara Putnam, and Brodwyn Fischer describe the use of the courts in defense of personal reputation in three starkly different settings: highland Bolivia, Rio de Janeiro, and Caribbean Costa Rica. Gotkowitz ties patterns in the language of insult to the evolving social and economic structure of Cochabamba, Bolivia, from 1880 to 1940. She highlights the continuity of racial invective in the face of sociopolitical change. Verbal attacks on "refined *cholas*" or debased *indias* served as rituals of power and marking, which linked racial degradation to sexual transgression. The expanding local court system became a prime forum for airing such affronts. Putnam analyzes insult suits in Port Limón, Costa Rica, hub of a vast banana plantation economy in the first decades of the twentieth century. Here as in Cochabamba insults and slander were among the most common of crimes brought to court. Prostitutes, female barkeeps, and prominent lawyers alike were enthusiastic litigants. Personal standing was defended through legal codes designed to restore honor, even by people who according to those codes should have had little honor to lose in the first place. Fischer explores slander cases in Rio de Janeiro in the 1920s and 1930s. The markers of honor were hotly debated in such cases, as litigants sought to define the credibility and moral worth of witnesses, accusers, and accused. In subsequent decades the porous boundaries of honorable citizenship would harden, as legal and administrative reforms under President Getúlio Vargas selectively incorporated some Brazilians and definitively marginalized others.

These essays show us honor systems in which women rather than men were the primary protagonists and judicial processes in which popular priorities rather than elite projects took center stage. Public insults and their adjudication were part of the conflictive negotiation of social boundaries, not so much between the haves and have-nots as between the have-somes, the had-somes, and the want-mores. In Quechua, Spanish, Jamaican Creole, and Portuguese alike slanderous words accused men of theft or dishonesty and women of sexual transgression. Promiscuous and unnatural acts with proscribed partners were everywhere the nadir of female sexual virtue, but what stood at the opposite end was open to debate within each setting.

The final two essays in part 2 uncover similar links between female honor and sexual propriety while exploring popular and legal understandings of male prerogative, female consent, and sexual violence. Eileen Findlay provides a close reading of lawsuits over elopement and rape in late-nineteenth-century Ponce, Puerto Rico. Findlay uses the metaphor of theater as a framework to explore the making of moral meanings, arguing that dominant scripts could be reworked or subverted by popular courtroom performances.[25] *Rapto* (formally abduction; in practice, usually elopement) was an established social practice in Ponce that included roles for parents, magistrates, and medical doctors. Findlay finds that while plebeian Ponceños had mixed attitudes toward both virginity and marriage, the possibility of *rapto* prosecution enhanced the leverage available to young women as they entered intimate relationships with men. She contrasts this with rape cases, in which judicial authorities rarely supported women's claims. The naturalization of male sexual aggression and female sexual passivity—which was reinforced by the reiterated performance of the *rapto* script—stripped such testimony of persuasive power before the courts.

Sueann Caulfield analyzes deflowering suits brought in Rio de Janeiro during the 1920s, 1930s, and 1940s. Caulfield finds that case participants agreed virginity was basic to female marriageability, even when they disagreed on how essential marriage itself was to honorable living. Like Findlay, Caulfield finds that a large minority of young women used nonmarital sex (and the judicial apparatus designed to recompense it) as a means of escaping from parental authority. As Rio's modern women claimed access to new forms of urban sociability and new pleasures, Brazilian jurists debated and ultimately widened the definition of criminal seduction while narrowing the definition of the "innocent woman" who could qualify as the victim of such a crime.

Together, the essays in part 2, like Chambers's and Barragán's essays in part 1, show that definitions of honor that tied female entitlement and male obligation to women's sexual virtue were not an unshakeable inheritance of the Iberian past, handed down from mother to daughter or judge to judge. It is true that nineteenth-century legal codes, reflecting a particular elite male ideology of female honor, shaped the possibilities of institutional redress and thus molded the arguments of generations of women and men. Yet when jurists came together to rewrite legal codes, their own dealings inside and outside the courtroom—with Arequipa's insistent citizens, with Rio's modern girls—shaped their vision of how law should work in their societies.

Police, Race, Nation

In contrast to the British common law tradition, which had established a stark boundary between investigation and enforcement, on the one hand, and judgment, on the other, the Continental tradition within which Latin American legal systems developed gave judges the role of both investigating crimes and assessing guilt. Meanwhile, minor offenses

—*faltas de policía*—were both pursued and judged by police officials. In the case of law as practiced in the judicial courts, the adversarial system created room for patron-client ties to be called into play by less powerful actors, who could thus ensure some adhesion to the rules. Police courts, in contrast, had far more latitude to mete out justice in an arbitrary way. At times, this benefited those whose formal standing before the law was unenviable—for instance, prostitutes who squared off against usurious landladies. At other times, the ad hoc nature of police justice left the door open for egregious abuse. The essays in part 3 focus on police and their interventions in the lives of poor city dwellers. Each author demonstrates that the policing of public space continuously reasserted the boundaries of honor.[26] They also shed new light on the changing politics of race and nation in the 1930s.

José Amador de Jesús provides a vivid portrait of lower-class leisure and cultural production in early-twentieth-century Ponce, Puerto Rico. As in many other cases presented in this volume, racialized judgments about sexual honor became central to class conflict and political projects here. Amador demonstrates the fluidity of such cultural politics over time. On the one hand, at the turn of the century elites and workers disputed the honorability of lower-class sexual arrangements and entertainments and disagreed on whether legal protections and access to public space might be restricted on the basis of respectability. On the other hand, the 1920s witnessed an expansive reworking of the boundaries of honor, cultural legitimacy, and citizenship, as evidenced by the elite adoption of once-disparaged *plena* music and by the shared opposition to the U.S.-imposed "anti-venereal campaign." Crucially, Amador points out, this expansive reworking occurred in the context of a colonial regime that left "cultural projects for the nation" as the only political projects open to local activism.

Cristiana Schettini Pereira describes prostitutes' contradictory relationship with the police and the courts in turn-of-the-century Rio de Janeiro. Like Amador, Pereira finds that honor was coded onto urban spatial divisions. In the 1890s older buildings in the city center were divided between rooms facing the street, acceptable for commerce or commercial sex, and rooms in the back of the building, appropriate for honest families. The campaign against collective housing destroyed this architectural pattern while recreating the same divisions—between residence and commerce, between decent areas and disreputable ones—on a citywide scale. According to Pereira, jurists selectively criminalized prostitutes without making prostitution itself a crime. At times the arbitrariness of police abuses and alliances undercut judicial attempts to impose a coherent program of social control. Yet overall, ad hoc police interventions served to increase popular vulnerability to judicial pressures and incentives, making extralegal abuse a de facto component of the legal system. Nevertheless, Pereira finds that some prostitutes managed to use the system for their own ends in struggles against abusive lovers or exacting landladies, a finding that echoes arguments about popular use of the courts put forward in previous sections of this volume.

Olívia Gomes da Cunha explores the role of police procedures and forensic science in the symbolic and ritual creation of individual and social identities. The setting is again Rio de Janeiro during the first four decades of the twentieth century. While the other authors in this section analyze how perceptions of dishonor motivated or justified police actions, Gomes da Cunha demonstrates that police were quite aware that their interventions *created* dishonor as well. For some jurists and bureaucrats, she suggests, this was a desired goal, a means to reinforce public order and prevent criminal acts. For other commentators it was a humiliating and unjustified betrayal of personal rights. The stigma of police identification and the creation of a permanent police file helped reshape the gendered contours of public propriety, as "idle" or "scandalous" behavior by women—especially black women—was criminalized through arrests for vagrancy or accusations of prostitution. Yet in the same years some police officials repudiated the use of race as a primary tool in identification, insisting that racial classification was humiliating and unscientific and should be abandoned altogether.

Race and race mixing and their implications for national character and national progress became central to public debate throughout Latin America in the 1920s and 1930s.[27] The salience of racial heritage to imagined political communities seemed self-evident. Whether collective honor would be staked on racial purity or on racial harmony was up for debate.[28] The essays presented here highlight the extent to which debates over race in the 1920s and 1930s drew on claims about lower-class danger and sexual dishonor that were developed a generation before in the context of police expansion and urban reform.[29] This tight connection between perceptions of race and notions of dangerous dishonor had important results in the decades that followed. When scientific racism was increasingly discredited in the North Atlantic world in the 1930s and 1940s, the concept of "decency" was waiting to take its place in naturalizing Latin America's economic inequities and political exclusions. In places like Rio, as depicted by Fischer, whole areas of the city and whole swathes of the population would be declared beyond the pale of honorable citizenship and denied access to the most basic public goods. They would be excluded from the populist pacts that united certain workers, wives, employers, politicians, and officers in pursuit of national progress.[30]

Conclusion: The Making of Modern Honor

These new coalitions, whose inclusions and exclusions were based on employment, deportment, and residence, were a far cry from the colonial system of corporatism. The establishment of republics marked the end of honor as the exclusive birthright of an elite whose status rested openly on class and race. Neither a descendant of the indigenous nobility of Mexico nor a French baroness in Rio could argue explicitly in court that they deserved special privileges. Yet the abolition of explicit noble and racial privileges did not eliminate status hierarchies. Modern ideals of respectability—education, a steady job, and a fixed household headed by a man who supported his wife—were beyond the reach of the great majority but well within the grasp of the small but growing middle class of doctors, lawyers, and public employees: precisely the class from which the professionalizing judiciary was drawn. The occasional person of color or humble background might attain some of these attributes, but the shifting jobs and addresses and domestic disorder imposed by urban poverty placed many beyond the pale of decency in the eyes of state officials.

The gendered nature of honor, by contrast, proved remarkably durable from colony to modern republic: the reputations of men continued to be judged primarily upon their honest conduct in economic and public affairs, while those of women depended upon sexual chastity and performance of their duties in the private sphere. Yet several essays show that some women began to push at the boundaries of what behavior could be considered respectable. Although virginity was apparently valued by people of all social classes, fidelity to one man was equally important to poor women, and a few young women might assert their feelings of desire and agency in sexual relationships. Many women also insisted that their hard work or support of children was evidence of their honesty despite their lack of a husband. Increasingly, "respectable" women participated in popular forms of public leisure—dancing in street festivals or dance halls, watching movies, riding on streetcars, sunning at the beach. Even prostitutes found ways to push the boundaries of respectability, using the courts to defend their wounded honor or civil rights. Finally, in a few cases, men accused of rape or sexual harassment might find their own reputations tied partially to their sexual conduct. Challenges to patriarchy were rarely successful in the courtroom. Yet at the same time, the economic disempowerment of many men, legally endowed by their sex with the right to rule, made their exercise of household authority fragile, unstable, and at times explosive.[31]

The simultaneous expansion of state judicial activism and rise of liberalism posed particular dilemmas for defining the boundaries of public and private. On the one hand, liberal ideology asserted the need for individual discipline in order to maintain public order and promote economic progress. Therefore, laws regulating moral norms were justified. On the other hand, the protection of civil liberties, such as a right to privacy, for those citizens who had proven their respectability, was also central to liberal legal philosophy. It is clear in each of the essays in this collection that honor played an important role in mediating liberalism's competing commitments to public order and individual rights, but the outcome varied according to historical context. Jurists across the region debated when an offense to honor was a private affair that could be prosecuted only at the initiative of the plaintiff and when the offense extended to families or even public decency. Some liberals lamented the permanent damage to the honor of those marked and recorded in police logs before being found guilty of any crime. State officials also had to make decisions about the regulation of public space: Which areas of a city would be set aside for brothels and dance halls and what kind of behavior could be tolerated in parks and plazas? Privacy could also become a badge of honor for those with the means to safeguard it. Dancing to the *plena* at a private party shielded the reputations of middle-class and elite *puertorriqueños* and distanced them from women and men of color who sang and danced in the streets. Likewise, Cariocas claimed differential status based upon where they lived within a burgeoning city.

In part, the idea that enforcing popular morality was necessary for the defense of national honor developed from the state's ever-expanding legal jurisdiction and judicial activism in cases pertaining to personal honor. In the colonial period, officials zealously guarded access to honorific privileges by requiring applicants to royal offices legally to prove their noble and racially pure lineages but more often simply served as arbiters when subjects themselves aired their disputes over status and reputation. Beginning in the eighteenth century, however, and intensifying under the independent republics, judicial officials and police played an active role in setting and enforcing standards of respectability and morality. By the end of the nineteenth century these changing practices were enshrined in new legal codes that defined increasing numbers of crimes as falling within the jurisdiction of the state to prosecute at its own initiative. The number of courts and judicial personnel also steadily increased, reaching far into the rural hinterland by the early twentieth century. Finally, there was increased reliance on technologies that marked individuals' very bodies and documented their reputations, including medical examinations, citizenship documents, anthropometric identification, and fingerprinting.

Undoubtedly many fell victim to this expanded role of the state: indigenous criminal defendants, female plaintiffs in rape cases, and rootless people of color on the urban streets, to name a few. Nevertheless, these essays reveal that humble citizens could maneuver the legal system in a variety of ways and that their notions of honor and status often presented challenges to the hegemony of the courts. As in the colonial period, plaintiffs, even those who would be considered by officials to be below the concerns of honor, continued to file lawsuits for slander. At the start of the nineteenth century, slaves in Brazil, members of indigenous communities in Mexico, and "honest" workingmen in Peru had demanded the fulfillment of their legal rights; by the twentieth century, prostitutes in Rio and Afro-Caribbean immigrants in Central America did so as well. Such plaintiffs achieved some victories owing to their ability to find allies among liberal jurists who believed that the state should both subject traditional seigniorial authority to secular power and safeguard the individual liberties of all citizens.

Such complexities did not belie the dominant ideology: in both the economic and political arenas of the public sphere, liberalism privileged individuals who had attained an independence that depended upon financial means, age, and gender. The legal philosophy of individual rights created spaces for contestation within the courts, but such spaces were relatively more constricted for those who were defined as dependents by their age or gender or as suspect by the color of their skin. Workingmen could at least claim an honor based upon liberal measures of merit, but women who similarly tried to push out the boundaries of respectability had to continue using the longstanding language of sexual virtue and domestic worth.

In Machado's short story, analyzed by Sidney Chalhoub, the canary of its title represents the myopic and self-serving view of Brazil's seigniorial elite. The bird describes the world as only that which he can see at the moment (a junkyard, his cage or the vast blue sky as the narrative unfolds): "Everything else is illusion and lie." We might say the same of the multiple uses of honor, whether invoked on the street, in law codes, or in the courtroom. The degree to which honor reinforced or challenged the evolving status hierarchies in modern Latin America depends upon whose shoulder the canary is perched.

Notes

1 Verena Martínez-Alier, *Marriage, Class, and Colour in Nineteenth-Century Cuba* (Cambridge: Cambridge University Press, 1974); Ramón A. Gutiérrez, "Honor Ideology, Marriage Negotiation, and Class-Gender Domination in New Mexico, 1690–1846," *Latin American Perspectives* 12.1 (1985): 81–104; Patricia Seed, *To Love, Honor, and Obey in Colonial Mexico: Conflicts over Marriage Choice, 1574–1821* (Stanford, CA: Stanford University Press, 1988); Susan Socolow, "Acceptable Partners: Marriage Choice in Colonial Argentina, 1778–1810," in *Sexuality and Marriage in Colonial Latin America*, ed. Asunción Lavrin (Lincoln: University of Nebraska Press, 1989), 209–246; Eni de Mesquita Samara, *As mulheres, o poder e a família, São Paulo, século XIX* (São Paulo: Marco Zero, 1989); Muriel Nazzari, *Disappearance of the Dowry: Women, Families, and Social Change in São Paulo, Brazil, 1600–1900* (Stanford, CA: Stanford University Press, 1991); Leila Mezan Algranti, *Honradas e devotas: Mulheres da colônia* (Rio de Janeiro: José Olympio, 1993); Mary del Priore, *Ao sul do corpo: Condição feminina, maternidades e mentalidades no Brasil colonial* (Rio de Janeiro: José Olympio, 1993), 68–80; Maria Beatriz Nizza da Silva, *História da família no Brasil colonial* (Rio de Janeiro: Nova Fronteira, 1998); Silva, *Sistema de casamento no Brasil colonial* (São Paulo: Queiroz/Edusp, 1984).

2 Steve J. Stern, *The Secret History of Gender: Women, Men, and Power in Late Colonial Mexico* (Chapel Hill: University of North Carolina Press, 1995); Mark A. Burkholder, "Honor and Honors in Colonial Spanish America," in *The Faces of Honor: Sex, Shame, and Violence in Colonial Latin America*, ed. Lyman L. Johnson and Sonya Lipsett-Rivera (Albuquerque: University of New Mexico Press, 1998), 18–44; Geoffrey Spurling, "Honor, Sexuality, and the Colonial Church: The Sins of Dr. González, Cathedral Canon," in Johnson and Lipsett-Rivera, *Faces of Honor*, 45–67; Sarah C. Chambers, *From Subjects to Citizens: Honor, Gender, and Politics in Arequipa, Peru, 1780–1854* (University Park: Pennsylvania State University Press, 1999); Silvia Lara, "The Signs of Color: Women's Dress and Racial Relations in Salvador and Rio de Janeiro, ca. 1750–1815," *Colonial Latin American Review* 6.2 (1997): 205–224; Richard Graham, *Patronage and Politics in Nineteenth-Century Brazil* (Stanford, CA: Stanford University Press, 1990); Silva, *Sistema de casamento*.

3 Muriel Nazzari, "An Urgent Need to Conceal," in Johnson and Lipsett-Rivera, *Faces of Honor*, 103–126; Silva, *História da família*, 208; Ann Twinam, *Public Lives, Private Se-*

crets: Gender, Honor, Sexuality, and Illegitimacy in Colonial Spanish America (Stanford, CA: Stanford University Press, 1999).

4 José Antonio Maravall, *Poder, honor y élites en el siglo XVII* (Madrid: Siglo Veintiuno, 1979); Javier Guillamón Alvarez, *Honor y honra en la España del siglo XVIII* (Madrid: Universidad Complutense, 1981); Richard Boyer, "Women, *la Mala Vida*, and the Politics of Marriage," in Lavrin, *Sexuality and Marriage*, 252–286; Burkholder, "Honor and Honors."

5 Twinam, *Public Lives, Private Secrets*; Nazzari, "Urgent Need to Conceal."

6 *Las siete partidas del rey Don Alfonso el Sabio: Cotejados con varios códices antiguos por la Real Academia de la Historia*, facsimile reprint of 1807 edition (Madrid: Atlas, 1972), 3:587; part 7, title 9 addresses the crime of dishonor; 574–589. See also Jacinto Martín Rodríguez, *El honor y la injuria en el fuero de Vizcaya* (Bilbao: Diputación Provincial de Vizcaya, 1973). Cândido Mendes de Almeida, *Código filipino ou ordenações do Reino de Portugal*, 14th ed. (Rio de Janeiro: Tipografia do Instituto Filomático, 1870), book 5, titles 42 and 84 address verbal and written insults.

7 For a good summary of Spanish family law, see Silvia Marina Arrom, *The Women of Mexico City, 1790–1857* (Stanford, CA: Stanford University Press, 1985), 53–81. Silva summarizes Portuguese family law in *Sistema de casamento*, 70–83, 191–198.

8 *Siete partidas*, part 7, title 20, 3:662. See also Mendes de Almeida, *Código filipino ou ordenações*, book 5, title 18, 1168–1170.

9 Martínez-Alier, *Marriage, Class, and Colour*; Seed, *To Love, Honor, and Obey*; Ramón Gutiérrez, *When Jesus Came, the Corn Mothers Went Away: Marriage, Sexuality, and Power in New Mexico, 1500–1846* (Stanford, CA: Stanford University Press, 1991).

10 Cheryl English Martin, "Popular Speech and Social Order in Northern Mexico, 1650–1830," *Comparative Studies in Society and History* 32.2 (1990): 305–324; Lyman L. Johnson, "Dangerous Words, Provocative Gestures, and Violent Acts: The Disputed Hierarchies of Plebeian Life in Colonial Buenos Aires," and Richard Boyer, "Honor among Plebeians: *Mala Sangre* and Social Reputation," in Johnson and Lipsett-Rivera, *Faces of Honor*, 127–151 and 152–178, Stern, *The Secret History of Gender*; Chambers, *From Subjects to Citizens*.

11 Sonya Lipsett-Rivera, "A Slap in the Face of Honor: Social Transgression and Women in Late-Colonial Mexico," in Johnson and Lipsett-Rivera, *Faces of Honor*, 179–200, Nancy E. Van Deusen, "Determining the Boundaries of Virtue: The Discourse of *Recogimiento* among Women in Seventeenth-Century Lima," *Journal of Family History* 22.4 (1997): 373–389; Arlene J. Díaz, *Female Citizens, Patriarchs, and the Law in Venezuela, 1786–1904* (Lincoln: University of Nebraska Press, 2004); Donald Ramos, "Marriage and Family in Colonial Vila Rica," *Hispanic American Historical Review* 55.2 (1975): 200–225; Priore, *Ao sul do corpo*, 68–80; Silva, *História da família*, 196–197; Sheila de Castro Farias, *A colônia em movimento: Fortuna e família no cotidiano colonial* (Rio de Janeiro: Nova Fronteira, 1998), 67. Even female slaves filed lawsuits to vindicate their sexual honor. See Christine Hünefeldt, *Paying the Price of Freedom: Family and Labor among Lima's Slaves, 1800–1854* (Berkeley: University of California Press, 1994); Sandra Lauderdale Graham, "Honor among Slaves," in Johnson and Lipsett-Rivera, *Faces of Honor*, 201–228; see also María Eugenia Chaves, "Slave Women's Strategies for Freedom and the Late Spanish Colonial State," in *Hidden Histories of Gender and the State in Latin America*, ed. Elizabeth Dore and Maxine Molyneux (Durham, NC: Duke University Press, 2000), 108–126.

12 Asunción Lavrin, "Sexuality in Colonial Mexico: A Church Dilemma," and Kathy Waldron, "The Sinners and the Bishop in Colonial Venezuela: The *Visita* of Bishop Mariano Martí, 1771–1784," both in Lavrin, *Sexuality and Marriage*, 47–95 and 156–177; María Emma Mannarelli, *Pecados públicos: La ilegitimidad en Lima, siglo XVII* (Lima: Flora Tristán, 1993); Guiomar Dueñas Vargas, *Los hijos del pecado: Ilegitimidad y vida familiar en la Santafé de Bogotá colonial* (Bogota: Editorial Universidad Nacional, 1997); Chambers, *From Subjects to Citizens*, 125–160. Ronaldo Vainfas demonstrates the relative leniency of the Inquisition in colonial Brazil in *Trópico dos pecados: Moral, sexualidade e Inquisição no Brasil* (Rio de Janeiro: Campus, 1989), 285–339. See also Laura de Mello e Souza, *O diabo e a terra de Santa Cruz* (São Paulo: Companhia das Letras, 1987); Luciano Raposo de Almeida Figueiredo, *Barrocas famílias: Vida familiar em Minas Gerais no século XVIII* (São Paulo: Hucitec, 1997); Fernando Torres Londoño, *El concubinato y la iglesia en el Brasil colonial* (São Paulo: CEDHAL, 1988); Eduardo Hoornaert, "A cristandade durante a primeira época colonial," in *História da igreja no Brasil*, ed. Eduardo Hoornaert et. al., vol. 2 (Petropolis: Vozes, 1979), 248–249. Elizabeth Anne Kuznesof provides excellent summaries of the conclusions of the historical literature on church vigilance of colonial morality in "Sexual Politics, Race, and Bastard-Bearing in Nineteenth-Century Brazil: A Question of Culture or Power?" *Journal of Family History* 16.3 (1991): 241–260, esp. 242, 244–245, and in "Sexuality, Gender and the Family in Colonial Brazil," *Luso-Brazilian Review* 30.1 (1993): 119–132, esp. 121–122.

13 Guillamón Alvarez, *Honor y honra*, 21, 169; Burkholder, "Honor and Honors," 41.

14 Twinam, *Public Lives, Private Secrets*.

15 See the 1795 petition from the City Council of Caracas to the king, translated and reprinted in *Latin American Revolutions, 1080–1826: Old and New World Origins*, ed. John Lynch (Norman: University of Oklahoma Press, 1994), 181–187; Rodulfo Cortés Santos, *El régimen de las "Gracias al Sacar" en Venezuela durante el período hispánico*, 2 vols. (Caracas: Academia Nacional de la Historia, 1978); Luis Pellicer, *La vivencia del honor en la Provincia de Venezuela, 1774–1809: Estudios de casos* (Caracas: Fundación Polar, 1996). For similar elite concerns in late colonial Argentina, see Eduardo Ricardo Saguier, "El combate contra la 'limpieza de sangre' en los orígenes de la emancipación argentina: El uso del estigma de la bastardía y del origen racial como mecanismos de defensa de las elites coloniales," *Revista de historia de América* 110 (1990): 155–198.

16 Seed, *To Love, Honor, and Obey*; Gutiérrez, *When Jesus Came*; Twinam, *Public Lives, Private Secrets*; Nazzari, *Disappearance of the Dowry*; Socolow, "Acceptable Partners."

17 Juan Pedro Viqueira Albán, *Propriety and Permissiveness in Bourbon Mexico* (Wilmington, DE: Scholarly Resources, 1999); Pamela Voekel, "Peeing on the Palace: Bodily Resistance to Bourbon Reforms in Mexico City," *Journal of Historical Sociology* 5.2 (1992): 183–208; Bianca Premo, "Pena y protección: Delincuencia juvenil y minoridad legal en Lima, siglo XVIII," *Revista histórica* 24.1 (2000): 85–120. The Church also bolstered its efforts at social and moral control in this period, particularly in Brazil, where royal authority was always stretched thin. See Mello e Souza, *O diabo e a terra de Santa Cruz*; Nazzari, *Disappearance of the Dowry*; del Priore, *Ao sul do corpo*; Figueiredo, *Barrocas famílias*; Maria Odila Silva Dias, *Power and Everyday Life: The Lives of Working Women in Nineteenth-Century Brazil* (Cambridge, UK: Polity, 1995).

18 Victor Uribe Uran found that government office still conferred prestige in Colombia until the 1840s, when bureaucrats were increasingly viewed as parasitical. See Uribe

Uran, *Honorable Lives: Lawyers, Family, and Politics in Colombia, 1780–1850* (Pittsburgh, PA: University of Pittsburgh Press, 2000). As state bureaucracies expanded throughout the modern period and civil servants made up a considerable proportion of the middle classes, they tried to project an honorable status that did not always match their economic means. See David S. Parker, *The Idea of the Middle Class: White-Collar Workers and Peruvian Society, 1900–1950* (University Park: Pennsylvania State University Press, 1998).

19 See Graham, *Patronage and Politics*.

20 Such exclusions were not unique to Latin American liberalism. Indeed, Uday Mehta has argued that they were embedded in the foundational philosophy of liberalism itself. Mehta, "Liberal Strategies of Exclusion," in *Tensions of Empire: Colonial Cultures in a Bourgeois World*, ed. Frederick Cooper and Ann Laura Stoler (Berkeley: University of California Press, 1997), 59–86.

21 See Elizabeth Dore, "One Step Forward, Two Steps Back: Gender and the State in the Long Nineteenth Century," and Maxine Molyneux, "Twentieth-Century State Formations in Latin America," both in Dore and Molyneux, *Hidden Histories*, 3–32; 33–81.

22 Dore, "One Step Forward," 21–23; Nazzari, *Disappearance of the Dowry*.

23 For a careful tracking of the secularization of kinship mediation and the nuances of that process, see Christine Hünefeldt, *Liberalism in the Bedroom: Quarreling Spouses in Nineteenth-Century Lima* (University Park: Pennsylvania State University Press, 2000); see also Eugenia Rodríguez, "Civilizing Domestic Life in the Central Valley of Costa Rica, 1750–1850," in Dore and Molyneux, *Hidden Histories*, 85–107; Arlene J. Díaz, "Women, Order, and Progress in Guzmán Blanco's Venezuela, 1870–1888," in *Crime and Punishment in Latin America: Law and Society since Late Colonial Times*, ed. Ricardo D. Salvatore, Carlos Aguirre, and Gilbert M. Joseph (Durham, NC: Duke University Press, 2001), 56–82.

24 See Carlos Aguirre and Ricardo D. Salvatore, introduction to Salvatore, Aguirre, and Joseph, *Crime and Punishment in Latin America*, 20. The valuable case studies in that volume can be fruitfully compared with the findings presented here: see for instance Juan Manuel Palacio, "Judges, Lawyers, and Farmers: Uses of Justice and the Circulation of Law in Rural Buenos Aires, 1900–1940," in Salvatore, Aguirre, and Joseph, *Crime and Punishment in Latin America*, 83–112.

25 For similar interpretive currents within legal anthropology, see Susan F. Hirsch and Mindie Lazarus-Black, "Performance and Paradox: Exploring Law's Role in Hegemony and Resistance," in *Contested States: Law, Hegemony, and Resistance*, ed. Mindie Lazarus-Black and Susan F. Hirsch (New York: Routledge, 1994), 1–31.

26 Across Latin America, programs targeting prostitutes spearheaded states' assertion of the right to enforce the spatial segregation of dishonor. See Donna J. Guy, *Sex and Danger in Buenos Aires: Prostitution, Family, and Nation in Argentina* (Lincoln: University of Nebraska Press, 1991); Juan José Marín, "Entre la disciplina y la respetabilidad: La prostitución en la ciudad de San José: 1939–1949" (Licenciatura thesis, Posgrado de Historia, Universidad de Costa Rica, 1993); Sueann Caulfield, "The Birth of Mangue: Race, Nation, and the Politics of Prostitution in Rio de Janeiro, 1850–1942," in *Sex and Sexuality in Latin America*, ed. Daniel Balderston and Donna J. Guy (New York: New York University Press, 1997), 86–100; Patricia Alvarenga, "Prostitu-

ción y control social en El Salvador, 1900–1930," in *Fin de siglo XIX: Identidad nacional en México y Centroamérica*, ed. Iván Molina and Francisco Enríquez (Alajuela, Costa Rica: Museo Histórico Cultural Juan Santamaría, 2000), 115–141; Katherine Elaine Bliss, *Compromised Positions: Prostitution, Public Health, and Gender Politics in Revolutionary Mexico City* (University Park: Pennsylvania State University Press, 2002); Cristina Garza-Rivera, "The Criminalization of the Syphilitic Body: Prostitutes, Health Crimes, and Society in Mexico City, 1867–1930," in Salvatore, Aguirre, and Joseph, *Crime and Punishment in Latin America*, 147–180.

27   Richard Graham, ed., *The Idea of Race in Latin America, 1870–1940* (Austin, University of Texas Press, 1990); Nancy Leys Stepan, *"The Hour of Eugenics": Race, Gender, and Nation in Latin America* (Ithaca, NY: Cornell University Press, 1991); Nancy P. Appelbaum, Anne S. Macpherson, and Karin Alejandra Rosemblatt, eds., *Race and Nation in Modern Latin America* (Chapel Hill: University of North Carolina Press, 2003).

28   Among the case studies that best capture the contradictory roles of racial thinking within national visions in this era are Steven Palmer, "Racismo intelectual en Costa Rica y Guatemala, 1870–1920," *Mesoamérica* 31 (1996): 99–121; Darío Euraque, "The Banana Enclave, Nationalism, and Mestizaje in Honduras, 1910s–1930s," in *Identity and Struggle at the Margins of the Nation-State: The Laboring Peoples of Central America and the Hispanic Caribbean*, ed. Aviva Chomsky and Aldo Lauria-Santiago (Durham, NC: Duke University Press, 1998), 151–168; Robin Moore, *Nationalizing Blackness: Afrocubanismo and Artistic Revolution in Havana, 1920–1940* (Pittsburgh, PA: University of Pittsburgh Press, 1997); Alejandro de la Fuente, *A Nation for All: Race, Inequality, and Politics in Twentieth-Century Cuba* (Chapel Hill: University of North Carolina Press, 2001); Alejandra M. Bronfman, "Reforming Race in Cuba, 1902–1940" (PhD diss., Princeton University, 2001); Michel-Rolph Trouillot, *Haiti, State against Nation: Origins and Legacy of Duvalierism* (New York: Monthly Review Press, 1990); Jeffrey Lesser, *Negotiating National Identity: Immigrants, Minorities, and the Struggle for Ethnicity in Brazil* (Durham, NC: Duke University Press, 1999).

29   Eileen J. Suárez Findlay, *Imposing Decency: The Politics of Sexuality and Race in Puerto Rico, 1870–1920* (Durham, NC: Duke University Press, 1999); William E. French, "Prostitutes and Guardian Angels: Women, Work, and the Family in Porfirian Mexico," *Hispanic American Historical Review* 72.4 (1992): 529–553; Sueann Caulfield, *In Defense of Honor: Morality, Modernity, and Nation in Early-Twentieth-Century Brazil* (Durham, NC: Duke University Press, 2000), chap. 2. See also the burgeoning literature on criminalization and policing in late-nineteenth- and early-twentieth-century Latin America: Carlos A. Aguirre and Robert Buffington, eds., *Reconstructing Criminality in Latin America* (Wilmington, Del.: Scholarly Resources, 2000); Robert Buffington, *Criminal and Citizen in Modern Mexico* (Lincoln: University of Nebraska Press, 2000); Pablo Piccato, *City of Suspects: Crime in Mexico City, 1900–1931* (Durham, NC: Duke University Press, 2001); Marcos Luiz Bretas, *Ordem na cidade: O exercício cotidiano da autoridade policial no Rio de Janeiro, 1907–1930* (Rio de Janeiro: Rocco, 1997).

30   See, for instance, Karin Alejandra Rosemblatt, *Gendered Compromises: Political Cultures and the State in Chile, 1920–1950* (Chapel Hill: University of North Carolina Press, 2000). On the redefinition of the boundaries of honor in this later period, with special attention to the role that employers and local elites attempted to play in the process, see Thomas Miller Klubock, *Contested Communities: Class, Gender, and Politics in Chile's*

El Teniente Copper Mine, 1904–1951 (Durham, NC: Duke University Press, 1998); Ann Farnsworth-Alvear, *Dulcinea in the Factory: Myths, Morals, Men, and Women in Colombia's Industrial Experiment, 1905–1960* (Durham, NC: Duke University Press, 2000); and Victoria González, "'El diablo se la llevó': Política, sexualidad femenina y trabajo en Nicaragua (1855–1979)," in *Un siglo de luchas femeninas en América Latina*, ed. Eugenia Rodríguez (San José: Editorial de la Universidad de Costa Rica, 2002), 53–70.

31 See, for instance, arguments in Heidi Tinsman, *Partners in Conflict: The Politics of Gender, Sexuality, and Labor in the Chilean Agrarian Reform, 1950–1973* (Durham, NC: Duke University Press, 2002); Lara Putnam, *The Company They Kept: Migrants and the Politics of Gender in Caribbean Costa Rica, 1870–1960* (Chapel Hill: University of North Carolina Press, 2002). Recent work on masculinity, sexuality, and honor in twentieth-century Latin America includes Roger Lancaster, *Life Is Hard: Machismo, Danger, and the Intimacy of Power in Nicaragua* (Berkeley: University of California Press, 1992); Peter Wade, "Man the Hunter: Gender and Violence in Music and Drinking Contexts in Colombia," in *Sex and Violence: Issues in Representation and Experience*, ed. Penelope Harvey and Peter Gow (London: Routledge, 1994), 115–137; Rocío Tábora, *Masculinidad y violencia en la cultura política hondureña* (Tegucigalpa: Centro de Documentación de Honduras, 1995); Marit Melhuus and Kristi Anne Stølen, eds., *Machos, Mistresses, Madonnas: Contesting the Power of Latin American Gender Imagery* (New York: Verso, 1996); Matthew C. Gutman, *The Meanings of Macho: Being a Man in Mexico City* (Berkeley: University of California Press, 1996); Klubock, *Contested Communities*; Lauren Derby, "The Dictator's Seduction: Gender and State Spectacle during the Trujillo Regime," in *Latin American Popular Culture: An Introduction*, ed. William H. Beezley and Linda A. Curcio-Nagy (Wilmington, DE: Scholarly Resources, 2000), 213–239; Sandra Gayol, *Sociabilidad en Buenos Aires: Hombres, honor y cafés, 1862–1910* (Buenos Aires: Signo, 2000); and Peter M. Beattie, *The Tribute of Blood: Army, Honor, Race, and Nation in Brazil, 1864–1945* (Durham, NC: Duke University Press, 2001). On the complex ways that performances of power between men are connected to the power hierarchies that surround them, see José E. Limón, "*Carne, Carnales*, and the Carnivalesque: Bakhtinian *Batos*, Disorder, and Narrative Discourses," in *Situated Lives: Gender and Culture in Everyday Life*, ed. Louise Lamphere, Helena Ragoné, and Patricia Zavella (New York: Routledge, 1997), 62–82.

I

LIBERALISM, STATUS, AND CITIZENSHIP

Private crimes, public order: honor, gender,
and the law in early republican Peru
Sarah C. Chambers

During the republican revolutions of the eighteenth and nineteenth centuries, the political concept of separate spheres became a central concern
of philosophers and statesmen.[1] The transition from a monarchy to a
republic in Peru similarly heightened the division between public and
private, at least in political theory. In practice, however, throughout the
nineteenth century, the state extended its regulatory reach into citizens'
everyday lives. Lawyers and judges in early republican Arequipa hotly
debated what constituted a "public" crime, and hence one that could be
prosecuted directly by the state. This essay will analyze how the negotiation of that legal boundary between public and private revealed understandings of honor and gender.
   The most basic distinction between public and private crimes in Peruvian legal codes was that the former affected the state or society, while
the latter harmed only individuals.[2] All civil cases were considered private. Nevertheless, most jurists recognized that drawing a clear line in
penal law was made more difficult by the fact that crimes against persons could cause enough fear among others to disturb public order.[3] In
general, republican prosecutors (*fiscales*) and judges in Arequipa pursued
significantly more cases on their own initiative (*de oficio*) than had been
the case in the late colonial period.[4] In particular theft and serious physical injuries, which had previously been prosecuted only at the initiative
of the plaintiff (*de parte*), came to be considered public crimes. Crimes
related to honor (such as slander or rape), however, continued to be tried
only at the initiative of the persons affected (the victim or family members), who had not only to file a complaint but follow through with the
calling of witnesses and the formal accusation. One of the justifications

most frequently offered for such a requirement was that plaintiffs should be able to decide whether the crime itself or the bringing of it to the court's attention constituted greater harm to their honor. A related concern was to protect patriarchal authority over the household. As Francisco García Calderón averred, even though there could be circumstances in which rape or seduction would disturb society enough to make it a public crime, to give prosecutors the power to file charges would "disturb the peace and secrecy that should exist in the domestic sphere."[5] For the same reason, physical injuries resulting from the "punishment" of dependents (servants, wives, and children) were usually considered "private" crimes, and the rights of the perpetrators carried more weight than the protections due to the victims, who were not, after all, citizens.

Even as republican judicial officials tried to balance the demands of public and domestic order, they continued a trend, begun with the Bourbon reforms, of increasingly claiming jurisdiction in those cases pertaining to marriage, family, and sexual honor, in which the affected parties did press charges. Formerly, such cases had fallen primarily within the jurisdiction of the church. Almost all the reported cases of domestic violence in Arequipa from the final decades of the colonial period, for example, can be found in the ecclesiastical archives. After independence, such complaints from wives decreased dramatically, and there is some evidence that church officials referred women instead to the secular authorities. Similarly, there are only three extant trials for *rapto* (the abduction and deflowering of a young woman) in the secular courts between 1784 and 1824; of these, two were for the kidnapping of a slave and a domestic servant; in the third, the mother was initially advised not to bring charges, and the case ended with no result. By contrast, nine *rapto* trials remain for the period between 1825 and 1854. More significantly, only after independence were there any trials for *estupro* (technically defined as the deflowering of virgins, but applied to rape in general), and most of these eighteen cases were pursued by the public prosecutor rather than the plaintiffs.

Evidence for this essay is drawn from the 184 extant criminal cases heard by the royal intendant (governor) between 1784 and 1824, and the 1,205 cases tried by either republican judges of first instance or the regional superior court between 1825 and 1854.[6] The following brief comments on Arequipa provide a context for the analysis of those cases. With an urban population of about twenty-four thousand in 1792, the city was an important agricultural and commercial hub in southern Peru, and the region became a key player in the nation's early republican politics and civil warfare. The men and women who appeared in criminal court ranged from agricultural laborers to landowners and merchants, with the largest single group drawn from the ranks of artisans. Surprisingly, given the racial prejudices of the period, local practice ignored Spanish regulations that the ethnicity of all parties be recorded in legal documents. According to official censuses, the city's population was predominantly white, with minorities of indigenous, African, and mixed descent; given the ambiguities of identity, however, many mestizos and mulattoes were included in the "Spanish" population. In particular, the label *mestizo* was seldom used in local documents, and in those rare instances it referred to those who exhibited indigenous traits of language or dress.[7]

During the transition from colonial to republican rule in Arequipa, growing concerns about crime and disorder spurred the development of a police force and a more activist criminal justice system. At the same time, however, political leaders and judges espoused liberal ideas that arrived with independence and were enshrined in the constitutions. Members of the popular classes who listened to speeches or read newspapers were not blind to such contradictions. With the help of lawyers, they seized upon these new principles to protest arrests and charges of criminality and to insist upon their right to be treated as citizens. In the process, they linked rights to their understanding of honor, shifting the emphasis away from status toward the concept of virtue. Although judges frequently recognized such claims, they simultaneously tried to reestablish social order by balancing rights with responsibilities. In addition to the differing definitions of respectability based upon class, honor was of course also highly affected by gender. Men were more successful at claiming protections of their civil liberties in return for fulfilling their duties within the public sphere. Women, in contrast, were expected to demonstrate their virtue within the private sphere, according to standards that were difficult to meet.

Personal independence had long enhanced male honor; now it also determined citizenship status. According to the constitutions in effect during this period (namely, those of 1823, 1826, 1828, 1834, and 1839), only men who were either married or of majority age (which varied between 21 and 25) and who either owned property, exercised an independent profession, or paid taxes were granted the privileges of citizenship.[8] Such requirements excluded many poor and nonwhite men and all women. Despite their dependent legal status, many women were self-

supporting; as much as 44 percent of households in one neighborhood census had female heads, and of women who dictated wills between 1780 and 1850, 25 percent were widowed, and 33 percent had never married.[9] Strict norms of morality also affected citizenship. Notorious gamblers, drunkards, "and others who offend public morals with their scandalous life," were subject to suspension of their citizenship. Such a penalty was also imposed on those undergoing criminal prosecution or "for not having employment, an occupation, or known way of life."[10] Finally, in order to enjoy the rights and privileges of citizenship, men had to serve in the military when called.[11]

Presumably, such restrictions were strictly applied in determining suffrage. In judicial proceedings, however, there seems to have been more latitude in determining who was independent and respectable, and thus enjoyed civil rights. Before the formulation of new republican codes, judges had to base their decisions upon the existing laws (when these did not contradict constitutional articles), but Spanish law provided for discretion in determining standards of evidence, the severity of the crime, and appropriate punishment.[12] Ultimately, I contend, the negotiation of rights using the language of honor, which occurred in the courts after independence in 1824, influenced the formulation of a new penal code in 1862. Its drafters, several of whom had practiced law in Arequipa, defined private and public crimes in accordance with gendered notions of honor and the sanctity of patriarchal authority.

Honorable Citizens in the Public Sphere

Liberal legal theory notwithstanding, honor had always been as much a public and political concept as a private trait. During the colonial period, the code of honor had emphasized status derived from family lineage, property, racial purity, and, for women, sexual reputation. Colonial honor, moreover, was based upon the monarchical system: the king, as the head of state, was not only the most honorable person within the hierarchical ranking but also the source of honor for all others. With Peruvian independence from Spain, the king's role as guardian of honor and its attendant ceremonies passed to the constitutions; as processions wound their way through the city, criers stopped in the main plazas to read these charters.[13] The crowd heard that all Peruvians were equal before the law and that hereditary privileges and offices had been abolished.[14] While lawyers would help people claim their new rights, it is no coincidence that those most often invoked—such as the right to one's reputation or patriarchal control of the household—coincided with the long-cherished value of honor.

The early constitutions explicitly recognized every citizen's right to his honor, guaranteeing "the good opinion, or reputation of the individual, as long as he is not declared a delinquent according to the laws."[15] Don José María Portugal cited this article directly in a lawsuit for libel, but more commonly it was used by defendants and their lawyers to win release from jail, since incarceration was considered to be dishonoring.[16] For example, cigar maker Victoriano Concha, arrested in 1829 on the suspicion of being a thief, was released when even the prosecutor asserted that the evidence against him was insufficient "to have persecuted a man damaging him in his person and honor."[17] Even more defamatory than imprisonment was the punishment of lashes; in the colonial period slaves and Indians had been whipped but "Spanish" people protested vociferously if subjected to the same treatment.[18] After independence, local judicial officials zealously enforced an 1821 decree protecting all free people from the lash as a fundamental republican principle. Prosecutor José Gregorio Paz Soldan argued in one case that "with the lashes given to a citizen all the principles were trampled, the entire public was insulted in [the body of] one man, the Government, the Constitution and the dignity of the Republic were violated."[19] Cases of honor, even if they targeted an individual, could have public consequences.

In addition to protecting a person's reputation, the early constitutions guaranteed that "the house of every Peruvian is an inviolable sanctuary."[20] To be insulted in one's own home had always been considered a particularly serious affront; the violation of a patriarch's house was one of the factors that made the abduction of daughters (*rapto*) such a serious affront. Under the republic, *arequipeños* strongly defended their right to privacy, seizing upon this constitutional guarantee to charge both officials and civilians with illegal breaking and entering.[21] In 1832 a group of youths pretending to be the police broke into the home of a shoemaker. The judge cut the case short, but the prosecutor protested that the crime was serious: "whatever the condition and wretchedness of the shoemaker Lázaro may be, and the poverty of his shack or house, it is a haven which should be considered according to the law as safe as that of the first magistrate of the Republic."[22]

The recognition of common men such as artisans and other manual laborers not only as honorable but as citizens deserving legal protections was a dramatic change from the colonial period. Nevertheless, officials were selective in identifying who qualified. When plebeian men claimed honor based upon their conduct, the authorities raised the standards of virtue. Even for humble men, civic virtue could be demonstrated on the battlefield, and soldiers were rewarded with the right to wear special insignias, inscription in official books of "meritorious citizens," and membership in Legions of Honor.[23] When farmer Nicanor Chávez was charged with insubordination for refusing to donate a mule to the army, he claimed an exemption based upon his military services. In defense of his claims, he presented a piece of paper on which the prefect had written: "The Governor of Tio shall treat with the highest consideration the citizen Nicanor Chávez, as he is a most honorable patriot."[24] Even as working men volunteered to defend the city, they avoided and protested forced impressment, and judicial officials often came to their defense against abuses by both real and imposter military officials.[25]

Military service was linked to honor and citizenship, but the region's landowners were increasingly concerned that conscription contributed to a labor shortage. Hard work, therefore, was promoted as another way that common citizens could contribute to the public good. "The citizen with a hoe in his hand is as useful as he who grasps a sword to defend the Fatherland," declared politician Miguel Abril in support of draft exemptions for workers.[26] Artisans and laborers referred to their dedication to work, therefore, to defend themselves against criminal charges. In 1831 José María Madaleno and José Torres, men of color who had migrated to the city from the coast, were picked up by a patrol as "suspicious" characters. They were able to present character witnesses to support their claim to have "always maintained themselves with honor and by means of their labor."[27] Despite their history of temporary and unskilled labor, the judge found them to be "honest men behaving themselves with honor and without any stain on their reputations." Indignant that they had suffered because of an unjust suspicion, he absolved them, "restoring them to their former good reputations and fame."[28]

Judges could be indignant when working people were arrested on mere suspicion, but the opposite was also true. In 1831 Victoriano Concha, who previously had been cleared on charges of suspicious behavior, was arrested a second time for complicity in a theft. As in the earlier case, the prosecutor admitted that there was little evidence against him but this time argued that his unemployment was proof enough. "A man without an occupation nor a known way of life," he asserted, "will most likely transgress in all matters."[29] When Enrique Nuñes complained that he had been illegally imprisoned, Judge Pascual Francisco Suero similarly retorted that he was a "vagrant, ne'er-do-well without an occupation, and therefore, not a citizen."[30] Poor men faced a more intrusive and punitive state after independence, but those who could present sufficient evidence of military service or employment could defend their civil liberties, including the rights to honor and privacy.

Dependents in the Private Sphere

While the rights of plebeian men were contingent upon their conduct, there were classes of people who were excluded despite their hard work. By requiring citizens at least to exercise an independent profession—and in some cases to own property or pay taxes—the constitutions excluded those who were dependent upon another for their living. Such dependents derived their juridical status from the private rather than public sphere, and lacked honor if male. Although race did not officially affect citizenship, men of African or indigenous descent, who were often employed in domestic service, were especially likely to be denied it. They won little sympathy in court, owing both to their dependent status and to the respect justices paid to the authority of heads of households.

In 1845, the police reported that they had discovered a "free" boy chained inside a house "contrary to our institutions and laws." Yet the same justices who could be so indignant when a man was whipped or imprisoned without proof decided that this case was not serious. The twelve-year-old servant, Mariano Parra, had been born in the highlands (a sign he was probably Indian) but raised in the household where he worked. His employers had put the chain on him when they left town because they believed he had stolen from them and were afraid he would run away. Ignoring the caretaker's testimony that the mistress had given explicit instructions to keep the boy chained, the prosecutor proposed that what appeared to be a "misdemeanor against humanity and the laws" was more likely an oversight.[31] The judge dropped the charges and even ordered that the chain be returned with a simple warning to report servants who committed serious crimes to the proper authorities for punishment. The authorities would not interfere in the governance of the household to protect a dependent minor of low class and ethnic status.

Gender could further limit the freedom of domestic servants. Even while defending the right of young women to choose their employers, justices believed they should not leave the private sphere. For example, when Petronila Fuentes complained that her employer was trying to force her to remain in her service, the prosecutor was quick to support her rights as a free person over the age of eighteen to change jobs. When Fuentes disappeared, however, the same prosecutor protested that "it should not be allowed that she go about on her own account without being subject to some person who will provide her shelter and protection at an age which still requires another's care and direction."[32] In a similar case, the defender of minors supported the right of a young woman to choose her employer but argued that she must be under the protection of a guardian, "especially when her age and sex puts her at many risks."[33] In order to protect sexual virtue, officials would assign patriarchs to young women lacking proper supervision.

Constitutional rights and protections applied to independent citizens as they acted in the public sphere but did not extend to the private realm, where patriarchs continued to rule over their dependents. As the prosecutor of the superior court argued with respect to the law prohibiting the use of the whip, "it does not penetrate into the domestic household nor put limits on paternal authority."[34] While some poor and nonwhite men found themselves in positions of dependency, only slaves and women were excluded as groups regardless of their conduct and status. The justification of women's inherent dependence upon patriarchal authority was a political fiction given the large numbers of self-supporting women from various classes.[35] But that fiction was compelling enough in legal deliberations to render insignificant apparent contradictions. The decision to allow lashes in the private sphere arose not from the punishment of a servant but from accusations that the teacher of a girls' school was whipping her students; presumably parental consent and the students' sex made the school an extension of the domestic realm.

Republican Mothers and Public Women

In addition to formal constitutional exclusion, the linkage of citizenship with honor circumscribed women's place within the republic. Compared to its male counterpart, female honor underwent only subtle transformations after independence: women continued to be judged primarily by their sexual purity and domestic virtue. Indeed, the standards of morality were raised. When doña María Rivera died in 1829 after supervising the foundling home for forty years, a full-page obituary praised her as an example of proper womanhood: "Austere with herself, sensitive and tender with the family given to her by Christian charity, she never showed that hardness often produced by the effort of closing off the heart to the emotions of love. So it is that she has been the model, not the imitator, of maternal tenderness."[36] Although this tribute reveals a particularly conservative notion of honor by depicting the ideal woman as both virgin and mother, it also suggests that women could put their domestic skills to use for the public good.[37] While women had cared for orphans and taught children before independence, their services gained a new recognition provided they fulfilled them in an "enlightened" manner.

While plebeian men invoked their work ethic to defend themselves from criminal charges, women realized that they could use the language of domesticity to better advantage. María Seballos, a self-declared merchant, claimed ignorance of a new regulation against distilling alcohol "as a woman who does not deal with anyone and lives withdrawn in the refuge and care of her family."[38] Despite her rhetoric, her account reveals that she had not heard of the new order because she was away on business, having left her children with tenants in her house. Clearly, women of the middle and upper classes had a degree of latitude in reconciling their words with their actions. While republican discourse actually increased the standards by which female honor was to be judged, therefore, it did reward virtuous ladies with, if not citizenship, at least a recognition of their social value as mothers and arbiters of morality.

Poor women, by contrast, had difficulty living up to the image of the republican mother, and therefore in claiming their parental rights. When her daughter ran away from home and took refuge with her employer, Catalina Aquina filed charges of *rapto*, claiming that "he has inflicted upon me a violent dispossession, depriving me of the maternal authority conceded to me by the Nature of the laws." The justice of the peace and the defender of minors countered that, by hiring her daughter out, she had exposed the girl to moral corruption and even prostitution. And in profiting from her daughter's labor, they continued, she failed to show the affections of a mother or to "fulfill the duties given her by Nature."[39] In this case the judge ultimately upheld the right of Aquina to decide where her daughter should live, but other women were not as fortunate. María Dolores Alcoser was awarded a small pension from the father of her illegitimate daughter, only to have him win a countersuit for custody of the child he still refused to recognize as his own. To bolster his case, he asserted that as a *chichera* (brewer), Alcoser would likely exploit her daughter's labor, raise her on leftovers and *chicha* (corn beer), and expose her to immoral and uneducated people.[40]

Because most forms of employment made it difficult to maintain even the appearance of domesticity, poor women had an anomalous place within the liberal theory of separate spheres. They were neither proper mothers whose modesty deserved to be protected nor citizens with civil rights in the public arena. The claims of motherhood, for example, failed to move justices to grant clemency to women convicted of crimes. After serving half of a year's sentence to work in the hospital, María Toledo petitioned for an early release based upon her good behavior and appealed especially as an "anguished mother" whose abandoned children were missing her "caresses" and support.[41] Her request was denied. Juana Pía, convicted of several thefts in 1833, similarly failed to win over the court because she did not live up to the proper norms of womanhood. In an attempt to play upon the justices' sympathies, her lawyer asked mercy for her six children, who, if they lost their mother's support, "would contract a powerful germ of corruption, of idleness and of worse habits than those of lifting items belonging to others." But the prosecutor convinced the judges to distance them from their mother's bad example by assigning them instead to workshops and domestic service, "in order to avoid in this way a race of bandits."[42]

Not only was it difficult for poor women to base claims upon their rights or duties as mothers, but the mitigating factors used by plebeian men were also denied them. A work ethic failed to redeem women since their virtue depended upon fulfilling their domestic roles. When Toledo requested an early release, for example, she emphasized that she supported her children on her wages as an agricultural laborer.[43] Just months before her request was denied, the sentence of an "honorable" man was reduced on the appeal of his wife, who pointed out that she and their children relied on his income to survive.[44] The role of hardworking provider was reserved for men.

Similarly, while men could appeal to their role in defending the nation, women associated with military service were presumed to be morally corrupt. Despite the critical support they provided to the troops and their participation at times in combat, the female camp followers (*rabonas*) were more likely to be scorned than appreciated by elites. The stewards of San Francisco, constrained perhaps from complaining about the soldiers quartered in their monastery, did protest to the prefect that "the women who have followed said troops have made the above cited cemetery their permanent home and place of their disorders."[45] According to French traveler Flora Tristan, several generals had tried to prohibit women from accompanying the troops, but the soldiers had always rebelled, fearing that the army would be unable to provide adequate food, medical care, and presumably sexual services.[46] Ladies might extend their mothering function to charitable institutions, but poor women were not to carry out their domestic tasks in public.

Because women who committed crimes were seen as "unnatural," officials were also less sanguine about their potential rehabilitation. An editorial in the official newspaper, *El republicano*, asserted that female prisoners should work, not because they would be reformed but "so that they are not consumed by a sedentary life, so that they feel in some way the punishment of their crime, so that their passions are not encouraged believing [their crimes] forgotten, and so that the public will have proof that crimes will not increase from impunity or misunderstood compassion."[47] Female criminals had forfeited their right to privacy and modesty; thus Pía's lawyer was unable to attain even a transfer of her labor duty from the jail to the hospital. The prosecutor argued that she had become a habitual thief "due to the perversity of a corrupted heart" and would therefore "put that holy place in disorder, continuing in her habits and scandalizing the institution."[48]

Given the difficulty of meeting the high standards of virtue after independence, plebeian women bore the brunt of efforts to enforce republican morality.[49] While it is unlikely that their behavior had changed in any significant way, their sexuality was increasingly seen as a threat to public order. When María Samudio was arrested for assaulting her lover, soldier José Valdez, even the prosecutor considered the wounds so inconsequential that the charges should be dropped. He argued, nevertheless, that Samudio should be punished for her loose morals and that the prefect should take stern measures against women like her because "this type of crime is repeated daily due to the toleration of the public immorality of these women, who abandoning modesty, social considerations, and family obligations, have the impudence to present themselves in public as prostituted persons."[50] The superior court ordered that Samudio be sent home to the port of Arica in order to end her relationship with Valdez.

Domestic Violence

The differential prosecution of public and private crimes by the republican authorities is further exemplified by the official attitude toward domestic violence. Given the emphasis after independence on respectability, one might expect the state to come to the aid of women who complained of dissolute, profligate, and abusive husbands. According to the constitutions, to abandon one's wife or to be at fault in an ecclesiastical separation was considered cause for the suspension of citizenship.[51] Republican officials in Arequipa did increasingly claim the authority to oversee marital affairs, a matter previously left primarily to the church. As Judge José Miguel Salazar argued, "the jurisdiction of our Prelates is purely in spiritual matters, and it is the responsibility of the Government to make sure that its subjects committed to the conjugal state comply with their pacts and do not offend each other."[52] Nevertheless, the civil authorities were hesitant to interfere with a citizen's patriarchal rights, including his prerogative to "correct" his wife.[53] As one judge optimistically affirmed of a propertied man accused of beating his wife, "the fear of scandalizing the community with actions foreign to an honorable citizen will be sufficient to moderate in the future the vigor of his temper and to make him more exact in the fulfillment of his duties in Holy Matrimony."[54]

Not only was it difficult for women to win cases against their husbands, by filing charges they opened their own domestic behavior up to public scrutiny as well. When Antonio Vilca was arrested for stabbing his wife, he was not the only one to receive a warning; after "making him understand that he should correct his wife using the moderation prescribed by marital love and by the considerations due to her weak sex," the court also advised his wife "that she respect and obey her husband, avoiding occasions for displeasing him."[55] Anselma López, who accused her husband, a shoemaker, of pursuing her with a knife and threatening to kill her, complained that the police not only refused to arrest him but had admonished her for fleeing their home.[56] Women did not even enjoy a posthumous protection from public criticism. In 1832, Gaspar Pango was absolved of killing his wife after he hit her with a stone while chasing her. The prosecutor pointed out that he could have killed her earlier had that been his intention, given "the perverse conduct of that woman, her habit and custom of fleeing from the side of her husband, without the singular meekness of this man or his suffering being able to oblige her to reform."[57]

Some abusive husbands were caught in the general rise in criminal prosecution, particularly when their drunken or violent behavior threatened public as well as domestic order. In 1852, for example, shoemaker Laurencio Salazar was arrested for knocking his wife unconscious. During the course of testimony it became clear that Salazar, having on previous occasions not only injured his wife but also killed animals for spite and cut his brother-in-law's hand, was dangerously violent. Even when his wife ran out of money to pursue the case and pardoned her husband on orders from her confessor, the court sentenced him to four months of labor on public works in addition to the five he had already served in jail.[58] Salazar's case, however, was unusual. In general, the republican courts defined narrowly the degree of violence necessary to constitute assault in domestic cases. When Francisca Obiedo, an Indian, complained that her artisan husband beat her with sticks, stones, and whips and committed incest with her daughter, the prosecutor asserted that even if the charges proved true, they would not constitute a public crime that could be tried by the state.[59]

The prosecutor's remarks are particularly striking if we compare them to official attitudes toward another form of violence against women: only after independence did judges in Arequipa begin actively prosecuting what today we would consider rape. Technically, *estupro* referred to the deflowering of virgins with good reputations, by either force or seduction but without abduction; in practice republican justices in Arequipa generally used the term *estupro* for violent sexual assault.[60] Although the number of rape trials was relatively small (eighteen between 1825 and 1854), and only minors were deemed worthy of protection, such cases marked a significant change from colonial practice and reflected increased concerns over sexuality. Between 1784 and 1824, there were only two comparable cases filed by mothers *de parte* under the category of *injurias* (physical or verbal injuries), and neither was carried through to completion.[61] In contrast, about half of the accused rapists after independence were convicted despite the efforts of their defense lawyers to depict their targets as promiscuous women. Even eighteen-year-old María Núñez, who accused tailor José María Peralta of sneaking into her room and getting her drunk in order to take advantage of her, convinced the judge of her honorable reputation.[62] Furthermore, the penalties for rape convictions were generally stricter than those for nonsexual assault: several months in jail while performing public labor and/or providing a dowry for the young woman.

However limited the definition of rape, it is remarkable that the courts were willing to defend the honor of poor girls. Indeed in one case the superior court increased the penalty applied by a lower court because the girl was "an unfortunate one who belongs to the lowest class of the plebe and lacking in fortune deserves more consideration and more legal protection."[63] The language used by judicial officials to describe such crimes contrasts starkly to their attitude toward plebeian women beaten by their husbands or lovers. In 1834, for example, the justices were outraged when a tailor attempted to rape a seven-year-old girl. Even if he had not been able to consummate the act, argued the prosecutor, "he reveals the utmost immorality and corruption, and if not repressed and punished, its contagion could upset the order of families and cause serious damage to innocence."[64] When defendants and their lawyers protested that such charges should be pursued only at the initiative of private plaintiffs, the courts countered that rape, like theft or homicide but apparently not wife abuse or incest, could be prosecuted by the state as "a true public crime because in addition to damaging the honor and morals of families, it attacks the liberty and the very person of an individual."[65]

Public and Private Crimes

The definition of what constituted a "public" crime was key because the rhetoric of honorable citizenship applied primarily to men's public rather than private conduct. Local ordinances made police responsible for all the scandals occurring in their districts but simultaneously prohibited them from "interfering in the private conduct of the residents [*vecinos*], unless with their exterior scandalous behavior they attack public morals."[66] The courts in republican Arequipa punished men whose violent behavior extended beyond their households, as when they attacked young women over whom they had no patriarchal authority. Indeed when poor girls were raped, the state often stepped in precisely because they lacked the protection of their own patriarchs. Only in the most egregious cases, however, was the state willing to intervene in marital relations. This delineation of public and private was often detrimental to wives, whose well-being and safety depended precisely upon publicizing their domestic disputes.

One space in which women felt safer was the *chicherías*, taverns serving corn beer that were run almost exclusively by women, often out of their homes. When women were assaulted in a *chichería*, they were usually defended by their female friends and the *chichera*. Yet these taverns were not granted the protections from forced entry that applied to the "sacred sanctuary of the home." When cook Juan Galiano was sentenced to exile for violently forcing his way into a *chichería* and punching the owner, his defense lawyer appealed on the grounds that "he entered the *chichería*, a public place, where everyone has the right to enter just like going to the plaza to drink from the public fountain."[67] Galiano's sentence was reduced to six months' service in the police force.

Differing definitions of privacy and honor clashed in an 1830 dispute between Toribio de Linares, the municipality's deputy for police, and María Escalante, the proprietor of a *chichería*. According to Linares, when he told Escalante not to throw out the fetid water from her *chichería*, she replied insolently "that she didn't recognize me as her Judge." Escalante countered that she had simply tried to explain to Linares that a recent rainstorm, not her *chichería*, had made the street muddy and that she would appeal her case to a higher authority. It was not an empty threat for she brought charges against Linares for violently arresting her without cause "since she was honorable, . . . and had not committed any crime for which she should be taken away with scandal." Escalante won the first round when Judge Zavala freed her from jail and ordered Linares to appear in court despite his position on the city council, "since all Peruvians are equal before the law."

Linares would not give up so easily, however, and took his case to the prefect. The city council complained that the court should uphold the authority of the police so that they would not become "the laughing stock of even *chicheras* like Escalante." Linares depicted *chicherías* as a perversion of private and public space "because it is clear that in all such establishments young people and servants are corrupted, and they are in the end offices of prostitution and shelters for criminals, vagrants, and ne'er-do-wells." When questioned by the judge whether he had violated the sanctuary of her home, Linares replied "that he was convinced that no *chichería* deserved the name of sanctuary." By appealing to gendered principles of separate spheres and honor, Linares managed to have jurisdiction transferred from the court to the executive branch, where the prefect upheld his authority.[68]

Conclusions

The transition from monarchy to republic in Arequipa sharpened the distinction between public and private spheres in the realm of law if not everyday life. In an effort to stabilize public order, the courts became more zealous in the prosecution of crime. The creation of the constitutional category of citizen, and the redefinition of honor as based upon merit rather than lineage, allowed at least some workingmen, with the help of their lawyers, to claim protections of their civil liberties. But rights carried with them obligations, and citizens were expected to defend their country, work hard, and abide by higher standards of respectability.

The recognition of citizenship was contingent upon not only conduct but also the exclusion of those identified as dependent. Race continued to color perceptions of honor as justices denied to slaves and indigenous domestic servants the protections they so fervently defended for workingmen. But the key factor these groups shared with all women was legal subjection to patriarchal control. Indeed it was only male heads of households, whose virtue was judged by their conduct in the public sphere, who truly enjoyed a right to privacy. As long as they worked to support their families and did not threaten the sexuality of women outside of their own homes, they could treat their wives, children, and servants as they saw fit.

These gendered principles of honor and privacy that developed in the judicial practice of early republican Arequipa (and likely elsewhere in Peru) apparently influenced the 1862 penal code, which linked strong protections of patriarchal authority and honor. The code ordered public prosecutors to proceed in all cases except those against "honesty" (i.e., female sexual honor), honor, domestic theft, abuse, and minor physical injuries.[69] Offenses to honor, including to one's wife or daughter, were considered extenuating circumstances in cases of assault and murder.[70] And the crime of violating one's domicile did not apply to "cafes, taverns, inns, and other public houses," enterprises often run by women in their homes.[71]

The first commissions established immediately after independence to codify both civil and criminal law in Peru rarely met, presumably owing to the political turmoil. The president of the Supreme Court, Manuel Lorenzo de Vidaurre y Encalada, took it upon himself to publish quite original and iconoclastic draft codes in 1828 (penal) and 1834 (civil), but they were not favorably received by most jurists and politicians.[72] From 1836 to 1839, during the period of the Peru-Bolivian Confederation, Peruvians were subject to the codes of Santa Cruz (analyzed in this volume by Rossana Barragán). With the relative stability established by President Ramón Castilla in the 1840s, new commissions were appointed that successfully wrote first the civil code (1852) and then the penal code (1862). Unlike Vidaurre, members of these commissions drew heavily from existing European codes.[73] The drafters of the civil code drew especially from the French code, although they rejected the proposal of some members of the commission, including José Luis Sánchez Gómez of Arequipa, to define marriage as a civil contract.[74] The penal code was modeled most closely upon Spain's 1848 code, praised by chair José Simeón Tejeda as both scientific and an appropriate guide, given that "the current customs of Peruvians are shaped by the imperishable molds of the laws and language of Castile."[75]

In light of this common practice of using existing codes as models, it is difficult to prove definitively that local judicial practice also influenced the formation of Peruvian law. Certainly, the members of the commissions had experience in the courts that must have shaped to some degree the way they evaluated the various codes consulted. And more specifically, the connection to the courts of Arequipa was strong. By the late 1830s, a majority of the justices on Peru's Supreme Court as well as several of its more notable prosecutors were from Arequipa. Of these, Manuel Toribio Ureta worked on the first draft of the criminal code, and at least one of the members of the commission appointed to review and revise that draft, José Simeón Tejeda, had also been educated and begun his career in Arequipa.

Given these links between the courts and the commissions, it is logical to assume that those elements of the 1862 penal code that departed from the Spanish model reflected the particular judicial practice of Peru. The generally milder punishments specified in the code, and the unique articles making lashing both a crime in itself (except when carried out by parents or teachers) and an aggravating circumstance in other offenses, suggest that the defenses put forward by poor but "honorable" men in court left a mark on the justices who went on to draft the codes.[76] Similarly, a later commentator was puzzled that the Peruvian code, unlike its Spanish model, specified illegal impressment as a crime, yet this had been a key issue of contention in the early republican courts of Arequipa.[77] The Peruvian code, therefore, implemented more measures than its Spanish model to protect the civil liberties of male citizens.

In contrast to the Spanish model, the Peruvian code also strengthened the power of husbands to the detriment of female victims of violence, by distinguishing domestic violence from general physical assault (*lesiones*) and making the former more difficult to prosecute.[78] More subtly, the Peruvian code eliminated the period of three days following childbirth established in Spain during which women could not be accused of infanticide, likely reflecting the attitudes in Peru toward female criminals as perverse and incapable of reform.[79] Finally, *estupro* (rape) was one of the few crimes punished more severely in the Peruvian than the Spanish code. Moreover, in contrast to most crimes, the penalty was increased if the perpetrator was a relative or other person with authority over the victim.[80] And although the Peruvian code specified that *estupro* should be prosecuted only by the plaintiff or her parents (*de parte*), except in the cases of orphans without guardians, the author of a comparative study of the codes in 1900 complained that the Superior Court of Lima, like the Arequipa courts before 1862, proceeded at its own initiative (*de oficio*) in all cases in which the victim was a minor.[81] This observation is an important reminder that the formation and application of the law may be distinct.

Though theoretically relegated to the domestic sphere, therefore, women found their private virtues subject to increasing public scrutiny after independence. Elite women who were able to maintain the appearance of fulfilling high standards of sexual purity, modesty, and maternal nurturing were denied citizenship but were at least recognized as arbiters of morality within the public sphere as well as the home. Moreover, the 1862 penal code offered such "honest" women greater retribution in cases of sexual assault and lessened their sentences in cases of abortion or infanticide undertaken to protect their reputation.[82] Poor women, however, who often lived beyond the control of a patriarch and continued to carry out their lives in public, bore the brunt of the increasing activism of the criminal justice system.

Notes

Sections of this chapter appeared previously in Sarah C. Chambers, *From Subjects to Citizens: Honor, Gender, and Politics in Arequipa, Peru, 1780–1854* (University Park: Pennsylvania State University Press, 1999), and are reprinted here with permission of the publisher. The title was inspired in part by Ann Twinam, *Public Lives, Private Secrets: Gender, Honor, Sexuality, and Illegitimacy in Colonial Spanish America* (Stanford, CA: Stanford University Press, 1999).

1   Jürgen Habermas, *The Structural Transformation of the Public Sphere*, trans. Thomas Burger (Cambridge: MIT Press, 1989).

2   Manuel Lorenzo de Vidaurre y Encalada followed this strict distinction in his proposed penal code, so that even murder was classified as a "private" crime, although some private crimes could be prosecuted by the state; Vidaurre y Encalada, *Proyecto de un código penal* (Boston: Hiram Tupper, 1828).

3   See Joaquín Escriche, *Diccionario razonado de legislación y jurisprudencia*, rpt. (Bogotá: Temis, 1981), 2:295; and José Viterbo Arias, *Exposición comentada y comparada del Código penal del Perú de 1863* (Lima: Librería e Imprenta Gil, 1900), 3:1.

4   Between 1785 and 1824, only 21% of surviving criminal cases were prosecuted *de oficio*,

whereas between 1825 and 1854, that number rose to 71%; Chambers, *From Subjects to Citizens*, table 4.3. According to Escriche, the same trend occurred in Spain (*Diccionario razonado*, 1:164).

5 Francisco García Calderón was a law professor in Arequipa who wrote the legal dictionary that would be widely consulted in Peru for many decades, the *Diccionario de la legislación peruana: Suplemento que contiene la teoría del derecho penal* (Lima: Imprenta de Aranda, 1864), 13.

6 Colonial cases can be found in Archivo Regional de Arequipa [hereafter ARAR], Intendencia: Causas Criminales [Int/Crim], and those after independence in Corte Superior: Causas Criminales [CS/Crim]. (Because the cases are bundled according to category but not individually indexed, I give the initial date to identify them.) The entire database was used to calculate the proportions of crimes by categories and type of prosecution; notes on testimony and judicial opinions were drawn from all colonial cases (except contraband) and sampled in alternate years for the republican period (with the exception of cases pertaining to sexual crimes and domestic violence, which were reviewed for all years).

7 For a full discussion of racial dynamics, see Sarah C. Chambers, "Little Middle Ground: The Instability of a Mestizo Identity in the Andes, Eighteenth and Nineteenth Centuries," in *Race and Nation in Modern Latin America*, ed. Nancy P. Appelbaum, Anne S. Macpherson, and Karin Alejandra Rosemblatt (Chapel Hill: University of North Carolina Press, 2003), 32–55.

8 Art. 17 (1823), art. 14 (1826), art. 4 (1828), art. 3 (1834), art. 8 (1839); Juan F. Olivo, ed., *Constituciones políticas del Perú, 1821–1919* (Lima: Imprenta Torres Aguirre, 1922), 38, 78, 110, 150, 205.

9 Chambers, *From Subjects to Citizens*, chap. 3.

10 Art. 24 (1823), art. 18 (1826), art. 6 (1828), art. 4 (1834), art. 9 (1839); Olivo, *Constituciones*, 39, 79, 111, 151, 206.

11 Art. 180 (1823), art. 12, num. 4 (1826), art. 175 (1834); Olivo, *Constituciones*, 65, 78, 183.

12 Sarah C. Chambers, "Crime and Citizenship: Judicial Practice in Arequipa, Peru, during the Transition from Colony to Republic," in *Reconstructing Criminality in Latin America*, ed. Carlos A. Aguirre and Robert Buffington (Wilmington, DE: Scholarly Resources, 2000), 19–39.

13 *El republicano*, July 19, 1834, 7.

14 Art. 23 (1823); arts. 142, 146, 147 (1826); arts. 157, 158, 159 (1828); arts. 158, 170 (1834); art. 160 (1839); Olivo, *Constituciones*, 39, 103, 140, 180–182, 234.

15 Art. 193 (1823), art. 164 (1828); Olivo, *Constituciones*, 68, 141.

16 Petition dated Jan. 26, 1835, in ARAR/CS/Crim (2 Jan., 1835), don Calistro Araujo contra don José María Portugal por injurias a su esposa.

17 Opinion of the *fiscal* on Aug. 7, 1829, in ARAR/CS/Crim (July 6, 1829), Contra Victoriano Concha por sospecharse que es ladrón. See also (July 3, 1833), Contra Pablo Aguilar por haberle encontrado con una gorra de policía; and (Sept. 2, 1834), Contra don Diego Begazo y su yernos por insubordinación a las autoridades.

18 ARAR, Cabildo: Causas Civiles, leg. 15, cuad. 380 (Aug. 10, 1780), Bartolomé Cutipa contra Josef Arrenasas, cobrador de los repartos.

19 ARAR/CS/Crim (May 20, 1843), Contra don Hermenegildo Rosas por haber azotado al menor Mariano Espinoza. Paz Soldan would go on to serve as a *fiscal* on the Supreme

Court. For other cases, see (Nov. 2, 1839), Contra don Mariano Rodríguez; (Aug. 3, 1844), Contra don José Villegas; (Nov. 6, 1846), Contra don José Franco; (Dec. 23, 1847), Contra el Sargento Mayor don Juan Cornejo, and (March 15, 1848), Contra Miguel Pas.

20 Art. 145 (1826), art. 155 (1828), art. 155 (1834), and art. 158 (1839); Olivo, *Constituciones*, 103, 140, 180, 234.

21 See ARAR/CS/Crim (Jan. 4, 1830), don Toribio de Linares, diputado de policía, contra María Escalante por falta de respeto; (Dec. 12, 1832), Contra Bernarda Torres y otras por haber herido a María Beltrán; (March 6, 1833), Apelación de don Domingo Santayana en la causa que sigue contra el Gobernador de Uchumayo por haber allanado su casa; (April 17, 1833), Contra Mateo Chávez por el homicidio de Manuel Pacheco y heridas a otros; (May 26, 1834), don Domingo Arias contra el alcalde de Yanahuara por injurias contra su esposa; (Aug. 25, 1838), Juan Batista Puma y otros indígenas de Cayma se quejan del mal comportamiento del Gobernador; and Prefectura (April 6, 1828) contra el Dr. don Francisco Paula Paez por injurias a Feliciana Zegarra.

22 Opinion of the *fiscal* Lazo on Feb. 1, 1833, in ARAR/CS/Crim (Jan. 31, 1833), Se remiten los autos contra Marcelino Esquivel y otros por robo.

23 See decree of President Orbegoso published in *El republicano*, April 11, 1835, 1–2; and letter from the military command to the prefect in *El republicano*, Oct. 8, 1836, 4–5.

24 In ARAR/CS/Crim (May 27, 1834), Contra don Nicanor Chávez por insultos al Gobernador y Municipalidad de Sachaca.

25 Chambers, *From Subjects to Citizens*, 156–159.

26 *El republicano*, supplement to Aug. 29, 1829, 4.

27 ARAR, Prefectura (Nov. 21, 1831), Expediente criminal sobre investigarse la conducta de Ramón Llerena, José María Madaleno y José Torres.

28 Sentence of Judge Mariano Paredes on Dec. 1, 1831, in ibid. See also ARAR/CS/Crim (Oct. 12, 1831), don José León Dongo contra Juan Salazar por robo.

29 Opinion of the *fiscal* España on Nov. 26, 1831, in ARAR/CS/Crim (Nov. 25, 1831), Apelación de los autos seguidos contra Victoriano Concha por robos. For a similar argument see the opinion of the *fiscal* Pedro José Bustamante dated Sept. 16, 1843, in (Aug. 31, 1843), Contra don Manuel Segundo Tapia, el cabo Cipriano Cáceres, y el soldado Mariano Quispe Guaman por reclutar sin autorización.

30 ARAR/CS/Crim (Sept. 2, 1826), Enrique Nuñes contra el juez de derecho Dr. don Pascual Francisco Suero por abusar su autoridad.

31 ARAR/CS/Crim (July 5, 1845), Contra doña Martina Hurtado por tener un menor con cadena al pie. Judicial officials displayed a similar lack of concern in the case of a young servant stolen from one master and sold to another; ARAR/CS/Crim (July 5, 1845), Contra Gregorio Gonzales por plagio.

32 ARAR/CS/Crim (Oct. 22, 1836), Petronila Fuentes se queja de doña Getrudis Lisardi por forzarla a quedarse en su servicio.

33 ARAR/CS/Crim (Jan. 8, 1841), Denuncia de Manuela Ampuero contra doña Petronila Olazabal por falta de pago por su servicio.

34 ARAR/CS/Crim (June 26, 1854), Contra doña Carlota La Rosa por haber castigado a sus alumnas.

35 For a similar situation in the United States, see Joan R. Gundersen, "Independence, Citizenship, and the American Revolution," *Signs* 13.1 (1987): 59–77; and Elaine R.

46   Sarah C. Chambers

Crane, "Dependence in the Era of Independence: The Role of Women in a Republican Society," in *The American Revolution: Its Character and Limits*, ed. Jack P. Greene (New York: New York University Press, 1987), 253–275.

36 *El republicano*, Jan. 17, 1829, 4. See also the obituary of señora doña María Moscoso y Pérez; *El republicano*, April 20, 1833, 7.

37 Such a role is similar to the "republican mothers" identified by Linda Kerber in the United States; Kerber, *Women of the Republic: Intellect and Ideology in Revolutionary America* (Chapel Hill: University of North Carolina Press, 1980); for Mexico, see Silvia Marina Arrom, *The Women of Mexico City* (Stanford, CA: Stanford University Press, 1985), 259–266.

38 Statement dated Jan. 21, 1841, in ARAR, Prefectura (16 Jan., 1841), Expediente seguido de oficio contra doña Francisca Bedoya por la denuncia de la destilación de aguardiente de higos. Although Ceballos's husband claimed to be the owner of the still, Bedoya had contracted with Ceballos to rent it.

39 ARAR/CS/Crim (Aug. 17, 1849), Catalina Aquina contra don José Santos López por rapto.

40 Archivo Arzobispal de Arequipa: Causas Civiles (April 14, 1847), seguido por doña María Dolores Alcoser sobre la filiación de sus hijos; and (March 31, 1849), seguido por don Carlos Arebato sobre que doña María Dolores Alcoser le entregue su hija natural. Although initiated in ecclesiastical court, the sentences were passed in secular courts, another indication of the state's increasing claim to jurisdiction in family law.

41 Petition dated Oct. 31, 1845, filed inside a separate case; ARAR/CS/Crim (Aug. 3, 1843), Contra Manuel Gutiérrez por la quiebra fraudulenta.

42 ARAR/CS/Crim (Aug. 3, 1843), Contra Juana Pía por robos.

43 See note 41 supra.

44 Petitions of Borja Cosme dated June 21 and 25, 1845, filed inside ARAR/CS/Crim (Aug. 3, 1843), Contra Manuel Gutiérrez por la quiebra fraudulenta.

45 Petition dated Dec. 29, 1828, in Archivo General de la Nación (Lima), R. J. Ministerio de Justicia, Prefectura de Arequipa: Culto, leg. 143.

46 Flora Tristan, *Peregrinations of a Pariah* (Boston: Beacon, 1986), 180.

47 *El republicano*, Aug. 24, 1833, 6. See also ARAR/CS/Crim (July 4, 1853), Contra Marta Cuadros por haber matado a su hijo.

48 ARAR/CS/Crim (Aug. 3, 1843), Contra Juana Pía.

49 Compare to Christine Stansell, *City of Women: Sex and Class in New York, 1789–1860* (Urbana: University of Illinois Press, 1987).

50 ARAR/CS/Crim (July 12, 1832), Contra María Samudio por heridas a José Valdez.

51 Art. 24 (1823), art. 6 (1828), art. 4 (1834), art. 9 (1839); Olivo, *Constituciones*, 39, 111, 151, 206.

52 ARAR/CS/Crim (Dec. 16, 1828), Don Alberto Anco apela la sentencia del juez de derecho que lo ha declarado adúltero. For similar jurisdictional disputes, see ARAR/Pref (Feb. 10, 1827), Contra don Juan Rodríguez y doña María Sánchez por haber sorprendido al cura del Sagrario; and ARAR/CS/Crim (Feb. 22, 1833), don Ramón Sea contra don José Antonio Berenguel por el rapto de su hija.

53 For more on domestic violence, see Sarah C. Chambers, "'To the Company of a Man Like My Husband; No Law Can Compel Me': Women's Strategies against Domestic Violence in Arequipa, Peru, 1780–1850," *Journal of Women's History* 11.1 (1999): 31–52.

54   ARAR/Pref (April 23, 1827), doña Faustina Tebes contra don Juan Antonio Acosta por sevicia.

55   ARAR/CS/Crim (Aug. 12, 1834), Contra Antonio Vilca por dos puñaladas a su esposa María Anco.

56   ARAR/CS/Crim (May 15, 1849), doña Anselma López contra su esposo don Pedro Ortega por maltratos.

57   ARAR/CS/Crim (July 24, 1832), Contra Gaspar Pango por la muerte de su esposa Ilaria Marantes.

58   ARAR/CS/Crim (Nov. 30, 1852), Contra Laurencio Salazar por graves heridas a su esposa.

59   ARAR/CS/Crim (April 24, 1850), Contra Carlos Herrera por maltratos a su mujer.

60   For an early-nineteenth-century discussion of the definition of *estupro*, see Escriche, *Diccionario razonado*, 2:526–530.

61   ARAR/Int/Crim (Aug. 19, 1809), Paulina Portugal contra Manuel Rondón por injurias reales a su hija María Rivero; ARAR/Int/Crim (Sept. 8, 1818), Catalina Bedregal contra Miguel Castro y Pedro Chaves por injurias a su hijo Josefa Salas.

62   ARAR/CS/Crim (Oct. 17, 1846), Contra José María Peralta por estupro en María Núñez, menor.

63   ARAR/CS/Crim (Aug. 11, 1846), Contra don Luís Gonsalen por haber violado a la menor Mercedes Murguía.

64   ARAR/CS/Crim (Aug. 19, 1834), Contra Mariano Villegas por el rapto y estupro de la menor Teresa Gómez.

65   The *fiscal* Tomás Dávila in ARAR/CS/Crim (Jan. 16, 1850), Contra Mariano Jara por haber violado a la menor Manuela Licarde. See also ARAR/CS/Crim (May 25, 1844), Contra Baltazar Cervantes por violación de la hija de don Silverio Cornejo.

66   *El republicano*, Nov. 28, 1835, 2.

67   ARAR/CS/Crim (Oct. 20, 1831), Contra Juan Galiano y Matías Bedoya por haber portado armas prohibidas, entrado a fuerza a una chichería y estropeado a las dueños de ella.

68   ARAR/CS/Crim (Jan. 4, 1830), Contra doña María Escalante por resistir al diputado de policía D. Toribio de Linares.

69   For this definition of public and private crimes, see art. 18 in Peru, *Código de enjuiciamientos en materia penal* (Lima: Imprenta Calle de la Rifa, 1862), 7–8.

70   Arts. 5, 234, 235, 247, 263 in *Código penal del Perú* (Lima, 1863), 5, 72, 75, 80.

71   Art. 317, in *Código penal* (Lima, 1863), 92.

72   For his penal code, see Vidaurre, *Proyecto de un código penal*.

73   On the history of the civil and penal codes, see Jorge Basadre, "Antecedentes del Código civil de 1852," *Revista de la Facultad de Derecho y Ciencias Políticas* 3.2 (1939): 283–319; Basadre, *Historia del derecho peruano*, 4th ed. (Lima: Librería Studium, 1988); José Hurtado Pozo, *La ley importada: Recepción del derecho penal en el Perú* (Lima: Centro de Estudios de Derecho y Sociedad, 1979); and César Luna Victoria León, "Código civil de 1852: Lo nacional y lo importado," *Derecho* 42 (1988): 73–100.

74   Basadre, "Antecedentes," 310–312; Basadre, *Historia del derecho peruano*, 371–373.

75   Quoted in Hurtado Pozo, *Ley importada*, 43.

76   On lashing, see Viterbo Arias, *Exposición comentada*, vol. 3, [90s] and 215. His comparative study also demonstrates that the Chilean penal code of 1875 adhered much more closely to the Spanish model and maintained harsher penalties than the Peruvian.

48   Sarah C. Chambers

77 Ibid., 3:283.
78 Ibid., 3:97–98; arts. 254, 256 in *Código penal del Perú* (Lima, 1863), 77.
79 Viterbo Arias, *Exposición comentada*, 3:50–53.
80 Arts. 269–278, in *Código penal* (Lima, 1863), 81–83.
81 Viterbo Arias, *Exposición comentada y comparada*, 3:180–181.
82 Arts. 242, 243, 273 in *Código penal* (Lima, 1863), 74, 82.

Community service, liberal law, and local custom
in indigenous villages: Oaxaca, 1750–1850
Peter Guardino

Anthropologists working in indigenous villages in southern Mexico have
long known of the vital connection between the individuals sweeping
the plaza and those governing the village. Community service is central
to authority in such villages. Only those who have faithfully discharged
their duties in a series of mundane posts accumulate the status that allows
them to rise to loftier positions. Villagers typically emphasize the antiquity of these systems, a crucial part of the vital and unchanging *cos-
tumbre* central to communal identity. Much of the early anthropological
literature on the history of these *cargo* systems began in some sense from
this premise, searching for their colonial or even pre-Hispanic origins. In
the 1980s several key works challenged this emphasis on antiquity. Scholars like Jan Rus, Robert Wasserstrom, and Judith Friedlander argued that
cargo systems changed significantly in the twentieth century due to external pressures.[1] John Chance and William Taylor extended the time hori-
zon farther, arguing that *cargo* systems only incorporated religious offices
in the nineteenth century after state policy destroyed the institutions that
had previously financed religious worship in communities.[2]

Although these newer perspectives have significantly improved our
knowledge of village life, they still pay scant attention to what is in my
view one of the most important formative moments in the history of
indigenous systems of authority. In the nineteenth century, villagers in
some communities adopted and domesticated key arguments of liberal
law, making them part of the indigenous ethic of community service.
This close encounter with the new legal basis of the modern nation-state
changed their indigenous communities in some very fundamental ways
but left some other basic characteristics of communal identity in place. In
essence, these communities embraced the egalitarian aspects of the new

concept of citizenship, while at the same time they retained their strong communitarian ethic of service.

Rossana Barragán points out in her contribution to this volume that law created the contested fields in which groups defined their identities. Moreover, Joanne Rappaport has argued eloquently and convincingly that for centuries in Latin America the law has been essential to indigenous identity. In her words, "Law constitutes a common idiom employed by community and state to formulate demands and to fashion and implement policy. At the core of the juridical idiom shared by Indians and the state is an acceptance of a legal definition of indigenous identity, one that originated in Bogotá but has been internalized by resguardo members. In effect, the European construction of the other, as it is interpreted in law, is basic to an indigenous definition of self."[3] Rappaport's argument, however, is about how indigenous people define themselves in relation to the state and outsiders, and Barragán takes what seems to be a similar tack. I believe that we can, and should, further extend these insights on the importance of law. I hope to show here how law shaped the way the members of indigenous communities related to one another and to their communities.

In this essay, I propose to explore a key moment in the development of indigenous political culture. I do not seek to affirm the basic compatibility between indigenous and modern forms of democracy, an argument that is encouraging but often overemphasized. I will also leave aside the question of how indigenous peasants sometimes used the very tools of the hegemonizing colonial and postcolonial state to resist impositions. Peasant appropriation of these arguments was not always a tool for resistance. The new ways of viewing politics were also available for use in conflicts internal to the peasantry.

What I am instead interested in is a different kind of encounter, one closer to the themes of this book. For want of better terms, I will call this an encounter between local custom and law, although, as we will see, for many years custom was essentially law. More important, custom was flexible, debatable, and changing, even as those who wielded arguments about custom in legal cases portrayed it as rigid, consensual, and ancient. The moment in which these communities assimilated liberal law to change some of their most basic political principles shows how these relatively autonomous, culturally differentiated indigenous communities were in important ways created by law, including the homogenizing kinds of law produced by the colonial and later republican state.

The material for this essay was drawn from the district of Villa Alta in the present-day state of Oaxaca. Even before the Spanish Conquest, polities in Villa Alta were relatively fragmented. The people in the district spoke five different mutually unintelligible languages, and villages were relatively autonomous from one another. The administrative and legal changes introduced by the Spanish reinforced this tendency toward fragmentation, and by the middle of the eighteenth century the area had 112 villages, none of which had formal political ties to its neighbors. Some were divided internally into barrios or parcialities, but none had subject towns. All were administered by an *alcalde mayor* seated in the small Spanish and mestizo town of Villa Alta.

Although the villages were fragmented from one another horizontally, they were tightly integrated in a vertical administrative and legal system. The *alcalde mayor* was an important figure because he adjudicated conflicts between villages. Yet his importance did not end there. Disputes between inhabitants of a single village also frequently ended up before the *alcalde mayor* when plaintiffs were dissatisfied with decisions reached by village officials. Furthermore, if the *alcalde mayor* did not resolve the problem in a satisfactory way, cases were appealed to higher courts in Oaxaca or Mexico City.

The most important village officers, the *gobernadores*, were elected, but only a few elders were allowed to vote in these elections. Most of these elders, often called *principales*, attained their status by faithfully serving the village in a number of service posts, beginning as young men with such menial jobs as sweeping the plaza or serving as temporary domestic servants for parish priests. From there, they progressed through a series of offices of greater and greater responsibility. Eventually males might be chosen to serve as the *gobernador*, the highest office in the communal system. Climbing this hierarchy of offices took years. Judging from their age, *gobernadores* usually had participated in the *cargo* system for twenty years or more.

In documents, the inhabitants of villages often referred to themselves as "children of the village," a phrase suggesting that villages were patriarchies. In village society, older men governed younger men, and all men governed women. In Villa Alta, as in the Sierra de Puebla region analyzed by Florencia Mallon, the importance of this hierarchy can be seen on one level in domestic arrangements and marital practices, where customs emphasized the respect and service that younger people owed to their elders.[4] Before marriage, young men spent a period as servants in the house of their future parents-in-law.[5] For several years after marriage young couples lived with the groom's parents, and the bride was effectively a domestic servant for her mother-in-law. Yet, as Steve Stern has pointed out for other regions of Mexico, patriarchy was also infused into the politics of village government.[6] Often this can be seen in gendered metaphors about politics. Moreover, at some key life-cycle moments village political officials played an important role in affirming the values of family life. For instance, during engagement ceremonies they received food and drink from the family and lectured the betrothed couple on the importance of fidelity.[7] Village political officials also worked with parish priests to enforce sexual morality.[8]

In principle, the *cargo* system that regulated access to village political power was egalitarian. All males had equal opportunity to climb the *cargo* ladder to authority. In practice, some males, either through perceived ineptitude or from lack of prestige, filled lower posts all of their lives. More important, some families claiming descent from *caciques*, or pre-Hispanic nobles, were exempt from service in lower offices, often entering the ladder of offices only a few rungs from the top. These peasant nobles inherited their status from their fathers. Moreover, peasant men could not achieve noble status by marrying the daughters of nobles. Typically, claimants had to justify their status with documentation of their ancestry.[9] As the eighteenth century went on, it became fashionable for men who had become elders through service to claim that this put them on a par with the pre-Hispanic noble families, able to pass their exemption from lower office on to their sons.[10] These families were using the two different meanings of the word *principal* to obscure their commoner origins. Strikingly, these pretensions were opposed not by noble families but by commoners, who feared that as the pool of labor available for necessary services dried up, the frequency with which they were called to service would become intolerable.

A representative case is that of Juan López of the village of Santa María Yabichui. In 1760 he complained that other villagers "wanted to treat me as a commoner, usurping the privileges acquired by my forefathers." They made him fetch fodder for the priest's horse and made his wife grind corn for the priest's meals. At first, the governor of the village claimed that in Yabichui all men served in low offices before becoming *principales*. When questioned, the *principales* supported the governor, describing the village *cargo* system in some detail. Later, a lawyer for the village qualified this argument, saying that in Yabichui there were two kinds of *principales*, "some that are *principales* by blood, and these are three known families. . . . the other kind of *principales* is the kind that is made by virtue of serving the village in low and laborious offices until becoming councilmen. Most *principales* are of this second variety, including the parents and grandparents of Juan López, and he will also become one this way, if he wants to subject himself to the same things that the others have done." The village government also pointed out that Yabichui's small size meant that any tendency to exclude people from service would make fulfilling village duties difficult.[11]

The oft-voiced concerns about finding sufficient labor for communal services help explain the longevity of *cargo* systems. They were a very effective method for these impoverished communities to provide collective necessities without imposing cash taxes. Many tasks were accomplished this way, and none of the people who did them were paid. Villages needed, for instance, tax collectors, a police force, and messengers. These posts, which were filled annually through the *cargo* system, were supplemented by other kinds of labor tax. Young families took turns providing domestic service to priests. Others served in religious offices as choirmasters or *fiscales*. All families participated in cooperative communal labor, or *tequios*, which might involve repairing public works or possibly tending communal fields whose harvest was dedicated to community religious or social projects.

Yet the essential tasks that families completed for the community came at a cost, as villages were relatively small. Every post took time, a precious commodity to peasants on the thin edge of subsistence. The burdens of maintaining a viable, independent community life weighed more heavily when people filled offices for more than one year or when they served in different offices from one year to another without a break. Thus in the eighteenth century, as more families sought to exempt their children from lower offices, other villagers had a strong incentive to keep the number of exempt persons low.[12]

Much of the labor for communal service was actually provided by wives as well as husbands. In fact, from the point of view of the *cargo* system, and for many other purposes in village life, husband and wife were considered two essential halves of a single person. Unmarried men served in the system but only as messengers.[13] The aid of a wife was considered essential to service in community offices. For example, when Francisco Vicente, *gobernador* of Yatoni, was accused of neglecting his duties in 1786, he explained that he did not "have anyone to help him," as his wife had died. Vicente asked to be allowed to resign, and this was permitted.[14]

Women also prepared the food for various banquets and celebrations associated with office. They routinely ground corn and prepared food for the priest, typically on a rotating basis. In this system a young couple would serve the priest together for a week at a time.[15] In the Yabichui case outlined above, Juan López was quite concerned not only with the duties assigned to him but also with those to be performed by his wife.

Nevertheless, in community service, as in other aspects of village life, the role of women was submerged. Judging from the available documents, women did not claim rights in relation to village government or even their own husbands on the basis of their service to the community. In domestic disputes women claimed a right to subsistence and support, and men asserted a reciprocal right to domestic services, but neither mentioned community service.[16] This submergence of women's role could be extreme. In most of these villages, women actually earned the cash villagers needed to pay taxes and buy articles from the outside. They wove cloth that was marketed on a viceregal scale before independence and on a regional one later. Yet in dozens of disputes about the role of colonial officials in this trade women never appear as plaintiffs. Instead husbands defended the rights of the couple, rarely mentioning the fact that the cloth was directly produced by women.

There was, however, one form of politics in which women were extremely visible. Both before and after independence women participated in, and often led, village riots.[17] The targets and aims of riots were varied, but the site was usually the central plaza, which contained the buildings that symbolized authority: the church, the priest's residence, and the municipal building, typically called the royal house in the colonial period and the community house after independence. In village riots, the hierarchies and tensions that characterized village political life could temporarily collapse into a homogeneous whole, even if the riot was actually directed against a village official. In these moments women could and did take a leading role.[18]

The *cargo* system was crucial to upholding patriarchal authority in villages, and the high stakes of the system often led to heated conflict within villages. Disputes had functional and social dimensions, but they also had legal and cultural aspects. The documents sometimes do not indicate where the material dimensions of conflict end and the cultural ones begin. For instance, it is difficult to tell whether those protesting their assignment to a particular office were concerned about the demands of the office or, alternatively, the status associated with it.

The general features of the *cargo* system were remarkably uniform from village to village, but in each village local custom determined the exact order that men followed in the system and who was exempt from lower offices. Yet, when individuals were unhappy with their appointments and what those appointments implied about their status, they appealed to the *alcalde mayor*, a Spanish official who did not speak the language and certainly did not have detailed knowledge of local custom. Spanish officials, who usually lacked training in even Spanish law, now had to decipher and enforce intricate local customs. These officials also had to verify the social identities of those who claimed noble status. This was not a simple task, as even before the Conquest the district's cacique families had not been particularly wealthy, and thereafter economic differentiation declined. John Chance points out that Spanish officials fell back on their experience with Spanish nobility, applying similar rules of descent.[19] Although I agree, I would also like to emphasize the degree to which officials investigated local customs to decide disputes. There was in fact ample legal justification for resolving conflicts this way. The Spanish colonial system acknowledged the importance of natural law, and local customs were to be respected wherever they did not contradict royal law or Christianity.[20]

Moreover, in the eighteenth century *alcaldes mayores* and their successors the *subdelegados* functioned in a legal and political system that was itself changing rapidly. The changes were complex, but basically a previous reliance on custom and detailed consideration of the social consequences of legal decisions was giving way to a new taste for uniform criteria, or, as it was most often stated at the time, "fixed rules."[21] Although this ethic of order did not by any means win out in every case, it could have drastic effects. In 1796 the Spanish legal advisor Luís Acosta swept aside Juan Tomás de la Cruz's effort to confirm his son's claim to cacique status and exemption from low offices. Acosta argued that in Spanish municipal law *principales* earned their status and exemptions by serving in demanding posts. Their status and exemptions were not passed on to their children, and the same rules applied to Indian villages.[22] Applying this uniform standard would eliminate the need to examine local customs about which families were noble and which offices noble families need not bother with.

Disputes over whether those who became *principales* through service could pass their status on to their children also should be seen in another, related context. In the late eighteenth and early nineteenth century many villages were fractured by fierce struggles over the rights and duties of even acknowledged noble families. Commoner groups were constantly trying to restrict both the privileges and powers of noble families. Often conflicts over whether a given family had achieved *principal* status through service or birth were folded into this more general field of contention, and arguments about both issues crop up in the same cases. The causes of this movement toward more egalitarian forms are difficult to ascertain. Certainly distributing burdens more equally was likely to be desirable to the less privileged. But it is also tempting to suggest that the Enlightenment erosion of corporatist paradigms was having an effect, particularly after the outbreak of the independence war and the emergence of Spanish liberalism.[23] Arguments of difference were losing the force they had enjoyed earlier in the colonial period, as the Spanish Bourbon state worked to collapse categories and create a more homogeneous body politic.

This situation became even more complicated after independence. The new state legislature of Oaxaca busied itself writing laws that would regulate municipalities, including indigenous village governments, throughout the state. Decisions based on custom no longer had legal standing. Instead, all cases were to be decided using a legal code backed by a constitution. This constitution was an exercise in egalitarian liberalism, and not an empty one at that. In theory the constitution should have eliminated most of the social glue that held indigenous villages together, replacing it with a basically administrative village government elected through universal male suffrage. Anyone who has read twentieth-century Oaxacan ethnography will understand that that particular development did not occur. Yet liberal egalitarianism did foster important innovation within villages. Commoners used the liberal egalitarian provisions of the state constitution and laws to reform the *cargo* system, eliminating all exemptions based on noble birth. In doing so, they ended the problem of families claiming that the exemptions earned through service could be passed on to their children.

The elimination of privileges based on birth was a momentous change for these villages. Disputes over such privileges had sparked dozens of lawsuits in the late colonial period and had been an important cause of village dissension. These conflicts were particularly uncomfortable because indigenous political culture sharply censured all divisions within villages.[24] Surprisingly, this dramatic change did not generate copious records. Noble village families, already buffeted by a rising tide of egalitarianism, slipped from view without a fight. In fact, what is striking about the records is the sudden silence about privileges based on birth. A type of conflict that generated dozens of trials from the 1750s to the 1820s abruptly disappeared.

Fortunately, another kind of dispute provides us with a small window on what happened. Although individuals no longer claimed exemptions based on birth, the *cargo* system continued to exist and generate conflicts. One of the most evocative occurred in the mestizo village of Villa Alta in 1834. Tomás Mijangos complained that the current *alcalde* of the village was trying to "impose new customs," in particular by forcing Mijangos to serve as a messenger. Although Mijangos hinted that his family was exempt from these servile posts, presumably by birth, Villa Alta did not have a history of noble families claiming privileges. Moreover, Mijangos did not make birth the center of his claim to exemption. Instead he argued that he should be excused due to his previous services, apparently as town councilman.

Alcalde José Eusevio Rojas replied:

> I don't know what legal exemptions citizen Mijangos has and even less his appraisal of the obligations he has as a citizen in whatever village he lives in; thus either the citizen Mijangos does not have rights as a citizen, or his exemptions are superior to those of others who with a better basis could claim exemptions, since it is well demonstrated that good citizens observe all parts of the laws. Mijangos, far from fulfilling the laws, wants to exempt himself from those duties, and, in trying this, not only is he not following the laws, he is failing in his obligations, hating them along with the prize of Citizenship that is conceded him on the basis of his labors. Article 10 of the regulatory law does not exempt any citizen from this obligation. . . . [offices] can be distributed among all the citizens because the common or town government never has had funds to pay people to do work and thus cannot exempt citizens.[25]

Rojas is referring here to article 10 of the 1825 law of municipal administration, which ordered municipal governments to take special care that obligations be distributed among all residents.[26] Despite the eloquence of the *alcalde*, this case is of limited utility in understanding the disappearance of claims of nobility. The *cargo* system did not have a particularly strong hold in Villa Alta, which was not an indigenous village and was also one of the smallest settlements in the district. The fact that it had any hold at all seems indicative of the interpenetration of indigenous and Hispanic political values.

A more likely explanation for the demise of such claims is provided not by the law of municipal administration but instead by the state constitution of 1825, which, in article 18, had abolished "hereditary distinctions, authority and power."[27] The constitution was promulgated in every village, and from 1825 village primary schools were required to teach its precepts using a "political catechism."[28] As early as 1826 peasant plaintiffs were citing the constitution in legal petitions.[29] The strength and clarity of this constitutional provision probably account more than anything else for the failure of noble families to officially protest the loss of their privileges. The constitutional language made winning their cases impossible, or at least so unlikely that they were unwilling to invest in costly and divisive legal procedures.

Notably, the liberal republican order did not abolish the authority of village governments to call on the labor of villagers. It instead codified this power in the 1825 law of municipal administration.[30] This law, which extended not just to indigenous villages but to all municipalities, demonstrates how features of the *cargo* system were as much Hispanic as indigenous. Hispanic municipal government had a long tradition of *cargas consejiles*, which an 1840 Spanish legal dictionary defines as posts "that all residents of a village must serve in turn."[31] In fact, one Bourbon lawyer had argued in 1796 that indigenous *cargo* systems were mere imitations of Spanish municipal practice.[32] Service to the community was not treated as involuntary "personal service," which was abolished by the liberal Spanish Cortes in 1812 and remained anathema to the postindependence liberal republicans.[33] Instead the legal system and apparently most villagers viewed community service as an undeniable duty of citizenship.

Villagers' acceptance of the new legal order was quite selective. In particular, they struggled with universal male suffrage, which eliminated the official electoral role of the elders or *principales*, at least for the highest offices. At first, it allowed men who had not ascended through the *cargo* system to be elected to the highest posts in the village, those of *alcaldes* and councilmen. These men often were vulnerable because the *principales* retained great prestige and moral authority. Villagers were also much more likely to challenge the power and legitimacy of younger officials. From the late 1820s through the abolition of the constitution and elected municipal government in 1836 there were many cases in which elected *alcaldes*, or mayors, ran afoul of the moral authority of village elders.[34]

When Mexican centralists eliminated elected municipalities in 1836, the situation in villages became even more confused. Justices of the peace appointed by Spanish and mestizo district administrators replaced elected municipal officials. Although in Villa Alta justices were almost always chosen from among residents of the villages they governed, they lacked both the old sanction of the *principales* and the new one of popular election. Their authority was at first particularly tenuous. They were often relatively young men, apparently preferred for these posts due to their greater exposure to both the Spanish language and Hispanic legal norms. These men might have served as village secretaries under more experienced officials in previous years. Now they were catapulted to the top office without having climbed the *cargo* ladder.[35] Those who wanted to defy their authority, often in public shouting matches, typically referred to their youth, pointing out that they were "muy muchacho," or very boyish.[36] Worse yet, to govern they needed the help of subordinates who were dutifully climbing the *cargo* ladder. Justice of the Peace Crisanto de Bargas of Yalalag put this very eloquently in 1840: "Unfortunately for me the *principales* have named as deputies two overbearing and haughty men, who, proud of having done the services customary in this village in their order and steps, treat me and the councilmen as pests, disobeying us and insulting us at every turn."[37] The new justices of the peace understood the weakness of their position and in some cases went to great lengths to show respect for the *principales*. In 1841 the district administrator named Juan Mario Santiago and Secundo Santiago justices of the peace of Lalopa. The new officials tried to continue the tradition under which incoming village authorities held a banquet for the *principales*, who, however, refused six different invitations. The *principales* also obstructed their administration and undermined their authority, claiming the justices were disrespectful of village custom. On this occasion even a concerted effort to show respect for the *principales* could not overcome the fact that the *principales* had not been allowed to choose the justices.[38]

District administrators had a substantial stake in preserving local peace. In the early nineteenth century, the indigenous villages of Villa Alta had few resources worth plundering. Their land was not suited to large-scale commercial agriculture, and the textile production that had connected the area's colonial economy to the outside world was no longer competitive. District administrators' only secure income was a share of revenues from the head tax, which was collected by municipal officials and later by justices of the peace. The justices needed the cooperation of the *principales*, and thus it became obvious that administrators' interests were best served by showing sensitivity to local social norms. Some evidence suggests that within a few years they began appointing justices of the peace nominated by the *principales* and rotating justices every year, as indigenous custom demanded for village leaders.

Elected municipal governments were restored after 1846. Thereafter conflicts over the authority of elected governments grew less frequent or at least more muted. Apparently, the *cargo* system and the authority of elders were brought back into harmony with the official means of selecting village officials. It seems likely that peasants accomplished this by using legal provisions for indirect elections, probably choosing *principales* as electors for municipal office. This move would bring two very different legal principles of authority together in the persons of the *principales*. These village elders continued to earn their status through faithful and lengthy service on the *cargo* ladder, following traditions established in the colonial corporate order. Yet when they were chosen by all adult males to serve as electors, they also became depositories of popular sovereignty legitimated by the liberal republican constitution.

The documents simply do not contain much evidence of this momentous transition. Villages reported final electoral results, but they did not submit lists of secondary electors. Again, we are forced to read between the lines of a related case. In 1852, the *principales* and commoners of Lachixila submitted a petition asking that their *alcalde*, Hermengildo Ayala be removed from his post because of drunkenness and womanizing. The petitioners wanted to replace Ayala with Mateo de Luna, whom they supported with "the votes of all the *principales* and all the village."[39] In this document, the *principales* have recovered an electoral role, and that electoral role is linked to that of the whole village. Notably, according to state law, if the *alcalde* were removed from office, his successor would be chosen by the secondary electors who had elected him. Apparently that is the legal provision the petitioners had in mind as they moved to depose Ayala and simultaneously to seat Luna. This interpretation of the Lachixila petition is reinforced to some degree by a similar petition written the following year in Temascalapa. The Temascalapa petition sought the removal of the *alcalde* Juan Molina but did not propose a replacement. It was written by, and in the name of, the councilmen and forty-two *principales*, who are listed by name.[40]

Reflections

At the outset of this essay, I argued that some of the most important political values of southern Mexican villages were formed in an encounter between law and custom in the early nineteenth century. Clearly some qualifications are in order. First, we need to keep in mind that villagers themselves apparently did not see custom and law as distinct categories. They were both to be obeyed, and the evidence suggests that for some they were the same thing. In 1843, Francisco Méndez of La Olla argued that he should be exempt from service as a *fiscal* due to his previous service as a justice of the peace. At different moments Mendez called the rule he appealed to either custom or law. To him, these were apparently interchangeable words, at least in this context.[41] Second, as the above remarks suggest, the encounter between previous norms and liberal law left very little direct evidence. Villagers clearly wrestled with the implications of this encounter, but their thoughts and arguments were not captured on paper. The best evidence of how the encounter played out is oblique.

Yet, even though the evidence of how this transition was worked out is sketchy, simply comparing what documents tell us about village political and social life in the mid-eighteenth century to the observations of anthropologists beginning in the early twentieth century leaves no doubt that the villages refashioned themselves. This transition can be seen as consisting of two equally important parts: what changed and what did not change. Each had a crucial role in shaping these communities and everything we know about their successors today.

The most important change was the end of hereditary distinctions within villages. The absence of hereditary distinctions has allowed anthropologists, led by Eric Wolf in the 1950s, to interpret the *cargo* system as a leveling device designed to assure that individuals did not accumulate wealth as they accumulated prestige.[42] It also shaped our entire vision of peasant communities as relatively egalitarian communities. Although this second observation only applies directly to interpretations of Mesoamerican communities, it had important influence on general views of peasant society and politics.[43] Here I have argued that the egalitarianism of these indigenous peasant communities was in part constituted by nineteenth-century Hispanic legislators.

Yet in history what does not happen is often just as important as what does. In this case, the great nonevent was the failure of republican liberal law to end the claims of indigenous communities on the personal labor of their members. This omission was probably both deliberate and pragmatic, as these communities could not maintain public works or even administer justice without this resource. Yet it also fatally weakened the liberal project of creating a nation of individuals, because this labor service was central to the indigenous vision of corporate identity. Lawmakers saw the necessity of the *cargo* system, but they overlooked its intense cultural significance. Although Hispanic lawmakers could justify community service as essential to citizenship, they did not understand the degree to which community service was linked specifically to village identity. By legally sanctioning the services villagers owed their communities, lawmakers fortified the communal identity of villages rather than the bonds between individual citizens and the sovereign national state. Belonging to the village, being a "child of the pueblo," required participation in the *cargo* system and its attendant institutions, communal work gangs and labor for the parish priest. Certainly communal identity was tied to communal land rights, but the membership of individuals in the community depended on service. For example, in 1832 the villagers of Santiago Lalopa dismantled the house of Plácido Martínez and used the beams and roof tiles to repair the village church. Martínez had emigrated to the city of Oaxaca sixteen years before, and the villagers felt he had lost the right to own a home there because "he had not served the village for anything."[44] The *cargo* system was important for village politics, but its importance also extended into social life. Far from a simple means to regulate access to political power, the *cargo* system and its attendant claims on the labor of families legitimated a more general village patriarchy in which the young served the old and women served men. The *cargo* system and communal service have persisted because the authors and interpreters of the law have allowed them to survive and sometimes even given them legal sanction. Thus it is possible to conclude that law shaped key elements of indigenous village identity.

Notes

1 Jan Rus and Robert Wasserstrom, "Civil-Religious Hierarchies in Central Chiapas: A Critical Perspective," *American Ethnologist* 7.3 (1989): 466–478; Judith Friedlander, "The Secularization of the Cargo System: An Example from Postrevolutionary Central Mexico," *Latin American Research Review* 16.2 (1981): 132–143.

2 John Chance and William Taylor, "*Cofradías* and Cargos: An Historical Perspective on the Mesoamerican Civil-Religious Hierarchy," *American Ethnologist* 12.1 (1985): 1–26.

3 Joanne Rappaport, *Cumbe Reborn: An Andean Ethnography of History* (Chicago: University of Chicago Press, 1994), 26. See also Rappaport, "History, Law and Ethnicity in Andean Colombia," *Latin American Anthropology Review* 2.1 (1990): 13.

4 Florencia Mallon, *Peasant and Nation: The Making of Postcolonial Mexico and Peru* (Berkeley: University of California Press, 1995), 66–74.

5 Archivo de Villa Alta (Hereafter AVA), Civil, exp. 1310 (1855).

6 Steve J. Stern, *The Secret History of Gender: Women, Men, and Power in Late Colonial Mexico* (Chapel Hill: University of North Carolina Press, 1995), 194–204.

7 For an example from Yalalag, see AVA, Penal, exp. 1241 (1857).

8 AVA, Penal, exp. 714 (1840).

9 AVA, Civil, exp. 790 (1816).

10 John Chance, *Conquest of the Sierra: Spaniards and Indians in Colonial Oaxaca* (Norman: University of Oklahoma Press, 1989), 137–146.

11 AVA, Civil, exp. 258 (1760). For other cases, see AVA, Civil, exp. 293 (1766); AVA, Civil, exp. 362 (1774); AVA, Civil, exp. 453 (1789); AVA, Civil, exp. 513 (1796); AVA, Civil, exp. 625 (1802); AVA, Civil, exp. 730 (1811); and AVA, Civil, exp. 790 (1816).

12 Chance, *Conquest of the Sierra*, 144–145.

13 AVA, Civil, exp. 1605 (1802).

14 AVA, Civil, exp. 430 (1786).

15 See, e.g., AVA, Penal, exp. 407 (1798); AVA, Penal, exp. 414 (1798); and AVA, Civil, exp. 268 (1760).

16 This fits the basic pattern of gender negotiation that Stern discusses in *Secret History*, 80–85. For examples in Villa Alta see AVA, Penal, exp. 515 (1827); AVA, Penal, exp. 520 (1828); AVA, Penal, exp. 529 (1829); AVA, Penal, exp. 536 (1830); AVA, Penal, exp. 554 (1831); AVA, Penal, exp. 891 (1844); and AVA, Penal, exp. 911 (1848).

17 For examples in Villa Alta see AVA, Civil, exp. 656 (1805); AVA, Penal, exp. 582 (1831); AVA, Penal, exp. 683 (1838); AVA, Penal, exp. 753 (1842); AVA, Penal, exp. 799 (1844); and AVA, Penal, exp. 995 (1851).

18 See Stern's analysis of this dynamic in *Secret History*, 204–209.

19 Chance, *Conquest of the Sierra*, 143–144.

20 Colin MacLachlan, *Spain's Empire in the New World: The Role of Ideas in Institutional and Social Change* (Berkeley: University of California Press, 1988), 28.

21 William Taylor, *Magistrates of the Sacred: Priests and Parishioners in Eighteenth-Century Mexico* (Stanford, CA: Stanford University Press, 1996), 13.

22 AVA, Civil, exp. 513 (1796).

23 See, for example AVA, Civil, exp. 790 (1816).

24 For the period in question see Peter Guardino, " 'Total Liberty in Casting our Ballots': Plebes, Peasants, and Elections in Oaxaca, 1808–1850" (paper presented at the Twenty-first Congress of the Latin American Studies Association, Chicago, Sept. 25, 1998). For the late twentieth century, see Philip Parnell, *Escalating Disputes: Social Participation and Change in the Oaxacan Highlands* (Tucson: University of Arizona Press, 1988), 5–6.

25 AVA, Civil, exp. 1079 (1834).

26 *Colección de leyes, decretos y circulares del estado libre y soberano de Oaxaca* (Oaxaca: Imprenta del Estado en el Instituto, 1851–1914), 1:213.

27 Article 18 of the constitution in *Colección de leyes*, 52.

28 See the law of municipal administration in *Colección de leyes*, 210. For the use of political catechisms in the Villa Alta district, see Archivo General del Estado de Oaxaca, Gobernación, box 29.

29 See for example AVA, Penal, exp. 502 (1826).

30 *Colección de leyes*, 213.

31 Joaquín Escriche, *Diccionario razonado de legislación civil, penal, comercial y forense* (Caracas: Imprenta de Valentín Espinal, 1840), 87.

32 AVA, Civil, exp. 513 (1796).

33 Terry Rugeley, *Yucatán's Maya Peasantry and the Origins of the Caste War* (Austin: University of Texas Press, 1996), 39.

34 The most dramatic example is found in AVA, Penal, exp. 631 (1834).

35 AVA, Penal, exp. 786 (1843).

36 See, for example, AVA, Penal, exp. 828 (1845).

37 AVA, Penal, exp. 706 (1840).

38 AVA, Penal, exp. 739 (1841).

39 AVA, Penal, exp. 1023 (1852).

40 AVA, Penal, exp. 1046 (1853).

41 AVA, Penal, exp. 786 (1843).

42 Eric Wolf, *Sons of the Shaking Earth* (Chicago: University of Chicago Press, 1959), 215–220.

43 See, in particular, the classic by James Scott, *The Moral Economy of the Peasant* (New Haven, CT: Yale University Press, 1976), esp. 3–7.

44 AVA, Penal, exp. 591 (1832). For another example of the tie between community service and community membership, see AVA, Penal, exp. 441 (1805).

The "spirit" of Bolivian laws: citizenship, patriarchy, and infamy
Rossana Barragán

On April 2, 1831, inhabitants of capital towns in Bolivia awoke to the sound of cannons announcing the reading of a presidential decree and the celebration of Te Deum masses in all the churches of the land.[1] The newspaper published a poem to honor the sun-father and source of light, who had ripped away the veil of infernal darkness and brought wisdom inscribed in sacred books.[2] That same day, "the most classical document of civilization in the youngest of republics" was dedicated to a woman who was both wife and mother.[3] These celebrations hailed the promulgation and publication of the civil and criminal codes and the code of procedure in 1831 and 1832.[4] The father-hero was none other than President Andrés de Santa Cruz. His wife, Francisca Cernadas, who celebrated her birthday that same day, received the codes into her safekeeping, recalling the manner in which Napoleon had paid homage to his wife, the empress Josephine. The preamble and dedication to Cernadas declared: "The penal code classifies crimes whose perpetration will cause you to invoke justice and punishments whose application will incite in you neither injustice nor cruelty but rather compassion for miserable human beings. In the civil code, the duties of spouse, mother, and tutor will complement your own sentiments, reflecting maternal feelings toward the sons of Bolivia."[5]

Three features stand out in this ceremonial presentation of the codes. First, the codes are, like the Bible, regarded as sacred books, which commemorate the foundation of the new republic. Second, the imitation of contemporary French political iconography highlights the themes of Enlightenment and "modernity." Last, the images reflect official conceptions about gender relations and social hierarchy: the philosopher-hero offers the product of masculine reason to his mythologized wife, who cradles justice in her lap and offers compassion. This chapter explores these themes, examining the relation between law and society in the nineteenth century in order to evaluate the degree to which the modernity claimed by Bolivian jurists marked a rupture with the colonial period. I argue that despite the establishment of formal equality, social hierarchy was subtly redefined in order to make it compatible with liberal principles. In particular, the law invoked gendered understandings of honor and infamy to legitimate the practice of differentiating among individuals according to their "quality."

Bolivia was one of the first countries in Latin America to formulate new legal codes. As early as 1825 and 1826, Simón Bolívar and Antonio José de Sucre called for new legislation in order to establish the nation upon a liberal framework.[6] Soon thereafter, Santa Cruz took on that task with the aim of establishing internal peace and stability, as well as a modern reputation in the eyes of European powers whose political and financial support he courted. The number of constitutions that Bolivia has had—a total of eleven in the nineteenth century[7]—reflects attempts by different presidents to legitimize themselves through a symbolic refounding of the republic. This was even more true of the law codes approved between 1830 and 1832, only five years after proclamation of the republic, since political autonomy, as represented in the constitutions, had to be matched by judicial and legal autonomy.[8] Old laws had to be abolished, as they were considered anachronisms in the new era; they belonged to "feudal times," the "horrors of serfdom," the spirit of "conquest . . . and oppression," and the perpetuation of colonialism.[9] They were declared an obstacle to entry into the new century, the age of Enlightenment, philosophy, freedom, and morality.[10]

Eager to modernize Bolivian law as quickly as possible, Bolivian jurists based their codes upon European models. The civil code belongs to the first wave of juridical changes in Latin America characterized by the adoption or at least strong influence of the Napoleonic Civil Code.[11] Carrying the force of the Enlightenment and of the French Revolution, this code was considered the culmination of liberal ideals. It consecrated private property, secularized society, and established the multiple rights and duties of citizenship.[12] Paradoxically, however, the Bolivian criminal code, which was to "break the chains with Spain," was a revision of the Spanish Code of 1822. Although this code was liberal, having been influenced by the Spaniard José María Calatrava, the Frenchman

The "Spirit" of Bolivian Laws   67

Benjamin Constant, and the Englishman Jeremy Bentham, it maintained older Spanish concepts of honor and infamy. This tension between modern and traditional concepts was even more marked in the Bolivian context, with its large indigenous population.

Two scholars have offered distinct explanations for the juxtaposition in Latin America of modern legal and political forms and a hierarchical society. Marie Danielle Demélas argues that the modern democratic system, based on the equality of individuals within a representative system of government, was imported rather than created. Hence, legal texts such as constitutions were completely divorced from Bolivian society, a stratified social order quite unlike that of modern social classes.[13] Francois-Xavier Guerra, in contrast, contends that the wars of independence were in fact cultural revolutions inspired by the Enlightenment, but that this modernity was the exclusive province of the elites.[14] Yet both see the coexistence of traditional society and modern political structures as the result of a long transition to an incomplete modernity. European models thus continue to be the hidden yardsticks against which the new Bolivian republic is measured.[15] This Eurocentric perspective highlights historical paradoxes and anomalies, incomplete and copied projects destined to fail, either because they did not correspond to reality or because the "masses" did not partake of the appropriate culture.[16]

Instead of these dichotomies between law and society, elite and popular sectors, I wish to offer a more complex and integrated interpretation of continuity and change. This essay focuses on the dominant discourse as expressed in republican legislation, specifically the various constitutions adopted, the civil and criminal codes, the procedural code, and the military code, because it is fundamental for understanding the complex interaction between modernizing elites and subaltern groups. I contend that the body of laws directly affected social conditions and cannot be considered merely ideological or divorced from reality. The presentation of the legal codes by Santa Cruz may therefore be described as a "solemn act of categorization," granting privileges to some while subordinating and excluding others, in the process of constituting the new nation.[17] In turn, the partial successes and failures of dominant projects were shaped by the strategies deployed by members of the popular sectors.

Honor was central to the effort to resolve the tension between juridical equality and de facto hierarchy. One's reputation affected the exercise of civil and political rights as well as the determination of punishments in criminal cases. Gendered definitions distinguished between virtuous and disreputable women and justified the maintenance of patriarchal privi-

68   Rossana Barragán

leges. Finally, paternalism characterized relations between elites and the indigenous population as well as between women and men. The first part of this essay analyzes the place of honor in the constitutions and codes, particularly in the determination of rights and penalties. In the second part, I critically examine the spirit of the laws, specifically the relations between citizenship and infamy, patriarchy and legalized violence, the differentiation between reputable and dishonorable women, and illegitimacy. In the third part, I consider the strategies of members of the popular sectors, especially indigenous groups, as they attempted to defend their rights in the courts. In the conclusion, I return to a consideration of continuity and change.

Crime, Punishment, and Infamy

The foundational Criminal Code of 1831 defined crimes and imposed punishments in order to regulate behavior according to the republic's needs. The criminal code was organized in three sections: the definition of crimes and punishments, crimes against society (in other codes the term *state* appears instead of *society*), and crimes against individuals. Classifying punishments as corporal, noncorporal, and pecuniary reveals the link between law and honor. This classification paralleled the attributes of the individual in his corporal nature, *fama* (honor), and property. Corporal punishments were those applied to the convict's physical body, such as death and different forms of the deprivation of liberty (such as incarceration).[18] Noncorporal punishments changed an individual's juridical status and suspended legal rights, both of which affected his public reputation. The civil code defined such a condition as civil death, according to which the individual could not be a guardian, act as a witness, initiate a legal demand, or participate in a trial.[19] The definition of crimes against individuals also paralleled these three attributes: acts against the physical being, such as murders, injuries, and rape; acts against honor and fame, such as slander and insults (*calumnias* and *injurias*); and acts against property.

According to Enlightenment philosophy, the severity of the punishment should correspond to the seriousness of the crime. This marked a break from the dark and barbarous past, as President Andrés de Santa Cruz emphasized and newspapers proclaimed.[20] As in Europe, reforms of the criminal code sought, as Foucault would put it, "not to punish less, but to punish better; to punish less severely . . . , to punish on more universal terms." Following the "Linnaean" scheme for crimes and punishments, the penalty should be proportional to the crime, and should "punish just enough to prevent it."[21] One might argue, then, that European "legal and criminal modernity" was rapidly and fully enforced by the new republic, but the coexistence of the liberal civil or Napoleonic code with the Spanish criminal code is revealing. Both held conservative dispositions regarding honor and patriarchy, and were thus far from incompatible. Despite the language of modernity, then, the Bolivian criminal code perpetuated colonial concepts of "infamy"[22] and of society as heterogeneous and hierarchical. Penalties were designed to fit not only the crime but also the perpetrator.

Infamy was the primary noncorporal punishment in the criminal code. Stemming from the Latin negative *in* and *fama*, it meant "without reputation."[23] In medieval Castilian laws (in force during the colonial period), *fama* was defined as "the good state of man," that is, he who "lived decently according to the law and good customs." Infamy was applied automatically to procurers, mountebanks, usurers, adulteresses; or it was imposed by law with a sentence for treason, falsehood, adultery, theft, robbery with fraud, bribery, and injuries.[24] The nineteenth-century definition of *hombre infame* combined these colonial antecedents with republican virtue: "Men hated because of their public behavior, but who act so as a result of their self-interested desire, regardless of the harm done to others, and against rules of morality and justice, as established by society. Infamous means without reputation, and reputation is only applied to those who act correctly with their fellow men and treat them with civility. To do the opposite, then, is to be infamous."[25]

Infamy, as a noncorporal punishment, involved three elements: (1) deprivation of political rights or the loss of citizenship; (2) deprivation (*interdicción*) of the legal and civil rights to act as accuser, witness, executor, or guardian; and (3) prohibition against holding public office (*inhabilitación*) and joining the army.[26] Infamy was a common punishment in cases of robbery, irrespective of the circumstances or the amount stolen.[27] In 1843, the law established that infamy should be applied in addition to other corporal punishments for all crimes except those punished with fines.[28]

Inequality before the Law

Despite the claims of modernity in the Bolivian legal codes, the laws were not based upon the assumption that society was composed of equal individuals. Although social distinctions were not always explicit in the criminal code, certain details reveal their presence. Four main areas clearly reveal the logic of hierarchy and difference: citizenship and infamy; paternalism and legalized violence; honest women versus prostitutes; and legitimate versus illegitimate children.

Citizenship and infamy

By determining who exercised political and civil rights, the constitutions distinguished between those who were citizens and those who were merely of Bolivian nationality. Bolivians were simply all people born within the republic, while citizens were those Bolivians who were male, over twenty-one years of age or married, literate, and not domestic servants. The division of Bolivians into citizens and noncitizens echoes the legal distinction between active and passive citizens in France, and even more so between Spaniards and citizens found on the Iberian peninsula.[29] In the case of Bolivia, the requirements for citizenship excluded the great majority of the population. The indigenous and mestizo majority spoke native languages that were oral, and they usually lacked Spanish literacy. Moreover, most could not exercise the political right to vote or be elected to office owing to their dependent status. Other criteria for social differentiation were sex and age. Because of their sex, women were not only excluded from citizenship, but they were not allowed to file accusations, except in cases in which they were directly and personally involved. Similarly excluded were minors and those whose occupation or profession did not yield a minimum annual income of three hundred pesos. Such requirements for citizenship were maintained in all Bolivian constitutions until 1938.[30]

In addition to setting standards of independence, the procedural code further distinguished between people of "good reputation" and those who lacked it. The former were granted the privilege of not being imprisoned together with delinquents or sentenced to major corporal punishments.[31] Moreover, if a crime was not serious enough for corporal punishment, people of "publicly known honesty and wealth" were not required to post bail.[32]

Such distinctions were particularly clear in the military code. Soldiers and officers were differentiated according to literacy, civic knowledge, and the power to give orders and to punish. In the case of the army, the power to inflict punishment corresponded to educational level, particularly knowledge about the republic and its laws. Soldiers, for example, were obliged to learn the "catechism of the political constitution" and had to pass a literacy test in order to be promoted to the rank of corporal.[33] Once they did so, they were given a stick with which they could punish enlisted men, especially drunkards, "not exceeding two or three strokes."[34] Corporals were required to read and write and to know the "catechism of the political constitution of the state." Sergeants had not simply to pass the literacy exam but also to know the four rules of arithmetic, keep up registries, and know the penal code; in return, they had the jurisdiction to arrest and jail their subordinates. Finally high-ranking officers were allowed to exercise authority over personal servants as well as those below them in the military hierarchy.[35]

The military code also distinguished among different kinds of crimes and established distinct punishments, according to the class, rank, and reputation of the defendant. For example, an article that applied to the "entire" army ended by stating that punishment should be imposed according to the "quality of the persons affected." Thus, a soldier who stole between six and twenty-five pesos was sentenced to eight years in prison and to death if the theft exceeded that amount; but in the case of an officer, robbery was called misappropriation, and he was merely suspended from employment while still receiving a third of his salary.[36] Drunkenness, moreover, was associated with specific "classes," and corporal punishments, like arrest and imprisonment, were mostly reserved for soldiers. Officers suffered, instead, a loss of employment or reduction of salaries.[37] The essence of the army was, of course, obedience.[38] If soldiers or corporals failed to carry out orders, even when not on active duty, they would receive one hundred strokes of the rod and four months' imprisonment.[39] Furthermore, everyone of lower rank "who spoke ill of his superior" should be "punished severely."[40]

The distinction between the high command and soldiers thus paralleled the differentiation between citizens and Bolivians. While the legal codes did not establish specific juridical categories based upon class or ethnicity, distinctions were made when administering and distributing punishments. There was no need for explicitly discriminatory laws since behind legal equality lay the practice of inequality. For example, applying corporal punishments to certain types of crime and noncorporal penalties to others meant that public officials (most of whom were of Spanish descent) were generally exempt from the former, except in the case of serious crimes.[41] Similarly, in the case of the army, soldiers and officers could commit the same offense but receive different punishments.

The identification of certain people as lacking in reputation reveals how concepts of honor and citizenship were intertwined. Dishonorable conduct could, according to the constitutions, result in a permanent or temporary loss of citizenship, as in the case of the insane, fraudulent debtors, drunkards, gamblers, beggars (constitution of 1826), and those involved in a criminal case or suffering either defamatory or grievous punishment or "degrading corporal punishment" (constitutions of 1831, 1861, and 1871). Thus infamy was a variant of "civil death" from the old legislation, since it meant loss of citizenship and the right to act as witness, executor, or guardian (except to one's own children), enter into public office, or serve in the army, militia, or navy.[42]

Paternalism and legalized violence

The rights granted to honorable heads of household extended from the public sphere into the domestic arena. *Patria potestad* in colonial legislation was "the power of parents over children and grandchildren, and over all those of their lineage born of honorable marriage."[43] In the republic *patria potestad* required that unmarried youth (under twenty-four years for men and twenty-two for women) respect and honor both parents.[44] Children could not marry without the explicit authorization of their fathers,[45] who enjoyed guardian rights (*tutela*) over them as well as the administration of their fortunes. Mothers could assume the same role only if the father was dead, and women who were not mothers could never take the role of legal guardians.[46]

In addition to the privileges of fatherhood, other articles granted men authority over their spouses. According to the civil code, for example, husbands should protect their wives, and wives should obey them. Moreover, women could not participate in trials, nor could they sell or buy without the permission of their husbands, although they could appeal to judges if husbands did not give their authorization.[47] Just as children were not allowed to leave home without paternal authorization or behave disrespectfully,[48] a wife who was disobedient and refused to change her behavior despite "warnings and moderate domestic punishments" could be taken before a judge to be reprimanded.[49] If a woman committed adultery, not only could she be sent to a reformatory for up to six years, she could also lose her dowry and her share of the joint marital property.[50] When a husband, brother, or father-in-law found his female relative committing a carnal act and killed the man, his punishment was less than that usually applied for murder.[51]

The authority of parents over children, of husbands over wives, and of masters over their servants also included legalized violence, a hold-over from the colonial period.[52] In addition to allowing "moderate domestic punishments," the laws did not punish "physical injury, offense, and physical ill-treatment" if they were inflicted "unintentionally" and without permanent injury by parents on their children or grandchildren.[53] Punishment meted out within the household thus reflected the same hierarchical gender, generational, and class relations as the penalties carried out by criminal and military courts.

Infamous women and illegitimate children

Given the patriarchal nature of the laws, it is not surprising that infamy took on particular meanings for women and children. The 1831 criminal code clearly distinguished between "uncorrupted women, those with good reputation," and those of blemished reputation or prostitutes, whether these women were victims or perpetrators of crimes. Punishment for sexual offenses committed against a prostitute was half that for a crime against women of good reputation.[54] Advocating this inequality in an 1834 congressional debate, one senator argued that honest women should not suffer the same punishment as "other" women because they always tried to behave according to the honor code. This attitude persisted among some of the elite a century later, when another jurist lamented that it was no longer considered acceptable for the law to discriminate between women with good and bad reputations.[55]

The differentiation among women according to their reputations was reproduced across generations in a hierarchy based upon legitimacy. This distinction was rooted in medieval customs that assumed the existence of a small female elite of good reputation, expected to be sexually chaste, as well as a group of "dishonorable" women. In medieval Spanish law, *patria potestad* permitted men to have concubines (*barraganas*), who were women over twelve years of age and not virgins.[56] We are thus confronted with a socially and legally specified class of women who were suppliers of extramarital sexual relations for men and, at the same time, the mothers of illegitimate children. Sexual virtue was expected only of certain women. The dishonor of many plebeian women thus underpinned the honor of gentlemen and ladies. A lady's honor was also linked to patrilineal norms of kinship descent: a married woman would be ascribed the "honors and dignity" associated with her husband, and above all the "highest honor" of having her children inherit her husband's patri-

74   Rossana Barragán

mony.[57] Illegitimate children, on the other hand, were considered to have been "conceived against law and natural reason" and thus had no right to property from their father's side.[58] In other words, the "quality" of the children also depended upon the condition and virtue of the mother.

In the Bolivian context, such premarital or extramarital unions frequently occurred across socio-ethnic lines, with the men of a higher social rank than the women. Republican law continued the colonial Spanish practice of identifying different types of offspring resulting from such unions. *Illegitimate* children were those not acknowledged by the father and conceived in circumstances socially or morally forbidden (e.g., outside of marriage) or those "stained" for some other reason (e.g., non-Catholic religious background). Such children could not inherit but had the right to financial support until they came of age at twenty-five years.[59] *Natural* children were those acknowledged by the father and conceived and born in circumstances in which the parents would have been able to marry. These offspring were allowed to demand a fifth of their parents' property.[60] Although the distinction was important for inheritance purposes, both illegitimate and natural children were characterized as "infamous" because of the conditions in which they were conceived and born, and thus both were despised by dominant groups because they embodied sin, shame, and frequently "illicit" interclass and interethnic unions.[61] The standards of reputation invoked in the laws, therefore, encompassed interrelated hierarchies based upon status, gender, lineage, and (implicitly) ethnicity.

Law and Infamy in Practice: Social Dynamics in the Courts

It is important to turn to the courts of justice in order to analyze the relation between the legislative corpus and society, as well as to identify particular strategies deployed by the popular sectors. While hegemonic class and gender ideologies certainly prevailed in the courts, regulating what should or should not be stated and in what manner, they also constituted arenas of struggle between elites and subaltern groups.

Lower-class men and women faced constant questioning of the validity of their legal testimony. To begin with, they had to justify their presence in court by declaring a socially legitimate trade or occupation. Some jobs, such as seasonal work on agricultural estates, performed mostly by indigenous laborers, were considered of such low status that they did not grant credibility. Those with only temporary employment fell into the category of "vagrants," defined by police regulations in 1845 as anyone whose "trade, occupation, destination, property, rents, or honest livelihood is unknown."[62] In a related category were those "dubiously engaged" (*mal entretenidos*), including artisans and other manual laborers who "do not apply themselves due to their vices and laziness." Apprentices, moreover, were seen as equivalent to dependents, estate workers, or domestic employees.[63] Ultimately, those identified as vagrants or dependents did not enjoy citizenship. Therefore, lower-class testimony could be easily rejected, as shown by the reply of a master accused of mistreatment:

> Article 786 . . . and 787 of the procedural code prohibits [*sic*] people from making accusations if it is not on their own behalf, if they do not have employment that brings in at least three hundred pesos annually, and in general if they do not exercise citizenship: you know very well that a few miserable estate workers [*colonos*] lack this franchise. The following article prohibits dependents [*criados*] from challenging their master; estate workers are nothing but domestic servants and dependents subject to the lord and owner of the estate.[64]

Let us take, as an example, the case of an indigenous hatter who sued a merchant over debts arising from a work contract. The merchant based his defense upon impugning the hatter's witnesses. First, he claimed, some witnesses were related to the plaintiff or were coerced, while others were living in his house or were "servants." One of the witnesses was a concubine of another, and furthermore she was "dimwitted and lacking in judgment." The merchant even identified several artisans as belonging to a "class that is barely visible," making them "obscure . . . unknown people," "miserable people . . . without any role in society." For all these reasons, he claimed, their testimony was suspect: the witnesses "do not merit credibility . . . due to their lack of or bad reputation."[65]

By insinuating intimacy between the witnesses and the hatter, the merchant implied a condition of dependency that would disqualify the witnesses. Thus, the witnesses for the prosecution were converted into accused who had to assert their status as citizens. This hatter, like others in similar straits, was forced to undermine his opponent's case by exercising the same logic: he had to discredit the opposing witnesses by demonstrating their condition of servitude and dependence while presenting testimony that his own were reputable workers and hence credible. Further, he sought to accredit his own character by asking the authorities of his community to provide assurances of his "conduct as a tributary [indigenous taxpayer] . . . and his behavior." He also requested the principal master of his guild to testify to the "honesty" with which he had "behaved as an artisan without the slightest mar to his character and honor." Finally, this information was channeled through the police, who issued a certificate of his "morally immaculate behavior."[66]

It is noteworthy that the attack against these witnesses focused on their being "obscure" and "unknown." Given the lack of any specific juridical status for persons of indigenous or mixed descent, elites tried to redeploy preexisting ethnic hierarchies while using a different language centered on the interrelated concepts of credit and credibility, competence and "invalidity," rationality and "lack of judgment." Similarly, the use of terms such as "concubine" and a woman "lacking reason" identified a female witness as dishonorable and dependent. To counter such accusations, subalterns had to appeal to character witnesses for recognition and validation. They also had to demonstrate personal ties to members of higher social strata who could act as guarantors, because without such backing, legal suspects could remain in jail for months even if they had been absolved of wrongdoing.[67] Yet such a strategy could also be a trap: without relations to those who were creditworthy, one was simply unknown; but with such relations, one could be taken for a dependent, a noncitizen, and someone subject to corruption.

Subalterns, therefore, often assumed the role of poor and ignorant victims who required the paternal protection of the authorities. In 1850, a group of indigenous people in La Paz, who had been subject to retaliation for having denounced a local official, called on the president of the republic, whom they described as a "fighter" for the "Indian caste," to defend them.[68] Such testimony clearly falls within a hegemonic state discourse, since popular sectors were seeking a favorable solution by taking on the role of "invalids" or, alternatively, by demonstrating honorable conduct as a response to imputations of discredit. It was an uphill battle because daily life was made up of actions considered by dominant groups to be morally unacceptable.

Nevertheless, subalterns also employed a strategy that obliged the state to follow through on its own liberal and egalitarian discourse. The same indigenous people who pled for presidential protection argued, for example, that they were as Bolivian and hence as free as anyone else.[69] Another indigenous couple appealed simultaneously to the patriarchal logic of the government and to the principle of juridical equality: "We wish to say that we unhappy Indians continue to suffer ignorance both in fact and in law, and therefore we have not improved in condition or fortune although the Supreme Government tries daily to provide relief for this unfortunate caste.... My Lord, you are authorized by the Nation and by the Law, acting in rigorous Justice, to protect Indians such as ourselves by showing us to be equal before the law."[70]

Such multiple strategies vis-à-vis their social superiors, which created an ostensible discrepancy between what subaltern subjects said and did, would help explain the deep disgust within the dominant society at the reputedly "two-faced" behavior of mestizos and Indians (best expressed by novelist Alcides Arguedas). This double attitude developed because the dominant sectors promoted a form of communication that required a discursive alignment with their norms and recognition of their patriarchal role. In effect, they encouraged humility and submission.

Conclusions

The coexistence in nineteenth-century Bolivia of a liberal body of law, which established the rights of citizens in a universal language, and a judicial practice based upon hierarchy raises the question of continuity and change from the colonial period. Ironically, less than a decade after independence, republican authorities modeled the 1831 criminal code on that of Spain rather than France.[71] They highlighted its modernity, however, as a break from the past. In a letter addressed to President Andrés de Santa Cruz, one of the authors of the criminal code stated:

> The criminal code ... is the product of wisdom and any criticism of it is groundless.... It was drawn up by eminent men of the Spanish courts. Not satisfied with Calatrava's six years' work ... it was revised by Benjamin Constant and the most profound of legislators, Bentant [Bentham]. According to the opinion of the former, this is the most perfect code ever issued in Europe. The latter's opinions were in the same vein.... Thus who in America would ever dare to condemn it? One would have to be superior to these notable men, or very arrogant.... After all, Sir, the code is wise, perfect, almost divine, and anyone who dares to find fault with it does not know what he is doing, and his lack of intelligence gives rise to his arrogance.[72]

Even if the codes did mark a change, adopting a foreign Spanish model implied an ongoing cultural and ideological if not direct colonial domination. I would assert that Bolivians followed the Spanish, rather than the Napoleonic, code because it allowed the maintenance of culturally engrained discrimination on the basis of reputation and social status, reserving citizenship for honorable and reputable men, as opposed to infamous and illiterate men, and civil rights to privileged women of good credit, not those of low or "unknown" reputation. There is certainly a recognizable relation between the colonial Spanish concept of civil death and the republican use of infamy as grounds for exclusion from or suspension of citizenship.

What, then, were the consequences of the new republican laws for the majority of the population, the indigenous sector whose very identity was a colonial creation?[73] Following upon the controversies provoked by the conquest, "Indians" were declared free vassals not subject to servitude.[74] Yet they paid tribute in recognition of the dominion of the Spanish kings and their role as protectors and administrators of the Indies.[75] Also, though unremunerated personal service for private benefit was prohibited, they were obliged by the state to carry out a series of tasks in the mines, on haciendas, and in public works. This corvée labor obligation was justified because of their "limited capacities," the "benefit" that Spanish intervention entailed for them, their similarity to "rustics" in Spain, and their "more apt nature" for labor.[76] Hence there was an apparent contradiction, since they were "free vassals" obligated to perform given services only incumbent upon indigenous people.[77] They also had a particular legal-juridical status as "miserable" individuals (*miserables*) "for whom we naturally feel pity due to their state, quality, and labors." This status was determined by their "imbecile nature" and poverty, their recent conversion to Catholicism, their lesser capacity for rationality, and their "inability to govern themselves."[78] The status of "miserable" individuals carried with it certain legal "privileges."[79] Their legal cases were to be expeditious, avoiding some of the usual juridical procedures, and they were represented in the courts by the Protector of Indians.[80]

After independence, in keeping with the ostensibly egalitarian principles of liberalism, indigenous people had no specific juridical status in either the constitutions or legal codes (penal, civil, or procedural). They were not even named in these texts, suggesting that they were considered along with all others in the categories of Bolivians and citizens. Given the general absence of a specific legal status for indigenous people, the colonial position of the Protector of Indians, and thus the limited legal privileges of indigenous status, disappeared. But another body of laws that were more conjunctural in nature—the laws, decrees, orders, and resolutions—displays an abundance of specific dispositions referring to "Indians" and reveals that in fact their legal situation was not altogether transformed. Among these dispositions, for example, was the legislation regulating the "indigenous contribution," a neocolonial form of tribute to the state. Despite initial attempts to abolish this differential tax, as a colonial vestige incompatible with enlightened liberal principles, the Bolivian state was fiscally unable to do without it.[81] Thus, as opposed to the Brazilian situation, where slavery became a real obstacle to the adoption of the liberal codes,[82] in Bolivia, theoretically universal codes coexisted with discriminatory regulations.

Within codified law, if not in the specific decrees and resolutions, the colonial terms of ethnic difference disappeared, but a new language ranked Bolivians according to their credit and credibility, competence or "invalidity," rationality or "lack of judgment," characteristics linked to republican understandings of honor and gender. The adoption of a single criminal code, civil code, procedural code, and constitution for all Bolivians could lead us to believe that the new legislation reflected an ideology of juridical equality for all individuals. Yet our analysis of the juridical corpus reveals that jurists still ranked individuals by their reputations. Although such differentiation was not explicitly linked to ethnic castes, in practice the markers of honor (education, property or steady employment, patriarchal authority, and legitimate birth) were out of reach for most of the indigenous population. Hence, indigenous people were generally regarded as infamous and noncitizens. The presumed modernity of the elites was bound up with a paternalism that extended from the household to the society at large. Bolivian leaders, as exemplified by the ceremony of Santa Cruz that opened this essay, saw themselves as bringing light, civilization, and progress to barbarous and backward people. A door was left open to equality, at least at a juridical level, but in order to attain equality and citizenship, indigenous people would have to undergo a process of "civilization."[83]

Despite the disappearance of explicitly colonial terms from the republican codes, two concepts from the past were key to the reformulation of social hierarchy in nineteenth-century Bolivia: patriarchy and honor. According to the criminal code, punishments were to fit not only the crime but also the character of individuals, especially women. Moreover, just as republican laws preserved patriarchal authority within the household, the indigenous population remained in a dependent relationship to the elite. Hence *patria potestad* permeated society in both the public and private spheres. Nevertheless, because the discrimination permitted in the law codes was subtle rather than explicit, the determination of one's social reputation became highly contentious. Interestingly, *fama* is related to the Greek *pheme* and the root word *bha*, which means "to talk."[84] Honor and the words related to it, therefore, were the language of argument in court, where laws were put into practice. Bolivians of indigenous and mestizo descent, as well as women of the popular sectors, marshaled strategies to defend their reputations in a context in which the exercise of not only political but also civil rights was at stake.

Notes

Some of the ideas in this essay are drawn from Rossana Barragán, *Indios, mujeres y ciudadanos: Legislación y ejercicio de la ciudadanía en Bolivia (siglo XIX)* (La Paz: Fundación Diálogo, with the support of the Royal Danish Embassy in Bolivia, 1999); and Barragán, "The Spirit of Bolivian Laws: Citizenship, Infamy, and Patriarchal Hierarchy," in *The Forging of Nationhood*, ed. Gyanendra Pandey and Peter Geschiere (New Delhi: Manohar, 2003). My thanks to Gyan Pandey, Peter Geschiere, Silvia Rivera, and Sudhir Chandra, and my colleagues Seemin Qayum, Tristan Platt, Sinclair Thomson, Sarah Chambers, and Ramiro Molina Rivero for their valuable comments on previous versions of this essay, as well as to Rose Marie Vargas for her assistance in drafting an earlier English translation.

1   "Decreto del 26 de marzo de 1831," *El iris de La Paz*, 31 March 1831, 2.

2   Cual suele el padre de la luz del día
Veloz marchando en carro luminoso
Rasgar el velo de la noche sombría
Imagen del averno tenebroso;
Así se ve brillar sabiduría
En las líneas sagradas, libro hermoso
Honor eterno al Héroe, cuya mano
Borró las leyes del poder Español!!!

[As the father of the light of day
Flying swiftly in a luminous carriage
Sweeping aside the veil of the night's shadow
Image of infernal gloom;
So wisdom shines forth
In the sacred lines, beautiful book
Eternal honor to the Hero, whose hand
Banished the laws of Spanish power!!!]
"A la publicación de los códigos," *El iris de La Paz*, 31 March 1831, 4.

3 "Dedicatoria a S.E. Francisca Cernadas de Santa Cruz," from José Manuel Loza in the first edition of the code. Andrés de Santa Cruz Shuhkrafft, "Notas y apuntes para la historia de don Andrés Santa Cruz: Génesis de la primera codificación republicana," in *Vida y obra del mariscal Andrés de Santa Cruz y Calahumana*, rpt. (La Paz: Edición de la Honorable Municipalidad de La Paz, 1992 [1976]), 40.

4 The Constitutional Assembly declared on July 15, 1831, that they be called the Santa Cruz codes; Santa Cruz Shuhkrafft, "Notas y apuntes," 33, 39. See also Valentín Abecia, "La obra legislativa del mariscal Santa Cruz," in *Vida y obra del mariscal Andrés de Santa Cruz y Calahumana*, 86.

5 One of the authors of the code, José Manuel Loza, wrote to Francisca Cernadas: "A literary genius offered the Napoleonic Code fashioned in elegant verse to the empress Josephine; I, a guest in the house of belles lettres, . . . present to you, Madam, the Santa Cruz codes." Santa Cruz Shuhkrafft, "Notas y apuntes," 40.

6 Decrees of Dec. 21, 1825, and Nov. 2, 1826; Santa Cruz Shuhkrafft, "Notas y apuntes," 22–23.

7 New constitutions were introduced in 1826, 1831, 1834, 1839, 1843, 1851, 1861, 1868, 1871, 1878, and 1880. See Ramón Salinas Mariaca, *Las constituciones de Bolivia* (La Paz: Don Bosco, 1989).

8 "Carta del Ministerio de Estado del despacho del Interior al Presidente de la Corte Suprema de Justicia," *El iris de La Paz*, Nov. 29, 1829, 2.

9 *El iris de La Paz*, March 31, 1831, 3; "Códigos. Decreto del Gran Mariscal Andrés de Santa Cruz," *El iris de La Paz*, March 31, 1831, 1; "Legislación," *El iris de La Paz*, June 12, 1830, 3; "El Iris," *El iris de La Paz*, March 31, 1831, 3.

10 See "Legislación," *El iris de La Paz*, June 12, 1830, 3; "El Iris," 3; and "Administración de justicia," *El iris de La Paz*, April 24, 1831, 4.

11 Other examples included Santo Domingo and Haiti in 1825 and Oaxaca, Mexico, in 1827–29.

12 See Carlos Ramos Núñez, *El código napoleónico y su recepción en América Latina* (Lima: Universidad Católica del Perú, 1997), 110. For an analysis of the French criminal code of 1792 and 1810 (known as the Napoleonic Code), see *Au nom de l'ordre: Une historie politique du code pénal*, ed. Pierre Lascoumes et al. (Paris: Hachette, 1989).

13 Marie Danièlle Demélas, *L'invention politique: Bolivie, Equateur, Pérou au XIXe siècle* (Paris: Recherche sur les Civilisations, 1992).

14 François-Xavier Guerra, *Modernidad e independencias* (Madrid: Mapfre, 1992).

15 For examples from Bolivian historiography, see Alipio Valencia Vega, *Historia política de Bolivia* (La Paz: Juventud, 1984–1986); and *El pensamiento político en Bolivia*, 4th ed. (La Paz: Juventud, 1991).

16 Partha Chatterjee, *The Nation and Its Fragments: Colonial and Postcolonial Histories* (Princeton, NJ: Princeton University Press, 1993).

17 Pierre Bourdieu, *Ce que parler veut dire: L'économie des échanges linguistiques* (Paris: Fayard, 1982).

18 Art. 28, chap. 3, *Código penal boliviano* (Paz de Ayacucho: Imprenta del Colegio de Educandas, 1831); and, with minor modifications, *Código penal boliviano* (Sucre: Imprenta de Beeche y Cia., 1845).

19 Arts. 14, 17, *Código civil Santa Cruz* (Paz de Ayacucho: Imprenta del Colegio de Educandas, 1831).

20 The marshall Santa Cruz commented: "The penal code presents to you a logical and well-classified nomenclature of crimes and penalties; a summary of the most accredited laws. . . . You will be emancipated from [the] barbaric yoke." Santa Cruz Shuhkrafft, "Notas y apuntes," 72. See also "Códigos," *El iris de La Paz*, Jan. 13, 1831, 4.

21 Michel Foucault, *Vigilar y castigar: Nacimiento de la prisión* (Mexico City: Siglo Veintiuno, 1993), 86, 97–98, 102–104.

22 Infamy as a legal concept lasted until the end of the nineteenth century. See José Medrano Ossio, *Derecho penal: Sus bases reales, su actualidad* (La Paz, 1951), 85.

23 Pierre Larousse, *Grand dictionnaire universel du XIXème siècle*, vol. 9 (Paris, 1873). In 1824 *infamia* was defined as: "quitar la fama, honra y estimación a alguna persona; el que carece de honra, crédito y estimación; lo que es mal y despreciable, vilis, abjectus; descrédito, deshonra," in *Diccionario de la lengua castellana por la Academia Española*, 7th ed. (Paris: Librería Hispano-Francesa de Rosea, 1824).

24 Part 7, title 6, law 1 in *Las siete partidas del sabio rey D. Alfonso el Nono, copiadas de la edición de Salamanca del año de 1555, cotejadas con varios códices antiguos por la Real Academia de Historia y glosadas por el licenciado Gregorio López del Consejo Real de Indias de S. M.* (Paris: R. Bouret, 1851), 4:468–473.

25 Roque Bárcia, *Primer diccionario etimológico de la lengua española* (Madrid: Alvarez Hermanos, 1881), 3:188.

26 Art. 73, *Código penal boliviano*, 1831.

27 Art. 699, *Código penal boliviano*, 1831.

28 Arts. 73, 63, *Código penal boliviano*, 1845.

29 It is worth underlining the similarity between the requirements for citizenship in Spain (political constitution of Cádiz from 1812) and Bolivia.

30 In the 1938 constitution, the condition of property and of being subject to another person as a dependent disappeared, while the condition of reading and writing as well as being registered in the civic registry remained.

31 Art. 822, *Código de procederes Santa Cruz* (La Paz: Paceña, 1852).

32 They were subject only to the simple "juratory caution." Arts. 841, 843, 844, *Código de procederes Santa Cruz*, 1852.

33 Arts. 96, 101, *Código militar para el réjimen, disciplina, subordinación y servicios de los ejércitos de la República Boliviana de orden de S. E. el Presidente* (Sucre: Imprenta de Beeche y Cia., 1843).

34 Art. 119, *Código militar*.

35 For the articles pertaining to common soldiers, see *Código militar*, esp. 13, 87, and 96; for corporals, see 101, 117, 119, and 130; for sergeants, see 183, 185, and 247; and for servants, see 501.

36 Arts. 291, 283, *Código militar*.

37 Compare articles 228, 230, and 231 of the *Código militar*.

38 Arts. 503, 504, *Código militar*.

39 Art. 249, *Código militar*.

40 Art. 506, *Código militar*.

41 Corporal punishments were applied preferably for crimes against persons, such as homicide and theft, while noncorporal punishment was applied for crimes against society, such as those involving public servants and family affairs. This implies that those guilty of crimes against society, except in the case of serious offenses, suffered

The "Spirit" of Bolivian Laws   83

only the loss of their employment and "honors." See, for example, art. 407, *Código penal boliviano*, 1831.

42 Art. 73, *Código penal boliviano*, 1831. On civil death, see Joaquín Pacheco, *El Código penal concordado y comentado* (Madrid: D. Santiago Saunaque, 1848–49), 343.

43 Title 17, law 1. José María Ots y Capdequí, *Manual de historia del derecho español en las Indias y el derecho propiamente indiano* (Buenos Aires: Losada, 1945), 94; part 4, title 17, law 4 in *Las siete partidas*, 3:149.

44 See title 9 of the first volume of the *Código civil*, 1831.

45 Art. 93, *Código civil*, 1831.

46 Arts. 196, 197, 230, *Código civil*, 1831.

47 Arts. 130, 132, 134, *Código civil*, 1831.

48 If they committed several offenses, they could be taken to a correctional house from anywhere between six months to two years (art. 519, *Código penal boliviano*, 1831).

49 Arts. 516, 521, 525, *Código penal boliviano*, 1831. In the opposite case, if a woman were able to prove that her husband was morally reprobate, he could be sentenced to a maximum period of one year. See art. 526 in *Código penal boliviano*, 1831.

50 Art. 629, *Código penal boliviano*, 1831.

51 Imprisonment was anywhere from six months to two years (arts. 575–576, *Código penal boliviano*, 1831). Another law referred to the death caused by parents and grandparents when they exceeded themselves in their "right to reprimand their children and grand-children." This case was considered as "involuntary homicide committed because of levity" and extended also to the masters' authority regarding "their servants, disciples, or other persons in their charge" (art. 581, *Código penal boliviano*, 1831). "Involuntary homicide" led to prison sentences of three months to two years and two years of exile" (art. 583, *Código penal boliviano*, 1831). Intentional murders were punished with the death penalty.

52 "The father can punish his son moderately, as the master his slave or servant and the master craftsman his disciple." Part 7, title 8, law 9 in *Las siete partidas*, 4:497.

53 Art. 614, *Código penal boliviano*, 1831.

54 For example, dishonest abuse and deception of women carried a penalty of three to six years of public labor and banishment or one to three years if the victim was a prostitute; molesting women "against their will" was punished with eight years of public labor and banishment, or four years if the victim was a prostitute. Arts. 620, 622, 625, 626, 644, *Código penal boliviano*, 1831.

55 Manuel Durán, *La reforma penal en Bolivia* (Sucre, 1946), 143.

56 Part 4, title 14, laws 1 and 2 in *Las siete partidas*, 3:127–128.

57 Part 4, title 2, law 7 in *Las siete partidas*, 3:24.

58 Part 4, title 15, laws 1 and 3 in *Las siete partidas*, 3:130, 132.

59 Art. 493, *Código civil*, 1831.

60 Art. 165, *Código civil*, 1831. The Toro's Law No. 11 in book 10 of the *Novísima recopilación*, which defined the natural son, was quoted in a trial; Archivo de La Paz [ALP], Corte Superior de Distrito, 1850, blue-covered dossier, Doña Ignacia Medina with D. Jacinta Medina, fol. 24v.

61 See the essay by Laura Gotkowitz in this volume.

62 Natural healers or ritual specialists, as well as those without fixed domicile, also fell under the category of vagrant; chap. 6, art. 68, Reglamento de Policía (June 10, 1845)

in *Colección oficial de leyes, decretos, ordenes (Primero de marzo de 1845 al 28 de febrero de 1846)* (Sucre, 1863), vol. 10.

63   Art. 26, title 2, chap. 1 in ibid.

64   Archivo Nacional de Bolivia [ANB], Corte Superior de Chuquisaca [CSC], 1851, no. 2, Criminal seguido contra el ciudadano Pedro Gironda por suponérsele haber seducido para revolución a los indígenas de su hacienda de Lajrachira y construcción de un cuartel en ella, fol. 18v.

65   ALP, Corte Superior de Distrito, 1849, C. 101, E. 2, fols. 21, 27–30, 42v, 44, 74.

66   Ibid., fols. 104–105v.

67   In 1845, for example, two indigenous people stated through their legal defender that they had been in detention for more than three months without being able to find guarantors; ALP, Corte Superior de Distrito, 1845, C. 80, Criminal contra Mariano Ortiz, fol. 10. In another case, an ironsmith had been held in prison for more than a year, despite having been declared innocent, because he had no guarantor; ALP, Corte Superior de Distrito, 1847, C. 88, Manuel Mamani contra Norverto Aguilar, fol. 84.

68   ALP, P.E., 1850, El Indio Quispehuana se queja de abusos.

69   Ibid.

70   ALP, Corte Superior de Distrito, 1846, C. 85, Expediente seguido por María Pabón, fols. 11–11v.

71   See, for example, the literal translation in the following articles: art. 561 of the *Código penal boliviano* of 1831 (CPB) and art. 605 of the Spanish Code of 1822 (SC); art. 569 of the CPB and art. 612 of the SC; art. 569 of the CPB and art. 613 of the SC. The list could be extended. The articles from the Spanish code are given in Pacheco, *El código penal concordado y comentado*.

72   Santa Cruz Shuhkrafft, "Notas y apuntes," 7.

73   We lack diachronic studies of the legal and juridical situation of indigenous people. My comparison of their situation in the colonial and republican periods is therefore necessarily general and does not account for changes that occurred over the three centuries of colonial domination.

74   Book 6, title 2, law 1, *Recopilación de leyes de los Reinos de las Indias*, 3rd ed. (Madrid: Andrés Ortega, 1774), 4:194.

75   Juan de Solórzano Pereira, *Política indiana*, book 5, chap. 19 [1648] (Madrid: M. Sacristan, 1739), 1:152.

76   Book 2, chap. 4, *Recopilación*; Solórzano, *Política indiana*, 1:71, 77; "That which is compensated by a greater good is not wrong" (book 2, chap. 20, *Recopilación*; Solórzano, *Política indiana*, 1:80); book 2, chap. 6, *Recopilación*; Solórzano, *Política indiana*, 1:77.

77   Solórzano, however, justified the contradiction: "It is not in opposition to say that in Spain free vassals are not obliged to perform similar services . . . because every province requires its own laws and customs" (see book 2, chap. 5, *Recopilación*; and Solórzano, *Política indiana*, 1:72–74, 79ff.).

78   Book 2, chap. 28, *Recopilación*; Solórzano, *Política indiana*, 1:203–205, 207–208.

79   Book 2, chap. 29, *Recopilación*; Solórzano, *Política indiana*, 1:211.

80   The law "exempted" miserables from some procedures since it was assumed that they would not be able to deceive others; Solórzano, *Política indiana*, 1:206–207. In the *Leyes de las partidas*, rapid or "verbal" trials were reserved for "poor and vile men";

part 3, title 22, law 6, *Las siete partidas*, 2:778. For the Protectors of Indians, see book 6, title 6, *Recopilación*.

81 William Lofstrom Lee, *El mariscal Sucre en Bolivia* (La Paz: Edición e Imprenta Alenkar, 1983).

82 See the essay by Keila Grinberg in this volume.

83 Silvia Rivera, "La raíz: Colonizadores y colonizados," in *Violencias encubiertas en Bolivia: Cultura y política*, ed. Xavier Albó and Raúl Barrios (La Paz: CIPCA Aruwiyiri, 1993); Tristán Platt, "Liberalismo y etnocidio," in *Autodeterminación no. 9: Análisis histórico-político y teoría social* (La Paz, 1991).

84 Larousse, *Grand dictionnaire universel*, vol. 9.

Interpreting Machado de Assis: paternalism,
slavery, and the free womb law
Sidney Chalhoub

In recent years, the literary critics Roberto Schwarz and John Gledson
have substantially modified the parameters of academic debate on the
literature of Machado de Assis, the foremost Brazilian novelist of the
nineteenth century. They have convincingly argued that, in telling his
stories, Machado de Assis sought to write, and often rewrite, the history
of nineteenth-century Brazil. Their work suggests that his novels convey
social and political meanings largely unnoticed by many of his contemporaries, as well as by subsequent readers and commentators.[1]

At this point, the historian enters the scene, hoping to engage literary critics in modes of historical thinking. The concept of paternalism
is at the core of Schwarz's reading of Machado; it is, therefore, a good
point of entry. In this essay, I will argue that by the early 1870s, if not
before, Machado de Assis had come to regard paternalism—the ideology of slaveholders—as pertaining to the field of ornithology. It was bird
cosmology. The short story "Ideas of a Canary" serves the purposes of
this argument, for it offers us a provisional, if ironic, definition of paternalism. When it was first published, in 1895, the institution of slavery
had been abolished and paternalism was perhaps no longer the dominant
ideology, though it continued to structure social relations to a great extent—certainly, it continued to structure Machado's interpretations of
historical changes in nineteenth-century Brazilian society.[2]

Canaries and the Ideology of Paternalism

Macedo was dedicated to the study of ornithology. The story he had been
telling his friends lately, however, seemed to indicate that he had gone

insane. While perusing in a junkshop, he had noticed a cage hanging next to the exit door. There was a canary inside, incessantly jumping up and down, and the more so as it perceived the visitor standing there watching. Macedo regretted the fate of that bird, hanging amid such a mess, and muttered words of indignation against the owner, calling the little bird "a ray of light" playing in "a cemetery." The canary replied: "Which owner? The man is my servant; he brings water and food to me everyday. He does that with such regularity that if I were to pay for his services it would cost me dear; but canaries do not pay their servants. In fact, since canaries are the lords of the world, it would be extravagant if they had to pay for what there is in the world."

Amazed by these answers, articulated in a language that appeared human, though coming in funny trills, as well as by the ideas, which seemed original, the ornithologist decided to investigate the phenomenon. He asked the canary if it missed flying freely in blue and infinite space. The bird interrupted him, as if it had heard nonsense: "My dear, blue and infinite space?" Macedo proceeded to ask what the canary thought of the world, how it conceived of it. "The world," answered the canary-become-professor, "The world is the junkshop of a secondhand dealer, with a small square bamboo cage hanging from a nail; the canary is the lord of both the cage it inhabits and the surrounding junkshop. Everything else is illusion and lie."

Macedo paid the price the dealer asked for the bird and left, determined to produce a major scientific study. The canary now inhabited a large circular structure, made of wood and wire, painted white. The cage was hanging from a wall on the verandah, from where the bird could see the garden, a fountain, and a little of the blue sky. Macedo devoted himself to studying the canary's language, seeking to transcribe it, understand its structure, and establish its connections to bird singing and music in general. He interrogated the bird on its aesthetic sentiments, wrote down its ideas and reminiscences. Upon concluding this philological and psychological investigation, he did some research on the history of canaries, then on the geology and ecology of the Canary Islands. After three weeks of hard work, he had to rectify some of his initial observations. Asked to repeat its definition of the world, the bird now trilled: "The world is a large garden with a verandah in the middle, flowers and bushes, some grass, clear air with a little blue above; the canary, lord of the world, inhabits a large circular white cage, from where it sees the rest. Everything else is illusion and lie."

The study presented difficulties Macedo had not anticipated; the canary had complex, often changing ideas. It was necessary to know them well before writing the paper that would be sent to the National Museum, the Brazilian Historical Institute, and the German universities. Macedo worked obsessively and thus became ill. His doctor recommended absolute rest. Once recovered, Macedo found that the canary had escaped from its cage. He thought of strangling the servant responsible, but the man defended himself by saying that the bird was astute and had deceived him. Macedo suffered, recovered once again, and finally decided to write the scientific paper using the annotations he had, however incomplete they might be. By then he had accepted an invitation to dine at a rich neighbor's estate.

Walking in the garden and chatting with his friend before the meal, Macedo was struck by a familiar trill: "Long life to you, Mr. Macedo, where have you been?" The neighbor thought the ornithologist had definitely gone insane, as he saw the man talking to the canary, insisting that he come back home, "to resume conversations, in our world composed of a garden, a verandah, and a large circular cage." Garden? Verandah? "The world, my dear," answered Macedo, exasperated. The canary was amazed: "What world? You haven't relinquished the bad habits of a professor. The world," the bird concluded solemnly, "is blue and infinite space, with the sun overhead." Macedo tried to argue with the canary, to say that it was contradictory, that if one were to give it credence, "the world could be anything. . . . it had already been the junkshop of a secondhand dealer." "The junkyard of a secondhand dealer? Are there indeed secondhand dealers?" The canary roared with laughter. "The world is blue and infinite space, with the sun overhead. Everything else is illusion and lie."

This story is one further variation on a theme to which Machado devoted much of his literature. His goal was a witheringly ironic portrait of paternalism: the ideology of the seigniorial class, which based its power on the institution of slavery and the production of personal dependence. The canary is a metaphor for a historically determined way of structuring social domination and articulating a worldview. In this perspective, the world was represented as a mere expansion of seigniorial wishes, and economic, social, and political power seemed always to converge on the same point, situated at the top of an imaginary pyramid. There are enough elements in Machado's work, both in this short story and elsewhere, to flesh out a picture of paternalism as viewed from within: a politics of dominance resting upon the idea of the inviolability of seigniorial will, in which workers and subordinates in general could only position themselves and think of their social places in relation to this supposedly unchallenged will. Furthermore, still viewed from within—that is, following the slaveowners' habits of thought—such a society was devoid of significant social conflicts because dependents tended to view their situation within the framework of values and social meanings imposed by masters.[3] The horizontal solidarities of class societies seem absent. Machado's novels are filled with characters that are convincing illustrations of this vision: Estácio (in the novel *Helena*), Jorge (*Iaiá Garcia*), Brás Cubas (*Memórias póstumas de Brás Cubas*), and Bentinho (*Dom Casmurro*), to mention just a few.

Lawyers are fond of the adage, "Whatever is not in the trial records is not in the world." One can imagine that Machado's character Dom Casmurro, himself a lawyer, appreciated this dictum; in fact, Dom Casmurro once observed that "whatever bears the appearance of truth is the whole truth."[4] Machado's Brás Cubas ruminated upon the effects of contemplating one's own nose for long hours, reaching the conclusion that the "equilibrium of societies" depended upon the "subordination of all the universe to just one nose." He proceeded to argue that such contemplation provided for the "elimination of external things."[5] As for the canary, as we saw he thought the whole world subordinated to his beak; everything else was illusion and lie. Dom Casmurro, Brás Cubas, the canary— this is a family reunion.

There is more to say, however, before taking up the concept of paternalism as a key to the interpretation of both nineteenth-century Brazilian society and the literature of Machado de Assis. Actually, if I were to remain on the same path, the necessary conclusion would be that the arbitrariness and inconstancy of the masters were the most important characteristics of that society. Roberto Schwarz concluded precisely this in his books *Ao vencedor as batatas* and *Um mestre na periferia do capitalismo*. In large part, he was correct. There remain, nonetheless, two major problems in Schwarz's interpretation. The first is conceptual and demands more reflection on the description of paternalism presented above. The second is more strictly historical, entailing anachronism in Schwarz's analysis.

For at least three decades, social historians have been demonstrating that it is insufficient to conceptualize any ideology, including paternalism, from the worldview of canaries and the like.[6] What the bird offers is only the self-description of seigniorial ideology. In this conception, paternalism is the world that masters idealized, the society they dreamed of realizing in daily life. In other words, the hegemony of paternalist ideology does not preclude social antagonism or horizontal solidarity. Rebecca Scott pointed this out over a decade ago:

> Perhaps the most striking feature of scholarship on slavery in the last decades is the way in which it has broken the association of subordination with stasis and passivity. . . . Scholars have found numerous ways to examine slave initiatives without denying oppression, to explore the creation of oppositional belief systems in the context of attempted ideological domination, to delineate the slave community while acknowledging the continual efforts at repression of many of its essential features. In postemancipation studies we are seeing a similar development, as monolithic portraits of peonage or marginalization are superseded by accounts that emphasize negotiation, initiative, and choice, though in a situation of extreme constraint and, often, violence.[7]

In this light, we can see Machado de Assis as a tireless interpreter of the possibilities for political action available to subordinate groups in those situations in which daily social intercourse always carried the danger of a slip that could provoke the masters' humiliating aggression. In a recent article, I sought to show that a reading of Machado firmly rooted in the now-outmoded tradition of Marxist social history reveals meanings otherwise unattainable: characters in positions of subordination in the novels—especially women—ceaselessly submit the logic of seigniorial domination to a devastating, though always dissimulated, critique. I beg the readers' indulgence, but in order to move further I need to reproduce here a key passage of that earlier article.[8]

In *Dom Casmurro*, Machado depicts a first-person narrator, Bento Santiago (Bentinho), who is urbane, wealthy, and formerly an owner of slaves and patron of dependent free people. The man believed his wife and childhood sweetheart, Capitu, had betrayed him with his best friend, Escobar. In a desperate search for answers, the narrator reinterprets past experiences, seeking to show that he had been a victim of the unfaithfulness and ingratitude of those under his protection, especially Capitu. In retrospect, he constructs Capitu as an ever-dissimulating character, skillfully leading him to do what she wanted him to do. The peculiar logic

dissimulating

of the allegedly cuckolded husband, writing his memoirs in old age and solitude, exposes the workings of gender and class antagonism in a paternalist society. Thus, according to this narrator, Capitu once explained to Bentinho precisely what I wish to point out. In order to convince Bentinho that José Dias, the *agregado* (a dependent person residing with the family), was their best ally in the campaign to avoid his being sent to the seminary, Capitu explained the following to her boyfriend:

> "Remember how you happened to go to the theater the first time, two months ago? Dona Glória was against it, and that should have been enough for José Dias; but *he* wanted to go, and he made a speech—remember?"
>
> "I remember: he said that the theater was a school of manners."
>
> "Yes, and he talked so much that your mother finally gave in and paid the way for both of you. . . . Go on, ask, order."[9]

The situation depicted in the passage is clear. The alleged subject of the conversation was Bentinho's desire to go to the theater for the first time. Dona Glória, however, was originally opposed to the idea. The conversation would have ended there if it were not for the fact that José Dias, the *agregado*, also wanted to go to the theater. A dependent man living with the Santiago family, José Dias could not challenge the widow's determination; the fact that the woman did not want her son to go to the theater should have been enough for him not to insist. Yet José Dias made a speech arguing that the theater was a school of manners. In other words, the *agregado* developed an argument seeking to demonstrate that it should be the widow's own will to send the boy to the theater—which, after all, had been turned into "a school." Dona Glória finally agreed to give her permission; that is, it then became her determination that Bentinho go to the theater. José Dias was designated to accompany the boy, whose desire to go to the theater for the first time was supposedly fulfilled. But perhaps it had been José Dias himself who had suggested to Bentinho that he should go to the theater for the first time. The *agregado* was the one who really wanted to go, and he found a way of going for free because the widow paid for both, as Capitu did not fail to remark.

If we observe this passage as an interpretation of the possibilities for political expression available to people submersed in extremely unequal social relations, characteristic of but not exclusive to paternalist domination, we may conclude first, that the prerogatives of seigniorial will were never openly called into question (quite the contrary, they were ritually reinforced at every step), and second, that the option left to dependents was to pursue their own objectives by trying to induce masters to take actions that benefited them, the dependents. In other words, not being able to struggle openly for their own objectives, José Dias, Capitu, and similar figures tried to reach their goals by making their masters imagine that it was the masters' decision to do exactly what the dependent wanted done.

It is thus possible to demonstrate that Machado de Assis, in several of his novels and other writings, systematically described and analyzed the viewpoint of the dependent—slave or free—in daily political situations. Roberto Schwarz, based on a definition of paternalism limited to canary cosmology, has been led to emphasize seigniorial arbitrariness and victimization of dependents as the two key elements in nineteenth-century Brazilian society. It seems, however, that Machado observed a great deal more. He crafted extraordinary passages in his writings to portray the political discourse of subordinate peoples.

This is such a crucial point that it is worth pursuing still further. It is possible to seek a homology between Machado's mode of analyzing the political discourse of dependents and the concept of literature he came to practice. Although he was never very explicit regarding what he thought literature was, he made it quite clear what he thought it ought not to be. His critique of Portuguese novelist Eça de Queirós was forceful. Writing in April 1878, he explained what displeased him in novels such as *O crime do Padre Amaro* and *O Primo Basílio*:

> Such a photographic and servile reproduction of minimum and ignoble things was unprecedented in our language. For the first time there appeared a book in which . . . the secluded and sordid were treated in minute detail and related with the exactitude of an inventory. Learned people read some passages with pleasure—they were indeed excellent—in which Mr. Eça de Queirós left behind, for a few minutes, the tenets of his literary school; . . . most readers, however, plunged into the inventory. And what were they to do, if not to admire the accuracy of an author who does not forget to mention anything, who hides nothing from view? Because the new poetics is just that, and it will only achieve perfection the day it tells us the exact number of threads present in a cambric handkerchief or a kitchen mop.
>
> Let me conclude, then, by suggesting to young talented writers in both lands of our language that they should not allow themselves to be seduced by a rotten, however recent, literary doctrine. Such

literary messianism has neither vitality nor universality; it brings decrepitude. It is of course useful to correct the excesses of some current doctrines. Nothing else. Let us observe reality excluding Realism; thus we will not sacrifice aesthetic truth.[10]

"Let us observe reality excluding Realism." In other words, literature seeks to describe and interpret reality, to convey truths about society, but that does not mean it should simply mirror the social relations it represents and often intends to change. Machado de Assis was interested in investigating the underlying motives of historical change, seeking to reveal what he knew remained opaque for those focused on the superficiality of political and social events. A proper literary rendering of an inherently complex and indeterminate historical process required a more sinuous narration, full of allegories and apparent inconsistencies. In the experience of readers, similar to that of dependents, literal meanings of words and situations did not exhaust possibilities — literary or historical; readers were permanently challenged to go beyond seigniorial (realist) ideology and eventually conceive of turning social and literary meanings upside down. José Dias, the *agregado*, wanted to go to the theater, preferably without paying for it; hence he manipulated the situation so as to convince Dona Glória that it was her desire and best interest to do precisely what he wished. In order to achieve his aim, the dependent knew he had to say only what others (masters) expected to hear. José Dias and Capitu followed the same methodology, so to speak, in their relations with masters: no matter how daring, how bold the ideas, "they were daring only in conception. In practice they were apt, sinuous, unobtrusive, and accomplished the end proposed, not at one leap but by a series of little leaps."[11] Author Machado de Assis — born to an *agregado* African Brazilian family himself — turned the daily political methodology of dependents such as Capitu and José Dias into a major tenet of his literature. He invented characters, dialogues, and narrators who seemed to adopt and express views that were rigorously compatible with the expectations of readers/masters; in so doing, Machado (Capitu? José Dias?) revealed a great deal about nineteenth-century Brazilian society.

Slavery and the Free Womb Law

As I have mentioned, a second problem in Roberto Schwarz's reading of Machado is anachronism — that is, his explanations are often too structural, failing to give a proper account of historical changes and the way Machado saw them. In *Ao vencedor as batatas*, Schwarz argued that Machado's aim in the novel *Helena* was to contribute to "the perfecting of paternalism."[12] According to Schwarz, the general theme of the book was that family values and Christian piety should soften social differences, hence preventing seigniorial humiliation of, and violence against, dependents. In other words, the ideology of the novel, frankly insipid, was that family and religion served the purpose of civilizing the rich and consoling the poor and subordinate, thus indicating that *Helena*—indeed all novels Machado wrote before *Memórias póstumas de Brás Cubas* (first published in 1880)—was "deliberately and disagreeably conformist."[13] The "underlying motive" in *Helena* according to Schwarz was the contrast between that "general civilizing and moderating intention" and the frequently turbulent and undisciplined behavior of the characters.[14] Such a conservative agenda, Schwarz continued, thwarted the potentially radical implications of Machado's rational and profound analysis of paternalism, an analysis that remained insufficiently critical because it did not aim to reveal social antagonisms.[15]

Besides the problems in Schwarz's conceptualization of paternalism, which prevented him from seeing much of the critical content of the actions and words of *Helena*'s title character, his reading fails to comprehend the novel's historical context. Machado wrote *Helena* in 1876, seeking to describe and interpret structures of domination prevailing in the 1850s. As made clear in several of his works, Machado thought the years of political and social agitation that led to the Free Womb Law of 1871—including the political crisis of 1868 and the Paraguayan War (1864–70)—were a turning point in the history of the Brazilian Empire. In fact, he attempted to come to grips with what had happened in those years and to understand its consequences in much of what he wrote thereafter. Machado knew about paternalist relations through both historical and personal experience; in *Helena* he showed, in a manner perhaps impossible before living through the events of the 1870s, the arbitrariness inherent in seigniorial power, as well as the suffering and ambivalence from which dependents had no escape.

It follows that the key to *Helena*, the novel, was the ambivalence of Helena, the character: on the one hand, she shared seigniorial ideology because she showed gratitude to her benefactors, understood their worldviews, and was able to uphold their values; on the other hand, she was critical of paternalist relations because she knew they were historically constructed and class-bound and thus reproduced by sheer force and intimidation. Helena's critical perspective allowed her a certain autonomy in most events related in the book; in the end, as the plot led her to the most abject dependence, the alternative was death—or historical change. Death followed, for *Helena*, discussing events unfolding in the 1850s, depicted the apogee of seigniorial hegemony. Historical change was to be the subject of *Iaiá Garcia*, the 1878 novel set in the period from 1865 to 1871. In sum, I do not think Machado could have had in mind, in *Helena* or in any piece written in the 1870s, "the perfecting of paternalism."[16] My argument depends, however, upon a better investigation of what Machado perceived was at stake in 1871: How did he see the political and social impact of the Free Womb Law?

The first difficulty here is to understand the novelist's position on the institution of slavery. On the one hand, it seems clear that for Machado the crisis of the Brazilian Empire originated in the struggles over the emancipation of slaves; on the other hand, references to the institution of slavery were neither frequent nor apparently central to his novels' plots. In *Ao vencedor as batatas* Roberto Schwarz offered a theoretical solution for this paradox: slavery provided "the basis for social relations of production," but it did not constitute the nexus of ideological life in nineteenth-century Brazil. The explanation for this was allegedly the fact that the subordination of slave workers was guaranteed solely by force.[17] In contrast, dependent free people found themselves woven into complex networks of paternalist practices, thus supposedly obtaining seigniorial protection in reward for fidelity and obedience. Schwarz proceeded to say that because slavery meant violence and banishment from civilization, paternalism and the social control of dependent free people became a more favored and appropriate theme for Brazilian intellectuals.[18]

Schwarz once argued that it was necessary "to see such reality as a structure: dependent, slave, landlord" and remarked that the situation of dependents "depended on the existence of slavery, was shaped by it"; consequently, what a dependent feared most was "to be treated as a slave —something he had to avoid at any cost."[19] The latter observation seems promising, but Schwarz failed to explore its potential. In other words, he postulated, but did not demonstrate, the existence of a structural link between slavery—that is, the institution that guaranteed the social control of slave workers—and paternalism—the politics of dominion that maintained the subordination of dependent free people. As a result, Schwarz excluded slavery as a theme in Machado's literature; that is, since the subject does not appear to be present, and indeed it is not there in any obvious way, then the literary critic concluded it was not there at all. Such a rationale, however, will not do.

Schwarz's remark that the situation of dependents "depended on the existence of slavery, was shaped by it," deserves further comment. First, it indicates that from the perspective of the slaveowning class the ideas of the inviolability of seigniorial will and the production of personal dependence constituted the politics of dominion of both slaves and subordinate free people. Chattel bondage was conceived as the condition of maximum dependence, and this fact clarifies the assertion that slavery shaped the situation of dependent free people. Second, dependents dreaded being treated as slaves for very concrete reasons, up to and including the danger of illegal enslavement. Indeed, there is evidence that a considerable number of former slaves and other free people, both white and of color, lived under the constant threat of a possible enslavement or reenslavement. The situation of people who had obtained their letters of manumission varied. Many had to fulfill a condition established in that letter of manumission in order to achieve full freedom. In the meantime, they experienced an ambiguous and uncertain status between slavery and freedom, especially because until the Law of 1871 masters retained the right to revoke manumissions by alleging freedpersons' ingratitude.

More systematic research is needed to determine the extent of illegal enslavement in nineteenth-century Brazil, but the tranquility with which slaveowners kept in bondage hundreds of thousands of Africans smuggled into the country after the law prohibiting the slave trade in 1831, as well as their descendants, boggles the mind. Also, we need to investigate more closely the common practice, in Rio de Janeiro and elsewhere, of detaining people of color under the allegation that they might be fugitive slaves.[20] What we know is that in a society characterized by the masters' private responsibility for the social control of workers, free people of color risked much when they left the surroundings in which they could be immediately identified with specific, personal relations of subordination.

With this in mind, I maintain that although he focused his stories on the antagonism between the propertied and their dependent free people, Machado de Assis actually aimed to describe the logic of social domination pertaining to nineteenth-century Brazil as a whole, including slavery, which provided "the basis for social relations of production." In so doing, his novels made yet another very subtle and effective comment on observed social reality: because narrated events invariably took place within the realm of seigniorial families and their relations in the capital, it would not have seemed proper to center plots on slavery. It is true that in the second half of the nineteenth century, Estácio, Brás Cubas, Bentinho, and other canaries lived in a world in which slavery remained obviously visible, however elegant, urban, and civilized that world pretended to be; nonetheless, such visible ostentation, especially after the Law of 1871, would be a mistake, a sin, or perhaps an unnecessary risk. Therefore, in choosing an urban seigniorial environment for his stories, Machado also displayed the social appearances that masters pursued, and he tried faithfully to describe the way they futilely hoped to be seen. The novelist surely knew that at least some contemporary readers—those who might identify with Helena or Capitu, for example—would be able to see through such appearances.

Machado's sardonic portrait of Brazil's slaveowning class in the face of the inevitable demise of slavery provides us an illuminating, if idiosyncratic, perspective on law—especially on one particular law—at the twilight of the Brazilian empire. If slave emancipation was the central drama of nineteenth-century Brazilian history, passage of the Free Womb Law in 1871 was its most decisive chapter. Writing in the 1890s, the eminent abolitionist Joaquim Nabuco compared the law to Niagara Falls in his attempt to render what he deemed "the whole truth" about that chapter of the nation's history. Brazilian society, he wrote, had been "a river, moving ahead smoothly, calmly, carelessly" until 1871. With the Free Womb Law, the river suddenly felt "the full weight of its waters . . . fall on open space," creating, for a period, the impression that "everything would pulverize into thin air."[21]

To clarify what was at stake in 1871, we may turn to Joaquim Manoel de Macedo, an important romantic novelist and an exalted liberal politician. Macedo tried his hand at political satire as well, thus producing, I think, his best works. In *Memórias do sobrinho de meu tio* [Memories of my uncle's nephew], first published in 1867–68, he created an outspoken, showy narrator, who allegedly remained anonymous in order to be able "to tell the whole truth about himself and his peers," all of them conservative politicians carrying the same "physical and moral belly."[22] There was also Macedo's alter ego, *compadre Paciência* (godfather Patience), an unredeemed liberal from the glorious struggles of the 1830s, who revealed his discontent with the cynicism and lack of scruples of the nephew and his group. On one occasion Paciência debated general proposals for public policies with a former cabinet minister at a meeting in the nephew's house. The question arose of slavery—"servitude," as they preferred to call it. Both Paciência and his opponent seemed to agree that emancipation was inevitable. The *compadre* also argued that the government should take the initiative and propose measures to guarantee that the problem be solved "with moderation, caution, and due respect for property rights." The former minister and his colleagues, in contrast, thought that politicians and public authorities should not interfere in such a question: "it would be impolitic." They feared that planters and slaveowners would resent such intervention, thus damaging their political careers.

The outlines of political debate in the late 1860s seem clear: Paciência, a liberal, favored government initiatives seeking to submit the private power of masters to the rule of law; conservatives opposed such a move.[23] Yet by the early 1870s, social tensions regarding slavery had mounted, and a Parliament with an ample conservative majority enacted the Free Womb Law. In its main articles, the Law of 1871 declared free all children born thereafter of slavewomen, provided for the protection of slaves' savings (the *pecúlio*), recognized slaves' right to freedom by self-purchase irrespective of masters' consent, established a compulsory slave registration system, and created an emancipation fund to increase the number of manumissions. On the whole, the Law of 1871 dealt a definite blow to a politics of dominance based on the inviolability of seigniorial will. As I argue elsewhere, the Free Womb Law not only provided for direct and intense state intervention in relations between masters and slaves, it also empowered bondspeople in their constant struggles—legal or otherwise—to achieve freedom.[24]

This account does not, however, do justice to the tensions pertaining to the enactment of such a law. Let us return to Joaquim Nabuco's metaphor of Niagara Falls and the frightening idea that society might "pulverize into thin air." The image reveals how dramatic the events leading to approval of the law appeared to contemporaries. Nabuco's comment, nonetheless, meant to encompass uncertainties regarding the law's *application* as well. In a preceding passage in the same paragraph, he had noted that "the truth about reforms of such a nature is that they do not operate mathematically, according to quantities and clauses fixed beforehand; they are not *exact, precise* solutions that can be expected to produce previously calculated results: they always involve decreeing the unknown; they are unpredictable by definition; they are general social molds from which new human types emerge" (emphasis in the original).[25] That is, on September 28, 1871, the Brazilian Parliament decreed "the unknown." And the first thing no one knew was whether the law would be executed in all its provisions with full force. In reality, the recent history of the empire had registered conspicuous examples of socially significant laws that had not been enforced at all—such as the law prohibiting the slave trade in 1831—or were only enforced weakly—as was the case with the Land Law of 1850.[26] In contrast, a new law abolishing the slave trade, enacted in 1850, had been fully carried out by the mid-1850s. In sum, regarding the Law of 1871, there was every reason to expect legal battles and other struggles to ensue. At this point, we return to Machado de Assis.

As a journalist, Machado had worked on a staunchly liberal daily paper during most of the 1860s, the *Diário do Rio de Janeiro*. There he crossed swords with journalists linked to conservative politicians and participated in a political group that dreamed of reviving liberal tenets of the 1830s against the "conciliation" of opposing parties then evolving.[27] In 1867 he joined the *Diário oficial*, becoming a government employee. In 1873 he moved to the Ministry of Agriculture; in 1876 he was promoted to head of the second department of the Directory of Agriculture in the same ministry. He remained in that post until the end of the decade and continued his career as a public official until his death in 1908. What matters for us here is that the department Machado de Assis headed in the late 1870s was the one in charge of monitoring the enforcement of the Free Womb Law.[28] Consequently, his work in the ministry may help to elucidate his views on slavery and the gradual emancipation law of 1871. In fact, it serves to recover, at least in part, his stance on decisive political events during the period he was conceptualizing and actually writing novels such as *Helena* (1876), *Iaiá Garcia* (1878), and *Memórias póstumas de Brás Cubas* (1880).

It will suffice to relate one case that had reached the second department shortly before Machado became its head.[29] As I have mentioned, the Law of 1871 required slave registration (the *matrícula*) throughout the empire. Slaveowners who did not register their bondspeople at municipal tax offices in the time period the law established would lose their property, and, as a result, their slaves would be declared free.[30] Masters in this situation could resort to Article 19 of the regulations for the Free Womb Law (issued December 1, 1871), which gave them the right to file a lawsuit to prove that captives remained under their dominion and that they could not be held responsible for not registering their property.

Otherwise, the Law of 1871, in Article 7, established that petitions for freedom were to follow summary proceedings. Furthermore, appeals to higher judicial authorities became mandatory in freedom cases initially resulting in a judgment for the continuation of slavery.[31]

The problem originated in Resende, a county in the province of Rio de Janeiro. The local authority in charge of slave registration was not sure he could enroll José Pereira da Silva Porto's slaves, as they had not been registered during the period specified by the law. The master, however, invoked Article 19 of the regulations and obtained a judicial decision in his favor. The municipal judge accepted the slaveowner's allegations that he could not be blamed for the fact that his slaves had not been included in the registration (*matrícula*) and, in addition, that he maintained the slaves under his dominion. Following the legal decision, the master applied for registration at the local tax office. The official, however, did not know whether he could enroll Porto's captives, considering the provisions in Article 7, paragraph 2, of Law 2040, of September 28, 1871. The article referred to was that which made appeals to a higher court obligatory in "lawsuits to promote the manumission of slaves" that resulted in a judgment against freedom. An appeal had not ensued from the municipal judge's sentence in favor of the master's right to register his slaves; therefore, the local tax official asked for guidance from the Ministry of Agriculture.[32]

The problem was difficult, and recent historical works on Brazilian slavery have demonstrated that legal questions such as these were important in slaves' and abolitionists' struggles against slavery in the final decades of the empire.[33] The interpretation given to the case would become a precedent that would guide public officials in their responses to similar consultations thereafter. Moreover, since the situation involved the government's attitude toward slaveowners who had not fulfilled the legal obligation of registering their chattel property, the decision might bear consequences regarding the enforcement of the Free Womb Law. An intense exchange of ideas followed in the Ministry of Agriculture and other bureaus of imperial administration. Diniz Villas-Boas, an official in the second department, declared his position in favor of the slaves and against the requested permission for *matrícula* on two different occasions. According to him, Article 7 of the Law of September 28, 1871, applied to the case described in Article 19 of the regulations of December 1, 1871: that is, slave registration could only happen if a higher court confirmed the sentence the municipal judge of Resende had pronounced in favor of the master.[34] Augusto José de Castro e Silva, then head of the Directory of Agriculture, maintained the opposite. Petitions for freedom mentioned in Article 7 were those concerning self-purchase. Article 7 did not apply to lawsuits dealing with masters' justifications for the lack of *matrícula*. Furthermore, "political powers in the empire are independent of each other, so the executive must comply with a judiciary decision; consequently, the tax official in Resende must be ordered to accept the registration of José da Silva Porto's slaves."[35] Xavier Pinheiro, another official in the Ministry of Agriculture, also concluded that the master should be allowed to enroll his bondspeople.

Because the question remained undecided, the ministry sought the opinion of the solicitor general for the Crown. Solicitor Sayão Lobato thought that a second legal decision supporting the master was necessary for the authorization of the *matrícula*. Soon afterward, however, Gusmão Lobo, new head of the Directory of Agriculture, said he could not agree with the solution offered by the solicitor and asked the head of the second department to provide his opinion on the matter. Lobo asked the department head, Machado de Assis, to accomplish the task "in a short period of time," as "was his custom," because the issue had remained unresolved for more than a year.[36]

I do not quite understand why Lobo demanded the opinion of the new head of the second department on a matter about which even the solicitor general had already expressed his view, but we must be thankful he did so. Machado de Assis wrote the most incisive and politicized piece in the whole series. His statement reminds us of the reasoning and political determination then becoming current in petitions for freedom:

> The question is the following: In the examples of Article 19, must there be mandatory appeals in the cases in which initial judicial decisions were against freedom?
>
> My answer is affirmative. A different answer to the question would imply making an untenable distinction between the two cases; in my opinion, such a distinction would be repugnant to the spirit of the law.
>
> The main argument I find in these documents supporting a negative answer is that the lawsuits pertaining to Article 19 of the regulations are not in favor of freedom, that is, they are not proposed by the slave, but by the master, in favor of slavery—actually, in favor of private property.

Such a difference is not essential but apparent and accessory. It is true that in cases originating in Article 19 the slave does not propose the proceedings, but the master does; the immediate objective is not to achieve freedom but to ascertain the master's allegations regarding property rights and reasons that prevented him from registering his slaves. But why should one consider that such a difference in the origin of legal proceedings must eliminate the most essential fact that the decision to be made concerns the freedom of a slave?

It does not really matter whether it is a master or a slave who initiates a legal suit; what one must notice is whether the outcome of the lawsuit will guarantee or revoke the freedom of an individual who was born a slave. Furthermore, in the case of Article 19, a judgment against freedom is one against the acquired liberty of an individual, for it annuls an effect of the Law of 1871, returning to slavery a person who already participates in free society; in this situation, as is also the case concerning Article 7, it is freedom that perishes; one must favor freedom in both situations. . . .

Besides, one ought not to forget the spirit of the Law of 1871. Cautious, impartial, and correct concerning the property of slave-owners, it is, nonetheless, a law of freedom; it is the interest of freedom that it upholds in all its parts and articles . . .; from the rights and opportunities provided for manumission to its main idea—its soul and essence—the Law of September 28 sought, first of all, to proclaim, promote, and defend freedom. Because the spirit of the law is such, it is clear to me that a person's freedom is the real object in lawsuits originating in Article 19; therefore, the legislator cannot permit freedom to perish without applying in its favor the guarantee indicated in Article 7 of the law.

This is my view.—July 21, 1876.—Machado de Assis.[37]

Director Gusmão Lobo admitted that the head of the second department had offered the "best reasons to favor freedom"; Lobo even urged changes in the regulations for the Law of 1871 in order to make clear that mandatory appeals applied to cases of liberty due to lack of *matrícula*. Until such changes were made, however, he thought impeding slave registration in these situations illegally contravened property rights. Because he deemed the question "serious," and "given the diversity of opinions," the director decided to consult the Council of State. Meeting on October 20, 1876, the council concluded that mandatory appeals were necessary in lawsuits originated under Article 19. Following Machado's reasoning, the councilors adopted the interpretation that "the spirit of the law" must be attended to in the case: "when there is uncertainty regarding the correct understanding of the law, one must follow the interpretation that conforms to the intention of the legislator."[38]

The episode reveals much about Machado's view on slavery and emancipation in the years following the enactment of the Free Womb Law. It also shows the strategic position in the struggle to enforce the Law of 1871 of the second department of the Directory of Agriculture—a department Machado headed with exemplary dedication and rigor beginning in 1876. Finally, the event illustrates the general conduct of the second department in monitoring the application of the law. The main points in the department's doctrine—so to speak—under Machado de Assis might be summarized as follows. First, there was no tenable argument in favor of slavery, which was against natural law; there remained, however, legal determinations upholding masters' property rights that had to be taken into consideration. Second, the aim of the Law of 1871 was to "proclaim, promote, and defend freedom"; thus, in case of doubt—or given the chance—one should pursue the "spirit of the law" against the interest of slaveowners. Third, and this follows from the preceding points, the department sought most generally to submit the private power of masters —that is, seigniorial power—to the rule of law.[39] In this, it struggled to make effective the most fundamental political tenet held by nineteenth-century Brazilian liberals, who saw this point as the critical basis for the creation of a modern nation. After all, citizenship rights and everything else on the liberal political agenda became a farce in the world of paternalism and slavery that they had inherited from what they considered a decrepit colonial regime.

I started out hoping to engage literary critics in the modes of historical thinking. Thus I argue, on the one hand, that as a public official Machado de Assis was one of the main artificers of the imperial government's strategies to enforce the Law of 1871; as a consequence, it is not surprising that his numerous literary allegories concerning this historical period were profoundly marked by that experience. It follows, on the other hand, that Machado knew perfectly well that the seigniorial class had suffered a decisive political defeat in 1871. Therefore, the politics of dominion based on the idea of the inviolability of seigniorial will and on the production of personal dependence—of slave and free people alike— seemed historically doomed, however important it continued to be in the shaping of social relations. The fact, then, is that in writing *Helena*, or any other piece in the 1870s, Machado was about the last living Brazilian who would have had in mind the "perfecting of paternalism," as Schwarz imagined. Schwarz's interpretation suffers from anachronism—a deadly sin for historians—and is inconsistent with known historical as well as allegorical and literary evidence of Machado's political stance during the period. It seems clear, however, that by inventing Brás Cubas, a slave-owner who was dead and buried but survived to tell us his story, the artist achieved new, complex ways to render in literary terms the ambiguities and uncertainties inherent in the historical struggles he experienced as a citizen.[40]

Notes

My thanks to Michael Hall and Micol Seigel for their corrections of my English and to Sueann Caulfield for her editing. The argument suggested in this essay is developed further in Sidney Chalhoub, *Machado de Assis, historiador* (São Paulo: Companhia das Letras, 2003).

1   John Gledson, *The Deceptive Realism of Machado de Assis: A Dissenting Interpretation of "Dom Casmurro"* (Liverpool: Francis Cairns, 1984); Gledson, *Machado de Assis: Ficção e história* (Rio de Janeiro: Paz e Terra, 1986); Roberto Schwarz, *Ao vencedor as batatas: Forma literária e processo social nos inícios do romance brasileiro* (São Paulo: Duas Cidades, 1981); Schwarz, *Um mestre na periferia do capitalismo: Machado de Assis* (São Paulo: Duas Cidades, 1990); Schwarz, *Misplaced Ideas: Essays on Brazilian Culture*, ed. John Gledson (London: Verso, 1992).

2   *Machado de Assis: Obra completa*, ed. Afrânio Coutinho (Rio de Janeiro: Nova Aguilar, 1986), 2:611–614. Unless otherwise stated, all stories and novels referenced in this essay are taken from this edition. This story was originally published under the title "Que é o mundo?" (What is the world?) in *Gazeta de notícias*, November 15, 1895; it appeared afterward in a collection of short stories, *Páginas recolhidas* (Rio de Janeiro: H. Garnier, n.d. [1899]), 91–98. It was then titled "Idéias de canário" (Ideas of a canary). For this information, see J. Galante de Sousa, *Bibliografia de Machado de Assis* (Rio de Janeiro: Instituto Nacional do Livro, 1955), 653.

3   Sidney Chalhoub, "A história nas histórias de Machado de Assis: Uma interpretação de *Helena*," *Revista do Departamento de História* (FAFICH/UFMG, Belo Horizonte) (July 1992): 19–43.

4   *Dom Casmurro*, 1:819. Translation by the author.

5   *Memórias póstumas de Brás Cubas*, 1:565.

6   See, e.g., E. P. Thompson, *Customs in Common: Studies in Traditional Popular Culture* (New York: New Press, 1993); and James C. Scott, *Domination and the Arts of Resistance: Hidden Transcripts* (New Haven, CT: Yale University Press, 1990).

7   Rebecca J. Scott, "Exploring the Meaning of Freedom: Post-emancipation Societies in Comparative Perspective," *Hispanic American Historical Review* 68.3 (1988): 407–428.

8   Sidney Chalhoub, "Dependents Play Chess: Political Dialogues in Machado de Assis,"
    in *Machado de Assis: Reflections on a Brazilian Master Writer*, ed. Richard Graham
    (Austin: University of Texas Press, 1999), 51–84; the passage cited is on pages 54–55.
    The original version of the article was published in Portuguese as "Diálogos políticos
    em Machado de Assis," in *A história contada: Capítulos de história social da literatura
    no Brasil*, ed. Sidney Chalhoub and Leonardo Affonso de Miranda Pereira (Rio de
    Janeiro: Nova Fronteira, 1998), 95–122.
9   *Dom Casmurro*, 1:830.
10 *Machado de Assis: Obra completa*, 3:904, 913.
11 *Dom Casmurro*, 1: 829
12 Schwarz, *Ao vencedor as batatas*, 89.
13 Ibid., 63.
14 Ibid., 90.
15 Ibid., 99.
16 Sidney Chalhoub, "A história nas histórias de Machado de Assis."
17 Schwarz, *Ao vencedor as batatas*, 16.
18 Ibid., 16.
19 "Machado de Assis: Um debate. Conversa com Roberto Schwarz," *Novos estudos*,
    CEBRAP, no. 29 (March 1991): 83.
20 On the dangers of illegal enslavement, see the documents presented in Robert Conrad,
    Children of God's Fire: A Documentary History of Black Slavery in Brazil (University
    Park: Pennsylvania State University Press, 1994), 322–331; see also Judy Bieber Frei-
    tas, "Slavery and Social Life: Attempts to Reduce Free People to Slavery in the Sertão
    Mineiro, Brazil, 1850–1871," *Journal of Latin American Studies* 26 (1994): 597–619.
21 Joaquim Nabuco, *Um estadista do Império* (Rio de Janeiro: Nova Aguilar, 1975), 732.
    First edition published in Paris and Rio de Janeiro by Garnier, 1897–99.
22 Joaquim Manoel de Macedo, *Memórias do sobrinho de meu tio* (São Paulo: Companhia
    das Letras, 1995).
23 Ibid., 458–461.
24 Sidney Chalhoub, *Visões da liberdade: Uma história das últimas décadas da escravidão
    na Corte* (São Paulo: Companhia das Letras, 1990). See also Joseli Maria Nunes Men-
    donça, *Entre a mão e os anéis: A lei dos sexagenários e os caminhos da abolição no Brasil*
    (Campinas: Editora da UNICAMP, 1999); Elciene Azevedo, *Orfeu de carapinha: A tra-
    jetória de Luiz Gama na imperial cidade de São Paulo* (Campinas: Editora da UNICAMP,
    1999); Eduardo Spiller Pena, *Pajens da Casa Imperial: Jurisconsultos, escravidão e a Lei de
    1871* (Ed. da UNICAMP, 2001); Keila Grinberg, *Liberata: A lei da ambigüidade. As ações
    de liberdade da Corte de Apelação do Rio de Janeiro* (Rio de Janeiro: Relume-Dumará,
    1994).
25 Nabuco, *Um estadista do império*, 731–732.
26 On planters' resistance to the Land Law of 1850, see Márcia Maria Menendes Motta,
    Nas fronteiras do poder: Conflito e direito à terra no Brasil de meados do século XIX (Rio
    de Janeiro: Arquivo Público do Estado do Rio de Janeiro, 1998).
27 On "conciliation" and nineteenth-century Brazilian politics in general, see Ilmar Roh-
    loff de Mattos, *O tempo saquarema: A formação do estado imperial*, 3rd ed. (Rio de
    Janeiro: ACCESS, 1994); and Richard Graham, *Patronage and Politics in Nineteenth-
    Century Brazil* (Stanford, CA: Stanford University Press, 1990); on Machado's po-

litical ideas and allegiances in the 1860s, see Marco Cícero Cavallini, "O *Diário* de Machado: A política do Segundo Reinado sob a pena de um jovem cronista liberal" (Master's thesis, UNICAMP, 1999).

28 Raimundo Magalhães Júnior, *Machado de Assis, funcionário público (no Império e na República)* (Rio de Janeiro: Ministério da Viação e Obras Públicas, 1958); Magalhães Júnior, "O burocrata Machado de Assis," in *Machado de Assis desconhecido* (Rio de Janeiro: Civilização Brasileira, 1957), 178–209.

29 For the story that follows, I rely on Magalhães Júnior's works cited in n. 28; see also Lenine Nequete, "Sobre a apelação necessária nas causas de liberdade," *Escravos e magistrados no Segundo Reinado* (Brasília: Fundação Petrônio Portela, 1988), 117–132; Manoel da Silva Mafra, *Prontuário das leis de manumisão ou índice alfabético das disposições da Lei n. 2040 de 28 de setembro de 1871, Regulamentos n. 4835 de 1°. de dezembro de 1872, n. 4960 de 8 de março de 1872, n. 6341 de 20 de setembro de 1876 e avisos do Ministério da Agricultura, Comércio e Obras Públicas e da Jurisprudência do Conselho de Estado, dos Tribunais das Relações e Supremo Tribunal de Justiça* (Rio de Janeiro: Tipografia Nacional, 1877), 278–298; and *Anexos ao relatório apresentado à Assembléia Geral Legislativa na Primeira Sessão da Décima Sexta Legislatura pelo Ministro e Secretário de Estado dos Negócios da Agricultura, Comércio e Obras Públicas Thomaz José Coelho de Almeida* (Rio de Janeiro: Tipografia Perseverança, 1877), 92–105.

30 Art. 8 of the Law of September 28, 1871, in *O parlamento e a evolução nacional, 1871–1889*, ed. Fábio V. Bruno (Brasília: Senado Federal, 1979), 1:294–295; art. 19 of the "Regulamento a que se refere o Decreto n. 4835 desta data, para execução do art. 8°. da Lei n. 2040 de 28 de setembro de 1871," in Luiz Francisco da Veiga, *Livro do estado servil e respectiva libertação contendo a lei de 28 de setembro de 1871 e os decretos e avisos expedidos pelos Ministérios da Agricultura, Fazenda, Justiça, Império e Guerra desde aquela data até 31 de dezembro de 1875* (Rio de Janeiro: Tipografia Nacional, 1876), 37–38.

31 Bruno, *O parlamento e a evolução nacional*, 294.

32 Document sent to the Ministry of Agriculture by the president of the Province of Rio de Janeiro, reproduced in Mafra, *Prontuário das leis de manumissão*, 278–279.

33 See, for example, the works cited in n. 24.

34 Mafra, *Prontuário das leis de manumissão*, 281–284.

35 Ibid., 284–285.

36 Ibid., 279–281, 288.

37 Ibid., 288–290.

38 Ibid., 290–298.

39 For this summary of the position taken by the second department of the Directory of Agriculture in the Ministry of Agriculture regarding the application of the Law of 1871, I rely on a variety of published and manuscript sources, such as the *Relatórios do Ministério da Agricultura, Comércio e Obras Públicas*, 1871 to 1884, microfilm reels numbered 028.11-80 to 028.26-80, Arquivo Nacional do Rio de Janeiro (AN); the consultations that the department often sent to the Council of State, "Pareceres do Conselho de Estado," AN; and other manuscript sources found in the series 1A-6, "Ministério da Agricultura, Diretoria da Agricultura, 2a. Seção" and "Ministério da Agricultura, Índice de Busca da Documentação Identificada (GIFI)," AN, though these two latter series contain documents primarily dealing with land policies, another issue pertaining in part to the department Machado headed. It should be clear that Machado and

his colleagues at the second department studied and suggested solutions to the problems that arose during the application of the Law of 1871, sometimes pushing for more "liberal" interpretations of its dispositions and, more often, just trying to make sure that masters would not easily circumvent the rights slaves had acquired; however, unlike the story I just narrated, higher authorities would not always go along with the suggestions of Machado and his team. In any case, I think it is fair to say that the imperial government was genuinely engaged in enforcing the Free Womb Law in the 1870s; of course, the law failed or produced meager results in some of its dispositions, but the reasons for that are complex and deserve careful scrutiny.

40   For an interpretation of Machado's *Memórias póstumas de Brás Cubas*, see Sidney Chalhoub, "What Are Noses For? Paternalism, Social Darwinism, and Race Science in Machado de Assis," *Journal of Latin American Cultural Studies* 10.2 (2001): 171–191.

Slavery, liberalism, and civil law: definitions
of status and citizenship in the elaboration of
the Brazilian civil code (1855–1916)
Keila Grinberg

From the time it was promised in 1823 as a priority of the newly independent nation, the Brazilian civil code took ninety-four years to complete.[1] In 1855, recognizing that a new code was taking a long time to
promulgate, Justice Minister José Thomaz Nabuco de Araújo contracted
with Augusto Teixeira de Freitas to prepare a compilation of existing civil
legislation, to be known as the Consolidation of Civil Laws (*Consolidação
das leis civis*).[2] A renowned judge, founding member of the Institute of
Brazilian Lawyers, and attorney for the council of state, Freitas seemed
the ideal candidate to undertake the task.[3] In 1859, after completing this
compilation, Teixeira de Freitas received another invitation, this time to
write an entirely new civil code. After publishing a draft (*esboço*), he abandoned the project in 1867, for reasons still debated.[4] This was the first in a
long series of failed attempts. Only after the abolition of slavery in 1888,
and the fall of the empire the next year, was the state able to contract with
a jurist who could see the project to completion. Clóvis Bevilácqua began
work in 1899 on the document that would finally become the Brazilian
civil code in 1917.[5]

A number of historians believe that the persistence of slavery until the
end of the nineteenth century was one of the main reasons for the delay
in the redaction of the civil code. It was impossible for jurists to reconcile a liberal code, in which the rights of citizenship should be shared
by all, with slavery, which was legally based on the distinction between
persons—those who were free—and *possessions*—slaves.[6] Authors such as
Paulo Mercadante, Pedro Dutra, and Eduardo Spiller Pena suggest that it
was impossible for nineteenth-century Brazilian jurists to codify civil law
without taking into account the "servile element," as it was then called.

And the problem extended beyond the code: any debate involving the definition of civil rights was forced to confront the reality of slavery.[7]

Along these same lines, I will demonstrate that the jurists who worked to craft the civil code found it impossible to create legal definitions for concepts they considered fundamental, such as equality and civil rights, while slavery still existed. Other unresolved issues also hindered their work, such as the relation between the state and the Catholic Church and the definition of women's legal status. Yet I will argue that the persistence of the social relations of slavery in Brazilian society was the most pressing problem for those struggling to elaborate the nation's civil code, or to create a liberal society, which nineteenth-century jurists believed was achievable through legislation.

"Liberty Is Indivisible": The Dilemma of Personhood in Nineteenth-Century Brazil

According to Brazilian imperial law, which like colonial Portuguese law drew from the Roman law tradition, a slave was a *thing*, deprived of civil and political rights and incapable of fulfilling any obligation. Yet Brazilian law denied masters' rights over the life and death of their slaves, penalized those who punished their slaves excessively, and made slaves personally responsible for their crimes. The penal code thus referred to the slave as a *person* who was responsible for his/her own actions: the slave could be brought before the law, tried, convicted, and punished. In addition, Roman law recognized numerous conditions under which slaves had the right to their liberty, making the slave, in legal terms, both a person and a thing.[8] In Brazil, this paradox reached its peak at the end of the nineteenth century, when the impending demise of slavery, the existence of an increasingly complex range of relationships among slaves, former slaves, and free persons, especially in urban areas, and increasingly frequent and successful demands by slaves for emancipation made it extremely difficult to define the terms of civil law.

Other aspects of social life were also affected by the failure to systematize civil law. The registration of births is one example. Since there were no civil registries of birth in Brazil until the beginning of the republic in 1889, the only way to verify a birth was through baptismal records (*assentos de batismo*). The local parish priest generally documented the baptism, recording information in separate registries for slaves and free persons. While the parochial registries vary greatly by period and region, in general the documents list the baptism and birth dates, and the name of the child, parents, godparents, and, in the case of slaves, masters. Since the master's presence was not obligatory, however, the priest often failed to note not only the master's name but the individual's status as a slave. Such an oversight was possible because nothing guaranteed that the priest who performed the baptism had any knowledge of the life of those brought to him to be baptized, who were not always infants and often not even children.[9] Thus, many slaves were baptized without having their "condition," or civil status, designated. When the information was transcribed in the record, which did not always occur immediately after the baptism, their names and baptismal information would end up in the registry of free persons.

Problems arose when alleged slaves appealed to the courts for their liberty and presented their baptismal records as proof of the legitimacy of their appeals. In these cases, the documents they presented contained either the words "free" or "free at the baptismal basin" or simply stated nothing in reference to their status. In the latter cases, the *Ordenações fili-pinas* stipulated that slaves should be given the benefit of the doubt. Many won their freedom this way.

The issue was practically irresolvable: legal reasoning made it evident that the baptismal records were unreliable, yet they were the only existing documents. Moreover, under the *padroado* (an agreement between the Portuguese crown and the Vatican dating to 1551) the state was obliged to consider ecclesiastical records to be legitimate civil documents.[10] Accepting ecclesiastical documents as proof of an individual's civil status meant allowing those same documents to prove—or deny—someone's property rights over a supposed slave. Thus, the slavery or freedom of countless people could be in the hands of any parish priest, who with one annotation could secure their status. This dilemma produced innumerable lawsuits over slaves' freedom until it was finally resolved in 1871, when the Free Womb Law created an obligatory registry for all slaves.[11]

Baptism is only a minor example of the legal uncertainty provoked by slavery. Imagine Teixeira de Freitas's situation, irrespective of his personal position on the morality of slavery, when obliged to resolve the incompatibility between slavery and the basic principles of civil law even though he believed that slavery itself would not last. It was for this reason that Teixeira de Freitas resigned the presidency of the Institute of Brazilian Attorneys upon finding himself positioned against the majority in a highly charged polemic over whether the children born after a slave's formal emancipation, but before his or her entry into actual freedom, should be considered slaves or free. This majority included attorneys Caetano Alberto Soares and Perdigão Malheiro, the former known for favoring slaves in judicial proceedings and for writing *Memória para melhorar a sorte dos nossos escravos* (Memorial to improve the lot of our slaves) and the latter renowned for his masterpiece *A escravidão no Brasil: Ensaio histórico-jurídico-social* (Slavery in Brazil: A historical-juridical-social essay).[12]

This debate involved the most important definition of status at the time: the status of free or slave, of innocent (*ingênuo*)[13] or freedperson (*liberto*). According to Soares and many others, the legal question, together with its enormous political implications, should be addressed by adapting Roman law and the Phillipine Code to modern times. Teixeira de Freitas, however, believed that Brazilian jurists should follow the letter of ancient Roman law regarding the issue. Thus, contrary to the position of all of his colleagues, he argued that the children of slaves granted conditional freedom that was not yet effective should remain in captivity. As he explained in his letter of resignation as the president of the Institute of Brazilian Attorneys:

> If you want a slave to be a man, then do away with slavery. If you want slavery, the slave will be a possession. . . . If you want, however, to improve the lot of slaves among us, since you cannot abolish slavery, place the unfortunate man in his real position and grant him every possible favor; but do not change the name of it. If you adorn the slave with the gracious title of freedman, you worsen your tyranny through mockery and will also be insulting liberty itself. Liberty is indivisible. If, in an explosion of enthusiasm, the slave in question is a freedman, you cannot take from him the body of rights that constitute liberty. . . . Will you be ready to accept all of the consequences?[14]

The phrase "liberty is indivisible" aptly demonstrates his legal position. An individual cannot simultaneously be a *possession* and a *person*. Since the most desirable circumstance, that is, that all be considered persons, was still not possible, then it was important that slaves maintain the status of *possessions*. The law could not be changed if reality was not changed. A short time later, the commission formed to review Freitas's Consolidation of Civil Laws, which included Soares and Nabuco de Araújo, among others, criticized Freitas for his failure to address the question of slavery. Although they advised drawing up a separate code that would deal with slavery, no further plans were made for such legislation.

Despite Freitas's reluctance to address the contradictions posed by slavery, he agreed that, in reality, civil relations did exist between slaves and free persons. His avoidance of slavery was not merely due to the limitations of his formalist conception of law. Even those most open to the possibility that legislation could reform society recognized that the failure to define slaves' legal status clearly created nearly irresolvable problems in diverse areas of civil law and legal practice.

While slavery was a great obstacle to the codification of civil law, it was not the only one. The debates surrounding the union of church and state were fundamental in making clear the need to establish a true public sphere in Brazil. The question of the *padroado* and the restrictions of rights associated with it were the object of intense debate beginning in 1873, when two bishops roiled formerly peaceful church-state relations by criticizing the existence of freemasonry in Brazil. Moreover, because church and state were so closely linked, there was no civil registry of any kind until the end of the empire. Only Catholic marriages and cemeteries were permitted, and only Catholics could be elected to public office. Non-Catholics were thus denied full citizenship rights, a situation criticized by Liberal Party members such as Nabuco de Araújo. Explaining his party's position on the "religious question" in 1873, Nabuco argued:

> The state owes the church full protection, the state should maintain the liberty and independence of the church; but the church should know that the state has laws to govern it, as it has for all citizens, and laws that are inflexible. . . . In effect, if the constitution states that all religions are permitted, how can we deprive the citizen of political rights because he is of a different religion than that of the state? . . . This is simply not possible . . . because it deals not with religious tolerance, but with civil or political tolerance.[15]

Nabuco opposed, however, attempts by other reformists to create civil birth, marriage, and death registries, for he believed that only a comprehensive civil code could resolve such questions.[16] In one of its first acts, the new republican government resolved some of the most grievous civil effects of the *padroado* by proclaiming it extinct in 1890. Comprehensive regulation of civil life, however, came only with the promulgation of the civil code twenty-seven years later.

In addition to the problems engendered by church-state relations under the empire, traditional family structures also hindered attempts to codify civil law. Debates concerning changes in women's status were the subject of an intense polemic among jurists.[17] The issue gained prominence in the republican period, when controversy emerged over the definition of "active" citizens (those who could vote and hold public office) under the constitution of 1891, which did not explicitly exclude women. Since references to the Brazilian people used masculine collective terms (*todos* and *os cidadãos*), legislators concluded that only men should hold these privileges. At the beginning of the twentieth century, debates over women's legal status gained unprecedented visibility, principally due to controversies generated by Clóvis Bevilácqua, who sought to expand women's citizenship rights in his proposal for the new civil code and attempted to introduce divorce, an issue the majority of legislators did not even want to consider. Nonetheless, the final text of the civil code did not incorporate any of these debates: women's legal status continued to be subordinated to that of men, and women continued to be defined according to their position within the family.[18]

All these factors suggest that the codification process reflected the broader movement, however slow and imperfect, of rationalization and secularization of Western societies.[19] What makes the Brazilian case different, however, is the persistence of slavery. The issues regarding women's status were not unique to Brazil, or even to Latin America. Likewise, the church was involved in various polemics during this period — such as those related to jurisdiction over church lands — in other Catholic countries such as France and Austria. The enormous impact of slavery on the law, however, was unique to Brazil.

The Dilemma of Labor Contracts in a Slave Society

The mark of slavery was especially visible in the regulation of free labor contracts under the empire. Beginning in the 1830s, legislators and cabinet ministers debated a series of laws that aimed to formalize contracts already in effect between employers and employees.[20] This alone would constitute a problem, especially since free laborers were a minority for much of the nineteenth century, when the country remained dependent on slave labor. But even that was not the central issue: the biggest difficulty was that labor relations in Brazil, from at least the mid-nineteenth century, involved formal agreements between free persons as well as between free persons and slaves. These agreements gave slaves rights and obligations that, in theory, could be held only by free persons.

The fact that slaves routinely entered into agreements between persons makes it easy to understand why Teixeira de Freitas could not adequately define certain concepts when he attempted to write the civil code. Even if he were not concerned with legal dogma, there was no way to regulate, for example, the provision of services that presupposes a contract between two parties, by which one of them pledges to lend services to the other for a specified time based on some type of remuneration. The problem in regulating this activity was that in urban centers, slaves sold their own services and paid a percentage of the remuneration they received to their masters. These were the "slaves for hire" (*escravos de ganho*) so frequently mentioned in the historiography of Rio de Janeiro in the nineteenth century.[21]

These slaves for hire received permission from their masters to lend a service or even obtain employment and had contact with such masters only when handing over to them the wages they owed. The slaves were thus practically free of their masters' subjugation, not only because they lived at their place of employment or in their own homes, but chiefly because they received remuneration—the *peculium*—which allowed them the autonomy to *govern their own lives*, even when they were unable to buy their liberty. Moreover, this form of labor made them similar to the freed slaves and free persons who labored in Rio de Janeiro in the middle of the nineteenth century. And such activities were not associated only with the city: slaves for hire could also be found working as intermediaries in the trade that brought milk, hay, coal, and wood produced in the interior to Rio and to runaway communities and merchants on the city's outskirts.[22]

In 1867, Perdigão Malheiro articulated the core of the problem. Lecturing on the *peculium*, he maintained that the masters of slaves in general did permit their slaves to govern their own lives, with the stipulation that the slaves pass on to them a portion of their earnings. In short, the slaves should live "almost exempt from subjugation, almost free."[23] Discussing the dictate of Roman law by which "the slave [could] acquire nothing . . . for himself; all goes to the master,"[24] he pointed out that Brazilian masters customarily permitted slaves to have possessions in a wide array of circumstances: when a pact existed between slave and master, when the master permitted the slave to buy something, when a slave inherited land or wealth, when a slave saved a portion of the provisions given him or her for subsistence and converted it into additional assets, or when a slave received an indemnity. In short, there were practically no restrictions on slaves' savings.

In court, judges had the option of interpreting the law in accordance with the intent of the legislator or of adapting the same law to contemporary circumstances, as, for instance, was authorized by one of the most widely cited laws of the time, the Law of Good Reason (*Lei da boa razão*).[25] Whether a particular judge or legal scholar opted for one or the other interpretation depended on his political views and how he regarded the relation between political reality and legal action. Most commonly, jurists cited the Philippine Code, book 4, title 11, paragraph 4, which states that arguments that favor liberty should always carry the most weight. This principle could be used to defend the liberty of a slave as well as the freedom to own a slave, through the argument that no one should be deprived of their property against their wishes.[26]

For many, this dichotomy made it impossible to distinguish, at least at first glance, who was the slave of whom, and who was a freed slave or free person. In Teixeira de Freitas's view, this dilemma highlighted the legal problem of attempting to regulate something that in practice was so disorderly.[27] In his outline of the civil code, the chapter "Of Contracting Services" ("De locação") provided only a broad definition of the subject, without specifically delimiting how services would be contracted or who could be parties to a contract.[28] Teixeira de Freitas thus did little more than copy already-existing commercial laws.[29] And, in the end, he really had no choice: the definition of the concept of *locador*, one who provides a service, would imply those workers who would be apt to undertake such labor. Since this labor was performed by both free persons and slaves, the term simply could not be defined. In fact, prior to the promulgation of the civil code, none of the lawsuits that sought to regulate labor relations was successful.

The history of the law regarding contracts for services exemplifies how difficult it was to regulate labor relations under the Brazilian slave regime. One must understand the urgent demand for regulation of labor contracts in the 1870s: it was necessary to outline new rules to take account of the diverse free labor relations created beginning in 1873, especially the case of foreign laborers, who were arriving in great numbers.[30] The principal concern of plantation owners was to guarantee workers' compliance with contracts and to create legal means of keeping laborers from abandoning their work.

The council of state discussed this issue in 1868, at the same time that a proposal calling for the emancipation of all slaves was also being considered. The proposal, authored by Nabuco de Araújo, called not for immediate emancipation but rather for the creation of an intermediary labor regime under which former slaves would be employed by their former masters through obligatory service contracts. In 1871, parliament passed the Law of the Free Womb, which freed all slaves born after that date. Further stipulations of this law resolved the issue of service contracts in part by stating that in order to earn money to purchase their liberty, slaves could, with the permission of their masters, hire out their services for up to seven years.

Other proposals for regulating service contracts, especially for farm labor, emerged in the mid-1870s. Without specifying the type of labor, many of these proposals referred to all possible workers: Brazilian or foreign; free or slave "contracted with permission of the master."[31] By 1877, the issue had been discussed at great length, and it became clear that a comprehensive law on labor contracts was indeed necessary. Since the civil code, then being drafted by Nabuco de Araújo, had still not appeared and there was enormous pressure from landholders, parliament passed a special law in 1879 to regulate agricultural labor.

The reason legislators gave for restricting the 1879 law to rural labor was that the agricultural sector had the most pressing need for regulation. One might argue, however, that it would have been impossible to do otherwise, because so many slaves were already participating in the urban labor market. In any event, the basic goal of the law was to make workers comply with the contracts set up by the plantation owners, or rather, to determine prison sentences for those who would not comply. The legal justification for such punishment was that since it was assumed that the laborer had no assets with which to guarantee his civil obligations, he/she would necessarily have to guarantee them by way of his or her *person*. In effect, this stipulation meant that the only form of payment was the loss of liberty. This formulation brings us back to the paradox of liberalism in a slave society: because slaves did not own their own persons, they could not guarantee their contracts.

Criticism of the 1879 law was so intense that it was never fully enforced.[32] As Nabuco de Araújo also had not finished the civil code, the issue remained unresolved until the beginning of the next century, when it was revived by the commission that reviewed Clóvis Bevilácqua's draft of the civil code. Even then, after years of debate, the part of the code that referred to the contracting of services remained "incomplete, anachronistic, and technically defective," as far as Bevilácqua was concerned. He came to this conclusion because congressional committees removed all clauses concerning protection of workers, along with articles prohibiting the hiring of minors. Bevilácqua's principal concern was assuring the basic rights of the worker, as was already being done in other countries. Against his wishes, however, the final draft of the code defined service contracts very broadly, in practice placing workers at a disadvantage vis-à-vis those who employed them.[33]

In addition to the difficulties inherent in the creation of labor contracts in any part of the world during this period,[34] Brazil faced a number of specific hurdles. The impossibility of defining the term *locador*, for example, is understandable, since there was still no consensus even on the concept of *person* and the relations that a person should establish in civil life. It follows that there was no way to define a *person* who, by the power of a labor contract, had been transformed into a *locador*.

In fact, one of the most piercing criticisms Bevilácqua received was precisely that in his proposal for the new code he had failed to define the meaning of *person*. All previous attempts at a code contained differentiations among persons, principally in relation to the acquisition of rights. Felicio dos Santos's project, for example, established, in article 75, that "the general capacity to acquire and exercise civil rights is inherent among all persons."[35] Although the statement did not refer expressly to slaves—because, legally, slaves were possessions and not persons—it nonetheless made clear that all could, at the very least, become persons, and, in this case, all had the capacity to acquire rights. Bevilácqua countered this criticism by arguing that in the twentieth century, this differentiation no longer existed. Since a person was anyone capable of having rights, there was no need for a definition, as it was self-evident. Among his intentions, according to his rebuttal to critics, were "to remove any doubt that the *human form* is the requirement for legal personhood" and "to establish that the civil code does not recognize slavery or any other institution that violates civil liberty. And if the subject does not carry the same importance as it did formerly, it has not lost all relevance, because there are slaves, servants, and those without civil rights in other countries, and the code assures that, within Brazilian territory, all enjoy the attributes of civil personhood."[36]

Evidently, the subject remained relevant, since there were still some who questioned the definition of "person." And the debate gained interest to the extent that the final text of the code itself still refers to it, in a note following the statement "every man is capable of rights and obligations in civil society."[37] The note, penned by Bevilácqua, explains: "The code offers everyone, regardless of whence they come, entry into the bastion of law and the security of legal order. Slavery and any other institutions that annul civil liberties are refused admission. Within the circle traced by the law to direct and harmonize human activity, man is free and can develop his energies, acquiring and conserving legal rights."[38]

It was important to demonstrate that slavery was no longer acceptable because the memory of its past and the legal relations it had engendered were still very much alive. As long as this was true, it proved impossible to regulate service contracts or any other relationship that somehow invoked the slave past. Only with the civil code were all remaining vestiges of slavery finally eliminated, at least in law.

History and Memory of the Civil Code

Much was written about the civil code while it was still being created. Those who wrote about it most prolifically were the codifiers themselves, many of whom authored narratives of this process between 1870 and 1930. Clóvis Bevilácqua, Sílvio Romero, Rui Barbosa, Cândido de Oliveira, and Epitácio Pessoa were only a few of those from different generations and schools of legal thought who took on this task.[39] As they composed their texts, most of which were introductions to commentaries on different proposals, the authors provided their individual interpretations of the process by which the law was codified, at the same time constructing their own visions of the history of civil law in Brazil.

None offered any particular explanation for the delay in promulgation of the code. Epitácio Pessoa gives a good example of how the process of creating the code was explained:

> I believe one can conclude: (1) that since 1855, with small interruptions from 1886 to 1889 and from 1896 to 1899, Brazilian thought has applied itself directly and forcefully to the construction of a civil code; (2) that such forces, maintained with perseverance over a period of forty years and courageously recommenced whenever death or other adverse circumstances have interrupted, constitute a continuous chain [in which] the same people were involved in two or more attempts [to write the code], solidifying the unity [be-

tween the different proposals]. Successive studies lessen the difficulties, providing experience and expanding judicial wisdom in ways that help to perform today's work. [The present draft] is the summation of those preceding it, with the addition of what we have learned from doctrine and comparative legislation.[40]

Many contemporaries agreed with Pessoa that circumstantial issues, such as death or carelessness, were to blame for Brazil's failure to produce a civil code on a timetable in keeping with other Latin American nations. The failure to mention possible larger impediments is, at the very least, curious, given the significance of the problem of slavery for those engaged in the political struggles of the 1850s and 1860s. Not even the monarchy, which was often considered to be the cause of almost all of the ills of the newborn republic, is cited as a cause, since more than twenty years of the new regime had passed without the finalization of the efforts to elaborate the code.[41]

The issue here is why none of the early-twentieth-century jurists mentions the so-called ills of the Brazilian Empire—in particular, slavery—when answering the question of why the code was so difficult and took so long to complete. Why does slavery, the most formidable obstacle to the elaboration of the code, disappear from theories regarding the history of civil law in Brazil? There are two possible answers. One is that an important event transformed the contemporary view of slavery. The most evident would be the passing of the Free Womb Law in 1871. The other possibility is that it was important to those writing at the turn of the century to hide the remnants of the slave regime in Brazilian society.

The Free Womb Law, which passed after intense debate, radically altered the status of the slave in Brazil. By freeing all children of slaves born from that point on, the law proclaimed what white Brazilians had awaited in fear: the end of slavery in their country. Thus, although it would take some time—an aspect criticized by many during the period—slavery's days were numbered.[42] For Nabuco de Araújo, this was of the greatest importance: "the bill has imperfections, as I have noted, but it has a magnificent inscription that obliges me to vote for it. The inscription is this: *In the land of the Holy Cross* [Brazil], *no one will ever again be born a slave.*"[43]

In fact, Nabuco seemed to believe what he said. There is no more mention of slavery in his notes on the elaboration of the civil code, work he began in 1872, sixteen years before an imperial decree emancipated all slaves. As far as he was concerned, in legal terms, the question had been resolved: the population that was then enslaved already had its future civil status guaranteed as free persons and citizens like everyone else. If many might object that this guarantee was not sufficient to ensure that such rights would actually be upheld—as, in fact, they were not—we must agree that, in regard to the formulation of the norms of civil law, the problem no longer existed. The law of 1871 might be considered to have established, as a principle, the end of the theoretical dilemma between liberty and property, although it did not mean the end of such a dilemma in practice.

Here we can understand, in part, why everyone writing after the passage of the Free Womb Law ignored the legal history of slavery when discussing the codification of civil law. For this history contradicted the very conception of slavery and liberal order defended by these jurists. For people such as Clóvis Bevilácqua, nineteenth-century Brazilian laws had progressed in the sense of a democratic evolution, which was considered to be something positive, but the presence of slaves represented the old colonial past, which they sought to eradicate. After all, with the abolition of slavery and the promulgation of the republican constitution, the racial issue should no longer exist, since everyone had been equally integrated into society with the concession of citizenship rights to all Brazilians.[44]

Bevilácqua, who believed that law could create an integrated society, dissociates slavery from the process of elaborating civil law, since he does not remember having encountered a legal institution in which race could be relevant:

> Precisely because the Negro race contributed to the formation of the Brazilian people as a slave, that is, without personhood, without legal attributes besides those that might be associated with a shipment of merchandise, [the Negro race] appears in our legislation only to testify to the slave regime that continues to darken our own time. In studying the laws of slavery, as they were written in our country . . . , we find the African element, but incontestably it appears without any peculiar attribute.
>
> It is a slave. What difference does the gradation of its pigment make? What difference does its ethnic origin make?
>
> With the elimination of the slave regime, blacks were definitively incorporated into a Brazilian society already formed and specifi-

cally distinctive. They could no longer be the object of the particular analysis of the historian nor the legal ethnologist.[45]

Bevilácqua makes it clear that he considered the absence of the influence of slavery fundamental for understanding how civil law was finally codified. For him, the great defender of the codification of law as the grounding of social organization, there could be no intersection between civil law and slavery. Yet it is worth emphasizing that history demonstrates precisely the opposite: slaves not only influenced Brazilian civil legislation but also played a fundamental role, from at least the eighteenth century, in the legal process of dismantling slavery. In fact, it was because of slaves' legal demands for liberty and the ways in which they fought for legal changes that the problem of slavery became the most urgent issue facing parliament by the 1860s.[46]

The firm belief in the incompatibility of slavery and civil law helps explain why the memoirs failed to mention the influence of slavery on the process of codification of civil law. As much as these jurists knew of the problems that plagued Teixeira de Freitas's period, and as much as they discussed the concepts of possession, property, and personhood in the new regime of free labor, there was one basic issue to attend to: the construction of the new nation, for which the codification of civil law was crucial. Law was the entryway to civilization and could not be contaminated by old colonial elements that, for many, should have been eliminated years earlier. This notion helped strengthen a fixed conception of liberalism, one glaringly incompatible with the slavery of the past. For the jurists who helped to create the civil code, the liberalism that had existed since the start of the empire had brought ever more rational laws and free trade. How might one reconcile this process, which could bring only benefits to the country, with the slavery that took nearly the entire nineteenth century to end, especially as liberals had desired the abolition of slavery since independence?

The theoretical character of the Brazilian civil code, disengaged, in some aspects, from reality, was related to this question. As far as its elaborators were concerned, to dissociate it from social customs was the only way that the law would contribute to the nation's transformation.[47] The educated elite who wrote the code understood that the system of norms they were consolidating would, in the end, extend to the organization of state and society. In the words of a famous jurist of the 1920s, "the liberalism of the Brazilian civil code is always the liberalism of a people who built a constitutional, rational, almost secular empire, and the scientific ambition and 'idealist justice' that motivates it is strongly reflected in its laws."[48]

Notes

1   Brazil became independent from Portugal in 1822 and, unlike the other countries of South America, established itself as an empire until 1889, when the republic was proclaimed. The law of October 20, 1823, decreed that "laws, regulations, charters, decrees, and resolutions promulgated by the kings of Portugal be provisionally in effect among us until the organization of a new code." While the criminal code had been promulgated at the beginning of the 1830s, the undertaking of a civil code was never more than a goal during the period of the empire. The political system of the Brazilian Empire stipulated that the emperor govern "in his councils" (advisories or courts): the council of ministers, the supreme tribunal of justice, the general assembly of the empire, and the council of state. The latter exercised numerous functions during the empire. During the First Reign (D. Pedro I, 1822–31), the counselors oversaw the formulation of the constitution of the empire, approved in 1824. Later, during the Second Reign (D. Pedro II, 1840–89), the council of state was responsible for advising the emperor on subjects such as conflicts involving jurisdiction among distinct authorities, cases of abuses by ecclesiastical authorities, and laws and proposals that the emperor had to present to the legislative assembly. See João Camilo de Oliveira Torres, *O conselho de estado* (Rio de Janeiro: GRD, 1965).

2   The following narrative regarding the first stage of the elaboration of the code project is based on Joaquim Nabuco, *Um estadista do Império*, 5th ed. (Rio de Janeiro: Topbooks, 1997), 2:1051–1074. José Thomaz Nabuco de Araújo (1813–1878), besides being a jurisconsult, served as a prosecutor and judge in Recife, representative of Pernambuco in the general assembly, senator, president of the province of São Paulo, and was minister of justice several times.

3   In addition to these positions, Augusto Teixeira de Freitas (1817–1883) wrote various books on civil and commercial law.

4   See Eduardo Spiller Pena, *Pajens da Casa Imperial: Jurisconsultos, escravidão e a Lei de 1871* (Campinas: Editora da UNICAMP, 2000).

5   In 1872, Nabuco de Araújo himself undertook the writing of the code, pledging to conclude the work in five years. There are some, like A. Coelho Rodrigues, in *Projeto do Código civil precedido da história documentada do mesmo e dos anteriores* (Rio de Janeiro: Tipografia Jornal do Commércio, 1897), ii, who say that this was the principal cause of his death in 1878, when he left behind dozens of volumes of notes but no text. Three years later, the attorney Felício dos Santos presented the government with a book of notes (*Os apontamentos*) as a proposal for the completion of the code. Since the commission appointed to evaluate the text did not approve it, they were themselves obliged to head a new project. The group rarely met and finally dissolved in 1883. The last attempt during the period of the empire came about too late: the final commission, formed during 1889, and composed of, among others, Afonso Pena, Cândido

de Oliveira, and even the emperor himself, dissolved with the end of the regime. The task was finally completed by Clóvis Bevilácqua (1859-1944), the author of numerous books and a specialist in civil law.

6   Although the slave trade to Brazil ended in 1850, slavery was not abolished until 1888.

7   Paulo Mercadante, *A consciência conservadora no Brasil* (Rio de Janeiro: Saga, 1965); Pedro Dutra, *Literatura jurídica no Império* (Rio de Janeiro: Topbooks, 1992); and Spiller Pena, *Pajens da Casa Imperial*.

8   Perdigão Malheiro, *A escravidão no Brasil: Ensaio histórico, jurídico, social* (Petrópolis: Vozes, 1988), 1:67.

9   Sheila de Castro Faria, *A colônia em movimento: Fortuna e família no cotidiano colonial* (Rio de Janeiro: Nova Fronteira, 1998), 308-312; José Roberto Góes, *O cativeiro imperfeito: Um estudo sobre a escravidão no Rio de Janeiro da primeira metade do século XIX* (Vitória: Secretaria de Estado da Educação/Lineart, 1993), 96-97.

10   The *padroado* was the right granted by the church to the Portuguese kings to administer religious affairs in the colonies, which included the nomination of bishops and payments from certain types of parishes. With Brazil's independence, this right was turned over to the emperors D. Pedro I and D. Pedro II. See Guilherme Pereira das Neves, "Padroado," in *Dicionário da história da colonização portuguesa no Brasil*, ed. Maria Beatriz Nizza da Silva (Lisbon: Verbo, 1994), 94.

11   See Law 2040, September 28, 1871, in *Coleção das leis do Império do Brasil* (Rio de Janeiro: Tipografia Nacional, 1880).

12   Caetano Alberto Soares (1790-1867), a priest and attorney, was a representative in Lisbon before Brazil's independence, served as president of the Institute of Brazilian Attorneys, and penned volumes concerning civil and commercial law, including *Memória para melhorar a sorte dos nossos escravos, lida na sessão geral do Instituto dos advogados brasileiros, no dia 7 de setembro de 1845* (Rio de Janeiro: Tipografia de Paula Brito, 1847). Agostinho Marques Perdigão Malheiro (1824-1881) was guardian of free Africans, procurator of the Agricultural Deeds, attorney in the Council of State, president of the Institute of the Order of Brazilian Attorneys, and author of various books on slavery and civil law.

13   *Ingênuos* were the children of slaves born free. The expression was coined in a law in the Constitution of the Empire: "Recognized as Brazilian Citizens . . . are those who were born in Brazil, be they Ingênuos, or freedpersons." Title 2, art. 6 in *Constituição política do Império do Brasil*, in Senado Federal, *500 anos de legislação brasileira* (Brasília: Senado Federal, 2000).

14   Letter of resignation of Teixeira de Freitas, from October 22, 1857, in Silvio Meira, *Teixeira de Freitas: O jurisconsulto do Império* (Rio de Janeiro: José Olympio/Instituto Nacional do Livro, 1979), 156. Eduardo Spiller Pena developed this argument in *Pajens da Casa Imperial*, 96-128.

15   Speeches of Nabuco de Araújo before the Senate on June 11 and 13, 1873, in Nabuco, *Um estadista do Império*, 2:968-973.

16   Nabuco, *Um estadista do Império*, 2:974.

17   The following discussion of women's civil rights is taken from Sueann Caulfield, *In Defense of Honor: Morality, Modernity, and Nation in Early-Twentieth-Century Brazil* (Durham, NC: Duke University Press, 2000), 26-30.

18   Although he did not propose to grant women complete equality—Bevilácqua be-

lieved that the maintenance of family values justified the suppression of some of women's civil rights—he intended to grant married women the right to represent themselves before the law, and he proposed changing the word "men" to "human beings" in the code's declarations regarding equality. This proposal was rejected by the commission named to revise the civil code. See Caulfield, *In Defense of Honor*, 26–30.

19 Max Weber, *Economía y sociedad* (Mexico City: Fondo de Cultura Económica, 1992), 603–609.

20 Concerning this topic, and especially the following law of 1879, see Maria Lúcia Lamounier, *Da escravidão ao trabalho livre: A lei de locação de serviços de 1879* (São Paulo: Papirus, 1988).

21 See, e.g., Mary Karasch, *Slave Life in Rio de Janeiro, 1808–1850* (Princeton, NJ: Princeton University Press, 1987); Sidney Chalhoub, *Visões da liberdade: Uma história das últimas décadas da escravidão na Corte* (São Paulo: Companhia das Letras, 1990); Flavio Gomes, *Histórias de quilombolas: Mocambos e comunidades de senzalas no Rio de Janeiro, século XIX* (Rio de Janeiro: Arquivo Nacional, 1995); Luiz Carlos Soares, "Os escravos de ganho no Rio de Janeiro no século XIX," *Escravidão*, ed. Silvia Lara, special issue of *Revista brasileira de história* 8.16 (São Paulo: ANPUH/Marco Zero, 1988): 107–142.

22 About the region of Iguaçú, see Flávio dos Santos Gomes, "Quilombos do Rio de Janeiro no século XIX," in *Liberdade por um fio: História dos quilombos no Brasil*, ed. João José Reis and Flávio Gomes (São Paulo: Companhia das Letras, 1996), 278.

23 Perdigão Malheiro, *A escravidão no Brasil: Ensaio histórico-jurídico-social*, rpt. (São Paulo: Cultura, 1944 [1867]), 2:116.

24 Malheiro cites the institutions of Gaio (II, par. 87; III, par. 167) and Justinian (II, par. 9; I, par. 8). Malheiro, *A escravidão no Brasil*, 1:58.

25 The Law of Good Reason or Good Sense, promulgated on August 7, 1769, decrees that, in the absence of specific legislation over a given issue, Roman law should be applied to contemporary situations in accordance with "common sense."

26 Keila Grinberg, *Liberata: A lei da ambigüidade—As ações de liberdade da Corte de Apelação do Rio de Janeiro no século XIX* (Rio de Janeiro: Relume Dumará, 1994), 91.

27 In this respect, Dutra argues that it is not possible (in reference to Teixeira de Freitas) "to stipulate obligations in which the slave figures as a subject, and likewise any sort of judicial negotiations under which social traffic demanded regulation." See Dutra, *Literatura jurídica no Império*, 108.

28 Art. 2282 of chap. 8 ("Of Contracting Labor") reads "There is contracting of services when, toward the end of transferring the use or temporary possession without actual ownership, one of the parties is obligated to turn over an item, or consent in the use and possession of it, and the other party to pay a price in currency for such use or possession." Teixeira de Freitas, *Código civil: Esboço* (Rio de Janeiro: Tipografia Universal Laemmert, 1864).

29 See art. 226 of title 10 in the Brazilian Commercial Code; Carlos Eduardo Barreto, *Código comercial brasileiro*, rpt. (São Paulo: Saraiva, 1968 [1850]). On the other laws, see Lamounier, *Da escravidão ao trabalho livre*.

30 The need for labor regulation increased beginning in 1870, when European immigrants, principally Germans and Italians, began arriving in Brazil in great numbers, partly through the incentives of landholders and the Brazilian government, which sought to encourage the replacement of slave labor with free labor. Regarding the Bra-

zilian immigrant projects, see Celia Marinho de Azevedo, *Onda negra medo branco: O negro no imaginário das elites, século XIX* (Rio de Janeiro: Paz e Terra, 1987).

31 Lamounier, *Da escravidão ao trabalho livre*.

32 Soon after its promulgation, a circular communication sent out by the government prohibited the enactment of the most critical articles; in 1890 it was completely revoked. Lamounier, *Da escravidão ao trabalho livre*.

33 In this respect, see Orlando Gomes, *Raízes históricas e sociológicas do Código civil brasileiro* (Salvador: Universidade da Bahia, 1958), 63–65; Sílvio Meira, *O Código Civil de 1917: O projeto Bevilácqua* (Italy: Giuffre editores, 1982), 403. This author believed it would have been impossible to include in the code sectors of social life that changed rapidly during the period, as was the case with the extension of social rights to workers; in this case, the contract of the hiring out of services would be situated at a "sociopolitical crossroads," between the strengthening of property rights and the guarantee of rights to workers.

34 See *Código civil dos Estados Unidos do Brasil comentado por Clóvis Bevilácqua* (Rio de Janeiro: Editora Rio, 1979), vol. 1, note to art. 1216. For a comparative analysis of the discussion concerning labor regulation and the rights of workers in other countries, see Angela de Castro Gomes, *Burguesia e trabalho: Política e legislação social no Brasil, 1917–1937* (Rio de Janeiro: Campus, 1979), 31 and 45.

35 Brazil, Chamber of Representatives, *Projeto do código civil brasileiro do Dr. Joaquim Felício dos Santos* (Rio de Janeiro: Typographia Nacional, 1882).

36 "Resposta do Dr. Clóvis Bevilácqua ao Dr. Coelho Rodrigues," in *Projeto do código civil brasileiro: Trabalhos da Comissão Especial da Câmara dos Deputados* (Rio de Janeiro: Imprensa Nacional, 1902), 2:296.

37 Art. 2, Bevilácqua, *Código civil dos Estados Unidos do Brasil*.

38 Ibid., n. 4.

39 See, for example, *Projeto do código civil brasileiro em 1889* (Porto: Imprensa Comercial, 1906); *Código civil brasileiro, trabalhos relativos à sua elaboração* (Rio de Janeiro: Câmara dos Deputados, 1903); Epitácio Pessoa, "Exposição" (to the revision of the proposal for the civil code), in "Relatório do ministro da justiça, março de 1901," *Revista de jurisprudência*, 11 (1901): 5–12. Sílvio Romero (1851–1914) was a juriscunsult, critic, essayist, and historian of Brazilian literature; influenced by the positivist school, he became known for his polemical positions. Epitácio Pessoa (1865–1942) was a federal congressman in 1890, minister of justice (1898–1901), Supreme Court justice (1902), and president of the republic (1919–22).

40 Pessoa, "Exposição," 5–12. For those who agreed with him, see, e.g., Paulo de Lacerda, org., *Código civil brasileiro precedido de uma síntese histórica e crítica* (Rio de Janeiro: Jacinto Ribeiro dos Santos, 1916); and Filinto Bastos, preface to Eduardo Espínola, *Sistema do direito civil brasileiro* (Rio de Janeiro: Francisco Alves, 1917).

41 See Bastos, preface, ii.

42 Nabuco de Araújo noted that this was no small matter when he said, "In this system there is a grand principle, a principle that satisfies our patriotism; in effect, it ends the law of slavery and substitutes for it only the reality of slavery, a transitory reality, which must become gradually extinct, because it cannot be extinct immediately" (speech given before the Senate on September 26, 1871, two days before the promulgation of the law, in Nabuco, *Um estadista do Império*, 2:840). Nonetheless, he often pointed to

the problems of installing a system in which children would be free while their parents were slaves. See, for example, the letter written by him to the Limeirenian Democratic Constitutional Society, in José Tomaz Nabuco de Araújo, *O centro liberal* (Brasília: Senado Federal, 1979), 117–122. After him, his son Joaquim Nabuco also pointed out the insufficiency of the law of 1871 in Joaquim Nabuco, *O abolicionismo* (Petrópolis: Vozes, 1977).

43 Speech given before the Senate on September 26, 1871, two days before the promulgation of the law. In Nabuco, *Um estadista do Império*, 2:845.

44 For more information regarding Bevilácqua, see Sílvio Meira, *Clóvis Bevilácqua: Sua vida, sua obra* (Fortaleza: Edições Universidade Federal do Ceará, 1990).

45 Clóvis Bevilácqua, "Instituições e costumes jurídicos dos indígenas brasileiros ao tempo da conquista," *Revista contemporânea* 1.1 (1894): 2–3.

46 See, in this respect, Chalhoub, *Visões da liberdade*; Grinberg, *Liberata*; Silvia Lara, *Campos da violência: Escravos e senhores na Capitania do Rio de Janeiro (1750–1808)* (Rio de Janeiro: Paz e Terra, 1988); Eduardo França Paiva, *Escravos e libertos nas Minas Gerais do século XVIII: Estratégias de resistência através dos testamentos* (São Paulo: Annablume, 1995); Azevedo, *Onda negra, medo branco*; and Maria Helena Machado, *O plano e o pánico: Os movimentos sociais na década da abolição* (Rio de Janeiro: Universidade Federal do Rio de Janeiro; São Paulo: Universidade de São Paulo, 1994).

47 See Gomes, *Raízes históricas*.

48 Francisco Cavalcanti Pontes de Miranda, *Fontes e evolução do direito civil brasileiro*, rpt. (Rio de Janeiro: Forense, 1981 [1928]), 456.

II

POPULAR

USES

OF THE

LAW

Trading insults: honor, violence, and the gendered culture of commerce in Cochabamba, Bolivia, 1870s–1950s
Laura Gotkowitz

A 1911 provincial court case recounts a conflict between two former lovers: Tomás Aviles and Catalina Claros.[1] Aviles, the plaintiff, claimed that Claros attacked his house with stones and a metal tube, insulted him with the words "thief of glasses and firewood . . . coward," and accused him of incestuous relationships with his daughter and sister. In a passionate plea to the court, Aviles refuted the slurs. "I am an honorable and moral person," he declared, "my daughter is a minor, incapable of sin, and my sister is married and observes good conduct." "Catalina Claros," he continued, "is a callous woman who does not fear God or anyone else." In her defense, Claros claimed that Aviles lodged the case because she refused to steal a glass from a *chichería*.[2] "I may be poor," she reportedly told him, "but I'm also honorable." Aviles became angry, she said, took her hat and shawl, threw her outside, and locked himself in his room with her things. "Why didn't you take that glass with you," she recounted him yelling, "I will never be *gente* [decent, respectable]." Claros denied that she had insulted Aviles. Instead, she claimed, Aviles beat her when she refused to help him steal, and accused her of sleeping with her own brother. Witnesses testified for both sides, but like so many other slander suits the case was dropped before the judge reached a verdict.

One of thousands of such actions lodged, and presently decaying, in abandoned court archives, this mundane incident illustrates the central themes that marked verbal conflicts in the Cochabamba valleys during an era of profound changes in land, labor, and commerce. First, there is the unruly behavior of a woman. Second, there are accusations of illicit sex. Such allegations were more commonly lodged against women, but they could also be a weapon against men. A third theme is robbery. In this particular instance, the accusation illuminates local meanings of morality and honor: outward signs of respectability, of being *gente*, could not be acquired by theft or other illicit means. If the case reveals that sexual morality might be a component of both female and male honor, it also shows that virtue alone was not the essence of women's status. Honesty mattered, too. Finally, there is conflict over social and racial status. The spark behind the altercation was the removal of two symbols of local status and identity, the plebeian woman's hat and shawl. When he swiped Catalina Claros's garments, Tomás Aviles stole her status as a mestiza and recast her as an *india*.[3] To reclaim her identity, she employed an eminently common weapon: insults.

This essay examines local conceptions of honor, status, and race as expressed in court cases over *injurias* and *calumnias* (insults and slander) of late-nineteenth- and early-twentieth-century Cochabamba. In looking closely at the social implications of slanderous words, it also explores why insults and insult litigation were such consistently central features of public life. Bolivia's modern criminal codes defined *injurias* and *calumnias* as the public expression of words that dishonored, affronted, vilified, or discredited another person, and made that person odious, despicable, suspicious, or ridiculous. *Calumnias* specifically implied that the insults attributed a crime to the injured individual. These laws also covered the revelation of secrets with the intention of harming another's honor, fame, or public image.[4] Together, such infractions against personal honor comprised the most common criminal offense in late-nineteenth- and early-twentieth-century Cochabamba. Although the proportion of insult crimes declined somewhat during specific years, court cases over sexual and racial slurs remained a highly significant judicial phenomenon during the entire period studied (see appendix 1). Cochabamba's modern legal culture, in short, was deeply marked by the idea that words had the power to harm.[5]

Lawsuits over dishonoring utterances provide a detailed sense of the moral and cultural criteria that local actors used to define boundaries of social inclusion and exclusion. They reveal the force of racial taxonomies, ideologies, and hierarchies even in a region where racial and social identities have generally been considered exceptionally fluid.[6] Insult suits also point to the strong connections drawn between racial classifications and exclusionary discourses of gender and sexuality. Over a seventy-year period of profound transformation, the negative stereotypes that

period spans 19th c. liberal reforms
and 1962 Revolution

gave rise to insult litigation continuously invoked images of refined, "disguised," or intrusive *indias* or *cholas*.

Subtle changes in emphasis nevertheless took place over time. A sample of cases examined for the late-nineteenth and early twentieth centuries reveals that violent, mocking words were often used to denounce or unmask a woman's social pretense: she was accused of being an *india* or *chola* feigning an improved state, with finer clothes provided by armies of men, married and unmarried. Such insults revolved around and inscribed notions of inferiority, poverty, and powerlessness. They employed images of uncontrolled or transgressive sexual activity and racial hierarchy, often linking the two. In the 1940s and 1950s, verbal expressions of anger and anxiety continued to focus on sex and race, but with a difference: the sexually transgressive, economically successful woman became a central figure of negative stereotypes. An even more frequently invoked insult of these decades was the label *alcahuete*, a double sign for "go-between" and harborer of criminals or stolen goods. Court cases that address this charge set into play a series of associations between female promiscuity, personal gain, and social liability. At a time of increasing competition and insecurity, the economically empowered, uncontrollably sexual and loquacious woman was transformed into a sign of great animosity.

My discussion of the changing—and unchanging—dynamics of insult crimes draws on 277 court cases heard between 1878 and 1954 in Cochabamba, the departmental capital, and in three provincial towns— Cliza, Punata, and Quillacollo—all located in the department's central valleys.[7] This period spans the late-nineteenth-century liberal reforms to the 1952 revolution and subsequent agrarian reform. The impact of the liberal reforms in Cochabamba contrasts sharply with their effects in other Bolivian regions.[8] Rather than the expansion of large estates, Cochabamba experienced the decline of the hacienda, the consolidation of a smallholding peasantry, and the emergence of new middle sectors. Crucial to regional patterns of verbal violence are the gender dynamics of this process. One key characteristic was women's central role in the booming *chicha* industry and local markets; their prominence, in many cases, was coupled with men's declining economic position. A second important aspect was the anxiety and tension that emerged precisely around many women's relative economic strength. True, women traditionally occupied an important place in the region's commercial life. Yet dramatic changes in land and commerce magnified the scale of competition and conflict during the early twentieth century. As hacendados lost control of the commercialization of *chicha* and other goods, female producers filled the void.

The transformation of local economic life along lines of gender is key to understanding the conflicts over power and identity that characterized insult litigation. This is not to say that material changes automatically determined the language of abuse, but rather to suggest that the abusive repertoire had a material basis. Above all, it was local actors' perceptions of changing land, labor, and commercial arrangements that shaped ideals of insult and honor.[9] I further propose that shifts in the gender dynamics of local trade were partly effected in the realm of insult litigation. Put differently, hurling, returning, and refuting slurs was central to middling women's struggles for social ascent, distinction, and honor. Like schools, courts are often considered purely state institutions, sites of punishment and the inculcation of hegemonic norms and values. Instead I take the court as a more open forum where social identities were formed and contested.[10] *Injuria* suits, in short, were not simply legal disputes over slanderous utterances. In late-nineteenth- and early-twentieth-century Cochabamba, insult litigation was integral to the "classification struggles" that characterize class formation.[11] Those who pursued such actions used the court to help distinguish themselves as members of a group of honorable people, as *gente*.

The study ends on the eve of the 1953 agrarian reform, which signaled the destruction of the hacienda in Cochabamba and the expulsion of rural landlords. Successful female merchants—resembling the upwardly striving litigants discussed here—occupied the ranks of the new rural elite that would replace the landlord class following the 1952 revolution.[12] For these enterprising women, insult litigation was a crucial but contradictory vehicle, for it brought them both honor and dishonor.

The essay first delineates women's prominent role in slander proceedings and links this juridical pattern with the gendered transformation of landholding and trade. The next three sections delve into the language of insult. The idiom of verbal violence in Cochabamba—as elsewhere—often centered on sex. Yet the disputes examined here were not exclusively concerned with sexual behavior. They focused on women's social mobility, pretense, and disguise, closely connecting sex with theft and "propriety" with honesty. Sex was central to insult crimes because it offered evidence of not working or of material gain by "illicit" means. The essay concludes with a discussion of local honor codes. No matter how forcefully litigants linked sexual politics with the race-class order, they did not simply affirm virtue or respectability in line with a dominant moral code enshrined in the law. As they refuted verbal affronts, participants in lawsuits revealed their own conceptions of honor and dishonor.[13] The insult could be central to both.

Why Women? Gender Dynamics of Social Change in the Cochabamba Valleys

The population that protagonized court cases over insults was nothing less than immensely heterogeneous. Small- and medium-property owners, rural workers (*labradores*), chicha producers and sellers (*chicheras*), market vendors (*regatonas*, *matarifes*, *ccateras*, and *chifleras*), and artisans of diverse trades pursued these contentious suits. Occasionally, landlords, lawyers, and local officials also litigated insult crimes. Men and women, young and old, rich and poor appeared as defendants, plaintiffs, and witnesses. Amidst this great diversity, however, middling sectors predominated. The bulk of the litigants appear to be upwardly mobile but not yet clearly established economically and socially. In general, they were an upwardly striving group engaged in multiple economic activities that bridged both urban and rural worlds.[14]

The women of these middling sectors, vendors and *chicheras*, are best identified by their emblematic clothing: the *pollera* (a layered skirt), shawl, and tall white hat.[15] Intellectuals and politicians generally referred to these distinctively dressed women as *cholas* or mestizas. Local actors of the late nineteenth and early twentieth centuries, however, employed *chola* almost exclusively as a derogatory term. And while the categories *mestizo* and *mestiza* prevailed in official records, litigants rarely used *mestizo/a* as terms of self-identification. To identify themselves, most litigants instead stated their occupation, or simply called themselves *vecinos* (residents) of a particular place.

The everyday struggles over power and identity waged by these diverse actors were played out against and shaped by a protracted crisis of the hacienda. Late-nineteenth-century economic reforms weakened Cochabamba landlords and the hacienda labor regime (*colonaje*) in the department's central valleys. During the first two decades of the twentieth century, a class of peasant smallholders with origins in the late colonial era expanded and became firmly established. The transformation of *colonos* (labor tenants on haciendas) into *piqueros* (smallholders) was a protracted process with profoundly uneven effects. Sometimes the new *piqueros* gained autonomy and even managed to accumulate wealth; often, however, their lives continued to be marked by poverty and servitude.[16]

A second, closely related characteristic of turn-of-the-century rural life was male out-migration. In the late nineteenth century, the nitrate boom in northern Chile drew men from Cochabamba, primarily to work in seasonal activities such as llama- and mule-train driving. In the first three decades of the twentieth century, *qhochalas* (Quechua for Cochabambinos) became laborers in Bolivia's booming tin mines and on Argentine sugar plantations. Men's wage labor in the mines and women's activities in the *chicha* industry helped generate the crucial capital to turn *colonos* into *piqueros*, and *piqueros* into owners of more extensive plots.[17]

A third facet of the slow and multivariegated process of agrarian transformation in Cochabamba was the development of new middle sectors. These were owners of small and sometimes medium-sized properties who combined agricultural production with commercial activities. Above all they profited from a burgeoning commercial economy rooted in the complex circuit of *chicha*. The fortunes of these new rural groups were volatile, rising and falling with successive generations. The successful ones would become the dominant rural elite after the 1952 revolution, when landlords were expelled from the countryside.[18]

The women of these new middle sectors took the lead in Cochabamba insult suits. Of course, men also litigated slander crimes, but women were the main participants. Over time, this gender imbalance deepened: Women comprised 55 percent of the participants in the early decades (1868–1929), and 68 percent during the later decades (1930–1954). And although men participated actively in both periods, they generally appeared with or against women. Lawsuits between men were few, and their numbers decreased over time, falling from 20 percent of all cases for the early period to just 8 percent for the later period. In contrast, the proportion of cases involving solely women remained steady at about 30 percent over the entire period studied. Further, women became the primary instigators of insult suits. During the early period, just about as many male as female plaintiffs initiated the cases, but more than twice as many plaintiffs (71 percent) were women in the later years. Why did women come to denounce insults more frequently in the courts? The answer lies in the peculiar gendering of race, rights, and honor; the discursive logics of judicial spheres; and the transformation of the regional economy along lines of gender.

Bolivia's late-nineteenth-century liberal economic reforms not only transformed land tenure arrangements and relations between landlords and peasants, they also changed patterns of commercialization and consumption, and altered the sexual division of labor. Until the mid-nineteenth century, Cochabamba's primarily male artisans produced and exported a variety of goods. With liberal reforms, the construction of rail-road lines, and an influx of inexpensive Chilean manufactures, artisans lost their extraregional markets and the local economy turned increasingly inward. By the end of the century, corn and its principal derivative—*chicha*—became the region's leading products. The four provinces studied were the center of Cochabamba's *chicha* industry; together they accounted for two-thirds of the production of *muko* and *chicha* in the entire department.[19]

In contrast to other artisan industries that were male-dominated, nearly every aspect of Cochabamba's *chicha* economy relied on women. At particular junctures, even hacienda *colonas* participated profitably in *chicha* production, for example, by producing small surpluses of *muko* for sale (*mukeo*).[20] There is no evidence that such *mukeras* in turn produced and sold their own *chicha*, however.[21] The *chicha* industry's main contenders were *hacendados* and independent female producers. Since *chicha* was the most lucrative business in early-twentieth-century Cochabamba, women's prominent role within it had an especially powerful valence. Women certainly sold *chicha* in the colonial era, but a clear division between sellers and producers characterized the industry at that time.[22] Cochabamba's early-twentieth-century *chicheras*, in contrast, oversaw production, distribution, and commercialization.[23] They accomplished this using family networks of real and fictive kin. Through such family economies, rural women also became central actors in town markets as vendors of agricultural goods. Their strategic significance and public prominence made these entrepreneurial women vulnerable to—and dependent on—local opinion, networks, and institutions.

If women's prominence in the local economy remained fairly steady across the entire period studied, the combined effects of world depression and the Chaco War with Paraguay (1932–35) deepened insecurities and tensions for both sexes after 1930. Most of Cochabamba's new smallholding peasantry acquired landholding status between 1860 and 1930, with the bulk of land sales to *colonos*, smallholders, and artisans occurring in the 1890s and the 1920s.[24] In some cases, rural laborers still acquired land after 1930, but the sales apparently declined with the Great Depression. One local symptom of the global crisis was the dismissal of thousands of Bolivian mine workers, who were abruptly pushed back to the countryside. Since a disproportionate number originated from Cochabamba, the layoffs increased pressure on land and other resources in the region, at a time of already heightened insecurity. Most *piqueros'* parcels were quite small, generally less than one hectare. Over time, tensions deepened, as population density increased and patterns of partible inheritance led to further subdivisions.[25]

In broad strokes, then, early-twentieth-century Cochabamba was typified by the decline of the hacienda and a flourishing peasant economy still containing deep pockets of dependence and poverty. There were signs of a new dominant class in the making, as well as tension and conflict around the volatility of that very process. These uneven paths of social and economic change had fundamentally gendered valences. *Chicha* was the only sector that continued to prosper within the deepening crisis, and it was women who controlled and benefited most from this essential source of family income. Migration, in turn, was one of the most important economic opportunities now available to men. In general terms, the profound changes of the era meant more social mobility for women and more physical mobility for men. Certainly, many women continued to depend on a male partner's income, but the overall dynamics of gender power shifted. Women's increasing participation in public affairs through their economic activities was punctuated by men's long absences and abrupt returns from long-distance trade, war, or labor in the mines. So were their private lives and intimate ties. "You dirtied yourself while your husband was away in the Chaco [war]," one string of insults reads.[26] Women sometimes competed for the absent men, or the ones who remained. They were also locked in tough commercial battles with each other. It is no wonder there were so many insults.

Refinement, Poverty, and Racial Slurs

Procedures for filing slander charges in rural and urban Cochabamba followed a fairly typical pattern. Plaintiffs generally lodged complaints before the police, *corregidor* (the lowest-level state authority), or *juez/alcalde parroquial* (the lowest-level judge, named by the municipal council). If evidence was compelling, the accused would be summoned for a statement. An arrest order might then be issued, the defendant(s) delivered for questioning to the *juez instructor* (next-level judge), and witnesses called to testify. Depending on the gravity of the case and the proof presented, the process might be remitted back to the *juez parroquial*, advanced forward to the *juez de partido*, or simply dropped. Sometimes, cases originating in provincial capitals (like Punata) were sent for consultation to Cochabamba's Superior Court.[27]

Transcripts of insult suits—from one page to over three hundred pages in length—testify to the ways in which multiple criteria of race and class combined and collided with gender and sexuality in contests over local position and power. This dynamic is especially apparent in the use of two common insults: *india* and *chola*. In the 277 cases examined, the word *mestizo* appeared only twice, and solely in the initial description of a witness' basic background. The words *chola*, *india*, and *indio* were uttered frequently, almost invariably as derogatory terms; *cholo* also surfaced, but much less frequently, and not exclusively as an insult. In one case, a man who was called "filthy *cholo* thief" said he could not tolerate such slander since he was a "citizen and artisan known for his honesty and irreproachable conduct."[28] *Cholo* was used in a positive sense in another case, however; it distinguished a higher-status artisan from a man who was merely a butcher (*mañaso*).[29]

There was no such ambiguity in the meanings that *qhochalas* ascribed to *chola* and *india*; these labels were unequivocally negative. Litigants frequently associated both terms with robbery and promiscuity. Yet there was one basic difference: *chola* tended to imply "refinement" and the attempt to profit from a sexual relationship with one man (often someone of power and position), while *india* was more closely connected to poverty and the sense of being the common prostitute of poor men.

An 1892 court case brought before Punata's Juzgado de Instrucción clearly illustrates these associations.[30] This case for insults exchanged between doña Ramona Gutiérrez (the daughter of a prominent lawyer) and Gregorio Mendoza (a medium-sized landowner) concerned a dispute at a birthday party in the home of Gutiérrez's *compadre* (co-godparent). In her declaration to the court, Gutiérrez stated that Mendoza pulled her by her hair to the ground and gravely injured her with the words "refined *chola*, home-breaking whore, adulteress." Mendoza countered that Gutiérrez had instead insulted him and his wife. A witness corroborated Mendoza's testimony, saying that she heard Gutiérrez comment at the party: "There are individuals who wear *polleras* to please their husbands, but the monkey, no matter how much satin she wears, is always a monkey." Mendoza insisted that Gutiérrez had directed these insults at his wife, along with the words "*chola*, disguised bigmouth." When he came to his wife's defense, Mendoza said, Gutiérrez also insulted him with the words "*cholo*, refined *indio*." Presumably as a kind of additional proof, Mendoza noted that Gutiérrez was nicknamed "viper" for her "bad and provocative conduct."

In the course of the proceedings, witnesses testified that Gutiérrez had in fact insulted Mendoza and his wife, calling them "*chola*, bigmouth," refined Indian cacique," and menacing him with "black, refined, impudent Indian . . . you're going to respect us." Described by the judge as a man of high social condition, Mendoza had been labeled with a lower status by Gutiérrez's insults. But the words hurled at Mendoza's wife were even more disparaging: they implied an elaborate disguise and deception, and the (failed) attempt to appear better by donning finer clothing.

Several other cases employed the term *chola* in just this mocking sense, to designate a woman apparently feigning a higher social status. Another common usage implied that a woman was the *chola* of a particular man. This embedded within the term *chola* the sense of being both a mistress and a servant.[31]

Chola, then, was associated with talking too much, deception, false refinery, and being supported by another woman's man. *India*, in contrast, tended to be linked with qualities like being mute, stupid, fawning, or poor.[32] Both *chola* and *india* could connote illicit sex, but *chola* implied the use of sex to advance socially while *india* generally connected sex with poverty, exploitation, and abuse. For example, a woman in one case was insulted with the Quechua terms *india qhola* (Indian prostitute), *t[h]antosa* (very poor), and *manupetaca* (someone in debt to everyone).[33] *India* and *chola*, in short, were subordinate categories that linked lowness with "improper" sex. If the *chola* disguised such lowness under fine clothes, the *india*'s lowness was depicted as something transparent and unmasked.

Sex, Theft, and Sex as a Form of Theft

While verbal assaults often linked sex with race, many affronts focused on sex itself. The "illicit" act in some such cases was sex with one particular married man. Numerous other *injurias* suits more randomly accused women of having sex with many married men.[34] Thus one man claimed that a woman "takes married men from one side to another."[35] And two women complained that they had not just been charged with the "crime of adultery" but were accused of committing it with "all men."[36] Some insults that focused on sex with many men overlooked marital status and zeroed in on the men's place of origin or trade. For example, one woman might accuse another of being the *chola* of all the drivers.[37] Or it might be said that she had "married after finishing with all the men in the Curtiduría [one of Cochabamba's most populated neighborhoods]."[38]

These varied accusations reveal a great deal about local moral codes, about what was considered acceptable and what transgressed norms. Sex outside of marriage, in and of itself, was not the subject of disdain. Unacceptable acts were those that destroyed established equilibriums. *Injurias* litigants condemned sex with other women's husbands, sex with many men, sex that destroyed relationships, and sex that left a woman alone with a married man's child.[39] A single woman sleeping with a single man was never the subject of an insult.

Another group of *injurias* and *calumnias* focused on theft or fraud and the resulting "immoral" social advance. Theft was no random act in these cases, and it rarely involved money. The indispensable and costly *perol* or *fondo* (pots) used in *chicha* manufacture were occasionally objects of robbery.[40] Most of the time theft involved basic commodities (*muko*, grain, or livestock) or signs of status and identity such as women's clothes and jewelry. The insults *sua*, *ladrón*, *ratera*, *pillo*, and *contrabandista*, all synonyms for thief in Quechua or Spanish, were received and contested frequently by both women and men.

Like sex, the accusation of theft was sufficient cause for insult litigation. But some cases went further, linking theft to sex as an explanation for sudden, unexplained social advance. The insults in a 1953 dispute, for example, connected "wandering every night in search of men" with assaulting and robbing people.[41] In another case, three women were called "thieving, corrupt whores" who not only robbed *polleras*, but stole money from their boyfriends.[42] Closely related to this theft-by-sex trope were accusations that women traded sex for economic support. When it allowed women to procure the outward signs of status and identity, especially *polleras*, the transgression was deep. A woman in one such case was said to have "good *polleras*" only because she was wearing those of her partner's former wife: "Now you're wearing the *polleras* of the woman who was previously with that old man, that's why you have good *polleras* now, before you only wore *bayeta* (rough woolen cloth)."[43] In an 1878 case one woman called another a *despachadora*, someone who literally dispatches all the men, and concluded saying, "I got married knowing only my husband, but your boyfriends, the potters, dress you. What, do you think I'm like her? Do my lovers make me *polleras* and boleros like they do for her?"[44] The insulted woman was not just "immoral" but unable to support herself.

Men, particularly those in positions of public authority, at times defended themselves against sexual slurs.[45] Both men and women could be accused of pretense, too. But insults that linked sexual misconduct with wealth, clothing, or social transgression were reserved for women. Sleeping with "all" the men was clearly more fiction than fact. It was a way of saying that a woman's wealth derived from sources other than her own legitimate labor.

As these many lawsuits illustrate, insults were rituals of social, racial, and moral marking, means to inscribe and consign someone to an inferior place.[46] The particular words that drove Cochabamba slander suits set into play a string of associations between Indianness, theft, poverty, female promiscuity, and sometimes also skin color or physical deformity, all of which implied permanent inferiority. Racial categories—*indio/a* and *cholo/a*—were not always explicitly employed in such verbal assaults. But just as many of the above insults suggested that "corruption" could not genuinely improve social or racial status, so it was implied that Indianness was an unchangeable state of corruption, immorality, and inferiority. Some of the insults can be seen as attempts to return an upwardly mobile woman "pretending" to be a *chola* to a state of misery deemed closer to Indianness. In a way, these verbal assaults also put *indias* and *cholas* on the same plane: both were considered irredeemable conditions rooted in the generation of wealth without work. For Cochabamba's litigious crowds, the differences between the *chola* and the *india* were subtle. The *chola* was an *india* in disguise, an *india* underneath the clothes one or many men procured for her.

Alcahuetas *and Household Strife*

Over the course of the early twentieth century, there is much continuity in the words that drove slander suits. Adultery in particular remained a common theme of insults in the forties, a "classic calumny" as one *chichera* so accused put it.[47] Slurs that labeled women as impoverished *indias* or sexualized *cholas* also continued to appear. One additional trope, already present in the 1880s, became ever more prominent in insult cases of the forties and fifties: that of the *alcahuete* or *alcahueta*.[48] Disputes that included this insult sometimes linked the management of sexual relationships with the exchange of *polleras*, the emblem of female merchants and artisans. Through this chain of meanings, *injurias* and *calumnias* established even deeper connections between unconstrained sex, robbery, and social or racial inferiority.

Alcahuete/a literally means pimp, messenger, or harborer of criminals and stolen goods. It also signifies a go-between who facilitates forbidden matches. Local actors associated the term with a range of things: corruption, seduction, meddling in romantic relationships, and pimping. Men were sometimes labeled *alcahuetes* in Cochabamba's verbal battles, but women received the slur more often, especially older women and female relatives of the slanderer. In contrast to the disparaging images of the poor and abused *india*, or of the refined *chola*, who only pretended to be rich, the *alcahueta* was usually associated with wealth and power. The *alcahueta* destroyed romantic bonds, sometimes also wealth, often both at once. Making and breaking matches for a profit was some of the trouble she wrought. "*Alcahuete*, you earn a living trading in people," one case reads, "you serve as an *alcahuete* for everyone."[49]

Cases with *alcahuetas* often involved family ties. For example, a 1940 case denounced a mother (the defendant) who had branded an older woman (the plaintiff) the *alcahueta* of her daughter. The mother had insulted the older woman, saying she compelled her daughter to marry the older woman's nephew "*alcahueteando* [luring her] with the offer of her house."[50] The young couple was now about to divorce, and the mother blamed the older woman for the breakup of the marriage. In a similar case from 1952, a son and daughter-in-law called their mother/mother-in-law an *alcahueta*: "You are *alcahueteando* [pimping] our daughters," they said. In the heat of the battle, the son reportedly also shouted that he did not need his mother's inheritance, "nor the old man's, who must be burning in hell." He concluded saying he would "teach her [his mother] how to talk."[51] Issues of inheritance, combined with references to the deceased father and the threat of retaliation if the granddaughters were interfered with, point to long-standing struggles over patrimony and power along lines of gender and generation. The conflict also suggests that the inheritance may have been conditioned on agreement to a particular match for the girls.

Two additional cases involve similar meddling in personal affairs, but add a connection to clothing. In a 1944 dispute, the defendant, Adriana Ortega, allegedly remarked in Cliza's public market that the plaintiff, Victoria Fernández, maintained illicit relations with "single and married men."[52] Ortega denied the charge and declared that Fernández had instead "denigrated [her] daughter with the expressions *ccara siqui imilla* [Quechua for poor Indian girl] you've already finished with all the men, but that has nothing to do with me." Fernández's apparently angry denial suggests that she had been accused of managing Ortega's daughter's relationships with men. Indeed Ortega declared further that Fernández had been watching over her daughter and loaning her *polleras*. Although Ortega did not call Fernández an *alcahueta*, their dispute alludes to the interference that local actors associated with the figure. In another case, a young woman called her mother an *alcahueta*, furious at the mother's attempt to profit from her successful business; her mother, she told the court, would not even allow her to make herself new clothes.[53]

In these familial and extrafamilial conflicts, the *alcahueta* was associated with unwelcome interference in interpersonal and community affairs. The verb *alcahuetear* referred to the arrangement of marriages that did not work out well. It signified control of the flow of wealth and riches (inheritance) through the management of relationships. It also implied the failure of economic alliances between families due to marriage arrangements gone awry. A trafficker in clothes, inheritance, marriage partners, and young women's fates, the *alcahueta* was cast as an economic and moral liability, a powerful woman who managed—or mismanaged —sexual relationships and thus the race-class order. As one woman who called another an "old *alcagueta*" put it, "my daughter wasn't made for that one-eyed man, she belongs with gentlemen."[54]

Although it is difficult to track definitive changes in *qhochalas'* varied insults, the meddlesome *alcahueta* clearly became a recurrent figure of violent verbal repartee over the course of the early twentieth century. Slander suits filed after 1930 point more frequently to conflict and disorder in intimate relationships: incest, inheritance, and failed marriage arrangements became common themes.[55] Some such cases show parents struggling to assert authority over children; others give glimpses of daughters exercising their autonomy. What made the intrusive *alcahueta* such a compelling icon of discord in the 1940s and 1950s? No single watershed event can explain this change. After 1930, however, the gradual effects of class formation were both crystal clear and undisputedly gendered. Migrant men returned home from long stints in the mines or the military to find increasing land pressure, social tension, and a commercial economy where women clearly held considerable force. The complex family economies that enabled *qhochalas* to weather the deepening crisis could equally be a source of stress and conflict, especially against the backdrop of a changing sexual division of labor. Women's new economic opportunities, in short, challenged social and household hierarchies. In these changing times, the image of the intrusive *alcahueta* not only appeared more frequently; it also came closer to home.

Honor Code or Codes?

Injurias and *calumnias* suits illuminate how local conceptions of race and class intersected with gender and sexuality. They also illustrate how *qhochalas* constructed distinctive codes of honor, and the role that honor played, more broadly, in community struggles over power and identity. People's definitions of honor and status certainly drew on legal codes and precepts, but a close look shows that their honorable ideals went beyond the court's gendered definitions of sexual virtue.

If the key socioeconomic phenomenon of the era was the decline of the hacienda, the crucial political feature was the expansion of the state into rural hinterlands. A fundamental symptom of this process was the gradual creation of courts in provincial towns. Available evidence suggests that the first provincial courts were established in the late 1850s.[56] In contrast to older and more private forms of conflict resolution (through landlords, priests, or community authorities), the court publicized both the details of the conflict and the terms of its resolution. The court could also impose new kinds of sanctions ranging from public apologies or signed statements promising good conduct (*actas de buena conducta*) to jail sentences.

In an overall context of still-weak state institutions, Cochabamba's new juridical forums were not simple instruments of governance. They also became popularized public realms. Local courts made it easier for rural litigants to seek the validation of state rules, officials, and processes. The laws and procedures invoked in insult crimes, however, were not airtight or even especially elaborate. Bolivia's criminal code delineated in general terms what constituted an *injuria* or *calumnia*, but did not list which specific slurs counted as crimes; thus the insults could be explicitly spelled out in the court proceedings.[57] These vagaries of the law left much room for plaintiffs and defendants to relive any given conflict in all its remarkable detail.[58] Insult cases, moreover, were classified as private crimes and thus initiated by the injured parties; the people—not the state—policed language and deference. Indeed, the plaintiffs in a full 44 percent of the cases dropped their complaints before an official judicial decision was reached. Even when a decision was attained, sometimes following years of appeals, the triumphant party might seize the jubilant moment only to desist.[59] Humiliation and the threat of punishment—ranging from small fines to jail time—often compelled desired apologies. Insult victims, in short, actively sought the court's intervention, but they molded law and procedure to fit local needs, not fully surrendering their own negotiations to state officials. In the process, they distinguished themselves from insulting, destructive, unruly "others," and articulated distinctive codes of honor. These local cultural codes, in addition to the legal norms, explain the powerful significance and unique gender dynamics of Cochabamba slander litigation.

This is not to say that the law played no role in defining the boundaries of honor. As elsewhere in Latin America, postindependence legislation in Bolivia assigned great weight to women's sexual virtue. The insulted woman's status as a *mujer honrada* (honest woman), for example, affected the gravity of *injuria* offenses.[60] Similarly, crimes such as *abuso deshonesto* (indecent assault), *rapto* (abduction), or *engaño* (fraud) called for distinct punishments depending on whether the victim was an "honest woman" or a *mujer pública* (prostitute).[61] In line with such precepts, the convicted defendant in one case invoked a legal disposition allowing "virtuous" married women to substitute house arrest for jail. The plaintiff protested the request, arguing that the accused possessed neither morality, social consideration, nor manners. The court upheld the original sentence of jail time, ruling that "the defendant's virtue had not been confirmed."[62]

If social climbing via sex and theft typified dishonor, *qhochalas'* honorable ideals centered on three principal qualities. The first was the simple fact of being married. The second had to do with being *gente*. Indeed *gente* is one of the few unequivocally positive identities in *injuria* cases. Sometimes combined with *bien*, *gente* literally means decent or respectable people, or people of a certain class. Locally, the term implied a publicly recognized position or status. "You're not *gentes* for anybody," the insults in one case read.[63] "They make me odious before the *jentes*," declared the plaintiff in another.[64] "I am a distinguished lady . . . respectful of the privileges of the *gentes*."[65] In addition to marriage and being *gente*, some litigants linked honor with a third quality: "culture" or "education." For example, a market woman in one 1953 case considered herself a "cultured" person who did not insult; she was esteemed by her acquaintances "for [her] acts of charity as for [her] culture," a witness said.[66]

Finally, litigants rooted honorability in work: I "live from my work" or I'm "hardworking," several declared.[67] Not only men made such claims. A female merchant in a 1917 case from Cochabamba stated that she was "an honorable working woman, engaged in commercial dealings . . . [and that she] . . . lived with her family without giving a single reason for complaint."[68]

In sum, Cochabamba slander litigants neither fully embraced nor fully rejected dominant notions of gendered propriety and decency. They valorized marriage, and denigrated "public" women, but not precisely the same ways that legal codes and experts did. Certainly the legal discourse of morality and respectability motivated individuals to adjudicate verbal conflicts before lawyers and judges. But the great variety of honorable claims militates against any sense of absolute scriptedness. Litigants did not univocally equate virtue with women's honor, status, or power. Nor did they invoke an absolutely rigid dichotomy between male and female honor; both men and women pointed to honesty, work, valor, and sexual virtue as evidence of their own honor and status. Sometimes, *injurias* litigants expected the very same kinds of dignity, conformity, and courage from men as they did from women. The region's litigious and inventive hurlers and receivers of insults not only elaborated multiple notions of honor but also embraced a common concern: defense of personal reputation from the injuries caused by words.

Conclusion: Acceptable and Unacceptable Insults

Public insults were hurled steadily in Cochabamba over the late nineteenth and early twentieth centuries, and judges willingly weighed the wounds those dishonorable utterances inflicted. Occasionally, legal experts decried this preoccupation with honor. Bautista Saavedra, a well-known lawyer and president during the 1920s, condemned the laws that allowed "exaggerated and illusory guarantees for personal honor and dignity"; he thought them "out of sync with modern ideas."[69] Why did public insults and insult suits persist, against the grain of the modern, as Saavedra put it? And why did women occupy an increasingly prominent place in the lawsuits?

Such concern with the social significance, gender dynamics, and historical trajectory of insult litigation has animated a growing body of literature on slander in Europe, North America, and Latin America. These recent works have considered public insults variously as forms of community control and moral regulation, as assertions of social and racial dominance, as public battles for prestige, and as signs of social transgression. Court cases over insults, in turn, have been called extensions of street battles for personal standing, evidence of peasant legalism, and struggles for respectability and honor, especially by sectors on the margins of the established middle class. Few studies of slander consider changes in insult litigation over time. Those that do point to the progressive decline of insult suits, and associate that decline with modernity and the rise of a new ethos that stigmatized both the public insult and insult litigation.[70]

Cochabamba slander suits seem unusual for their endurance into modern times. During a seventy-year period of profound social and political change, slander litigation remained prominent, with insults precisely enumerated and honor expressly defined. This persistence points to an elemental consensus: reputation mattered deeply, and words could do harm. Cochabamba slander litigation also shows that honor, in its modern renditions, was not just a sign of sexual virtue but a symbol of social-racial precedence, as it was in colonial times.[71] It might thus be said that *injurias* suits proliferated because honor codes both persisted and became more fully suffused with demands for virtue.[72] Indeed, Bolivia's modern legal codes grounded a woman's status in sexual honor. For all its significance, however, the law is only an approximate tool.[73] Legal prescriptions for honor mattered greatly, but they do not fully explain the peculiar weight of insult suits in Cochabamba. While honor had and has enormous legal significance in Latin America, it does not seem that insult litigation persisted everywhere to the same degree.[74]

The reasons why *injurias* suits proliferated in early-twentieth-century Cochabamba, and the reasons for the predominance of women in those cases, lie in the relationship between local culture and economy. In part, the endurance of insult suits by and against women was rooted in the gender dynamics of class formation and commerce. The transformation of the regional economy in the early twentieth century was a gendered process that provided women with new opportunities for upward mobility. Women's economic power was simultaneously indispensable, highly public, and concurrent with a deepening regional crisis; this made women both targets of insults and especially concerned with their own honorable status.

Insult suits also endured because local actors attributed particular powers to the spoken word, especially to bad words. A review of judicial and nonjudicial sources reveals that the insult was not simply a sign of lowness but an accepted feature of life. Under certain circumstances, the insult might even be highly valorized. Sexual and racial slurs could be the stuff of raucous street fights and marketplace disputes. They might also be weapons of women who led political marches, or of men who pioneered rural labor strikes, or of women who resented economic competitors. Although insults were said to be uttered by "disreputable" people, they could also be employed by moralizing ones to disclose reprehensible behavior and enforce conformance with community norms. Of course, acknowledging an accepted place for insults should not mask their violent effects or neglect the significance of "virtue" and "prudence" for local status and identity. But to view insults only as a sign of dishonorable conduct would misapprehend the acknowledged place for the woman who could sling an admirable string of ignoble verse.

Finally, the ongoing force of public insults and insult suits has much to do with the contested meanings of *mestizaje*. As recent studies have shown, *mestizaje* was not only a fundamental characteristic of the region but a contradictory process, both valorized and denigrated by local actors.[75] As they rose socially and economically, and moved between countryside and city, Cochabamba's market women and *chicheras* remade their own identities, shedding Indianness and displaying visible signs of newfound status as *mestizas*.[76] The insult cases reveal how valuable, and how contentious, those signs could be. Some verbal battles were precisely about who should wear the most elegant *polleras*. Many more were disputes over who truly belonged to the established "moral" group with means. Insult suits, in sum, evidence the complex risks, conflicts, and potentials associated with the process of *mestizaje* in Bolivia.[77]

In different ways, Cochabamba slander cases were quite simply about the meanings of the "bad tongue." That insults were simultaneously considered unacceptable and an essential trait of female middle sectors—women of the town—made the local court not just a key site of class formation but an eminently gendered domain. As such, the court also constituted a public arena where women, excluded from formal citizenship rights, exercised civic authority. For the upwardly striving women who so zealously pursued slander suits not only defended their own reputations and injured the reputations of others; they also engaged in debates over moral norms, social obligations, and the very legal culture that recognized in words the power to do harm.

Appendix: Insult Crimes as Percentage of All Criminal Cases per Decade (Cochabamba)

Years	Average total insult crimes per year	Average total crimes per year	Insults as average percent of total crimes per year (%)
1870–79	5.8	22.6	26
1880–89	10.2	35.7	29
1890–99	14.3	56.9	25
1900–09	17.3	74.1	23
1910–19	24.2	99.9	24
1920–29	7.2	60.1	12
1930–39	11.4	102.9	11
1940–49	61.8	301.4	21
1950–59	75	362.8	21

Source: Corte Superior de Cochabamba, registries for Juzgados de Instrucción Penal 1 and 3 and Juzgados de Partido Penal 1 and 2.

Notes

A longer version of this essay appeared in the *Hispanic American Historical Review* 83.1 (2003): 83–118.

1 Archivo Municipal de Quillacollo (AMQ), T. A. vs. C. C., 1911. I use pseudonyms in the text and initials in the notes.

2 A tavern where people drink *chicha*, an alcoholic beverage made from corn.

3 For a similar dynamic, see Marisol de la Cadena, *Indigenous Mestizos: The Politics of Race and Culture in Cuzco, Peru, 1919–1991* (Durham, NC: Duke University Press, 2000), 224.

4 República de Bolivia, *Código penal concordado por Hernando Siles* (Santiago de Chile: Barcelona, 1910), 489–505.

5 For the period 1870–1959, the registries of the Corte Superior de Cochabamba contain 11,164 entries of more than one hundred different crimes. *Injurias* and/or *calumnias* accounted for 2,272 (20.4 percent) of those entries.

6 In this context, I use "race" to mean the attribution of innate characteristics that have less to do with phenotype than with the cultural or social attributes often referenced by "ethnicity."

7 The cases were selected randomly. One hundred and sixty of the total 277 reviewed span the years 1868 to 1929; 117 cover the period 1930 to 1954. Approximately 15 percent of the cases reviewed combined *injurias* and/or *calumnias* with other charges such as threats or stone throwing.

8 Robert H. Jackson, *Regional Markets and Agrarian Transformation in Bolivia: Cochabamba, 1539–1960* (Albuquerque: University of New Mexico Press, 1994); Brooke Larson, *Colonialism and Agrarian Transformation in Bolivia: Cochabamba, Bolivia, 1550–1900* (Princeton, NJ: Princeton University Press, 1988), 305–21; María Lagos, *Au-*

tonomy and Power: The Dynamics of Class and Culture in Rural Bolivia (Philadelphia: University of Pennsylvania Press, 1994); José M. Gordillo and Robert H. Jackson, "Mestizaje y proceso de parcelación en la estructura agraria de Cochabamba," *HISLA* 10 (1987): 15–37.

9 For similar perspectives, see Heidi Tinsman, "Household Patrones: Wife-Beating and Sexual Control in Rural Chile, 1964–1988," in *The Gendered Worlds of Latin American Women Workers: From Household and Factory to the Union Hall and Ballot Box*, ed. John D. French and Daniel James (Durham, NC: Duke University Press, 1997), 264–96, quote on 267; and David Warren Sabean, *Property, Production, and Family in Neckarhausen, 1700–1870* (Cambridge: Cambridge University Press, 1990).

10 On the court as a space where negotiations over power and status are carried out, based on strategic use of the law, see Laura A. Lewis, "Colonialism and Its Contradictions: Indians, Blacks, and Social Power in Sixteenth- and Seventeenth-Century Mexico," *Journal of Historical Sociology* 9.4 (1996): 410–31; and Rossana Barragán, *Indios, mujeres y ciudadanos: Legislación y ejercicio de la ciudadanía en Bolivia (siglo XIX)* (La Paz: Fundación Diálogo, 1999).

11 On the importance of classification struggles for the formation of group identities, see Pierre Bourdieu, "What Makes a Social Class? On the Theoretical and Practical Existence of Groups," *Berkeley Journal of Sociology* 32 (1987): 1–17. For a similar approach, focused on dance in Peru, see Zoila S. Mendoza, *Shaping Society through Dance: Mestizo Ritual Performance in the Peruvian Andes* (Chicago: University of Chicago Press, 2000).

12 Lagos, *Autonomy and Power*, 22–47.

13 On the manipulation of honor codes, see Patricia Seed, *To Love, Honor, and Obey in Colonial Mexico: Conflicts over Marriage Choice, 1574–1821* (Stanford, CA: Stanford University Press, 1988). On contests over competing codes, see Steve J. Stern, *The Secret History of Gender: Women, Men, and Power in Late Colonial Mexico* (Chapel Hill: University of North Carolina Press, 1995); and Eileen J. Suárez Findlay, *Imposing Decency: The Politics of Sexuality and Race in Puerto Rico, 1870–1920* (Durham, NC: Duke University Press, 1999).

14 See Jorge Dandler, *El sindicalismo campesino en Bolivia: Los cambios estructurales en Ucureña* (Cochabamba: CERES, 1983).

15 *Polleras* ranged, and range, from cheap to extremely expensive. On the history of the *pollera*, and its transformation into a self-conscious mark of identity, see Rossana Barragán, "Entre polleras, lliqllas y ñañacas: Los mestizos y la emergencia de la tercera república," in *Etnicidad, economía y simbolismo en los Andes*, ed. Silvia Arze et al. (La Paz: Hisbol, 1992), 85–127.

16 See Larson, *Colonialism and Agrarian Transformation*, 313–19; Jackson, *Regional Markets*; Lagos, *Autonomy and Power*; and Gordillo and Jackson, "Mestizaje y proceso de parcelación."

17 Xavier Albó, "Andean People in the Twentieth Century," in *The Cambridge History of the Native Peoples of the Americas*, vol. 3, part 2, ed. Frank Salomon and Stuart Schwartz (Cambridge: Cambridge University Press, 2000), 756–871, quote on 774; Gustavo Rodríguez O. and Humberto Solares S., *Sociedad oligárquica: Chicha y cultura popular* (Cochabamba: Serrano, 1990), 46–48; Jackson, *Regional Markets*; Larson, *Colonialism and Agrarian Transformation*.

18 Lagos, *Autonomy and Power*, 22–47.

19 Rodríguez and Solares, *Sociedad oligárquica*. *Muko*, the raw material of traditional *chicha*, is chewed corn flour.

20 Wálter Sánchez, "Hacienda, campesinado y estructura agraria en el Valle Alto de Cochabamba, 1860–1910," *Retrospectiva, Boletín del Archivo Histórico Municipal de Cochabamba* 1.1 (1993): 41–54.

21 On relations between *chicheras* and *mukeras*, see Archivo del Juzgado de Instrucción de Cliza (henceforth AJIC), *juicio verbal civil* presented to the Alcalde Parroquial, P. V. vs. L. Z., 1887; and AJIC, to the Alcalde Parroquial, 1885.

22 Jane Mangan, "Enterprise in the Shadow of Silver: Colonial Andeans and the Culture of Trade in Potosí, 1570–1700" (PhD diss., Duke University, 1999), chap. 3.

23 Rodríguez and Solares, *Sociedad oligárquica*, 92–93.

24 Jackson, *Regional Markets*, 150–159, 167–194.

25 Ibid.; Larson, *Colonialism and Agrarian Transformation*; Rodríguez and Solares, *Sociedad oligárquica*, 45.

26 AJIC, N. V. and M. F. vs. E. R., A. R., and S. C., 1940.

27 Manuel Ordóñez López, *Leyes penales de la República de Bolivia* (La Paz: Boliviana, 1918), 149–212.

28 AJIC, N. C. vs. A. G., C. I., and J. I., 1897.

29 Archivo de la Corte Superior de Cochabamba (henceforth ACSC), no. 2904 21P, 1915. *Cholo* was used five times, *chola* twenty-two times.

30 Archivo del Juzgado de Instrucción de Punata (henceforth AJIP), G. M. vs. R. G., 1892.

31 The insults *chola de* or *mi chola* appeared about twenty-two times.

32 *India* and its Quechua equivalent, *imilla*, appeared thirty-three times. *Indio* and its Quechua equivalent, *llocalla*, surfaced thirty-one times.

33 ACSC, A. R. and S. Z. vs. A. P. and R. P., 1931.

34 More than forty-nine women were called adulteresses and eight were called home-wreckers (*descasadoras*); five men were called adulterers.

35 AJIC, R. V. and S. O. vs. J. E., 1950.

36 AJIC, P. P. and F. P. vs. C. A., 1905.

37 ACSC, B. M. de C. vs. V. S., 1940. See also ACSC, L. L. vs. M. V., 1878.

38 AJIC, M. P. vs. J. M. J. and M. A., 1888. See also AJIC, B. V. vs. P. V., 1888; and AJIC, V. F. vs. A. O. E., 1944.

39 See, e.g., ACSC no. 3661 21P, 1953.

40 AJIC, F. E. vs. M. V., A. L., and S. N., 1905.

41 ACSC, no. 2963 21P, 1953.

42 AJIC, E. R., I. C., J. R., and P. S. vs. S. F. and D. F., 1905.

43 ACSC, no. 2939 21P, 1953.

44 ACSC, L. L. vs. M. V., 1878. See also AJIC, D. U. vs. F. T. and L. A., 1889; and ACSC, no. 3687 21P, 1948.

45 See, e.g., AJIC, J. G. vs. A. V. and P. N., 1954; and AJIC, M. M. S. vs. S. F., 1888.

46 On everyday rituals of racial marking, see Thomas C. Holt, "Marking: Race, Race-Making, and the Writing of History," *American Historical Review* 100.1 (1995): 1–20.

47 ACSC, no. 2986, 21P, 1953.

48 There were twelve such insults against women for the years 1868 to 1929, seventeen for the years 1930 to 1954. *Alcahuete* was used against men eight times in the early decades and eight times in the later decades.

49   AJIC, P. G. vs. J. N., 1892.
50   AJIP, E. T. vs. I. A. and A. G., 1940.
51   AJIC, M. R. vs. F. J., 1951.
52   AJIC, V. F. vs. A. O. E., 1944.
53   ACSC, no. 2981, 21P, 1953.
54   AJIC, H. P. and T. Q. vs. A. T., T. V., and S. V., n.d. See also ACSC, no. 3148, 21P, 1948; and ACSC, no. 2095, 1PP, 1881.
55   Eleven cases mention incest; two are dated prior to 1900, nine are from the 1940s and 1950s. For an analysis of links between incest accusations (and other sexual slurs), and conflicts over inheritance and household authority, see Sabean, *Property, Production, and Family*, 336–40.
56   See Marcelo Galindo de Ugarte, *Constituciones bolivianas comparadas, 1826–1967* (La Paz: Amigos del Libro, 1991), 692–93; and art. 32 of the *Ley de la Organización Judicial* (Sucre: Imprenta de Beeche, 1863), 10.
57   My discussion of the law draws much inspiration from Jane Burbank's "Insult and Punishment in the Rural Courts: The Elaboration of Civility in Late Imperial Russia," *Etudes rurales* (1999): 147–71.
58   With the exception of just five cases, all of the slander suits recorded specific insults, often in Quechua as well as Spanish, usually at enormous length.
59   See, e.g., ACSC, C. P. vs. B. S. de G., 1947.
60   See art. 594, Bolivia, *Código penal*, 504.
61   Bolivia, *Código penal*, 371–72, art. 420; 476–478, arts. 548–554. See Barragán, *Indios, mujeres y ciudadanos*, for a detailed analysis of the ways that gender structured Bolivia's criminal code, esp. 37–42.
62   ACSC, C. P. vs. B. S. de G., 1947. See also ACSC, J. P. G. vs. B. R. and others, 1921.
63   AJIC, A. S. vs. S. V., 1940.
64   AJIC, B. V. vs. P. V., 1888.
65   AJIC, C. V. vs. S. de B., 1925.
66   AJIP, F. C. vs. T. N. and V. V., 1953.
67   ACSC, de oficio vs. A. O., 1932; C. V. vs. T. O., 1915; J. S. vs. J. N., 1952; AJIC, M. M. S. vs. S. F., 1888; S. G. vs. H. G., 1925; M. T. vs. G. F., 1932.
68   ACSC, M. J. M. vs. J. R., 1917.
69   Bautista Saavedra, *Estadística Judicial, 1897–1898* (La Paz: Tipo-Litográfico, 1900) 12, 18. For a similar view, see *Discurso del presidente de la Corte Superior del Distrito Dr. Desiderio Gandarillas* (Cochabamba: Mercurio, 1922).
70   The most detailed study of change over time is Robert B. Shoemaker, "The Decline of Public Insult in London, 1660–1800," *Past and Present* 169 (2000): 97–131. For citations of other works, see n. 130 of the longer version of this article cited in the first, unnumbered note above.
71   On honor in colonial Latin America, see discussion and sources cited in the introduction to this volume.
72   Recent studies stress the increasing importance of virtue and morality for meanings of honor since independence. For different perspectives on the gendered implications of this process, see Sarah Chambers, *From Subjects to Citizens: Honor, Gender, and Politics in Arequipa, Peru, 1780–1854* (University Park: Pennsylvania State University Press, 1999); and Barragán, *Indios, mujeres y ciudadanos*. On the "modernization" of honor,

Trading Insults   153

see also Sueann Caulfield, *In Defense of Honor: Sexual Morality, Modernity, and Nation in Early-Twentieth-Century Brazil* (Durham, NC: Duke University Press, 2000); Kristin Ruggiero, "Honor, Maternity, and the Disciplining of Women: Infanticide in Late Nineteenth-Century Buenos Aires," *Hispanic American Historical Review* 72 (1992): 353–373; and Elizabeth Dore and Maxine Molyneux, eds., *Hidden Histories of Gender and the State in Latin America* (Durham, NC: Duke University Press, 2000).

73 Olivia Harris, introduction to *Inside and Outside the Law: Anthropological Studies of Authority and Ambiguity*, ed. Olivia Harris (London: Routledge, 1996), 3.

74 Honor is the subject of an extensive literature, but "insult studies" are in their infancy. For a recent study that demonstrates the decline of insults in twentieth-century Latin America, see Putnam's work on Limón, Costa Rica: *The Company They Kept: Migrants and the Politics of Gender in Caribbean Costa Rica, 1870–1960* (Chapel Hill: University of North Carolina Press, 2002), chap. 5.

75 On mestizaje, gender, and violence, see Silvia Rivera Cusicanqui, "La raíz: Colonizadores y colonizados," in *Violencias encubiertas en Bolivia*, ed. Xavier Albó and Raúl Barrios (La Paz: CIPCA, 1993), 27–139; and Rivera Cusicanqui, "Mujeres y estructuras de poder en los Andes: De la etnohistoria a la política," *Escarmenar* 2 (1997): 16–25. On contests over meanings of *mestizaje*, see Rossana Barragán, "Los múltiples rostros y disputas por el ser mestizo," in *Seminario mestizaje: Ilusiones y realidades* (La Paz: Museo Nacional de Etnografía y Folklore, 1996), 63–106; and José M. Gordillo, *Campesinos revolucionarios en Bolivia: Identidad, territorio y sexualidad en el Valle Alto de Cochabamba, 1952–1964* (La Paz: Plural, 2000). On the dangers attributed to *mestizaje* in colonial Bolivia, see Brooke Larson, "Cochabamba: (Re)constructing a History," in *Cochabamba, 1550–1900: Colonialism and Agrarian Transformation in Bolivia*, expanded ed. (Durham, NC: Duke University Press, 1998), 322–390; and Thomas A. Abercrombie, "*Q'aqchas* and *la Plebe* in 'Rebellion': Carnival vs. Lent in Eighteenth-Century Potosí," *Journal of Latin American Anthropology* 2.1 (1996): 62–111.

76 In *Indigenous Mestizos*, de la Cadena argues that *mestizas* of Cuzco cast off an inferior social status without rejecting indigenous cultural practices. The same holds true for Cochabamba.

77 See Rivera, "Mujeres y estructuras de poder"; and Barragán, "Los múltiples rostros."

Sex and standing in the streets of Port Limón, Costa Rica, 1890–1910
Lara Putnam

For a few heady decades at the turn of the nineteenth century, Port Limón was a boomtown beyond compare. Bananas were first planted commercially in Costa Rica in the 1880s, on lands granted to railway magnate Minor C. Keith as part of the contract for his construction of the first rail line from the coffee-producing Central Valley to the Caribbean coast. Keith's banana export business would prove enormously profitable, and in 1899 he merged his Costa Rican holdings with Jamaica-based Boston Fruit to create the United Fruit Company. Vast tracts of lowland rain forest were cleared and planted in the province of Limón in those years, including tens of thousands of acres directly managed by United Fruit and at least twice that in the hands of smaller planters, who included both Costa Rican entrepreneurs and well-placed immigrants. In the first decades of the century, United Fruit's Limón division was among the largest in the world, and all bananas grown there, whether on company plantations, private farms, or peasant smallholds, were shipped from the docks of Port Limón.[1] The boomtown port's atmosphere must have been something like Gabriel García Márquez's Macondo once the banana company arrived: a "tempest of unknown faces, of awnings along the public way, of men changing clothes in the middle of the street, of women with open parasols sitting on trunks, and of mule after mule dying of hunger on the block by the hotel."[2]

People and goods had long circulated among the islands and rimlands of the Western Caribbean. The scale of such movement grew enormously in the second half of the nineteenth century as direct foreign investment on the rimlands offered wage-earning opportunities to workers displaced by the collapse of Jamaica's sugar economy. More than twenty thousand

Jamaicans would come to Limón during the banana boom, along with thousands of migrants from elsewhere in the Caribbean, including Barbados, St. Lucia, and St. Kitts. Many came via Colón, where canal construction under French and then U.S. direction drew West Indians by the hundreds of thousands during these years. Migrants also came to the coast from Costa Rica's Central Valley, although there the still expanding agricultural frontier, and favorable international coffee prices, meant that most workers found opportunities for independent or waged agricultural labor closer to home.[3] Others came to Limón from Colombia to the south, from Nicaragua and points north, and from Cuba and elsewhere in the Spanish-speaking Caribbean. Former indentured workers from the Indian subcontinent arrived by way of Jamaica; Syrian peddlers traded in dry goods and sundries; Chinese merchants set up *pulperías* and *cantinas* (corner stores and popular bars). The streets of Port Limón, the local police chief wrote in 1912, looked as if "practically the majority of the nations of the globe—Costa Ricans, Europeans, North and South Americans, Antilleans, Africans, and Asians—all have arranged to meet here."[4]

This essay is about the politics of honor in Port Limón; about how individual and collective status was asserted, challenged, and defended; and about the contradictory roles that state institutions and actors played in that process. I begin with two anecdotes. In 1899, Louise Gordon sued Jane Parker for insults before the *alcalde* (mayor) of Limón, claiming that the previous morning at nine, while she was chatting with Annie Cummings at her stall in the market, Parker had yelled across to her "that I was a whore, a filthy pig. . . . I asked, who are you talking to? and she repeated herself, saying it was me she was insulting, since I was talking about her."[5] On a nearby street in 1902, as the governor of Limón telegraphed to his superiors in San José, "due to personal disputes motivated by despicable articles published in one of the so-called 'newspapers' of the capital, don Eduardo Beeche gave don Lucas Alvarado several blows with his cane: there were no serious consequences."[6] Beeche and Alvarado were both wealthy and influential citizens, active in electoral politics; Alvarado was a former *alcalde* himself. Their conflict seems far removed from that of the two Jamaican market women (certainly Beeche and Alvarado would have insisted that it was). Yet in the following pages, I hope to show both the parallels and the direct connections between battles for status in each of these social worlds.

Much of this essay will be based on an analysis of insults (*injurias*) suits filed in the Limón judicial system during the heyday of the banana boom. The preserved insult cases offer an intriguing set of paradoxes. First, insult suits were quite common in Limón, much more so than in the rest of the country. Seventeen times as many insult cases were filed per capita in the province of Limón than in San José in these years.[7] Second, the majority of insult suits were brought by a category of migrant invisible in much of the official record and little discussed in the secondary literature on the banana economy: West Indian women. Third, according to the Penal Code of 1880, *injurias* consisted of expressions or actions intended to bring "dishonor, discredit, or scorn" that harmed the recipient's "reputation, credit, and interests."[8] Yet the women who sued for insults—washerwomen, peddlers, prostitutes—were precisely those women with the least honor to lose, in the eyes of elites and officials. In contrast, the men who filed such cases as often as not were themselves local elites and officials: plantation owners, contractors, police commanders. Finally, while the gender ratio and social standing of insult participants varied markedly across ethnic groups, the specific content of insults did not. Women were accused of sexual impropriety (with lavish and varying detail), and men were accused of theft or dishonorable business dealings.

Two hundred and two insult suits from Limón are preserved in the Archivo Nacional de Costa Rica, dating from 1892 to 1910. The breadth of participation is remarkable. Spanish storeowners and St. Lucian laundresses, Colombian madams and Tunisian traders, fruit magnate Cecil V. Lindo and the men who hauled his bananas on the docks: all appear among the ranks of those who filed suit for *injurias* in turn-of-the-century Limón. Just over half of parties to insult cases were women. Patterns in national origin differed sharply by gender. Four-fifths of female plaintiffs were West Indian, while only half of male plaintiffs were the same. Put differently, male plaintiffs equaled or outnumbered females in every national group *except* Jamaicans, among whom women outnumbered men by more than two to one. Costa Rican men were twice as likely to sue as to be sued. West Indian men were half again as likely to be sued (almost always by West Indian women) as to sue. Eighty-five percent of cases involved parties from the same region of origin. West Indian women, West Indian men, Hispanic women, and Hispanic men were each twice as likely to sue someone of their own origin and gender as anyone else. This matches a basic pattern of status similarity between participants. Such cases involved two stages of confrontation: the original act of insult and the subsequent decision to sue. For a case to result, at the first stage one party had to find the other neither too inferior to bother with nor too powerful to risk offending, and at the second stage the other party had to make the same evaluation. Insult cases embodied "the logic of challenge and riposte, in which a challenge both validates an individual's honor by recognizing him as worth challenging, and serves as a 'provocation to reply.'"[9] Not infrequently, the case itself served as an additional provocation to reply, inspiring the filing of a countersuit.

By definition, insult cases had their origins in public defamation. The exchanges recounted in court testimony took place on the streets, at the market, in boardinghouse patios, inside and outside *cantinas*, at train stations. Almost without exception, cases were urban in origin. A few began in the junction towns along the rail lines that led to the plantation zones, but the vast majority took place in the port itself. Thus, absent from these cases are the temporary camps and plantation barracks where the male laborers who made up the bulk of Limón's population resided and worked, clearing jungle, planting, and harvesting bananas. But it was precisely that plantation production, albeit at one remove, which shaped the social spaces where insult cases did originate. Banana exports fueled the booming port economy in all its guises, not only the scores of dockworkers needed to load fruit into each outgoing steamer but also the burgeoning employment in local government, the municipal improvement contracts with their associated boondoggles, the land speculation, the *cantina* world of brothels and bars. This last sector blended at its edges into the cheap hotels and boardinghouses where women performed the labor of daily social reproduction that sustained the largely male workforce employed in export production. Here women provided cooked meals, clean laundry, and companionship, under a variety of monetary and nonmonetary arrangements.[10]

The patterning of cases, with respect to the relationship between the parties and the substance of the inflammatory accusations, has much to tell us about the bases of male and female honor and the connection of intimate lives to public stature in Limón. Classic descriptions of honor in the Mediterranean depict men's control over the sexual behavior of female dependents as the centerpiece of the honor/shame system and argue that male hypersensitivity to affront evolved both to defend and to display this patriarchal power.[11] Yet as a motive in insult actions, male defense of the reputations of mothers, sisters, or wives (or lovers) is most notable by its absence.[12] Sexual impropriety was indeed the substance of almost all actionable insults against women. But in Limón, female sexual honor was not a symbol in status struggles between men. Rather, women's sexual choices were seen as instrumental to their own social and economic status, their standing vis-à-vis other women as well as men. This is clear, for instance, in the two suits for insults filed days apart by Martha Brown and Isabel Jamieson in 1907. Brown had called the younger woman over to her doorway, saying, "I'll tell you not to keep company with my son anymore" or, in another witness's version, "You evil woman, you took all my son's money last payday." Jamieson answered, "Oh, I take [or "fuck": the meaning is ambiguous in the interpreter's Spanish rendering, as it probably was in the original Creole] any thing I want if there's money behind it," to which Brown replied, "If you want to be a whore I'll go the governor and have him ship you out as a prostitute." Brown turned her back, saying, "Don't you break my ass this morning."[13]

In this case the imputations against the woman's sexual honor seem to stem logically from the substance of the conflict. But in fact sexual dishonor was the idiom through which women's status was challenged and defended, no matter who the women were and no matter what the conflict was. Thus Matilda Thompson sued Edith MacLean for saying "that she was a 'whore,' that she was always getting money from a man to sleep with him, that when that man goes to her house, she shuts herself up with him and three others and they keep cohabitating [sic] until midnight." Queried about the parties to the case, the local justice of the peace reported that the two women were constantly in disputes stemming from a conflict over the title to a piece of land.[14]

Meanwhile, men defended their own honor and status through court cases but rarely with reference to sexual behavior, whether their womenfolk's or their own.[15] Rather, in this dynamic boomtown of striving entrepreneurs, business disputes were frequently the occasion of actionable insults, and accusations of thievery and dishonesty were exchanged with angry gusto. Thus in 1902 Frederick Davis denounced Jerome Bright for saying publicly, "You were a thief in Jamaica, a thief in Colón, and a thief here." The occasion, according to Davis's witness, was that Bright had tried to collect "the rest of the pay owed him for a job that they had done together in Banana River, to which Davis replied that he didn't owe anything, as the remaining money the company commissary had deducted for goods Bright had bought on credit; and Bright said this was a lie, and Davis a lying thief." In Bright's version of the encounter, Davis responded to his request for the money owed by saying "that he didn't have the means to pay me now, and anyhow that *negros* as stupid as I should work for free." When Bright answered in kind, Davis "called me a son of a bitch and threatened to take me up before the authorities," as indeed he did.[16] A similar business dispute occurred between two Cuban contractors in 1906. When Manuel Ulyett went to collect the one hundred *colones* that Miguel Xirinach owed him for carpentry work, Xirinach said "that he owed me nothing because I had taken some of the lumber for myself, that I had no right to complain about the cow I said I had given him, and that anyway he had lost money on the business of building the hospital in Guápiles; to which I answered that if he had lost money on that contract it was because he'd been planning to steal a profit of four to eight thousand *colones*," upon which "he threw himself at me, and attacked me, calling me a *bandido* [crook], *sinvergüenza* [shameless one], and thief."[17]

In some cases the feud between the parties was long-standing, as in the conflict between Florence Thompson and her cousin, who had accused her of stealing the pound sterling that he had given her to take to his mother in Jamaica; or that between Sarah Simon and David Newcome over her brand-new market basket, full of forty eggs and three pounds of coffee, which she claimed he had taken off the train at Zent Junction while her attention was elsewhere.[18] In other cases the relationship between the parties was ephemeral, yet personal pride was still at stake. Ethel Forbes sued Harold Franklin in 1902 after he called her "in English, 'Jamaica Bitch' which is to say in Spanish *jamaicana puta perra puta*." His prepaid laundry had not yet been ironed when he came to pick it up.[19] Likewise disputes over a few cents' change, at the pharmacy or the butcher's shop, led to court cases in which the parties invested many times that amount.[20] One could place an oral accusation at the *alcalde*'s office for free, but to pursue a case further involved increasing outlays, for stamps, witnesses' depositions, and legal writs. While the latter were by no means required, fully two-thirds of the participants in the cases reviewed turned to professional lawyers to pursue their cases.[21] Local lawyers made a variety of arrangements with clients, including quid pro quos and patron-client ties.

Such ties are exemplified by a case involving Juan José León, the prominent leader of the local Chinese merchant community. León sued two young Jamaican women in 1909 for calling him (in his lawyer's account) a "thief, *bandido*, *sinvergüenza*, and other words so against morality that

I omit to mention them, although I am forced to add that they also said that his mother was a Chinese whore." The accused Emma Charles explained that the conflict had begun on the day when presidential candidate Don Ricardo Jiménez came to visit Limón: "the *chino* saw that I was wearing a Civilista badge [that of the party opposing Jiménez] and began to insult me, saying that I was a vagabond, *bandida*, and that only *sinvergüenzas* and thieves and drunkards wore Civilista badges, because the Civilistas were idiot sons of bitches." Despite this affront, she returned to make a purchase a few weeks later. "In the moment that one of the *chinos* was cutting the meat, as they were speaking in their language I laughed, and so the *chino* who apparently is the owner of the establishment asked me if I liked to have sex with *chinos*, to which I replied that only a woman who was totally shameless could sleep with a *chino*, as it's well known that *chinos* are really filthy." Incensed, León sued, contracting the services of a prominent lawyer tied to Jiménez's Republican Party. The anti-Jiménez electoral effort was being bankrolled at the time by United Fruit Company president Minor Keith, and former *alcalde* don Lucas Alvarado was local counsel for the company. Alvarado joined the case on the girls' behalf, and soon after the suit was dismissed.[22]

Like this case, the majority of insult cases never made it past the initial writ of complaint and perhaps a few witnesses' declarations. Less than one in seven actually reached judgment, and in at least half of these cases the defendant was absolved. All told, less than 5 percent of accusations ended in conviction.[23]

The bulk of accusations stemmed from conflicts between neighbors, in which monetary disputes, malicious gossip, and moral judgments were inextricably mixed. Such cases highlight the relation among built environment, social networks, and popular culture in Limón. Working folk in the port city lived either on the outskirts, in wooden shacks built on the public domain, or in the center of town, in boardinghouses and multifamily dwellings. These, known as *casas de vecindad* or *chinchorros*, were usually two-story buildings, in which lines of eight to ten single rooms opened onto a corridor along the first floor and a balcony on the second. In the patio behind the building there would be a standing water pipe and sometimes a separate kitchen to reduce the risk of fires. Many insult cases had their origins in words shouted "from the *altos* [second floor]," from doorway to doorway, or through the partitions that separated rooms (a row of planks that often stopped several feet from the ceiling). Even more than the public market, the *casas de vecindad* facilitated the informal economy of workingwomen. They were the centers not only of laundry and food preparation but also of money-lending, small-scale retailing, and services like dressmaking and hairdressing. Here there could be little distinction between public and private domains. Such a division had no spatial basis in a world in which only five flimsy boards separated your bed from your neighbors'; in which you literally washed your dirty linen in public; in which your financial borrowing power depended on your upstairs neighbor's opinion of the man you had been keeping company with. In the *casas de vecindad* social networks, economic well-being, political connections, and intimate liaisons were all linked, and information and judgments about all of these came together in personal reputations.

It was not uncommon for a dozen or more neighbors to testify to a particular verbal battle they had all witnessed, giving versions that differed dramatically depending on whose side they had chosen to take. In a 1908 case, Roberta Thompson said she and her husband had been sitting peacefully in front of their door when Edith Carter called out, "Why is this bitch laughing at me, why don't you go to Jamaica and whore with the man you left behind there?" to which, one witness claimed, Thompson had responded "that [Edith] was a damned nothing, 'patio princess.'" Other neighbors, testifying on Edith Carter's behalf in the countersuit she filed, remembered a more colorful response: "that [Edith] was a whore all her life, that she had given birth in a chamber pot; that she smelled worse than chicken shit; that she was a shaved-head, no more than a vulgar woman of her class; and that if she didn't like it, she could take it to the judge."[24] Such cases were not unique to West Indian women. Similarly intimate public conflicts occurred among Costa Rican and Central American boardinghouse tenants. The conflict between Costa Rican Vicenta Hernández and Isabel Montoya, a Nicaraguan eighteen-year-old, began in the public market with insults and accusations of malicious gossip, involving several other women as well, and carried over into a string of insults in their shared patio (including the classic repartee, "She said '*tu madre*' to which I replied '*la tuya*'"). According to Montoya's testimony, the fight culminated with Hernández declaring, in front of Montoya's male partner "that I [Montoya] am a whore, so low that I whore with *chinos*."[25]

In the tight quarters of boardinghouse life, struggles over status sometimes became fights over space, as the attempt to "keep someone in her place" was enacted literally. One morning in 1900 Amelia Esquivel, a Colombian woman who "lived as if married" with *cantina* owner Isidor

Stein, nailed a canvas sheet along the corridor behind the *cantina* to prevent Maud MacPherson from walking past and announced "that filthy whores like her could not pass here." In response MacPherson paraded back and forth, milk jug in one arm and baby in the other, daring Esquivel to stop her and taunting "that if she was dirty it was from caring for her one husband and her child" (implying that Esquivel was morally dirty for living with Stein). "One Colombian woman there was urging Amelia to hit [MacPherson], but Amelia instead brought out her chamber pot as a sign of disrespect and put it in front of Maud saying that she should talk to the chamber pot, that she [Esquivel] wanted no more trouble." Meanwhile Stein came out of the store and began insulting MacPherson as well, at which point MacPherson's mother joined the fray, demanding to know why Stein was calling her daughter a whore. Esquivel spoke little English and MacPherson no Spanish: bystanders and partisans had translated for each throughout (although Esquivel's attorney, don Lucas Alvarado, wrote of MacPherson that "she knows how to swear well enough in Spanish, and besides which, Señor Alcalde, anyone who hears 'God Dam Son of a Bitch' [in English in original] knows he has been called *hijo de una perra*, even schoolchildren know that").[26]

Amelia Esquivel belonged to a category of women clearly overrepresented among insult plaintiffs: women who ran *cantinas* owned by their male partners.[27] The line between *cantinas* and brothels was blurry, as was the line between a materially advantageous consensual union and commercial sex. Such female entrepreneurs were sometimes former prostitutes themselves and were always suspected of remaining so. Their honor was precarious and perhaps hard won, and they defended it with a vengeance. Ramona Méndez sued Fidel Gómez for insults in 1907 because, when she refused to serve him twenty *céntimos* of cane liquor on credit, he yelled "very loudly that I couldn't cure a burn I have on my hand because I had been the concubine of *chinos* and was syphilitic." The offense occurred while she was supervising the *cantina* owned by Ramón Sárraga—with whom, she emphasized, "I have lived honorably and maritally for more than three years."[28] Arabella Levi sued Isaac Fraser for insults in 1899 (both were Jamaican). She had served Fraser a drink "in my *cantina* establishment. . . . He brought the glass to his nose and then said that those of us working there were 'dirty' and that I in addition was 'a daughter of a whore,' 'damned' 'a prostituted *mulata*.'" Fraser's lawyer countered by promising to prove that "Arabella Levi is an unmarried woman, and she has lived for more than four years with [*cantina* owner]

José Fontaine," who had abandoned his wife and children in Jamaica because of her. Levi quickly settled out of court.[29]

Accusations of prostitution undercut the rising social and economic status of female entrepreneurs in the profitable liquor-and-entertainment sector and prompted vigorous responses. It seems harder to explain the frequent insult suits filed by individual prostitutes themselves, in which they claimed that their honor and reputation had been damaged by people (more often than not other "public women") who had called them whores. In 1906 Martha Darling sued Bell Brown and Jessie Smith for publicly insulting her in a port brothel known as Noah's Ark. Brown had declared "that Martha Darling had stolen clothing in Jamaica and in the market on said island had stolen yams and hidden them up her ass." When Martha replied in kind, Jessie said to Bell, "I'm your cousin and no one can insult you, much less Martha Darling, whom I've known for a thieving whore since Jamaica."[30] The following year Darling sued a couple for insults, claiming that when she had attempted to collect some money they owed her, Samuel Brown said, "Here is your money damned bitch," and Wilhemina Brown had added, "You can't talk to me because, when you go to the Lines, you execute carnal acts in the banana fields like a female dog."[31] Two years later Darling was visiting the same Jessie Smith in a different brothel and got into a fight with one Mary Jane Brooks, calling her a "rotten-assed whore who was full of putrefaction." This time Brooks sued Darling, and Smith testified in her former adversary's defense.[32]

How can we understand the apparent contradiction of prostitutes filing legal suit to restore the honor they claim was injured when other prostitutes accused them of being prostitutes? The answer illuminates the dynamics of insult suits as a whole. As the cases presented above demonstrate, insult accusations frequently grew out of public slanging matches similar to those described by anthropologists from across the Caribbean. This was a street theater of personal honor, fueled by righteous indignation and animated by the aesthetics of verbal artistry. Insult accusations were brought by people who felt they had been bested in such public battles for prestige. It was a way to trump one's opponent, to continue the same argument by other means. By taking the case to the *alcalde*, the plaintiff proved that she had the money or connections necessary to carry a case through the criminal system—or bluffed that she was willing to do so. As discussed above, one could place an oral accusation for free or pay a few *colones* for a single lawyer's writ, but the costs for both parties grew heavier as the case moved on. To file for insults proved that one was willing and able to raise the ante. Indeed, bragging about one's ability to afford to carry cases through the courts became part of the standard repartee of public insults. An extreme case is that of Roberta Thompson, the "patio princess" above, who apparently kept former municipal judge Enrique Jiménez Dávila on retainer for just such occasions. According to one neighbor, she "makes a habit of insulting her neighbors, bragging that she has money, and has already paid a lawyer for the year to carry her defense."[33]

Furthermore, the act of mobilizing supporting witnesses flexed the muscle of the parties' social support. The process of "putting witnesses," calling on onlookers to testify on one's behalf in a court case, seems to have become a ritual part of public verbal duels. The mention of "putting witnesses" in the 1898 case between Hermione Edwards and Letitia Phillips is typical. Edwards and her friend Leonore Green had been sitting in the corridor outside one of the port's biggest stores, talking "about the bad state of business," when Phillips interjected, "What are you going on about, don't you remember the time [when things were so bad that] you stole yams from that *coolie* and hid them under your bed?" Edwards said to Green, "What do you think of that offense?" and Green replied "that she should not get angry, but just go to the authorities, and so she did, she put witnesses and didn't answer Phillips back."[34]

To sue for insults opened a new forum for conflict and occasioned a repetition of the original public performance, as participants and witnesses came forward to repeat lines from the first engagement. But the valences attached to statements were crucially different in this forum, in many ways reversed. Cleverly detailed insults counted against the speaker; sexual boasting lowered one's standing in the eyes of the law. Thus in 1901 the Barbadian carpenter Alexander Barnes sued "Mistress French" on behalf of his wife, saying she had "accused his wife of having illicit relations with one 'Barefoot,' a neighbor of French's." His wife, who identified herself pointedly as Cassandra Maxwell *de* Barnes, included a copy of their marriage certificate as part of her formal complaint. Her writ of accusation declared that, "since the act that was imputed to me consists of grave insults, as I am a married woman and this could bring about the dissolution of my tranquil home and bring down the wrath of my husband, I come before you, Señor Alcalde, to demand restitution for my injured honor." Yet the substance of the alleged insults takes on a rather different tinge in the testimony of Barnes's own witnesses. Apparently Barnes had gone to another woman's room in order to purchase some vegetables. Mistress French, who happened to be visiting there, had picked up a yam and boasted, "My man [*mi marido o concubino*] John Belfore can get any married woman he wants with that yam of his."[35] In a petition written by lawyer Lucas Alvarado, Mistress French claimed she never meant to offend. "I have a very high regard for Mrs. Barnes, if I said anything, which I don't remember, it certainly wasn't referring to the plaintiff, as the testimony so far makes clear." It seems likely, however, that at the time, the vulgarity of the jest was very much intended as an affront to *la señora de* Barnes and her pretentious propriety.

Strong parallels for such competitive wordplay can be found in the ethnographic literature on "slanging matches" in Providencia, "cussing out" in Barbuda, "tracings" in Jamaica, or "the dozens" among Afro-Americans in the United States.[36] But in Port Limón, this was not an exclusively West Indian phenomenon. The heterogeneous city blocks facilitated casual contact among migrants of every origin, and, when conflicts arose, standing was challenged and defended in much the same terms whether it was within or across group lines. Mistress French's comment exemplifies one of the few clear ethnic differences in the substance of insult accusations: West Indian women's creative references to male and female anatomy ("My husband slipped you a yam and a bit of coal"; "In Jamaica your ass dropped down and your mother had to tie it up with rags"; "Your ass is so worn out from whoring that you need to get a new one").[37] But in general, even the specific content of insults was shared. For instance, not only did Nicaraguans, Costa Ricans, and Jamaicans all use "whoring with *chinos*" as emblematic of the worst female degradation, but among all groups insults having to do with Chinese men were most commonly uttered by debtors confronted with their inability to pay.[38]

What are we to make of the similarity of insults among migrants of every origin in Limón and more generally the similar strategies through which they sought to affirm their public standing? Contemporary observers from both sides insisted that West Indians and Costa Ricans were culturally different and that that difference had much to do with appropriate gender roles, domestic arrangements, and sexual morality.[39] Such convictions had real impact on the public politics of race in Limón and on the future of the region and its populace in the wake of the banana boom. But that contemporary conviction of difference, and its political salience, has served to mask real similarities between the cultural heritage of the two regions, similarities accentuated by the self-selection of migrants to the zone. The uncertain prospects of the banana boom did not draw all potential workers evenly. It took a certain degree of "facetyness" simply to arrive, whether from Kingston, Colón, or Cartago.[40] In addition, the built environment of the city, particularly the *casas de vecindad*, favored certain social developments for migrants of both groups. Specifically it enhanced the importance of female social networks, as well as the informal economy associated with them, and thrust intimate relationships into the public domain.

The very notion of regional cultural difference is predicated on a concept of cultures as bounded and consensual systems that is itself increasingly questioned. As conflict and power differentials take center stage in ethnographic and historical analysis, culture begins to look less like a matter of shared norms and occasional deviance and more like an ongoing dispute over meaning: a "language of argument."[41] This notion illuminates the cases at hand. Think back, for instance, to the insult case between Maud MacPherson and Amelia Esquivel. The former spoke only English, the latter only Spanish, yet clearly the two shared a "language of argument." Underlying the exchange of insults and its aftermath were a series of common understandings—indeed the insults could not have been insulting if this were not the case. Esquivel had tried to assert class privilege, barring MacPherson from the corridor behind her store and calling her a dirty tramp. MacPherson replied that she was dirty but not from whoring: that she was dirty from caring for her husband and legitimate child. She challenged Esquivel's claim to superiority by implying that Esquivel's economic status came from her advantageous but immoral sexual liaison with the store's owner and insisted that her own domestic strategy—church-sanctioned marriage and hard work—entitled her to a higher standing.[42] The women relied on bystanders to translate the words of this exchange, but the content of the insults made perfect sense to each. Both assumed that access to public space was symbolic of social privilege; that sexual practice and public status were linked; that the ways women negotiated this link were grounds for moral judgment; and that resultant claims to decency and precedence could be made either on the streets or in the courts, either by brandishing a chamber pot or by buying a lawyer's time.

In one sense even the judicially sanctioned version of female honor was not so distant from those versions espoused by MacPherson and Esquivel or even by public woman Martha Darling and her friends. Honor for women meant sexual propriety. It was simply the definition of sexual propriety that varied. In the letter of the law, sexual propriety meant fidelity to a lawfully wedded husband; on the streets of Limón, it meant not sleeping with *chinos* for cash (or not "cohabiting" with three men at once in the kitchen or not having sex in the *bananales*). Both West Indian and Latin American popular cultures drew on European traditions, as developed in colonial caste societies, in which elite male privilege included sexual freedom and poor women's vulnerabilities included sexual vulnerability. Thus when the working-class women who participated in public verbal duels laid claim to personal status, they did so by asserting their sexual subjectivity. They claimed sexual virtue not as virgins but as willful actors who enforced their own moral discriminations.

At the beginning of this essay, I noted the apparent paradox that such cases were filed by the lowest of women and the highest of men. What these groups had in common was their use of public space for personal conflicts. In each case, the streets served as settings for individual conflicts within the group, while at the same time the very claim to a street presence was a collective act with political implications. This was true of Jamaican market women like Louise Gordon and Jane Parker, whose slanging battle was described above, and it was equally true of local elites like don Lucas Alvarado and don Eduardo Beeche, who came to blows on a nearby street. By "local elites" I refer not to those ranking United Fruit Company officials who would move on once their tour of duty was over but to the handful of wealthy and well-connected residents who had made fortunes in the region and sought to make more. Such men included Costa Ricans as well as immigrants from Colombia, Cuba, North America, and Europe, many of whom married into prestigious Costa Rican families. Their wealth and political activism went hand in hand, since the national and local governments controlled almost all potential sources of income not already in the possession of the United Fruit Company—in particular, land concessions and municipal contracts. Court documents and internal government correspondence record intraelite battles as boisterous, public, and vindictive as those of any *casa de vecindad*. Elites' economic and kin-based alliances were institutionalized in party structures, and because their rituals of public assertion involved *fiestas cívicas* and electoral tallies in addition to cussing out and ritual shaming, the political nature of their conflicts has been comparatively easier to see. But like the popular struggles embodied in insult cases, elite conflicts were expressed in the idiom of gendered honor; they were fought out in public with words and occasionally with blows; and they united social connections, economic leverage, and personal prestige.

Limón's elite rivalries were unusually personal and rowdy, even by the standards of the day. In the words of one exasperated governor, "If anywhere in this country there's a big ants' nest, it's here."[43] Conflict was endemic between the centrally appointed governors and the locally elected *regidores* (municipal chiefs), whose cycles of collusion and obstinacy with regard to the United Fruit Company rarely seemed to coincide. In general the local elites who controlled the municipality identified their own interests with those of the company, while the central government periodically adopted a more oppositional stance.[44] The dynamics of the regional political economy were expressed on the local scale in battles over office space and social clubs, in the securing of a prime secretarial position for the protégé who "is like a son to me," in the cultivation of networks of clients whose legal petitions (appealing, say, eviction orders) could make life hell for a rival businessman.[45]

Thus in 1906 Governor Ricardo Mora complained to his superiors in San José regarding his difficulties with the *regidores municipales*. Not only had they approved a street construction swindle that was going to cost the government thirty-five thousand *colones* for the extension of a single avenue (not coincidentally, the avenue that led to the newly completed home of *regidor* don Carlos Saborío), but they had made common cause with the official port doctor and insulted Mora loudly within his hearing in the streets. The origin of the most recent incident was the governor's opposition to the *regidores'* attempt to impeach municipal treasurer Eduardo Beeche (he of the 1902 caning) for embezzlement. "So far things have gone no further, but it's clear that if they continue in this manner and repeat the affronts that they have been committing against my authority and my person, I will have to demand my respect as an authority and suffer personally the consequences that would follow, because if it comes to that I will not be lacking that which it is necessary I not lack."[46] Mora threatened to take the law into his own hands—which, he implied, he would certainly have the balls to do—in order to "make himself respected as an authority." Thus male honor was figured as a necessary component of legal authority even as the vindication of that honor was predicated on disregard for the rule of law.

The men involved in these quarrels were no second-tier provincial burghers. Their families were at the core of Costa Rica's commercial and agricultural elite.[47] Yet just as with other port residents, elite power struggles depended on public demonstration of individual daring and social support. And just as boardinghouse dwellers pulled elite actors into their interpersonal conflicts, as they denounced neighbors before the *alcalde* or hired lawyers to press their claims, so too elite conflicts had need of working-class actors. Recall the case of Chinese storekeeper Juan José León, who sued two Jamaican teens for calling him a son of a Chinese whore. Their quarrel began when the girls came into the store wearing the red ribbons and badges of the Partido Civilista, while León had decorated his store with blue banners in support of the Partido Republicano. León was a naturalized Costa Rican citizen and thus eligible to vote, but the teens were foreign women and therefore doubly disenfranchised. Clearly that did not prevent them from taking part in the public display and personal affronts that were an embedded part of party politics.[48]

Of course such parallels and ties should not blind us to the fact that the resources elites fought over—that is, access to the state and its spoils—were immensely more valuable than those up for grabs in any boardinghouse conflict. This is symbolized by the contrast between William William's fifteen-cent nails, or Sarah Simon's market basket full of coffee and eggs, and the four to eight thousand *colones* that Miguel Xirinach had allegedly planned to skim off the hospital construction contract (an accusation that may well have been accurate, if Governor Mora's contention regarding street construction is anything to go by).

Almost never did working-class men sue each other. Economics cannot be the explanation: poor and workingwomen sued each other frequently and enthusiastically; their male counterparts did not. Of course, comparatively more women and elites lived in the port, and thus had easier access to judicial institutions, than did the bulk of workingmen, who resided on the plantations and in the rainforest camps spread out from the rail lines to the north and south. But in absolute numbers workingmen predominated even in the port of Limón. Many men chose to live in the city in between money-earning stints of plantation labor; others came through on weekends or paydays; still others worked in the port itself as dockhands, construction workers, or day laborers. Such men do indeed show up in judicial records, not in insult suits but in cases of assault, brawls, and homicide. Not infrequently the conflicts and insults that led to such outcomes were identical to those that led other men, and many women, to file insult accusations. But when the conflict was between two young, able-bodied, working-class men, they didn't take it to the judge: they took it outside.

The "culture of male bonding and rivalry that blends play, risk, and a ratification of masculine courage amidst life's adversities" has played a central role in accounts of both the honor/shame system in Latin America and cultural resistance in the British Caribbean.[49] While scholars of Latin America have usually taken this as evidence of the downward spread of elite Iberian values, whose effect was to increase the legitimacy of the social hierarchy, scholars of the Caribbean have seen in confrontational working-class masculinity a reaction against the elite imposition of British respectability and the last, best defense against internalized colonial dependency.[50] The similarities between West Indian and Latin American male street culture in Limón should make us question these divergent accounts of causality and impact. Above I suggested that the overlap among women's claims to sexual honor in Limón reflected commonalities in notions of gender and kinship created under conditions of race-based colonial domination. Similarly, competitive claims to honor among men in the port both echoed traditions of dominance and sometimes subverted them in the process.[51]

Thus there were multiple models for how to claim precedence in public; for when to defend honor with words, when with fists, when with a legal writ. Patterns in the use of different models varied by gender and class, but individuals were not wholly constrained by those patterns. Rather than speak of class-specific, culturally specific, or gender-specific "norms," one might think of these models as familiar scripts available for performance. The meaning of the scripts varied with the context in which they were performed, and neither actors nor audience members had the ultimate power to affix meaning. This formulation undercuts interpretations of respectability as a matter of ideological dependency on bourgeois or colonial cultural forms. When Maud MacPherson bragged to Amelia Esquivel that she was legally married and dirty from caring for her husband and legitimate child—in contrast to Esquivel, who was dirty by virtue of loose living—she was asserting her personal virtue through one of the multiple codes available to working-class women. She was no more a dupe of bourgeois femininity than Eduardo Beeche was exposing his internalization of working-class masculinity when he smacked Lucas Alvarado with his cane. Workingwomen in Port Limón remade honor in their own image, or at least on terms to which they could reasonably aspire; simultaneously, they used the legal apparatus, built to safeguard other people's honor, to stake their own claims to status and space.

Notes

This chapter is an abridged and modified version of Lara Putnam, *The Company They Kept: Migrants and the Politics of Gender in Caribbean Costa Rica, 1870–1960* (Chapel Hill: University of North Carolina Press, 2002), chap. 5.

1 Aviva Chomsky, *West Indian Workers and the United Fruit Company in Costa Rica, 1870–1940* (Baton Rouge: Louisiana State University Press, 1996), chaps. 2–3; Carmen Murillo Chaverri, *Identidades de hierro y humo: La construcción del Ferrocarril al Atlántico, 1870–1890* (San José, Costa Rica: Porvenir, 1995); Philippe Bourgois, *Ethnicity at Work: Divided Labor on a Central American Banana Plantation* (Baltimore: Johns Hopkins University Press, 1989), chap. 2.

2 Gabriel García Márquez, *Leaf Storm and Other Stories*, trans. Gregory Rabassa (New York: Harper and Row, 1972), 2.

3 Elizabeth M. Thomas-Hope, "The Establishment of a Migration Tradition: British West Indian Movements to the Hispanic Caribbean in the Century after Emancipation," *International Migration* 24 (1986): 559–571; Elizabeth Petras, *Jamaican Labor Migration: White Capital and Black Labor, 1850–1930* (Boulder, CO: Westview, 1988).

4 Costa Rica, Ministerio de Gobernación y Policía, *Memoria* (1912): 570.

5 Archivo Nacional de Costa Rica (henceforth ANCR), Serie Jurídica, Limón Alcaldía Unica (henceforth LAU) 443 (1899). All translations are mine unless otherwise noted, and all parties' names have been changed except for those of public officials or well-known figures, such as Lucas Alvarado and Eduardo Beeche below.

6 ANCR, Serie Policía 449, telegram of June 21, 1902.

7 This figure is calculated from the yearly totals provided in the official *Anuarios estadísticos* from 1907, the first year of their publication, through 1913, the end of the first boom of banana exports, as will be discussed in more detail below. More than two hundred insults cases from Limón are preserved in the Costa Rican National Archives' judicial section, whose holdings cover roughly the period 1880 to 1910. This is slightly more than the number of preserved cases of *lesiones*, or assault, and far more than the number of preserved homicide inquiries. Thus, in Limón insults were the most common of the various "crimes against persons" established by the 1880 Penal Code.

8 *Código penal de la República de Costa Rica* (San José, Costa Rica: Imprenta Nacional, n.d. [1880]), title 8, chap. 5, art. 437.

9 Lila Abu-Lughod, *Veiled Sentiments: Honor and Poetry in a Bedouin Society* (Berkeley: University of California Press, 1986), 90, citing Pierre Bourdieu on the Kabyle bedouins.

10 Cf. George Chauncey Jr., "The Locus of Reproduction: Women's Labour in the Zambian Copperbelt, 1927–1953," *Journal of South African Studies* 7.2 (1981): 135–164.

11 Jane Schneider, "Of Vigilance and Virgins: Honor, Shame, and Access to Resources in Mediterranean Societies," *Ethnology* 10.1 (1971): 1–24.

12 In part this reflects the gendered division of labor, which concentrated men on the plantations and women in the port and militated against the establishment of rigid or

172   Lara Putnam

isolated domestic units. Even if the men who came to Limón had wished to be patriarchs, they had no patriarchal households over which to rule. Only a few cases suggest that a male partner was urging the female plaintiff to sue: ANCR, LAU 535 (1901), LAU 467 (1900), LAU 470 (1901).

13 ANCR, LAU 3411 (1907).

14 ANCR, Serie Jurídica, Limón Juzgado Civil y del Crimen (henceforth LJCYC) 730 (1903). "Que era una 'puta' que acostumbraba recibir dinero de un hombre para luego vivir con él; y que, cuando ese hombre va a su casa, se encierra con él, y con tres mas y duran cohabitando hasta las doce de la noche."

15 Although the words "hijo de puta" or "son of a whore" were frequently cited in insult suits, it seems clear that the phrase was a formulaic humiliation whose link to one's actual mother's actual sex life was beside the point.

16 ANCR, LAU 510 (1902).

17 ANCR, LAU 3406 (1906).

18 ANCR, LAU 399 (1898); LAU 472 (1899). In each of these instances the insult accusations followed months of criminal and civil accusations for theft.

19 ANCR, LAU 508 (1902).

20 See ANCR, LAU 466 (1900), LAU 476 (1900), LAU 544 (1901).

21 This included plaintiffs and defendants alike. Legal representation ranged from the purchase of a single-page writ of complaint, to specifying a lawyer's office for the receipt of subsequent notifications (and presumably getting legal advice on the decisions notified), to officially registering an *apoderado* to act on one's behalf.

22 ANCR, LAU 3441 (1909). For more on the 1909 elections in Limón, see n. 44, below.

23 Of seventy-four cases subjected to detailed review, forty were not pursued by the parties after the first complaint was made or the first round of witnesses testified; twelve were ended by the parties through an extrajudicial accord. For the majority of those cases that settled out of court there is no record of a monetary accord. The remaining one-third of them settled for costs so far: nine *colones* in one case, thirty-one to seventy-seven *colones* in the others. Twelve cases were carried through to the point of *enjuiciamento* and then dismissed by the judge for lack of evidence or because the insults had been "reciprocal and thus compensated." Only ten cases actually reached judgment, and in at least five of these, the accused was absolved. A day laborer in these years earned between one and a half and four *colones* per day, and rooms in boardinghouses rented for around ten *colones* per month.

24 ANCR, LAU 3487 (1908).

25 ANCR, LAU 3494 (1908).

26 ANCR, LAU 460 (1900); LAU 447 (1900). Despite Don Lucas's efforts to minimize the issue, discrepancies over which language MacPherson had issued the insults in were cited by the Sala de Casación as grounds for overturning the lower court, which had ordered MacPherson to pay 101 *colones* in damages, plus costs.

27 ANCR, LAU 522 (1901), LAU 409 (1898), LAU 426 (1899), LAU 460 (1900), LAU 447 (1900), LAU 3417 (1907). In our sample, such cases make up the majority of suits with Hispanic female plaintiffs.

28 ANCR, LAU 3417 (1907).

29 ANCR, LAU 426 (1899). According to the *Código penal*, evidence that the content of insults was true could only be used as a defense if the plaintiff "habitually and pub-

licly" engaged in the behavior of which he or she had been accused (fornication, fraud, etc.). Even if the objectionable insults were proven to be both accurate and common knowledge, the effect was not to exonerate the defendant but to decrease the fine by two-thirds. In the above case, the threat of publicity was surely more significant than the legal impact of the promised evidence.

30 ANCR, LAU 3398 (1906).

31 ANCR, LAU 3485 (1907).

32 ANCR, LAU 3495 (1908).

33 ANCR, LAU 3487 (1908).

34 ANCR, LAU 408 (1898).

35 ANCR, LAU 537 (1901); LAU 539 (1901). This case was one of the few in which a husband took an active role in defending his wife's honor against sexual insult. The suit Barnes filed was annulled because he could not legally sue on his wife's behalf, and she appeared at the *alcalde*'s office to file suit herself the following day.

36 The most comprehensive cross-cultural account of this is Roger D. Abrahams, *The Man-of-Words in the West Indies: Performance and the Emergence of Creole Culture* (Baltimore: Johns Hopkins University Press, 1983). See also Richard D. E. Burton, *Afro-Creole: Power, Opposition, and Play in the Caribbean* (Ithaca, NY: Cornell University Press, 1997), chap. 4.

37 ANCR, Limón Juzgado del Crimen [LJCrimen] 297 (1911); LAU 3471 (1908); LAU 3472 (1907).

38 ANCR, LAU 3494 (1908), LAU 422 (1899), LAU 522 (1901), LAU 3417 (1907), LAU 422 (1899), LAU 3441 (1909), LAU 3467 (1908), LAU 3494 (1908). I suspect this reflects Chinese men's role in small-scale retail across the country. For many working people the *pulpería del chino* was a site of unending petty debt.

39 See Lara Elizabeth Putnam, "Ideología racial, práctica social y Estado liberal en Costa Rica," *Revista de historia* (San José, Costa Rica) 39 (1999): 139–186.

40 The *Dictionary of Caribbean English Usage*, ed. Richard Allsopp (Oxford: Oxford University Press, 1996), defines *facety* as "bold and bare-faced; brazen; impudent."

41 David Warren Sabean, *Power in the Blood: Popular Culture and Village Discourse in Early Modern Germany* (London: Cambridge University Press, 1984); cf. Steve J. Stern, *Secret History of Gender: Women, Men, and Power in Late Colonial Mexico* (Chapel Hill: University of North Carolina Press, 1995), 386–387, n. 25. Stern further develops this concept in his own analysis of gender conflict in colonial Mexico.

42 MacPherson's lawyer in fact tried to make cultural difference the basis of his defense. He called on four West Indian men (one originally from Belize, two from Barbados, one from Jamaica—all long-time residents of Limón) to testify that "the word 'bitch' or 'puta' is very common among Jamaicans and among them, it is a grave offense when directed at a married woman, but not when it refers to a woman who, not being married, lives or has lived maritally with some man." Three out of four of his handpicked witnesses disagreed with this statement. ANCR, LAU 460 (1900).

43 ANCR, Policía 1567, letter of March 11, 1907.

44 For example, in the 1909 presidential election campaign Minor Keith gave financial and other support to Rafael Iglesias, candidate of the Partido Civil, because, as a congressman several years earlier, Partido Republicano candidate Ricardo Jiménez had denounced the most recent government contract with the United Fruit Company.

Some of the nature of the "other support" Keith provided is indicated by the election results for that year. While Jiménez won 71 percent of the popular vote nationally, he won only 24 percent of the vote in Limón. Limón, the province with the smallest number of electors apportioned (33 all together, as opposed to 288 for the province of San José), accounted for over a third of the *civilistas'* 81 electoral votes nationwide. See Orlando Salazar Mora, *El apogeo de la República Liberal en Costa Rica (1870–1914)* (San José: Editorial de la Universidad de Costa Rica, 1990), 155 and 230–231. On the role of fraud in Costa Rican electoral processes, see Mario Samper, "Fuerzas sociopolíticas y procesos electorales en Costa Rica, 1921–1936," in special issue of *Revista de historia* (San José, Costa Rica) (1988), 157–222; Iván Molina and Fabrice Lehoucq, *Urnas de lo inesperado: Fraude electoral y lucha política en Costa Rica (1901–1948)* (San José: Editorial de la Universidad de Costa Rica, 1999).

45 ANCR Policía 1550, letter of March 1, 1905; Policía 1120, letter of July 2, 1908; Policía 06196 (1911); Gobernación 3419, letter of Nov. 15, 1912; Policía 1567, letter of March 11, 1907.

46 ANCR Serie Gobernación 2084, letter of Jan. 31, 1906. See also ANCR, LJCYC 729 (1903); Gobernación 3419, letters of March 28, 1912, and Nov. 15, 1912; Policía 1565, letter of Sept. 12, 1907.

47 For instance Saborío, Beeche, and Alvarado would all soon build residences in Barrio Amón, a chic new neighborhood in San José that became home to the nation's wealthiest families. See Florencia Quesada Avendaño, "Los del Barrio Amón: Marco habitacional, familiar y arquitectónico del primer barrio residencial de la burguesía josefina (1900–1930)," *Mesoamérica* 31 (1989): 215–241. (I am grateful to Florencia Quesada for providing me with additional biographical data on these families.)

48 ANCR, LAU 3441 (1909).

49 Quote is from Stern, *Secret History*, 320.

50 It is worth noting that Peter J. Wilson's earliest work on male "reputation" claimed this as a Caribbean-wide phenomenon, not merely an Anglo-Caribbean one, and made explicit reference to research on Puerto Rico that would be influential in shaping scholarly approaches to Latin American "machismo." See Wilson, "Reputation and Respectability: A Suggestion for Caribbean Historians," *Man* [n.s.] 4 (1969): 70–84, esp. 73, 75, 82–83.

51 Cf. Lyman L. Johnson, "Dangerous Words, Provocative Gestures, and Violent Acts," in *The Faces of Honor: Sex, Shame, and Violence in Colonial Latin America*, ed. Lyman L. Johnson and Sonya Lipsett-Rivera (Albuquerque: University of New Mexico Press, 1998), 127–51, esp. 129; Burton, *Afro-Creole*, 168.

Slandering citizens: insults, class, and social
legitimacy in Rio de Janeiro's criminal courts
Brodwyn Fischer

On March 11, 1931, a scandalous article appeared in *A batalha*, a polemical Rio de Janeiro daily. Prominently displayed between a fiery denunciation of incompetent health officials and a darkly suggestive account of a
boy's disappearance, the blandly titled story seemed innocuous enough.
Its contents, however—graphic allegations of sexual harassment carried
out by a prominent public servant—left little doubt that it could hold its
own in such sensational company:

> Senhora Doralícia Costa, a married woman with a sick husband,
> depends mainly on her seventeen-year-old daughter, Srta. Francisca
> da Costa, who serves as her strong arm and helps to maintain seven
> younger siblings.
> Srta. Francisca Costa used to be employed as a typist in the office
> of the Superintendent of Public Sanitation, and her boss, an old man
> of about seventy named Senhor Joaquim Virgílio Teixeira Leite . . .
> spent all of his time joking with the young ladies who assisted him,
> directing toward them certain indecorous jokes and carrying out in-
> decorous acts, purposely sitting down next to them so that he could
> rub his legs against theirs.
> Srta. Francisca Costa earned 300 *mil-reis* a month, and the old man
> told her that if she wanted to earn 550, she would have only to sub-
> mit herself to his desires. For this reason, on October 22 of last year,
> the young lady—unable to put up with the old man . . . any longer—
> abandoned her place of work.
> Now, with the triumph of the new republic, her mother took
> her complaint to the superintendent of Public Sanitation and to

the interim mayor . . . but neither of them paid the least bit of attention to this zealous mother, who went to them to claim Justice and also some measure that would guarantee the decorum of public employees. . . .

We are thus calling for the attention of some competent authority who . . . is willing to take the steps that this case merits![1]

By Doralícia's account—or at least her lawyer's—she, "a poor mother," publicized her story as a last resort. Abandoned even by agents of Getúlio Vargas's "revolutionary" new republic, Doralícia had taken matters into her own hands in a desperate attempt to "guard the honor and good name of her young daughter, who was constantly threatened by the exaggerated despotism and indecorous invitations" of Joaquim Leite.

Her appeal did not, however, render "justice" as Doralícia might have defined it. Scarcely a week after the story appeared, Joaquim retaliated, charging in a criminal case that Doralícia and her daughter had illegally threatened *his* honor with the public dissemination of their tale. Although the presiding judge quickly threw the case out on technicalities, Joaquim immediately—and possibly illegally—resubmitted his complaint. This time, the accusation stuck. Doralícia and her daughter found themselves at the center of a legal maelstrom from which neither would escape unscathed and that would ultimately turn on issues with ramifications far beyond the relatively narrow confines of their lives or Joaquim's.

Doralícia's case, like numerous Brazilian slander trials of the late 1920s and early 1930s, forced witnesses, lawyers, and judges to define what "honor" was, which exterior characteristics signified it, who was capable of possessing, recognizing, or assaulting it, and what degree of responsibility the judicial system—and the state—would take for defending it. In certain respects, these trials resembled the legal and extralegal rituals that had long negotiated honor around the globe. Trial participants, whatever their social class, generally accepted the same highly gendered notions of honor and insult that reigned in the Mediterranean world; for women, "honor" connoted sexual purity and monogamy, while for men it entailed honesty in public life, an ability to control women and dependents, and a willingness actively to defend themselves and their families against attacks or insults.[2] These trials also suggested that the concept of honor transcended boundaries of class and race; participants spanned the socioeconomic spectrum of Carioca (Rio) society (see figs. 1–3).[3]

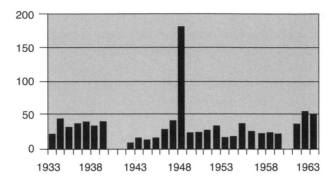

1 Number of Honor Crimes Tried in Rio de Janeiro's Criminal Courts, 1933–1963. Source: *Crimes e contravenções, 1942–1963*; *Anuário estatístico do D.F., 1933-1934*. Years with no cases listed indicate gaps in the data sequence.

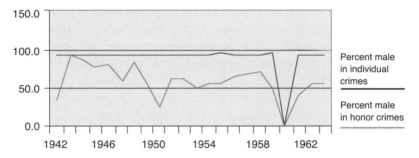

2 Masculinity Index of Honor Crimes, 1942–1963. Source: *Crimes e contravenções, 1942–1963*. Years with no cases listed indicate gaps in the data sequence.

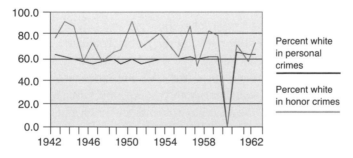

3 Race Index of Honor Crimes, 1942–1963. Source: *Crimes e contravenções, 1942–1963*. Years with no cases listed indicate gaps in the data sequence.

The Carioca slander trials also revealed the peculiarities of their historical moment. They suggested that Carioca society—despite its general acceptance of specific moral and cultural conceptions of male and female honor—was deeply divided on the question of what social attributes signified such honor and what role social status played in its conceptualization. Participants here confronted the contradictions of a highly stratified society that was nonetheless relatively free of legally recognized divisions between individuals—divisions of race, class, and breeding that, in other places and earlier times, had allowed both courts and societies to formulate status-based definitions of the particular gradations and shades of honor that the state and local communities were willing to protect.[4] In the absence of these formal divisions, Carioca trial participants had to construct their own notions of what made any individual—the accused, the accuser, the witnesses, even the lawyers and judges—honorable in the eyes of the law; every actor, in short, constructed her or his own notion of honorable citizenship.

Such intricate dynamics would merit historical interest regardless of their context. But these Carioca slander trials occurred just as Getúlio Vargas ascended to the presidency in 1930, a watershed not only in Brazil's social and political history but also—as surprisingly few historians have noted—in the country's legal history. Some of the fiercest debates of the Vargas era concerned precisely the question of how certain forms of personal honor and virtue—the ability to hold a steady job, maintain a marriage, establish a place of residence, and, above all, recognize the state's authority to define and legitimize personal worthiness—would translate into full social, political, and economic rights. In the end, one of Vargas's most important legacies was the widespread dissemination of legal documents, many previously unknown, that served as formal signifiers of worthy citizenship. Work cards, marriage and birth certificates, formal property titles, formal rental contracts, detailed police rap sheets, and national identity cards—all of these papers first gained critical importance for Brazil's urban population during the Vargas era. They established, in effect if not always in intent, a new legal stratification based on access to documents and bureaucratic agility that closely mirrored economic, racial, and social divisions already apparent in Brazilian society at large.[5]

Given this context, the slander trials of the late 1920s and early 1930s are particularly suggestive. Despite their scant number—my sample of some eight hundred criminal cases from 1927 to 1964 unearthed only seventeen insult accusations, most from 1927 to 1933—these cases are micro-cosms of the others, encapsulating the intricate and conflicting symbolizations of honor and worthiness that shaped the lives of Cariocas of every social stripe at the beginning of the Vargas era. They suggest that many Cariocas ratified the associations Vargas would make, both in rhetoric and in law, between honor and residence, work, marital status, and (more obliquely) race. But these links were still far from hegemonic, even within social classes. In demonstrating the lively conflict that surrounded these symbolic linkages, the slander trials reveal the social meaning of Vargas-era decisions to write them into law. The trials suggest who would be favored by these legal transformations and who would be prejudiced; which sorts of people would gain new rights to honorable citizenship under Vargas and which groups would lose whatever tenuous claims they previously had. At the same time, they capture the clashes and commonalities between popular perceptions of honor and those of the lawyers and jurists whose job it was to define and defend it—and whose opinions would, ultimately, most directly influence Vargas-era legal transformations. This is the larger significance of the following tales.

The Meanings of Honor in Brazilian Law and Jurisprudence

In order to understand the seriousness with which Brazilian judges approached attacks on individual honor in the 1930s, a brief history is useful. In 1905, Carioca appeals judge Virgílio de Sá Pereira confronted an interesting dilemma. A lower court judge had condemned Mário Madureira Ramos for committing "physical offenses" against Bonifácio Garcia. Bonifácio had provoked the crime by bumping into Mário on a busy downtown street. Mário complained, and Bonifácio, in the judge's words,

> let out a stream of clamorous and atrocious insults and, satisfied, . . . went on walking, leaving his victim in the uncomfortable position of being the center of public curiosity, and perhaps even ridicule. Nevertheless, after walking a few steps, Bonifácio repeated his insults, calling them out so that everyone could hear, an action that was only stopped by the victim, who stepped forward and hit him a couple of times with his cane, whereupon the two men immediately came to blows.[6]

The insults included the common but highly offensive terms *safado* (degenerate) and *caftén* (pimp). Bonifácio then accused Mário of physical assault, for which he was arrested and convicted. In Sá Pereira's view, the validity of the condemnation hinged on two critical questions: "Did the defendant act in defense of his honor? And does the defense of honor legally qualify as legitimate self-defense?"[7]

In his decision, the judge responded positively to both questions, articulating a definition of honor and an affirmation of its importance that lay at the heart of Brazilian judicial thought well into the twentieth century. Quoting the Italian jurist Pietro Cogliolo, Sá Pereira wrote: "With the word honor, we refer to the esteem and good name that go along with good and honest conduct . . . the most sacred and precious patrimony of any man. No right is thus more essential to human beings than the right to honor. This right is one of the founding principles of social life; an individual whose honor is attacked is offended in every aspect of his personal activity."[8]

According to the 1890 Brazilian Penal Code, Sá Pereira reasoned, the right of self-defense "included the defense of all rights that might be attacked."[9] And Brazilian jurists—among them the renowned João Vieira —had consistently defined these rights as including honor and modesty, along with life, health, and liberty. Sá Pereira thus concluded that Mário was fully within his rights to defend his honor and that, given the situation, only physical action would have preserved it: "He could have fled, but no man with even a minimum of self-respect could have judged such an action as anything but cowardly and shameful. . . . it is not reasonable to expect a man who has been stopped in the middle of a public street and faced with loud and atrocious slanders, which cause a public scandal, to slink away ignobly to the nearest police station and call for help."[10] Given this, Sá Pereira reversed Mário's conviction.

In defining honor as one of a human being's dearest rights, Sá Pereira represented the mainstream of Brazilian juridical thought. The Penal Code of 1890 was a far cry from the colonial Philippine Code, a document permeated by rigidly hierarchical, status-based conceptions of public honor and draconian punishments for its infringement. Yet it still enshrined a broadly defined concept of honor as a fundamental individual right and attribute.[11] According to the code, honor's protection constituted legitimate self-defense, attenuating even serious charges such as homicide. Beyond this, the code proclaimed public responsibility to defend at least two forms of honor. First, Title 8 criminalized various forms of sexual transgression, including the rape of "honest" women, as well as the corruption, seduction, or deflowering of virgin girls. The "honor" envisioned in these clauses was essentially feminine, a combination of modesty, sexual purity, and good repute.[12] Damage to this "honor" reflected not only upon the woman or girl in question, but also upon her family and society at large.[13] Female honor, thus conceived, was as much an emblem of civilization as an individual possession.[14]

Other offenses, while still ultimately conceived of as socially dangerous, were understood as violations of an individual right to honor, which the courts would protect in much the same way as they did the individual rights to property or physical integrity. The provisions of Title 11 ("Crimes against Honor and Good Reputation") shielded individuals from printed or spoken words, gestures, or acts that would harm either their good name and reputation ("external" or "objective" honor) or their internal sense of self-worth and dignity ("internal" or "subjective" honor).[15] The offenses detailed fell into two categories. First, article 315 defined *calúnia*, "the false imputation, made to an individual, of an act that the law defines as a crime." A *calúnia* had to be made in bad faith, with full knowledge of its falsity, conditions assumed unless the offender could prove otherwise. Unlike other verbal honor offenses, *calúnia* could not be excused when it occurred as a response to equally offensive words or actions. Written *calúnias* and those pronounced against public employees were most harshly punished, with fines and prison terms of up to two years.

Second, article 317 defined *injúria* (slander) as "the imputation of vices or defects, defined specifically or generally, that might expose a person to public hatred or contempt," "the imputation of facts that are offensive to an individual's reputation, decorum, and honor," or "a word, gestures, or signal considered offensive by the general public." Barring special circumstances, even true or commonly accepted *injúrias* were considered criminal.[16] The courts could excuse reciprocal *injúrias* or those spoken in good faith. The punishments were less severe than those for *calúnia*, with one- to nine-month prison terms, depending on whether the *injúria* was verbal or written, carried out in public or private, and committed against a public employee or a private individual. Both *injúria* and *calúnia* constituted "private" crimes—that is, they were judged in public courts by public judges but would only be prosecuted at the initiative of the victim, who could always desist from the case and whose private lawyer would effectively take on the role of prosecutor.[17]

In the face of an actual honor crime prosecution, the clarity of definition and purpose articulated in both the law and the juridical discourse
of its interpreters dissipated quickly. This was true partially because of
the importance of another sort of "honor" in procedural law: witnesses
were themselves judged even as their testimony contributed to the judgment of others. In Galdino Siqueira's words, "(witnesses') credibility depended both on their knowledge and on their moral conscience," and
they were considered "suspect" or "defective" if they lacked a "good
reputation," if they were suspected of partiality to one of the parties,
or if they were subordinates of the accused or the accuser.[18] For most
honor crimes, material proof was scarce, and judgments concerning the
moral quality of witnesses only added to the ambiguity of decisions already hinging on subjective judgments about the honor and reliability of
the accused and the accuser.[19] In the eyes of almost every actor in these
small dramas, only honorable victims had honor to lose; only dishonorable perpetrators were capable of the most heinous verbal offenses; and
only honorable witnesses had the moral authority to judge whether an
offense against honor had occurred or not. Inevitably, such cases thus unmasked the conflictual conceptions of honor and its symbols that underlay Carioca society. As the five brief tales that follow demonstrate, the
resolutions of such cases in the late 1920s and early 1930s revealed little
consensus among lawyers and jurists as to which of these conceptions
Brazilian law would ultimately protect.

Paper Honor in Tatters: The Baroness of Icarahy

Few argued for the importance of personal identity in determining an
individual's juridical right to honor more categorically than those who
saw social class as honor's defining feature. And, among these, few participants in Carioca criminal trials defined the symbols of class as rigidly
as Eugénie Juliette Carneiro Leão de Barros de Icarahy—the French-
born, widowed (and self-styled) "baroness of Icarahy."[20] In February
1930, Eugénie's lawyer, valiantly touting her inherited, decrepit noble
title, filed an *injúria* complaint with Rio de Janeiro's third criminal *pretoria* (lower court).[21] The complaint accused a lawyer, José Santos Camara
Lima, of intentionally slandering Eugénie by declaring—on the steps of
a police station, no less—that she had stolen furniture and habitually
"maintained" a young man who lived in her company; in later testimony,
he was referred to as a *caftén*. According to the lawyer, these accusations,

inherently "highly slanderous," were especially vicious because they had been spoken in a highly public setting, and Eugénie was "a person of fortune and social position, with business transactions in the neighborhood of the police station."

The complaint was only slightly unusual. Honor crimes were among the few whose clientele spanned the class spectrum, and a larger than average proportion of plaintiffs and defendants in such cases were women or foreign natives.[22] Like most *injúria* cases, the complaint was apparently the culmination of a long-simmering conflict. Eugénie and José had met through her deceased husband four years before, later becoming friends and business associates. After the baron's death, the association had begun to unravel when a rancorous dispute arose between José and a young Belgian, whom Eugénie referred to as her nephew and José claimed was her lover (and a thief to boot!). A few months before the alleged *injúria*, the two men had already come to blows, and Eugénie had tried, with little success, to prosecute José for physical assault. Finally, in what Eugénie characterized as a desperate attempt to escape José's persecution, she had abandoned Rio entirely for the summer resort of Petrópolis. When Eugénie's two moving men returned to Rio, José had them hauled into the local police station for questioning, demanding to know where Eugénie was and insisting that the authorities detain the men for transporting stolen goods. The moving men refused to disclose anything, at which point José used his influence to have them sent on to the reputedly fearsome Fourth Delegacia Auxiliar for further questioning. En route, Eugénie claimed, José spoke the injurious words.

The *injúria* complaint may have been a genuine response to wounded honor. More probably, it was Eugénie's latest attempt to settle an old vendetta, a tit-for-tat response to José's legal harassment. In either case, it came to naught. After a trial fraught with legal maneuvers and mutual character assassinations, Judge Leonardo Smith e Lima found José not guilty. But the verdict, in this case, mattered less than the arguments put forth. According to Eugénie's lawyer, José's crime was defined not so much by the words he had spoken as by whom they referred to and who had heard them. In his final statement, after noting that accusations of thievery and insinuations about being the protectress of a pimp would be at least mildly offensive to anyone, the lawyer came to the crux of his argument:

> It is important to note that high society, of which the victim is a part, does not tolerate or pardon people who act in these ways; this

is obviously not true of the lower social classes where such acts are forgivable. It is also important to note that the accused, when he proffered the insults, did so in front of people from inferior social classes, who have no notion of secrecy or decorum, and who . . . might easily spread these insults as rumors. . . . Evidently, the defendant . . . sought to stain and denigrate the reputation of the victim, seeking to expose her to public scorn, imputing to her facts that were offensive to her station, her honor, and her decorum, attempting to vilify her by comparing her to a prostitute, a thief, and a concubine, all in an obvious attempt to place her in an unsustainable and unbearable position in the society she frequented.

The severity of an honor offense, in this conception, depended on the victim's social status, defined by wealth, lineage, and title. Eugénie's possession of all three entitled her to a higher degree of honor than those of lower social station; words that, to them, may have seemed common and forgivable were, when spoken against her, criminally offensive.

José did not deny outright this link between social status and enhanced rights to honor. His arguments focused rather on the nature of social standing itself. In describing the conflict's history, he asserted not only that Eugénie and her "nephew" were illicit lovers but also that a French court had convicted the pair of an unnamed crime. He further claimed that both had once vulgarly insulted him at his home, in front of his wife and children, forcing him to defend his family's honor with blows. Finally, he impugned the social origins of Eugénie's nephew and of her witnesses. Implicit in all of these arguments was a comparison of Eugénie —a woman who, despite her formal claims to social status, had no friends or family willing to support her—and José, an established lawyer, who presented himself as a family man, zealous of his honor, who obviously had useful connections with well-placed individuals within the Carioca justice system. In ruling against Eugénie, the judge privileged behavior and personal connections over the tattered paper title of a woman with few useful friends and questionable social habits.

"Pelo Telefone": Slander and Dirty Talk among Rio's Respectable Poor

In October 1927, Maria José Cherre—an Italian-born widow who lived with her common-law husband in a poor but respectable downtown rooming house—filed a very different sort of complaint with Judge Antônio Bernardino dos Santos Netto.[23] In it, she alleged that her neighbors, the Portuguese couple Ascendino and Innocência Gonçalves, had spread a terrible rumor. On August 23, in the midst of dinner in the rooming house dining room, they had announced that Maria José was "a woman of bad behavior" and that she worked "accepting sexual telephone calls for a brothel." In Maria José's view, this was obviously an attempt to "expose her to public disdain" and therefore a criminal *injúria*. She claimed no special rights and made no reference to her own social status; her complaint was that of an ordinary citizen who sought protection from the courts because her honor—that of a plain, decent woman—had been illegally trespassed.

The testimony of Maria José's companion—Plínio de Abreu Coutinho, a humble treasury employee—revealed the importance that a seemingly trifling malicious rumor could assume among people whose claims to formal status were few and whose reputations were thus doubly important in defining their personal and social relationships.[24] Largely because a respectable man like Ascendino told the tale—and because the allegations involved that rare, modern, and somewhat mysterious instrument called the telephone—Plínio refused to write the rumor off as women's idle gossip ("disse"—"me disse"). He instead set off on a furious quest to interrogate everyone who might have overheard Maria José's phone conversations. Plínio was convinced that the entire affair was a malicious concoction only after repeated assurances that all of Maria José's telephone partners had been women discussing gossip, clothing, or petty business. His common-law wife's good name—and, by extension, his male honor—were secure; the only task remaining was to bring the rumormongers to justice.

Maria José's neighbors shared Plínio's zeal. Although Ascendino and Innocência tried to stain Maria José's reputation further (claiming that she was a disruptive element in the rooming house and had even abused Ascendino's children), Maria José's friends and neighbors flatly contradicted such testimony. Maria José had cared for Ascendino's children when they were sick, they said, and Ascendino himself had gone so far as to rebuke Innocência for failing to emulate Maria José's good conduct. Maria José had, furthermore, lived with the same man for more than ten years, a badge of honor requiring no legal sanction in the eyes of these poor, working women. Their solidarity had its intended effect. Ascendino and Innocência, apparently unsure of their ability to defend themselves, officially recanted their slander, affirming in writing that they considered Maria José "dignified and irreproachable," thus hastening an informal judicial settlement. Maria José had succeeded in regaining her prized womanly honor; even destitute of official signs and symbols. A humble woman whose community was willing to come to her aid had succeeded where a wealthy but socially isolated baroness had failed.

Race, Class, Marriage, and Honor in a Carioca Tenement

Five years later, however, another *injúria* case showed that other members of the Carioca popular classes did not share Maria José's conception of female honor and its signifiers. The case began in December 1932 as a run-of-the-mill domestic conflict among residents of a tenement in Espírito Santo, one of Rio's most decadent downtown neighborhoods.[25] Alfredo Fernandes—a barely literate Portuguese native who declared pointedly that he was married and employed as a chauffeur—claimed that his wife, Alcira, had been quietly attending to her domestic chores one day when her downstairs neighbor, Aurora Villela, banged on the door to complain "in aggressive terms" about the noise made by Alcira's children. When Alcira opened the door, Aurora "almost physically attacked" her and made her "the target of terrible abuses," which included accusations that Alcira was "a vulgar whore [*uma puta muito ordinária*]" and "a well-known slut [*uma vacca muito conhecida*]." Aurora ended her tirade by saying that she "was amazed that her [Alcira's] husband still put up with her." All of these insults, Alfredo claimed, had been shouted so that all of the tenement residents could hear them. They were thus "declarations that affected not only his wife's honor but also his own and that of his children" and therefore criminal *calúnias* and *injúrias*.

Some of the arguments that surfaced in the subsequent trial aired well-worn and generally accepted symbolizations of poor women's honor. According to Aurora, Alcira lacked honor because she was an obnoxious, slandering, vulgar neighbor, blind to her own children's defects and insensitive to the reasonable needs of Aurora's ill, bedridden common-law husband. Cleverly, she also claimed that Alcira had actually insulted *her* and that the abuse had been so vulgar that she—a humble, illiterate, woman, informally married but honorable and obedient nonetheless—could not repeat it "out of respect for the judge." Witnesses on both sides indicated that they did not think that it was proper to interfere in their neighbors' lives, and argued about whether Aurora or Alcira had most gravely violated the codes of conduct and mutual respect that made tenement life minimally bearable.

Other aspects of both the witnesses' testimony and the lawyers' arguments, however, revealed deeply conflicting notions about the proper significations of female honor. Laudelina de Souza, an illiterate widow testifying for the defense, claimed not only that Alcira had done most of the slandering but also that her most grievous insult had been to say that "she [Alcira] was a married woman and didn't want anything to do with a tramp," a clear reference to Aurora's informal civil status. Another defense witness claimed that Alcira had called Aurora a "nigger" who "wasn't even married." Both made it clear that they viewed race and marital status as entirely illegitimate measures of honor and social worth and that Alcira's references to them weakened her own claims to respectability.

Alfredo and Alcira's lawyer confronted this attitude head on, asking the judge to compare Alcira, "a married woman who lives with her husband and two children, obeying every requirement of law and morality, defending these principles with great ardor," with Aurora, who, in audaciously admitting cohabitation with a man who was not her husband, showed herself to be a person "who doesn't even know what morality is, who thinks that the entire world has the same low principles as she does and lives by the same immoral customs!" In a tautological appeal to judicial self-importance, he also presented the very fact that Alfredo and Alcira had brought the *injúria* suit as a badge of honor, claiming that "even though they were poor, they would not hesitate to gather some money, with incalculable sacrifice, with the intent of justly punishing" offenses against their honor. Thus the battle lines were drawn: on the one hand, an appeal to informal rules of conduct that deemed references to race and marital status vulgar preening; on the other hand, a view that state-sanctioned symbols of honor constituted its only legitimate measure.

If any of the participants expected a judicial resolution, they were ultimately disappointed. After the final arguments, the case was misfiled or forgotten until after the statute of limitations had run out, and the matter was closed. This kind of informal dismissal happened often in Brazilian judicial trials of the early 1930s; such "misfilings" may have occurred in error, or they may have represented a conscious judicial decision to let slide certain kinds of cases. Either way, the judge had refused to make a point of punishing Aurora, and Alfredo and Alcira received for their trouble only a public airing of their dispute. The questions the case had raised remained unresolved: Were racial epithets as offensive to honor as attacks against a woman's sexual reputation? And did legal marriage denote entitlement to a special class of honor?

Barnyard Witnesses: Favelados *in Search of Honorable Poverty*

In the first decades of the twentieth century, middle-class and elite Cariocas generally regarded downtown tenement houses like those inhabited by Aurora, Alcira, and Alfredo with scorn and horror. Politicians, social workers, and public health officials considered them breeding grounds for criminality, immorality, and infectious disease, and few minced words when describing them. But these descriptions paled in comparison with the diatribes reserved for Rio de Janeiro's favelas. One 1926 speech given at Rio's Rotary Club referred to the favelas as a "plague," and an "aesthetic leprosy," constituting "not only an impudent crime against aesthetics but . . . a grave and permanent menace to the tranquility and health of the public."[26] Alfred Agache, a prominent French urban planner who drafted an elaborate urban renewal plan for Rio in the late 1920s, described the favelas as places "made up of a seminomadic population and completely lacking the basic rudiments of hygiene."[27] Given such attitudes—which rarely acknowledged the humanity, let alone the honor, of favela residents—it seems somewhat surprising that they would go to the courts to settle questions of honor. But on February 11, 1930, favela resident Elvira Rodrigues Marques did just that.[28] The resulting trial not only unveiled conceptions of honor and dishonor held by Elvira, her husband Antônio, and their neighbors; it also hinted at the conflicting images of "honorable" and "dishonorable" poverty that shaped the thinking of lawyers, prosecutors, and judges in any matter that concerned the lives of favela residents.

Elvira's and Antônio's complaint resulted from a long, smoldering neighborhood dispute. The Portuguese-born couple lived in a tiny favela called the Morro da Cyprianna. Like many favelas that developed during these years, theirs was not a full-fledged shantytown. Unlike the adjacent hillside settlements of Mangueira and Telégrafo, which, combined, contained about 1,600 residences in 1933, the Morro da Cyprianna consisted of just a tiny, extralegal group of ramshackle dwellings, built at the steep, mountainous end of an established street in a busy, lower-class railway suburb.[29] According to Elvira, two of her neighbors—Antônio Augusto Serafim and his wife, carefully referred to as *Dona* Humbelina de Jesus— had, for the last several months, mounted a "campaign of defamation" against her, culminating in a string of slanders.[30] Among other things, Humbelina had said publicly that Elvira was "a known prostitute" and that "Elvira's residence was worse than a whorehouse when her husband was not home." In addition, Elvira claimed that Antônio Augusto had come to her door on the evening of February 9, "armed with a stick," and called her a prostitute and her husband Antônio a cuckold (*cabrão*). These words, in Elvira and Antônio's view, constituted criminal *injúrias*.

The trial that followed was the judicial equivalent of a neighborhood brawl, and lawyers on both sides dove into the melee. The defense lawyer questioned Antônio's virility, stating that an honorable man would have come to blows with Antônio Augusto over a verbal insult such as *cabrão*. He characterized Elvira as a nasty, quarrelsome woman "of poor moral fabric" and lauded Humbelina and Antônio Augusto as "rustic workers who turn themselves over every day to the heavy labor of their unlucky existence," who "would never have time to worry about the lives of their neighbors, their ailments, and their wretchedness," and who had only the "compassion of well-formed souls" for an unhappy wretch such as Elvira. For good measure, the defense lawyer also attacked one of the witnesses for the prosecution as a dissolute "concubine" who used a false name.

Witnesses for both sides — favela residents, unschooled or barely literate — traded eyewitness accounts and disputed the irascibility, hardworking nature, and neighborliness of all four participants.[31] The prosecution's lawyer descended into the most remarkable tirade. He underlay his claims that the defense witnesses "had no moral authority and were all social outcasts," with the observation that two of them lived in the Mangueira favela and the third in the Morro da Cyprianna in a house without a legal street number, addresses that plainly indicated "the character of these barnyard witnesses (*testemunhas de viveiro*)."[32] Never mind that his own clients also resided in a little favela (a pesky fact indeed); the mere address of these witnesses precluded their credibility as honorable citizens.

The judicial system proved no less divided than the trial participants. Unusually, the lower-circuit judge found Humbelina guilty — sentencing her to one month's jail time and a fine equivalent to approximately one month's salary.[33] But the superior court reversed the conviction on technical grounds. Not surprisingly, given legal constraints that still prohibited outright consideration of personal character, status, or circumstance in criminal verdicts, none of the judges referred to the honor-related arguments made over the course of the trial. Nowhere did they acknowledge that the defendants were hardworking, well-mannered, and kept to themselves; nor did they consider openly the connections made by both parties between legal marriage and purity, work and trustworthiness, and place of residence and moral character.

But the arguments' absence in the written verdicts did not strip them of their significance; this was far from the only trial featuring similar rhetorical strategies.[34] In other *injúria* cases, lawyers would repeat the allegations that favela residents could not be relied upon and that they were all "barnyard witnesses"; still others would argue that favela residents and other poor people were so morally hardened that they could not possibly be insulted by words that would bruise tenderer sensibilities. Even in cases not ostensibly involving honor, arguments hinging on questions of individual worthiness appeared with more and more frequency over the course of the 1930s, as judges and lawyers alike adopted positivistic notions of criminal law that placed an enormous emphasis on the personal circumstances and moral character of defendants.

The problem, as Elvira and Antônio's case and so many others revealed, was that there seemed to be no consensus, either among the popular classes or among Cariocas in general, as to what constituted the appropriate signs and symbols of personal honor and worthiness. Most Cariocas seemed to have come to a general agreement—at least in the courtroom—about what constituted honorable characteristics, especially among the popular classes; poor Cariocas indicated that they valued discretion, hard work, good manners, and sexual fidelity (especially among women), and most lawyers, judges, and wealthier Cariocas concurred. Likewise, everyone seemed to agree that certain terms and accusations were offensive to honor for people of any social class—for women, the worst insults implied loose character or sexual impropriety; for men, they alleged thievery, cowardice, an inability to control a wife or companion, or the use of women's sexuality for material gain.

What, though, were the signs that symbolized concretely such abstract notions of honorable conduct? What role would class and race play in their definition? Here, few concurred, and in this sense the honor cases unmasked a deep contradiction. Although Brazilian law formally separated social status from legal rights in criminal cases involving honor, attitudes on the ground were much more complex. In the early 1930s, Rio de Janeiro may not have been a place where a wealthy baroness, simply by virtue of her title, could claim in court a unique grade of honor. But it was a place where some associated honor with certain exterior signs of status—place of residence, manner of speech, occupation, color, formal marriage—while others vehemently rejected such links, favoring instead less rigid measures of worth.[35] Clearly, personal characteristics mattered in determining judicial treatment. Yet, equally clearly, nobody agreed for sure about which particular characteristics indicated special worthiness. Carioca society in the late 1920s and early 1930s had reached no consensus as to which "rites of institution," to borrow Pierre Bourdieu's notion, could legitimately endow individuals with a right to honor.[36] Without such a consensus, it was very difficult for the courts to know either what constituted "honor" or how to measure its infringement. It would be still more difficult for the Brazilian state as a whole—as it set about selectively expanding social, economic, and political rights over the course of the 1930s and 1940s—to determine which lower-class Brazilians were worthy enough to claim the privileges of honorable citizenship.

Doralícia Revisited: Papers, Honor, and Justice in the Vargas Era

Which brings us, however circuitously, back to the case of Doralícia and Joaquim. The article that had provoked Joaquim's charges stated that Doralícia and her daughter, Francisca, had not dared to complain to the municipal authorities about Joaquim's advances until "the triumph of the Republic." This suggested that Doralícia, like many other poor Brazilians, took the words of provisional president Getúlio Vargas at face value when he claimed that his 1930 revolution sought "the construction of a new Nation, equally welcoming of the great and the humble, open to the collaboration of all her children."[37] Vargas's intentions, though, were rarely so transparent. Although his explicit initiatives to include urban popular classes in his idealized "national community" led many to hail him as the "father of the poor," his interest in lower-class Brazilians was generally more tutelary than egalitarian. As Vargas himself stated in a 1933 speech, he was convinced that "every Brazilian *will be able to be* an admirable man and a model citizen"; this by no means implied that Vargas believed that every Brazilian already possessed these qualities, or that he or she deserved the benefits of citizenship without them. It signified, rather, that the Vargas government intended to take a more active role in morally and academically educating the Brazilian poor, so that they would eventually be ready to take their place as honorable citizens. It also meant that Vargas's government would assume an active interest in formalizing differential citizenship, depending on an ever expanding array of legal documents—birth and marriage certificates, identity cards, labor cards, police records, property titles, rental contracts, memberships in unions and social security institutes—that would both signify that an individual had attained honorable civic standing and serve as passports to an exclusive arena of social and economic privileges. These documents represented the "institutions" of honor that had been lacking before 1930.[38] Such papers were not a fair measure of social or moral worthiness—even in Rio de Janeiro, most were notoriously difficult to obtain, especially for rural migrants, women, the illiterate, and the informally employed or housed—and most lower-class Cariocas only instrumentally accepted their symbolic meaning.[39] But these instruments were important signifiers of honorable citizenship in many arenas of *public* life, and especially in the courts, where their manipulation became an essential element by the 1950s.[40]

When Joaquim charged Doralícia with *injúria* in April 1931, this process of formal certification of honorable citizenship had only just begun. But the moral and sociological requirements for such certification had already become apparent, and, in these terms, Doralícia proved no match for Joaquim. As a respected municipal doctor and professor at Rio's state medical school, Joaquim had three decades' worth of paper to support his honor claims. He was also married, with a house in a decent neighborhood and a squad of his subordinates—respectable public employees all—backed up his story. Joaquim also hired an excellent lawyer who stopped at nothing to convict Doralícia and destroy her daughter's reputation.

Doralícia, for her part, was a rural migrant, probably dark skinned, with no documents to prove her good name.[41] Although she was married, her ill husband never appeared in court, and the addresses she listed over the course of the trial were located near the borders of small favelas. A few neighbors—a seamstress, a mechanic's assistant, and a textile worker—proved willing to attest to the women's good character, but Doralícia and Francisca apparently moved too frequently to be well known. Doralícia did have a particularly passionate and attentive public defender, and he did present some proof that her allegations were true— a fact that should have proved legally significant, given that the accusations concerned Joaquim's behavior as a public employee in his place of work. But these advantages alone did not amount to much in the eyes of the two judges who, successively, presided over the case.

Lawyers for both sides argued their claims partially on straightforward, evidential grounds. Joaquim called his subordinates in to testify that Doralícia had come to his office and accused him loudly of being a "dirty old man [*velho cretino*]" who had offered Francisca a raise in exchange for sex, told all of the girls who worked in his office that they would do better working as prostitutes, and purposely sat close to them so he could rub his legs against theirs. These witnesses further claimed that Francisca had left her job because, days before, Joaquim had censured her when he discovered that she had been hauled in to a police *delegacia* for nighttime carousing with a young man.[42]

Doralícia's lawyer, for his part, introduced witnesses who, though ignorant about the events in Joaquim's office, were willing to swear that Doralícia "behaved well," that "Francisca's behavior was always exemplary," and that "Francisca's family are good people, and Francisca is a hardworking, serious, moral young woman." The lawyer also called Francisca herself to make the shocking claim that, a few days before she quit her job, Joaquim had taken her to a doctors' office, drugged her, and asked the two presiding doctors to determine whether or not she was still a virgin. Incredibly enough, the lawyer later produced a signed affidavit from both doctors saying that this event had in fact taken place.

But Doralícia and Joaquim's case did not, as it turned out, hinge on facts. Throughout the case, both the public prosecutor and the presiding judges showed remarkable favoritism toward Joaquim. First, they accepted the case, even though procedural laws stated clearly that it belonged under the jurisdiction of the judge who had thrown out Joaquim's original complaint.[43] They also ignored open violations of other procedural laws, including abuses that prevented several defense witnesses from testifying. Even more remarkably, the judge took the extraordinary step of asking Joaquim's superintendent to send him a full report containing testimony of coworkers concerning Francisca's and Joaquim's moral characters. The resulting document had only praise for Joaquim—the employees' "beloved boss"—and only disparagement and innuendo for Francisca. Despite the fact that this testimony came from people professionally subordinate to Joaquim, neither judge expressed any hesitation in admitting it as wholly reliable.

As if all of this were not enough, Joaquim's lawyer mounted a final, frontal attack on whatever was left of Francisca Costa's good name. He claimed that the report from Joaquim's office revealed that Francisca "consistently demonstrated that she had a degenerate character, practicing acts of passive pederasty with other employees" and that Francisca "was already a prostitute, frequenting bawdyhouses and brothels . . . and giving herself over to cheap prostitution with the assumed name of Nancy da Costa." The lawyer concluded that Doralícia had forgotten that she was dealing with "a citizen with various titles to his name, a professor, the head of the municipal office with great and important responsibilities and, above all, a doctor" who "would never have practiced the acts that had been imputed to him, in the middle of his office, or in any other place, and less still with a minor who was wanton, shameless, and anti-hygienic, seeing as how she had had anal and oral sex with several of his employees." This was a case of an honorable, established citizen, with the credentials to prove as much, who had been viciously attacked and dishonored by a miserable, undocumented, rootless woman with so little moral fiber that she had allowed her daughter to become a whore.

Doralícia's lawyer bitterly protested this "slander," chastising Joaquim for using his fortune and social connections to "drag a member of the opposite sex, who is incapable of having committed the acts of which she is accused, through the streets of bitterness, driving her to despair." Neither this nor the lawyer's repeated protests against the trial's procedural irregularities held any water with the judge. He fined Doralícia and sentenced her to one-and-a-half months of prison, without even granting her the commutation to which she was legally entitled as a first offender. Although Doralícia's lawyer pursued the case through two appeals, a highly unusual action—particularly in a case involving a public defender—the conviction stood.[44]

"Truth" here proves elusive. Francisca might very well have been a sexually loose young woman who told her mother a tall tale to explain her abrupt unemployment, and they may have brought their story to *A batalha* out of spite or vengeance. Joaquim might well have been a sexual harasser who propositioned Francisca and orchestrated the entire trial out of fear that her charges might find some credibility. But, if the accuracy of the judge's decision remains unclear, the inconsistencies in the way he reached it stand in bold relief. Legally, irregularities that invalidated numerous other trials hardly played a role in determining the outcome of this one, and both judges granted considerable judicial leniency to Joaquim. It is difficult to escape the conclusion that this case hinged on the status differential between Joaquim and Doralícia, a gap that gained juridical legitimacy both because of Joaquim's access to the key signs and symbols of honorable citizenship and because of his extraordinary ability to manipulate them.

Over the course of the 1930s and 1940s, these signs and symbols became both more important and more widely disseminated, and their importance in Carioca criminal trials only increased. The concept of "honor" remained central in determining the credibility of victims, defendants, and witnesses during these years; if anything, it only gained influence with the rise of positivistic legal theories. But the manner in which this honor was defined changed radically. In the late 1920s and the 1930s, associations between honorable citizenship and formal marriage, formal employment, or formal residential status remained loose and highly contested, an important, but rarely determinant, factor in most *injúria* trials. By the 1950s, Vargas-era legal transformations had institutionalized such associations, creating a system of legal stratification that closely mirrored the city's economic, racial, and gender hierarchies and facilitating the legal marginalization of a large portion of the Carioca population. In the courts, paper symbols such as national identification cards, *carteiras de trabalho* (work cards), positive police character assessments, and clean rap sheets had become virtual talismans against everything from indictment and conviction to imprisonment and civil rights violations, and informal residential circumstances had become a virtual guarantee of poor treatment.[45] In an expanding and increasingly anonymous metropolis, legal arguments grounded in popular notions of honor but unsanctified by its formal symbols fell on increasingly deaf ears. We can only speculate on how this process was understood by Doralícia, Aurora, Maria José, and others whose claims to honor rested more on popular morality than on formal significations, and whose poverty and legal ignorance limited their ability to acquire the signs and symbols of public worth. But it is not much of a leap to surmise that this new world of paper honor would have seemed to them a confusing and illegitimate one, in which full citizenship depended more on power than on moral worth and in which the state could not be relied upon justly to distribute the rewards of lives honorably lived.

Notes

1 Arquivo Nacional (henceforth AN), 9th Criminal Division, box 2380/173; 5th Criminal *Pretoria*, CF 70.12275.

2 See the essays by Gotkowitz and Putnam in this volume; see also Julian Pitt-Rivers, "Honor and Social Status," in *Honor and Shame: The Values of Mediterranean Society*, ed. J. G. Peristiany (Chicago: University of Chicago Press, 1966), 19–77; Lyman L. Johnson and Sonya Lipsett-Rivera, eds., *The Faces of Honor: Sex, Shame, and Violence in Colonial Latin America* (Albuquerque: University of New Mexico Press, 1998); David Garrioch, *Neighborhood and Community in Paris, 1740–1790* (Cambridge: Cambridge University Press, 1986); Garrioch, "Verbal Insults in Eighteenth-Century Paris," in *The Social History of Language*, ed. Peter Burke and Roy Porter (Cambridge: Cambridge

University Press, 1987); Peter N. Moogke, "'Thieving Buggers' and 'Stupid Sluts': Insults and Popular Culture in New France," *William and Mary Quarterly*, 3rd ser., 36.4 (1979): 524–547; and Mary Beth Norton, "Gender and Defamation in Seventeenth-Century Maryland," *William and Mary Quarterly*, 3rd ser., 44.1 (1987): 3–39.

3 Note similarities to cases cited by Gotkowitz and Putnam. There are no detailed statistics on Carioca insult cases before 1942, but my own sample followed patterns evident in official statistics from 1942 to 1963 (see figs. 1–3). On the racial and class aspects of honor, see Garrioch, *Neighborhood and Community*; as well as Lyman L. Johnson, "Dangerous Words, Provocative Gestures, and Violent Acts," and Sandra Lauderdale Graham, "Honor among Slaves," in Johnson and Lipsett-Rivera, *Faces of Honor*, 127–51, 201–28.

4 On the breakdown of legal divisions in nineteenth-century Brazil and Latin America, see the essays in this volume by Guardino, Barragán, Chalhoub, and Grinberg.

5 Brodwyn Fischer, "The Poverty of Law: Rio de Janeiro, 1930–1964," PhD diss., Harvard University, 1999; Olívia Maria Gomes da Cunha, *Intenção e gesto: Pessoa, côr e a produção cotidiana da (in)diferença no Rio de Janeiro, 1927–1942* (Rio de Janeiro: Arquivo Nacional, 2003), and "1933: Um ano em que fizemos contatos," in *Dossiê povo negro: 300 anos*, special issue of *Revista USP* 28 (Dec. 1995–Feb. 1996): 142–163; Wanderley Guilherme dos Santos, *Cidadania e justiça: A política social na ordem brasileira* (Rio de Janeiro: Campus, 1987); Sérgio Carrara, "A ciência e doutrina da identificação no Brasil: Ou do controle do eu no templo da técnica," *Religião e sociedade* 15.1 (1990): 83–105.

6 Virgílio de Sá Pereira, quoted in Oscar de Macedo Soares, *Código penal da República dos Estados Unidos do Brasil*, 7th ed. (Rio de Janeiro: Garnier, 1910), 124–25.

7 Ibid., 125.

8 Ibid., 125, quoting Pietro Cogliolo, *Trattato de Diritto Penal*, vol 3, 88.

9 Ibid., 125.

10 Ibid., 127.

11 Like most civil-law systems, Brazilian law defined honor offenses as crimes rather than as civil violations.

12 These clauses also served to prosecute pederasty and adultery.

13 The 1890 code, unlike that of 1830, classified these as offenses "against the security, honor, and honesty of families and public modesty and decency" rather than as "crimes against honor or good reputation." Law No. 2992 (Sept. 25, 1915) added "the corruption of minors" to its label. On female honor as a familial and societal good, see Muriel Nazzari, "An Urgent Need to Conceal," and Sonya Lipsett-Rivera, "A Slap in the Face of Honor," in Johnson and Lipsett-Rivera, *Faces of Honor*, 130–26, 179–200; and Sueann Caulfield, *In Defense of Honor: Morality, Modernity, and Nation in Early-Twentieth-Century Brazil* (Durham, NC: Duke University Press, 2000).

14 Francisco José Viveiros de Castro, introduction to *Os delitos contra a honra da mulher*, 4th ed. (Rio de Janeiro: Freitas Bastos, 1942). See also Caulfield, *In Defense of Honor*; and Martha de Abreu Esteves, *Meninas perdidas: Os populares e o cotidiano do amor no Rio de Janeiro da belle époque* (Rio de Janeiro: Paz e Terra, 1989).

15 Macedo Soares, *Código penal*; João Vieira de Araujo, "Parte especial," in *Código penal interpretado*, vol. 2 (Rio de Janeiro: Imprensa Nacional, 1901–2); Galdino Siqueira, "Parte especial," art. 411, in *Direito penal brasileira* (Rio de Janeiro: Jacyntho, 1924).

For the years after 1940, see Nélson Hungria, *Commentários ao Código penal*, vol. 4, arts. 137–154 (Rio de Janeiro: Forense, 1942–55). Although this conception mirrors Pitt-Rivers's, legal practice, following Roman precedent, often did not sanction offenses against "internal" honor.

16 Here, Brazilian law diverged from others; see, Moogke, "'Thieving Buggers' and 'Stupid Sluts,'" on eighteenth-century New France.

17 Galdino Siqueira, *Curso de processo criminal*, 2nd ed. (Sao Paulo: Magalhães, 1924).

18 Ibid, arts. 268–277. In the absence, before 1942, of a national procedural code, Siqueira's commentary drew upon regional laws and practices, but it did accurately reflect Rio's 1924 Procedural Code and legal practices.

19 Exceptions include written *injúrias* or *calunias* and sexual honor cases admitting medical "evidence" of virginity. On the declining importance of such medical evidence after 1920, see Caulfield, *In Defense of Honor*.

20 AN, box 2658/2436.

21 The end of the empire stripped Brazilian noble titles of official worth, but their informal meaning endured much longer. Eugénie's surname, Carneiro Leão, suggests that her late husband was descended from a Portuguese merchant who, in the late eighteenth century, amassed one of the most enormous commercial fortunes in Brazil and whose widow was one of the first Brazilians to receive the title of baroness. On nobility, see Eul-Soo Pang, *In Pursuit of Honor and Power: Noblemen of the Southern Cross in Nineteenth-Century Brazil* (Tuscaloosa: University of Alabama Press, 1988).

22 Figures 2 and 3 demonstrate white and female overrepresentation in honor crimes between 1943 and 1964; my own sample of eight hundred cases between 1927 and 1964 confirms this, also showing increased numbers of middle- and upper-class defendants. This may be due to social taboos on physical violence as a method of conflict resolution between men and women or between individuals of different social classes. For colonial parallels, see Johnson and Lipsett-Rivera, *Faces of Honor*.

23 AN, box 3658/849.

24 On honor and the lower classes, see Johnson, "Dangerous Words," and Lauderdale-Graham, "Honor among Slaves," in Johnson and Lipsett Rivera, *Faces of Honor*. On eighteenth-century Paris, see Garrioch, *Neighborhood and Community*.

25 AN, 8th Criminal *Pretoria*, 1932/524. Espírito Santo was adjacent to Santana, the area where Maria José had lived a few years before, but the neighborhoods differed greatly. Santana was more central, whiter (85%, vs. 79%, according to the 1940 census), more literate (84% vs. 80%), and had only about 36% as many tenements as Espírito Santo. Maria José's residence, located blocks from prominent government buildings and the central railway station, was distant from the Espírito Santo tenement, near numerous shantytowns in an area famous as an early center of Afro-Brazilian counterculture.

26 "Para a remodelação do Rio de Janeiro," Rotary Club speech, Nov. 12, 1926, quoted in Denise Cabral Stuckenbruck, *O Rio de Janeiro em questão: O Plano Agache e o ideário reformista dos anos 20* (Rio de Janeiro: Observatório de Políticas Urbanas e Gestão Municipal, 1996), 86.

27 Agache, *Cidade do Rio do Janeiro: Extensão, remodelação, embellezamento* (Paris: Foyer brésilien, 1930), 20.

28 AN, CF 70.10840.

29 Brazil, Ministério de Trabalho, Indústria e Commércio, *Estatística predial, Distrito Fed-*

eral, 1933 (Rio de Janeiro: Ministério de Trabalho, Indústria e Commércio, 1935). On Rio de Janeiro's social geography, see Mauricio de Almeida Abreu, *Evolução urbana do Rio de Janeiro*, 2nd ed. (Rio de Janeiro: Jorge Zahar, 1988); Teresa Meade, *"Civilizing" Rio: Reform and Resistance in a Brazilian City, 1889–1930* (University Park: Penn State University Press, 1997); and Fischer, "Poverty of Law."

30 *Dona* denotes respect for a mature woman; in this context it probably was also meant to emphasize Elvira's own civility.

31 The witnesses included a housewife, a carpenter, a gardener, a day laborer, an unemployed commercial employee, and a small-scale contractor. Four could read and write rudimentarily, two were illiterate. According to the 1940 Brazilian census, 15.5% of the people in Andaraí—the Morro da Cyprianna's neighborhood—were illiterate; the citywide figure was 21.6%.

32 Among lawyers, *testemunha de viveiro* meant a false witness, one specially prepared to appear in trial. In the early 1930s, however, I have only found this derogatory term used with regard to favela witnesses.

33 Between 1942 and 1963 (when figures are available), only 2.9% of honor crime defendants were convicted (27 out of 934). In the category "crimes against individuals" as a whole—which included murder, physical assault, attempted abortion, injuries inflicted by a vehicle, as well as honor crimes—12% were convicted (21,937 out of 182,108). *Crimes e contravenções, 1942–1963*.

34 In my sample of 251 cases from 1927 to 1940, judges mostly adhered to the 1890 Criminal Code, which followed the classical law tradition in leaving no room for open consideration of personal characteristics or circumstance. Lawyers and prosecutors, though, frequently signaled the informal importance of such factors. On the classical and positivist conceptions of law, see Fischer, *"Quase pretos de tão pobres?* Race and Social Discrimination in Rio de Janeiro's Twentieth-Century Criminal Courts," *Latin American Research Review* 39.1 (2004): 31–59; Caulfield, *In Defense of Honor*; Carlos Antonio Costa Ribeiro Filho, "Clássicos e positivistas no moderno direito penal brasileiro: Uma interpretação sociológica," in *A invenção do Brasil moderno*, ed. Micael M. Herschmann and Carlos Alberto Messeder Pereira (Rio de Janeiro: Rocco, 1994); and Peter Fry, "Direito positivo versus direito clássico: A psicolização do crime no Brasil no pensamento de Heitor Carrilho," in *Cultura e psicanálise*, ed. Sérvulo A. Figueira (São Paulo: Brasiliense, 1985).

35 This seems to have held true generally. In the 1920s and 1930s, a variety of "negative" social characteristics—including informal marriage, migrant status, illiteracy, low-status employment, residential circumstances, and race—correlated with negative judicial outcomes for defendants. See Fischer, *"Quase pretos."*

36 Pierre Bourdieu, "Rites as Acts of Institution," in *Honor and Grace in Anthropology*, ed. J. G. Peristiany and Julian Pitt-Rivers (Cambridge: Cambridge University Press, 1992), 79–90. Bourdieu claims that a "rite of institution . . . leads towards the consecration or legitimization of an arbitrary boundary, that is to say, it attempts to misrepresent the arbitrariness and presents the boundary as legitimate and natural" (80). It is also "an act of communication, but of a particular kind: it signifies to someone his identity, but at the same time as it expresses that identity and imposes it on him, it expresses it before everyone . . . and authoritatively informs him of what he is and what he must be" (84). In borrowing this notion here, I argue that, in Brazil's First Republic, while

most Cariocas had their own "rites of institution" bestowing social honor, few were recognized at once by every sector of society and also by the state. One of the Vargas administration's legacies was the partially successful introduction of a number of bureaucratic "rites" that would reward individuals with status as "honorable citizens."

37 Vargas, "Nova organização administrativa do país," speech from Nov. 3, 1930. Vargas, *A nova política brasileira* (Rio de Janeiro: J. Olímpio, 1946), 69–103.

38 On documents and the legal formalization of Carioca society, see Fischer, "Poverty of Law." See also dos Santos, *Cidadania e justiça*; Carrara, "A ciência e doutrina"; and Olívia Maria Gomes da Cunha, "1933: Um ano em que fizemos contatos."

39 See Fischer, "*Quase pretos*."

40 In my 263-case sample from the early 1950s and 1960s, worker identification cards, police character assessments, and other paper measures of worthiness predicted impressively a defendant's judicial fate, eclipsing all other personal characteristics. See Fischer, "*Quase pretos*."

41 Although Doralícia's skin color is never mentioned, Francisca is identified by doctors as *parda* (brown); Doralícia likely shared her daughter's skin color.

42 When Doralícia's lawyer attempted to verify this story, police authorities denied it.

43 According to the 1924 Procedural Code, *Pretoria* jurisdiction depended on a crime's location. See Cándido Mendes de Almeida, *Código do processo penal* (Rio de Janeiro: Imprensa Nacional, 1925), 40.

44 Public prosecutors were rarely appointed and notoriously lax in the early 1930s, rarely scribbling more than a few sentences in their clients' defense.

45 Fischer, "*Quase pretos*."

Courtroom tales of sex and honor: *rapto* and rape in late-nineteenth-century Puerto Rico
Eileen J. Findlay

Courtrooms—and the documents they generate—are exceedingly important for historians writing about the laboring classes. We historians have reveled in our discoveries, based largely on judicial records, that Latin American peasants and plebeians developed their own understandings of politics, morality, and social relationships, which influenced as well as borrowed from those of elites. Here I will continue in this tradition, arguing that "dishonored" Puerto Rican women appearing in court often analyzed the workings of power in heterosexual relations differently from magistrates, their parents, and the men with whom they had had sexual encounters.

For all our creativity in the use of criminal records, it seems to me that we historians have neglected two possible avenues for analysis that I will begin to explore in this essay on late-nineteenth-century Puerto Rico (1880–98). First, we have tended to sidestep the role of court personnel and the legal process itself in creating cultural norms in Latin America.[1] This essay will take some preliminary steps toward a more detailed examination of how the legal process and its agents shaped the interpretations of sexuality and gender power relations that plebeian Latin Americans brought to the courts. In the judicial arena, a wide variety of parties fought over and collaborated in the creation of moral meanings, which then helped shape broader cultural norms. Second, and perhaps more important, this article will show that we can unravel additional important nuances of the power-laden interpretive courtroom struggles by analyzing *how* witnesses crafted their narratives, instead of simply examining *what* they said in their testimony, as social historians have traditionally done.[2]

Rapto (the abduction and deflowering of a young woman) and rape cases in late-nineteenth-century Puerto Rico provide an illuminating forum for this exercise. This was a period of growing Liberal political power and social prominence. By 1893, the Liberals dominated local offices in Ponce's municipal government, and in 1897 they won autonomy from Spain for the entire island. The Liberal presence in the courts was most plainly demonstrated, at least in *rapto* and rape cases, by the increasing emphasis on using "scientific" medical evidence to prove women's sexual pasts. Ironically, this reliance on allegedly objective, rational facts often prejudiced women seeking physical and moral protection from the courts.

The plaintiffs, defendants, and most witnesses in the vast majority of these cases were laboring Puerto Ricans; the middle and upper classes seem to have resolved these types of conflicts privately, without resorting to the courts. In nineteenth-century Ponce, *rapto* proceedings frequently provided some measure of protection for the honor of workingwomen and their families, whereas rape was one of the most difficult crimes for women to prove. Between 1880 and 1898, 60 percent of all the Ponce *rapto* cases (which totaled 211) ended either in conviction of the "seducer," marriage of the two parties (and thus restoration of the woman's honor), or an acceptable arrangement worked out between parents and youthful couples. This is quite striking considering that, additionally, almost 30 percent of the cases were dismissed because the "seduced" girl insisted that she had not been a virgin upon leaving her parents' household with her sweetheart. Rape cases present a starkly different picture. Only fifteen were brought to court in this period; all but two of the accused men were acquitted. Both of the convictions involved assaults on very young girls, with corroborating witnesses.

The legal definitions of both crimes, however, were built on the same gendered assumptions about honor and sexuality. Honorable women were virginal and sexually passive; honorable men were sexually aggressive and protective of "their" women; heterosexual sex was naturally consensual. Plaintiffs, defendants, and other witnesses often built their testimony on these dominant scripts but also deliberately played with, subverted, and sometimes even challenged them, drawing on and helping to create a broader, more flexible plebeian sense of respectability. In their interpretations of the law, however, jurists generally refused to acknowledge the subtleties of power relations that characterized heterosexual sexual interactions, upon which laboring women's testimony often insisted.

Finally, despite their legal definitions as separate crimes, in practice the interpretive boundaries distinguishing *rapto* from rape sometimes blurred. Prosecutors frequently could not decide in which category to place criminalized sexual encounters. In turn, defendants and attorneys in rape cases drew on the familiar *rapto* script when reinterpreting coercive sexual acts in the courtroom. Bringing a criminal charge, whether for *rapto* or rape, followed a formula that was relatively standard procedurally but that complicated the question of courtroom narrative authorship. The plaintiffs arrived at court to file a declaration describing the crime committed and the circumstances surrounding it. Even this initial narrative, though constructed by the plaintiff, was filtered through the pen of a court scribe. The *fiscal* (prosecutor) then gathered declarations from the defendant and other witnesses, the written court record again shaped by the attorneys' interrogation. All the testimonies in a legal transcript, then, were produced by a variety of people, usually through adversarial courtroom proceedings that must have been quite intimidating to uneducated Puerto Ricans.

Obviously this process, and the legal scripts that permeated it, molded the stories told in court by plebeian Puerto Ricans. We should not assume, however, that attorneys, scribes, and the formal legal discourses they brandished exercised complete control over unlettered witnesses' meanings and narrative structures. Most witnesses, particularly plaintiffs and defendants, probably came to court with stories already prepared—stories that they could only hope would convince the rich, white, educated people who wielded power in the court, but their own stories nonetheless. Even while pinned in the straitjackets of prosecutors' questions and scribes' legal terminology, laboring Puerto Ricans produced a number of narratives about gender, sexuality, and power that asserted their authorial and interpretive integrity. Popular narrative agency in the courtroom did not always manifest itself in alternative discourses, however. Sometimes the straitjackets themselves served plebeian purposes. Working people's repeated use of them helped reinforce the legal scripts' power.

The initial testimonies of a case were the richest source for plebeian courtroom tale spinning. Subsequent trial phases showcased the legal and medical experts. After the complaint and the interrogations of witnesses, medical examinations of the crime scene and women's bodies were carried out, and the testimony of the physician recorded. This moment often marked a pivotal point in the courtroom struggles over ownership of the truth. The prosecuting and defense attorneys then made legal arguments, and finally the magistrate rendered his verdict, consisting of a series of "proven facts" and his final judgment regarding guilt and sentencing. The medical and legal authorities spun their own courtroom fables of interpretation, but unlike the lay witnesses' accounts from which they borrowed, the experts' stories were cloaked in scientific claims to objective truth and wielded punitive state power. Thus, the legal transcripts and judicial practice enshrined them as the ultimate authority, regardless of how plebeian Puerto Ricans may have interpreted or reacted to their pronouncements.

Stories of Seduction

Rapto was both a legally defined crime and a well-established social practice among Puerto Rican working people by the late nineteenth century. After having established a romantic relationship, a young woman would leave her parents' home and go with her boyfriend to the house of a friend or relative of his. If the young man had saved money and had planned the move for some time, he sometimes had his own house or rented room prepared. Once away from parental surveillance, the couple would have sex, the man, in the process, "taking possession of" the woman's virginity. They would then set up "marital life together," sometimes remaining in the household to which they had originally gone and sometimes moving off on their own.[3]

Since he had stolen the young woman's honor, according to the dominant script, the *raptor* was required by law either to marry his sweetheart or to suffer the punishment of one-and-a-half years' imprisonment, plus the payment of one thousand pesos to the woman as reparation for lost honor, as well as formal recognition and provision of financial support for any child who might have been conceived during the liaison. This theft of honor was deemed legally not to have been committed against the woman, since she had consented to the sexual act, but against her family and public morality.[4]

Magistrates did their best to enforce the moral codes adhered to by the most powerful sectors of Puerto Rican society. Control over women's sexuality was a cornerstone of the dominant honor code. Among the Puerto Rican elite, respectable women were required to be virginal prior to marriage and unswervingly faithful to their husbands once married. Most Puerto Ricans also expected men to control and protect their "own" women from male marauders while sexually conquering others.

Once destroyed by sexual activity, rape, or rumors of such encounters, a woman's reputation could only be fully restored by marriage, usually to the man who had "conquered" her.[5] Thus, female virginity and an explicit male offer to marry prior to the *rapto* were essential prerequisites for the courts' protection of women's assumed interests. The man also had to be established as the sexual agent in the *rapto* drama, in keeping with the dominant norms for masculine behavior.

Magistrates' final sentences in *rapto* cases routinely used language such as the following: "Galo Antonio Velásquez carried seventeen-year-old Catalina Vega away from her paternal home. He then enjoyed her honor and purity, taking possession of her virginity."[6] Judges generally found that if a young woman initiated the sexual encounter, no *rapto* had taken place. Thus, in the eyes of magistrates, *rapto* sex was inherently consensual but always presumed sexual passivity for women and sexual aggression by men. Any other scenario ruptured the gendered norms of honor that *rapto* cases were meant to uphold.

Such categorizations were buttressed by medical doctors in *rapto* cases. Traditionally, testimony of family friends and community members about whether a woman was "reputed to be pure" had established the "fact" of virginity (or lack thereof) in *rapto* cases. Through the early 1880s, then, legal certification as a virgin depended primarily on one's public reputation and community standing. But by the 1890s, Liberal, rationalist methods of determining women's "moral condition" began to prevail in court. Now medical physicians routinely examined young women's genitalia to ascertain "scientifically" how long ago, and under what circumstances, they had been "deflowered." This did not necessarily yield conclusions favorable to the women in question. Scarring and wounds in the vaginal area that seemed not sufficiently fresh or too abundant, a hymen that was "improperly" ripped, all signaled a lack of purity.[7]

Medical evidence was often the trump card in resolving conflicting testimonies, such as those of doña Cecilia Amoros y Toro and don Félix Fernando y Pacheco. Doña Cecilia claimed that she had lost her virginity to don Félix and deserved marriage as recompense. In a rare departure from the usual male assertions of virile sexual conquest, don Félix insisted that their relationship had never been consummated. After examining both parties more than two weeks after the "offending act," the medical doctor pronounced that despite doña Cecilia's lack of a hymen, clearly no "foreign body" had entered her vagina. Neither did don Félix display any physical signs that he had "introduced his penis" into his sweetheart.

Consequently, no *rapto* had occurred.[8] Despite its dubious reliability, such scientific inquiry established supposedly incontrovertible truths and revealed "natural facts." By the turn of the century, medical courtroom stories were the most powerful of all, outweighing the earlier, more debatable truths of public reputation, which plebeian parties to *rapto* proceedings still frequently invoked.[9]

In nineteenth-century Ponce, *rapto* cases were generally filed by the parents or other close relatives of the young woman involved in the elopement. Their responses to the couple's move usually took one of three forms. The first response was to accept the young people's move and not bother attempting to enforce marriage. Since this type of parental response never appeared in court, and thus created no historical record, we have no idea how frequent it was. The second response, and by far the most common in court documents, was immediately to report the girl's disappearance to the local *comisario de barrio* and start judicial proceedings to enforce the couple's marriage. The third response was to extract a promise from the girl's lover to marry her within a set period of time; such agreements were reached either through informal negotiation or the *comisario de barrio*'s mediation. If the wedding was not carried out as agreed, the girl's family, sometimes joined by the girl herself, appealed to the court to enforce it. These delayed petitions were frequently successful.[10]

Plebeian parents probably believed to some degree in the importance of female virginity and marital compensation for women's "damaged honor," but above all they seem to have been seeking social and financial security for their daughters. Sixty-five percent of the very parents who insisted so vehemently on their daughters' marriage in *rapto* petitions were not married themselves; they had probably set up their first household in the same way their daughters had. Those parents who trusted that their daughters' lovers would be financially dependable partners may well not have even thought to enter the courts and raise the issue of marriage. Thus, the parental concern for marriage expressed in the *rapto* cases may have been based largely on the "older and wiser" knowledge that women needed some insurance against future economic troubles.[11]

Examining nineteenth-century *rapto* cases in conjunction with *juicios verbales* petitions, in which women attempted to win economic support from long-term partners who had now left them, suggests that many women of the popular classes also became interested in marriage only when they could no longer trust that male income would be regularly available. Marriage also became a more attractive option for women once they had children; motherhood meant increased monetary needs, less time to be able to earn one's own income, and potentially more difficulty in finding a steady lover who would be willing to support several people.

Only 25 percent of the young women in nineteenth-century Ponce *rapto* cases, however, stated that they wanted to marry their *raptores*: 30 percent explicitly rejected marriage in their testimony, and another 45 percent did not express any desire to marry, although their parents were eager for them to do so. For 75 percent of the 211 women involved in contested *raptos*, then, marriage appears not to have been the ultimate economic aspiration or proof of social worth. Childless, and reassured by their sweethearts' interest in living with and supporting them, at least for the time being, these young women did not clamor to be married. The female plaintiffs in *juicios verbales*, all of whom either had children or had been in their relationship for several years and now complained of abandonment by their partner, faced a very different situation than the majority of the *rapto* women who were in the early stages of consensual unions, had no children, and whose young men were prepared to live with and support them for the time being. In marked contrast to the *rapto* women, in *juicios verbales* 82 percent of white plaintiffs and 85 percent of plaintiffs of acknowledged African heritage requested marriage, the only social status recognized by the state through which women could make financial claims on their sexual partners. Financial stability, thus, not rich people's respectability, was most plebeian women's bottom line. Marriage was only one among various honorable options.

Indeed, working Puerto Ricans, at least in the plantation-based coastal regions such as Ponce and its hinterlands, did not limit their definitions of feminine respectability to virginity or marriage. Rather, plebeians also considered serial female monogamy a perfectly honorable lifestyle: many young women seem to have preferred it, since marriage did not allow a woman to leave the relationship if her present partner became abusive or failed to provide economic sustenance. Women's virginity may have been preferred, but flexibility in partner choice and economic stability seem to have been of paramount concern to laboring Ponceños. Plebeian women and men had differing expectations of consensual "marital life," however. Women sought steady financial support as well as freedom from familial surveillance and physical and sexual aggression. Men, on the other hand, often tried to contain women's attempts to choose acceptable partners freely and did their best to keep women under close control.[12]

Whether or not they fully subscribed to them, all working people knew the terms of the dominant honor code and were fully aware that the law of the rich was based upon them. Therefore, when plebeian parents went to court, they used arguments that they knew would be familiar, and hoped would be convincing, to the presiding magistrates. In order to be "vindicated" by the courts, young women had to be successfully presented as innocent victims, done in by their boyfriends' insistent pressures. Inés Serna's mother echoed scores of other parents when she insisted that she "had no idea why the girl might have left so suddenly—Juan must have pressured her to do so."[13] Another woman insisted that the policeman Pedro Beltrán had carried her daughter off to his room, "keeping her there in his power" and taking her virginity. "He who has dishonored her should restore her honor," she cried.[14]

The narrative structure of parents' stories of honor and morality helped create accounts that resonated with the dominant *rapto* script. Parental denunciations almost always began with a declaration of the girl's disappearance from her home, followed by an accusation against the young man, who certainly had taken their daughter away and was now living in concubinage with her. They inevitably closed with an assertion, backed up by several neighbors, that the girl had indeed been a virgin before her "robbing." The written record of these familiar accounts was often relatively brief: no extra detail was needed to convince judges of their legitimacy. They probably were of little interest to the scribes who recorded scores of them each year. Whether consciously produced or not, these narratives did, however, powerfully assert a specific set of assumptions that served parental interests in the *rapto* struggles. The sole actor in parents' seduction narratives was the young man. The girls appeared only fleetingly, as pale, inert embodiments of moral purity. Thus, the very structure of parental statements privileged female virginity and sexual passivity as well as predatory male sexuality.

This belied the widespread acceptance of nonmarital sexual activity for women and recognition of the power of female sexuality expressed by plebeian Puerto Ricans outside the courtroom walls.[15] It also completely erased any role that the parents themselves may have played in the *rapto* events. Finally, the near rote testimonial pattern implicitly presented *raptos*—even (perhaps especially) those unpredictable ones needing prosecution in court—as ritual, preordained steps leading irrevocably to the appropriate outcomes of conviction or marriage, not as the more complicated struggles over youthful female agency and familial power that emerged from the younger generations' testimonies. The requirements for parental judicial success were quite clear. Thus, parents' narrowed representation of popular moral norms and practices in the courts resonated strongly with magistrates' assumptions about honor.

Young *raptores*, on the other hand, had to manage a much more delicate balancing act. They were defending themselves on a variety of fronts; their testimonial tales often were more complex than those of the accusing parents. In order to avoid imprisonment, *rapto* defendants needed to convince the magistrate of their respect for the law and for female honor. Consequently, most accused *raptores* began and ended their testimony with assertions of their own civility and willingness to play by the customary courtship rules. Most defendants in *rapto* cases also wanted to maintain some type of ongoing relationship with their sweetheart, whether or not they wished to marry her eventually, and so could not trample too heavily upon the young woman's reputation in their desire to win acquittal. Only two of the defendants alleged in contradiction to their lover that she had not been a virgin prior to their relationship.

But popular codes of masculinity also required that young men depict themselves as virile sexual conquerors, even if this meant risking conviction. All but one of the 211 men accused of *rapto* readily stated that they had had intercourse with the woman in question, thus setting themselves up for a prison sentence. One potential way to resolve the dilemma this posed was to acknowledge some female agency in *rapto* events, implicitly destroying the presumption that they had dishonestly seduced a passive girl. Accused *raptores* frequently reported that their girlfriends had suggested the elopement, begging to be taken away. This strategy subtly portrayed their lovers as less-than-pure women, perhaps not meriting a court defense of their honor, while maintaining the appearance of male control of *rapto* events. Manuel Pato proclaimed that he had not seduced his sweetheart Lorenza, "pues, fue ella la que se fue con él" (since it was she who had left with him).[16] In these narratives, boyfriends also routinely presented themselves as virile protectors of their sweethearts, saving them from abusive parents, then enjoying the sexual fruits that were their natural due.[17] Thus, although they did not reproduce the *rapto* script of passive feminine acquiescence and male conquest as faithfully as protective parents or court magistrates, defendants in *rapto* cases generally attempted to affirm male power and dominant moral definitions even while acknowledging female agency.

The stories told by a slight majority of the young women in court fit the *rapto* script as well. Courting and accepting invitations to marry, being carried off to a nocturnal "dishonoring," quietly hoping for some sort of dependable commitment from their lover—all these confirmed the stereotype of passive, virginal womanhood swept along by a torrent of male desire. But approximately 45 percent of the women wove a different type of tale. They depicted themselves as active agents, structuring their stories around not predatory male machinations but their own experiences, feelings, and strategies. In a *rapto* case brought by her parents, Daniela Colón y Collazo, for example, recounted how her parents happily allowed her boyfriend Juan Enrique to visit her at their home. However, after eight to ten months of courtship, "the passion that she felt for her sweetheart was too great," and so she proposed that she leave her family's house with him. Juan Enrique refused, afraid of her parents' wrath; only after following him some distance to the local watering hole was Daniela able to convince him to "take her away" to his sister's home, where they could make love. Colón y Collazo also took care to point out that she had been a virgin when she made love with Juan Enrique. She thus insisted that she could be simultaneously sexually assertive and respectable, rejecting the magistrate's rigid moral dichotomy while attempting to preserve some of her *rapto* rights.

Daniela's testimony contrasted tellingly with her boyfriend's reconstruction of events. Juan Enrique stated that "upon indications from Daniela, he found it not inconvenient to seduce her [*raptarla*], carrying her to his sister's house, where immediately upon arriving, he enjoyed her virginity." Juan Enrique's declaration managed almost completely to bury Daniela's unequivocal assertion of female desire and sexual initiative. He reestablished himself as the sexual actor so effectively that the magistrate convicted him, in a terse summary that destroyed all traces of Daniela's agency: "while filling water buckets at the creek, Daniela Colón y Collazo was seduced by Juan Enrique Colón."[18] Daniela's honor had been confirmed and her marriage decreed by law. But in the process of the *rapto* proceeding she had been reduced discursively and legally from a passionate virgin to a passive instrument of her boyfriend's lust.

Many young women must have had yearnings similar to Daniela Colón's but been unwilling to discuss them in court—such overt discussion of female sexuality was rare. Not so for the struggles between children and parents, however: 35 percent of the women insisted that they had eloped primarily to escape familial violence. In these girls' stories, boyfriends represented their hope for a life free of abuse but never appeared as the authors of the girls' actions. On the contrary, the women were the ones who "obliged," "insisted," and "were determined" to leave with their sweethearts. Isidora Salustiano, for example, told how her sweetheart José Troche "went to her house to say goodbye before leaving to work in Ponce. Fearing that his absence would last a long time and not wanting to suffer her mother's constant beatings, she abandoned her home, looking for Troche along the road. When she reached him, she obliged him to take her with him, since she was determined not to return home."[19]

Thirty-five percent of the women in *rapto* cases also stated openly that they were not virgins when they left with their boyfriends. Some claimed that prior to the elopement they had only had sex with their current sweetheart, but many testified that this was not the first man with whom they had made love. Everyone knew that such admissions usually immediately destroyed any possibility of the courts' intervening to ensure their marriage; parents tried desperately to deny their daughters' testimony. Not being virgins did not, however, appear to provoke shame in the girls. Neither did it deter the young men involved from publicly recognizing the relationships and intending ultimately to marry their sweethearts in the few such cases where the girls wished to do so.

Thus, many young women crafted narrative strategies that diverged significantly from those of magistrates, parents, and even boyfriends. They rejected these parties' often monocausal, morally rigid versions of the *rapto* script. In the girls' stories women could seduce men, morally concerned parents could beat their daughters, and female purity and sexual activity could coexist. Such women spun tales of power struggles and alliances between men and women, parents and daughters, but they invariably positioned themselves as principal authors of the *rapto* drama.

Unfortunately, their stories of female agency and moral shades of gray did not fit within the terms of honor formally recognized in the legal arena. Magistrates' final summaries and sentences carefully erased all references to parental violence and intervention in daughters' lives. They also invariably reduced the women to one end or other of the moral spectrum: either they were respectable virgins, worthy of the law's protection and therefore passive recipients of their lover's sexual attentions, or they were "fallen," already sexually spoiled before undertaking their latest immoral foray. The heavy hand of the law could tolerate few of the subtleties offered by youthful witnesses.

In contrast to *rapto*, rape was legally defined as nonconsensual: sexual intercourse that was achieved through force or intimidation, or with a woman who did not have full use of her reason or a girl under twelve years of age, both presumed unable to give free sexual consent. The force required to qualify a sexual assault as rape legally did not have to be "overwhelming," but "the aggressor's acts [had to] demonstrate clearly that the force was not meant for other purposes."[20] Again, the law and the jurists who interpreted it assumed that heterosexual sex was naturally consensual, and men naturally sexually aggressive. These were very difficult presumptions for women to challenge.

Indeed, the judicial record reveals that magistrates considered it practically impossible to rape a woman. During the entire nineteenth century, only two men were convicted of rape in the judicial district of Ponce, which encompassed most of Puerto Rico's southern coast. Both had assaulted young children (one his own daughter) and were unlucky enough to face the testimony of direct witnesses and damning medical evidence. Not surprisingly, women seem to have been very reluctant to charge men with rape in the courts. Only fifteen cases were brought to Ponce magistrates in the entire second half of the nineteenth century. The women who made these charges appear to have been particularly socially vulnerable: impoverished, unlettered, and, most important, unconnected to familial or community networks of men who would intervene informally on their behalf to punish their assailant.[21] Salomé González, whose testimony follows, fit this profile. She lived, in 1887, in a rural shack with several other Afro–Puerto Rican women, memorable to the men deposed only because "there were no men there."

> Salomé González, native and resident of Ponce, presently living in the *barrio* of Sabanetas, single, occupation laundress, twenty-five years old, declares: that about 10:00 on a Sunday night, about two weeks ago, the declarant was sleeping in the house in which she lives in [the rural neighborhood of] Sabanetas, and along with her were an old woman named Concha and a young woman named Juana Paula García, when they felt someone pounding on the door. They called out and after Concha opened the door, a member of the *guardia civil*, whom the witness does not know by name, came over to her and asked about her husband's whereabouts. The witness an-

swered that she did not have a husband but that the man with whom she lived, the father of her son, had left for Santo Domingo.

Then this *guardia* invited her to go to the house of the *comisario del barrio*, and she who testifies invited Concha to accompany her, and Concha having accepted her invitation, the three left together, but when they had walked only a short way from the house, the policeman told Concha to leave, that it was not in her interest to accompany them, and Concha returned the way she had come, and now that the witness was left there alone with him, he took her to a grove of banana trees some distance from the house, and there pulled out a coin, which he showed to her and then offered to her so that she would commit carnal acts with him, all of which the witness refused with great determination, but when she saw his insistence and the severe manner in which he treated her, all this provoked great fear in the declarant, and she gave in to his desires; thus he managed to have relations with her.

From there, he went with her back to Concha's house, meeting up with another policeman and the Comisario Guillén on the way, and all of them together arrived at the aforesaid house, where the officer who had raped her expressed his desire to drink coffee, which Concha made for them, and they drank it. After having drunk this liquid, the *comisario* left, along with Concha, to look for a girl named Irene, who had left the house in great fear, and the other officer whom they had met on the road also disappeared, leaving the original policeman, the declarant, and Paula García alone, Paula in the adjoining room. Then the policeman closed the door to the room and throwing himself upon the witness managed to rape her once again, leaving immediately afterward. Concha arrived just then and found the declarant crying, and she told her all that had happened to her.

The other women's testimony followed the same story line as Salomé's, enriching the tale with detail about the subtleties of the officer's coercion. Concha recounted how the *guardia civil* "penetrated the threshold of the house, passing before the beds of the other women, looking at them closely, and, stopping before Salomé González's cot, asked her the whereabouts of Cruz, and when she [Salomé] protested, not knowing, he told her that she had to come with him to the *comisario*'s house." Concha accompanied them, at Salomé's request, "but when they had walked some distance from the house, the *guardia* stopped and ordered her [Concha] back to the house. She insisted on remaining with them, but he responded to her in a very vulgar way that she had better leave, so she finally turned around and left."

Another resident of the household, Paula García, also told of Salomé's fearful exit from the house, her tearful return and confession to her friends of the violation she had suffered, the mounting fear of the girl Irene Oppenheim as the Spaniards sat at the table drinking coffee, Irene's being escorted away by two of the men, "and Salomé being left alone in her room with the guard, the declarant sensing from her own room that the officer was having relations with Salomé. Asked if she had heard the officer intimidating Salomé in order to achieve his ends, she said: she did not hear such a thing, but if Salomé gave in to his desires, it was from fear. This man was a *guardia*, and Salomé was afraid that he could hurt her."[22]

Female plaintiffs and other supporting women witnesses in rape cases wove stories that followed a discernible pattern. They inevitably opened their testimony by situating the rape victim in a tranquil domestic setting or engaged in domestic work, thus establishing her as an honorable woman, respectful of gendered spatial boundaries. Like Salomé González, Rufina Santiago was asleep with her mother in their room in the farmworkers' barracks. Eleven-month-old Antonia González played by her sister's side, as the teenager worked in the kitchen. Several women told of washing clothes by the river in the company of friends or sisters.[23]

In women's rape narratives, men brutally disrupted this feminine domestic peace, following up their symbolic violation with a physical and sexual one. Ruperta Rivera told how Ramón Rodríguez ripped open the front door one night and attacked her daughter with a knife as she lay in bed. Carmen Muñoz related how her assailant broke into the patio of her home, grabbed her as she stood up to put her infant son to bed, and fled over the patio wall again after she successfully fought him off.[24] These images of seemingly random attacks by unfamiliar men were rendered potentially more believable by popular assumptions of natural male sexual aggression—an ever present threat that could arise inexplicably and without warning strike any woman in its path. Such a characterization of male attackers also implied that the women had done nothing to provoke the violence. Finally, it distanced the plaintiffs from the defendants, implicitly asserting that the defendants were strangers to the women, despite their frequent actual position as neighbors or previous boyfriends. Such a testimonial strategy is not surprising, considering the overriding presumption of consensual sex that the women faced in the courts and, probably, in their communities. Admission of prior sexual relationships appears to have doomed a woman's charge of rape to dismissal by the magistrates—all of the men in such cases were acquitted.

Women related a variety of reactions to the sexual assaults; some talked of valiant physical struggles, others of verbal attempts to dissuade the attacker, others of apparent compliance. But whatever their immediate response to the rape, fear and its silencing power, expressed in tears, permeated women's testimony. In these narratives, women's sobbing proved they had been traumatized, despite their frequent inability to explain what had happened to them. Both Salomé González and Irene Oppenheim cried before they could speak coherently about what they had experienced. Margarita Marcucci told how, "after having obtained what he desired, he told her that she could leave now, since he had taken his pleasure with her. She left crying for her house, where she arrived unable to speak." The proof of the baby Antonia González's sexual assault, according to her mother and sister, lay not only in her wet genitals and the man surprised lying on top of her in a neighbor's back room but in her inconsolable crying.[25]

Indeed, women's tears often formed the only visible sign of the coercion they contended that they or their loved ones had experienced. Faced with magistrates' and prosecutors' persistent questioning about whether defendants had ripped their clothes, bruised or bloodied them with beatings, women witnesses consistently rejected the determinant power of these "material proofs" of rape. Instead, they articulated an alternative definition, one which recognized that even if physical violence was not directly used, sexual encounters could be coerced and therefore constituted rape if a woman was afraid or did not wish to have sexual contact. They thus challenged the presumption of consensual heterosexual sex that underpinned both magistrates' reasoning and men's testimony. Antonia González's mother and sister named their baby's emotional and physical trauma rape, despite the court doctor's finding that her vagina had not been penetrated. Cecilia Rodríguez brushed away the prosecutor's scornful comments that her daughter's clothing showed no traces of blood or semen; the young woman's cry for help and the male schoolteacher's lowered pants were proof enough of rape for her. Paula García reminded the court that Salomé González's fear of the rural police was sufficient coercion; no physical force was necessary.[26]

Sexual consent, in this feminine definition of rape, was conditional.

Even once given, it could later be revoked. Several women and their supporting witnesses insisted that the sexual encounter in question was, indeed, coerced, despite admitting prior romantic relationships with their alleged assaulters.[27] Neither was consent subject to external proofs. María Rodríguez echoed Salomé González in her story of a man offering her a coin before raping her with a stick. Both women rejected their symbolic labeling as dishonored prostitutes and stoutly denied that they had willingly accepted the men's sexual advances.

Indeed, the elderly Concha's bitter, clipped recounting of how the three Spanish men required her to prepare and serve them coffee in her home against her will serves as a more appropriate analogy for Salomé's rape. The Spaniards "prevailed upon [Concha] to make them coffee, which she did not want to do, but she finally complied, after they insisted." An act of apparent hospitality actually signified men's coercive power in women's lives. For Concha and the younger women in her household, this was one more punishment—seemingly insignificant but redolent with meaning—among many imposed upon them in the country shack that night. Only Irene Oppenheim's fearful sobs exposed the women's true experience of that tense moment.[28]

Men spun quite different tales in rape investigations. Not surprisingly, they generally presented themselves as hardworking, civil individuals and, like the women, faithful to respectable gender expectations. The Spanish rural policeman Juan Arbosa, accused of raping Salomé González, said that he was simply doing his job as an upholder of public order. In fact, he noted his companions' generosity in bringing coffee with them to the old woman Concha's home, so that she could prepare it for them. Ramón Rodríguez admitted that he might have had too much to drink the night he assaulted Rufina Santiago but argued that this was the only reasonable way for "a hardworking plantation hand" to deal with the stresses of life. The magistrate accepted his drunkenness as a manly excuse for his violence, since it appeared not to be habitual.[29]

Consensual exchanges between men and women were the central threads of male testimony in rape cases, recasting women's stories of fear and domination. At times these interactions set the symbolic and narrative context for a direct denial of sexual relations. Don Francisco Guillén, the *comisario* of *barrio* Sabanetas, echoed his companion Juan Arbosa in claiming to remember nothing of Salomé González's presence but told of Concha's serving them coffee in a gesture of welcome. Those men who admitted having had sexual relations with their accusers insisted that they could not have coerced them. Eladio Maldonado reasoned that it was impossible for him to have sexually forced his girlfriend because he had visited her several times previously at her mother's house to make love. José Nicolás Baldiris pointed out that he had had intercourse with Juana Montalvo in the past and had also provided her with occasional financial support, thus creating the presumption of sexual consent in the present.[30]

Medical testimony sometimes cemented such assertions. The court-appointed physician found no physical traces of the beating María Margarita Marcucci claimed to have received from her assailant, despite noting the blood stains on her clothing. When she refused to let the doctor examine her vagina, he pronounced that not only had she not been raped, she "had gone to the sexual act with pleasure," a judgment repeated by the magistrate in his final decision. More often than proving consent, however, the doctors' evaluations simply nullified the possibility of sexual coercion, noting the lack of sufficient genital damage, blood, or "signs of struggle." Physicians also declared coercion impossible in cases where women were deemed to have been previously sexually active. Upon examination a full two months after the alleged assault, one adolescent's hymen was reported to be extensively scarred, "proving" that her deflowering had happened long ago and that therefore she could not have been raped. Unmarried, allegedly sexually active women had already stepped beyond the dominant moral pale. Thus, in rape, as in *rapto* cases, they did not deserve the protection of the law.[31]

Such judgments were extremely powerful. Magistrates seem to have found medical testimony the most convincing of any story told in court. Every single judicial sentence followed the lead of the medical examiner, often repeating his intertwined physical and moral evaluations verbatim. Medical evidence was also the basis of verdicts in the extremely rare case of a rape conviction. In declaring Juan Miguel Ortiz Padilla guilty of raping his thirteen-year-old daughter, the judge gave the most weight not to the girl's testimony but to the doctor's findings of "recent deflowering," the presence of semen, and despite no evidence of "material violence," a definite "control over her will through fear and intimidation."[32] Apparently only male doctors, not female plaintiffs, could convince magistrates of the coercive power of fear.

Magistrates thus appropriated scientific verdicts, increasingly available to court personnel after 1890, to enhance their own judicial authority. Their final decisions—organized around their own interpretation of events and relationships, now labeled as a series of "proven facts" —rang with the certainty of having produced objective truth. Rape, as one judge proclaimed, had to be proven with "material evidence": "facts that were clear, determinant, and of undeniable force, creating evidence of robust value." Judicial opinions erased women's attempts to highlight the subtleties of coercion, recognizing only consent or ruthless violence as sexual possibilities. "Consent, not brute force, must be assumed as the basis for carnal acts between men and women. . . . This is the natural order of things."[33] Time and time again, magistrates fell back upon the presumption of consensual sex in their decisions. Women observed in a sexual encounter were assumed to have willingly acquiesced if they could produce no corroborating witnesses to confirm their stories of struggle or intimidation.[34] The magistrate in Salomé González's case did accept her story sufficiently to conclude that she had had sex with the rural policeman. But Juan Arbosa was not found guilty of rape—the judge's recapitulation stripped the encounters of all traces of coercion. "The officer returned to González's house and without using force or intimidation, had relations with her, as Paula García and Juana Rivera have testified, and as the medical examination of the plaintiff's body and genital organs demonstrates. Proven facts."[35]

In rape cases, then, magistrates rendered men's tales of naturally consensual sex more powerful than women's images of natural male sexual aggression. Socially vulnerable women stood little chance in challenging the unified front of scientific opinion and men's invocation of patriarchal moral norms. Even the rules of logic limited the possibility of women's vindication in court: if men were naturally sexually aggressive, how could their assaults be deemed criminal?

The line distinguishing rape from *rapto*—in large part a question of coercion versus consent—could be quite fragile. Sometimes courtroom disagreements surfaced over how to classify a sexual encounter. Especially in cases where the two parties had carried on a prior relationship, defense attorneys insisted that the events only merited consideration as a *rapto*, not as rape. Male plaintiffs, too, drew on the *rapto* script in their testimony, speaking of young women "going away with them" and "acquiescing in their seduction." Those *fiscales* who emphasized the apparent coercion of the act argued for prosecution under the rape clauses of the penal code.[36] They always argued in vain; the cases were invariably dismissed, or the defendant acquitted.

Indeed, these instances of blurred definitions suggest that the power of the dominant *rapto* script—which incorporated both consensual sex and a male aggressor—helped create a legal and broader cultural context in which it was almost impossible to win a rape conviction. The basis upon which Puerto Rican courts protected women's honor and bodily integrity had high costs, not only in rendering women passive but in practically denying the possibility of rape. The *rapto* script's potency came not just from the medical doctors and magistrates who stripped the subtleties from working women's testimony about sexual agency, respectability, and coercion. Plebeian parents, boyfriends, accused assailants, neighborhood onlookers—even other "wronged women"—also helped reinforce a discourse about honor and sexuality which ensured that in the courts of late-nineteenth-century Puerto Rico, women generally lost, even when they won.

Notes

1   A number of Brazilianists are exceptions to this rule. See Sueann Caulfield, *In Defense of Honor: Sexual Morality, Modernity, and Nation in Early-Twentieth-Century Brazil* (Durham, NC: Duke University Press, 2000); Sidney Chalhoub, *Trabalho, lar e botiquim: O cotidiano dos trabalhadores no Rio de Janeiro da belle époque* (São Paulo: Brasiliense, 1986); and Martha Abreu de Esteves, *Meninas perdidas: Os populares e o cotidiano do amor no Rio de Janeiro da belle époque* (Rio de Janeiro: Paz e Terra, 1989).
2   See Natalie Zemon Davis's by now classic work on the gendered narrative structures of early modern judicial petitions, *Fiction in the Archives: Pardon Tales and Their Tellers in Sixteenth-Century France* (Stanford, CA: Stanford University Press, 1987). For another example in a colonial setting, see Ann Laura Stoler, "In Cold Blood: Hierarchies of Credibility and the Politics of Colonial Narratives," *Representations* 37 (1992): 151–189. Daniel James is one of the first to apply systematically the technique of narrative structure analysis to modern Latin American social history. See his *Doña María's Story: Life History, Memory, and Political Identity* (Durham, NC: Duke University Press, 2002). See also *The Gendered Worlds of Latin American Women Workers: From Household and Factory to the Union Hall and Ballot Box*, ed. John D. French and Daniel James (Durham, NC: Duke University Press, 1997). Essays in French and James's volume focus on the narrative structure of oral storytelling and interviews, however, not on the production of written documents in a judicial setting.
3   See Archivo General de Puerto Rico [henceforth AGPR], Ponce, Judicial [henceforth Jud.], Criminales [henceforth Crim.], box 19, "Por rapto de Ercilia Reyes," Sept. 10, 1896, for plebeian youths' wonderfully rich description of their methods of flirtation, courtship, and preparation of "marital space" prior to running off together.
4   Title 9, chap. 5, art. 465; and title 13, chap. 1, arts. 261–262 in *Código penal para las islas de Cuba y Puerto Rico* (Madrid: Góngora, 1886). The first Spanish colonial penal code written specifically for Puerto Rico was approved in 1848 and reformed two years later. A second penal code, which would stand until the United States took over colonial

control of the island in 1898, was penned in 1870 by Liberals in Spain and reformed in 1879 in an effort to incorporate the abolition of slavery in Puerto Rico. Ibid., 5–17.

5   These tenets emerge clearly from the testimony of witnesses in the hundreds of slander, *rapto*, and rape cases that survived from the nineteenth century. Accusations of sexual promiscuity or infidelity were the most common insults slung at women in attempts to dishonor them. The dominant honor code's requirements for women are also laid out in *Código penal*, title 9, chaps. 1, 2, and 5.

6   For examples, see AGPR, Jud., Ponce, Crim., box 23, *Tomo de sentencias, 4° trimestre de 1893*; AGPR, Jud., Ponce, Crim., box 19, "Por rapto de Inés Serna Lugo contra Juan de la Cruz Lugo conocido por Baerga," 1896; and AGPR, Jud., Ponce, Crim., box 21, "Sobre rapto de Daniela Colón y Collazo, dicen Vásquez, contra Juan Enrique Colón," 1897.

7   See, e.g., AGPR, Jud., Ponce, Crim., box 6, "Violación contra Juan Concepción Velásquez," 1890; and AGPR, Jud., Ponce, Crim., box 66, *Sentencias dictadas el segundo trimestre*, 1891, rulings 138 and 154.

8   AGPR, Jud., Ponce, Crim., box 66, *Sentencias dictadas el segundo trimestre*, 1891, ruling 154. See also AGPR, Jud., Ponce, Crim., ruling 138; and AGPR, Jud., Ponce, Crim., box 6, *Minutas de sentencias del año 1890*, ruling 164.

9   Martha de Abreu Esteves finds a similar trend in early republican Brazil, when increased attention to "scientific" definitions of women's virginity resulted in more rigid moral categorizations by the courts. *Meninas perdidas*, 15–16, 19–34.

10 See AGPR, Jud., Ponce, Crim., box 42, *Tomo de sentencias, 4° trimestre de 1892*, ruling 316; and AGPR, Jud. Ponce, Crim., box 66, *Minutas de sentencias de 1889*, "Por rapto contra José Rosendo Troche y Serrano." Of the 211 surviving *rapto* cases from the nineteenth century, 50 percent included no mention of how long the parents had waited to file their complaint. Forty-six percent of all parents went to court within a week of the *rapto*; the remaining 4 percent filed after waiting several months or longer.

11 Eileen J. Suárez Findlay, *Imposing Decency: The Politics of Sexuality and Race in Puerto Rico, 1870–1920* (Durham, NC: Duke University Press, 1999), 18–52.

12 See ibid. for a detailed analysis of the various codes of honor circulating in late-nineteenth-century Puerto Rico's coastal regions. For a contrasting study, see Sueann Caulfield's essay in this volume, where she finds that plebeian women in Rio de Janeiro consistently preferred marriage but were willing to settle for consensual union.

13 AGPR, Jud., Ponce, Crim., box 19, "Por rapto de Inés Serna Lugo," June 14, 1896.

14 AGPR, Jud., Ponce, Crim., box 100, "Sobre rapto de Ramona Carabello," 1902; see also AGPR, Jud., Ponce, Crim., box 24, *Tomo de sentencias, febrero a septiembre de 1894*, ruling 219; AGPR, Jud., Ponce, Crim., box 38, "Sobre rapto de Teresa Astacio," 1894; AGPR, Jud., Ponce, Crim., box 50, "Por rapto de Martina Santiago," 1897.

15 Lillian Guerra provides rich material on workingmen's fascination with and fear of women's sexual powers in *Popular Expression and National Identity in Puerto Rico: The Struggle for Community, Self, and Nation* (Gainesville: University Press of Florida, 1998), 248–264.

16 AGPR, Jud., Ponce, Crim., box 105, "Contra Manuel Pato sobre rapto de Lorenza Torres Rivera," 1900.

17 AGPR, Jud., Ponce, Crim., box 91, "Sobre rapto de Dolores Rivera," 1886; AGPR, Jud., Ponce, Crim., box 31, "Sobre rapto de Juana Lugo," 1888; "Por rapto contra José Rosendo Troche y Serrano," 1889; AGPR, Jud., Ponce, Crim., box 14, [no formal title;

rapto proceedings against Don Miguel Santiago], 1893; AGPR, Jud., Ponce, Crim., box 50, "Por rapto de Martina Santiago," 1897; and "Sobre rapto de Daniela Colón y Collazo," 1897.

18 "Sobre rapto de Daniela Colón y Collazo," 1897. Daniela's assertion of virginal purity apparently carried more weight than her claim to sexual agency, aided by her boyfriend's claim of having seduced her.

19 "Por rapto contra José Rosendo Trochey Serrano," 1889; see also "Sobre rapto de Dolores Rivera," 1886; AGPR, Jud., Ponce, Crim., box 48, "Sobre rapto de Dolores Vega," 1895; AGPR, Jud., Ponce, Crim., box 66, *Audiencia de Ponce, sección segunda, minutas de sentencias, 1889*, minute 88, Oct. 28, 1889; AGPR, Jud., Ponce, Crim., box 26, *Audiencia de lo Criminal de Ponce, sentencias dictadas en el primer trimestre de 1892*, "Por el delito de violación contra Juan Miguel Ortiz Padilla," ruling 71; AGPR, Fondo de Gobernadores Españoles, box 145, Juan Bautista Rivera to governor of Puerto Rico, Nov. 11, 1862; AGPR, Ponce, Jud., Crim., box 2, "Contra Juana Garay Hernández sobre hurto de dinero y ropa a Olivorio Garay," case 1711, 1894. In her essay in this volume, Sueann Caulfield finds a similar pattern in Brazilian deflowering cases.

20 *Código penal*, title 9, chap. 2, art. 453.

21 The judicial record is replete with instances of men defending the honor of "wronged" female relatives. These were consistently classified as "riñas" between men, however, not as rape or sexual assault cases. Steve J. Stern notes this pattern in colonial Mexico as well in *The Secret History of Gender: Women, Men, and Power in Late Colonial Mexico* (Chapel Hill: University of North Carolina Press, 1995), 55–58. For a few examples, see AGPR, Jud., Ponce, Crim., box 28, "Sobre lesiones a Miguel Fernández," 1880; AGPR, Jud., Ponce, Crim., *Tomo de la Audiencia de lo Criminal de Ponce, minutas de sentencias de año 1890*, "Lesiones contra Juan Domingo Martínez y González," ruling 26.

22 AGPR, Jud., Ponce, Crim., box 31, "Sobre violación de Salomé Gonzalez," 1887.

23 See AGPR, Jud., Ponce, Crim., box 9, "Sobre tentativa de violación de la niña Antonia Gonzalez," 1888; AGPR, Jud., Ponce, Crim., box 9, "Contra Ramón Rodríguez (a) El Indio y Simón Santos sobre tentativa de violación el 1° y lesiones el 2°," 1886; AGPR, Jud., Ponce, Crim., box 42, "Por delito de violación a Juana Montalvo," ruling 372, 1892; AGPR, Jud., Ponce, Crim., box 27, "Sobre violación de María Margarita Marcucci," 1885.

24 AGPR, Jud., Ponce, Crim., box 26, *Audiencia de lo Criminal de Ponce, sentencias dictadas en el primer trimestre de 1892*, "Contra Ramón Rodríguez," 1886; see also "Por el delito de violación contra Juan Miguel Ortiz Padilla," ruling 71; AGPR, Jud., Ponce, Crim., box 2, "Tentativa de violación contra Carlos Muñoz," case 676, roll 847, June 8, 1897; AGPR, Jud., Ponce, Crim., box 27, "Sobre violación de María Margarita Marcucci," 1885.

25 "Sobre violación de María Margarita Marcucci," 1885; "Sobre tentativa de violación de la niña Antonia González," 1888.

26 "Sobre violación de Salomé González," 1887; "Sobre tentativa de violación de la niña Antonia González," 1888; AGPR, Jud., Ponce, Crim., box 14, "No hay procesado," 1899; AGPR, Jud., Ponce, Crim., box 43, "Declaración de Cecilia Rodríguez" (loose leaf), 1904; AGPR, Jud., Ponce, Crim., box 92, "El pueblo de Puerto Rico vs. Eladio Maldonado, por violación," 1907.

27 "Por delito de violación a Juana Montalvo," ruling 372, 1892; "El pueblo de Puerto

Rico vs. Eladio Maldonado, por violación," 1907; AGPR, Jud., Ponce, Crim., box 27, "Sobre violación de María Margarita Marcucci," 1885.

28   "Sobre violación de Salomé Gonzalez," 1887; AGPR, Jud., Ponce, Crim., box 14, "No hay procesado," 1899; "Declaración de Cecilia Rodríguez" (loose leaf), 1904; "El pueblo de Puerto Rico vs. Eladio Maldonado, por violación," 1907; "Sobre tentativa de violación de la niña Antonia González," 1888; "Contra Ramón Rodríguez," 1886; "Por delito de violación a Juana Montalvo," ruling 372, 1892; "Sobre violación de María Margarita Marcucci," 1885.

29   "Sobre violación de Salomé González," 1887; "Contra Ramón Rodríguez," 1886.

30   AGPR, Jud., Ponce, Crim., box 14, "Sobre amenaza y hurto contra no hay procesado," 1899; "Sobre violación de Salomé González," 1887; "Sobre tentativa de violación de la niña Antonia González," 1888; "El pueblo de Puerto Rico vs. Eladio Maldonado, por violación," 1907; "Por delito de violación a Juana Montalvo," ruling 372, 1892. See also "Declaración de Cecilia Rodríguez" (loose leaf), 1904; and "Sobre violación de María Margarita Marcucci," 1885.

31   "Sobre violación de María Margarita Marcucci," 1885; "Sobre tentativa de violación de la niña Antonia González," 1888; "Sobre amenaza y hurto contra no hay procesado," 1899; "Declaración de Cecilia Rodríguez" (loose leaf), 1904.

32   AGPR, Jud., Ponce, Crim., box 26, *Audiencia de lo Criminal de Ponce, sentencias dictadas en el primer trimestre de 1892*, "Por el delito de violación contra Juan Miguel Ortiz Padilla," ruling 71.

33   "Por delito de violación a Juana Montalvo," ruling 372, 1892.

34   AGPR, Jud., Ponce, Crim., box 6, *Tomo de la Audiencia de lo Criminal de Ponce, minutas de sentencias del año 1890*, "Violación contra Juan Concepción Velásquez," ruling 164; AGPR, Jud., Ponce, Crim., box 66, *Audiencia de lo Criminal de Ponce, sentencias dictadas el segundo trimestre, 1891*, ruling 138; AGPR, Jud., Ponce, Crim., box 42, *Tomo de la Audiencia de lo Criminal de Ponce, sentencias de 1892*, ruling 372; AGPR, Jud., Ponce, Crim., box 14, "Sobre amenaza y hurto contra no hay procesado," 1899.

35   "Sobre violación de Salomé González," 1887. Ramón Rodríguez was also acquitted, notwithstanding the testimony of several men who saw him threatening Rufina Santiago with a knife and forcibly holding her down in her bed. The magistrate had seen no proof that Rodríguez was attempting specifically to rape her, "especially considering that he was inebriated." "Contra Ramón Rodríguez," 1886.

36   See, e.g., AGPR, Jud., Ponce, Crim., box 38, "Delito: Violación de la jóven Guadalupe Rosa contra Luciano Alcántara," 1896; AGPR, Jud., Ponce, Crim., box 13, "Contra Angel Santoni sobre violación de Lorenza Pardo y Rivera," 1902; AGPR, Jud., Ponce, Crim., box 102, "Violación de Hemeteria Cruz," 1900; and AGPR, Jud., Ponce, Crim., box 102, "Contra Andrés Nieves Serrano, preso, sobre violación de Juana Teodora Pérez y Torres," 1900.

The changing politics of freedom and virginity
in Rio de Janeiro, 1920–1940
Sueann Caulfield

In 1898, Francisco Viveiros de Castro attributed what he perceived to be a recent increase in crimes against the honor of women to the changes brought by turn-of-the-century urban life. Referring to Brazil's capital city, Rio de Janeiro, where he sat as judge, Viveiros de Castro complained that factory work and "modern upbringing" were leading women from "the silent intimacy of the home" and exposing them to "all kinds of seduction." The rise of new attitudes among women was the most damaging effect of these changes. The "modern woman," he warned, "dominated by the erroneous, subversive idea of her emancipation . . . does all she can to lose the respect, the esteem and the consideration of men."[1]

To some nostalgic jurists in Rio in the 1920s and 1930s, however, Viveiros de Castro's era seemed one of innocence, a time when women were "zealously preserved in ignorance of the evils of the world."[2] Judges needed to adapt the 1890 penal code to the realities of their day, according to post–World War I legal authorities such as Judge Nelson Hungria, because "the modern social environment, with its leniency and licentiousness, presents us with a very different type of young woman than that of a half-century ago."[3] Yet the "modern women" he described would have sounded familiar to Viveiros de Castro. "Modern girls," Hungria explained, "have participated actively at the vortex of daily life, spreading out into offices, public buildings, and commercial establishments, and they have thus lost that feminine reserve that was their greatest enchantment. . . . They removed themselves from the vigilance and discipline of the family and became precocious in the science of sexual mystery."[4]

Apart from the occupational classification of "modern women"—factory hands in Viveiros de Castro's day, white-collar workers forty years later—the rhetoric of these prominent representatives of two generations of jurists on the lost innocence of independent working women is strikingly similar. Yet although both judges were writing about the need for new guidelines to distinguish between honest and dishonest women in trials of sexual crime, they diverged sharply on the criteria for such guidelines. For Viveiros de Castro, it was imperative that the courts defend what he considered the civilized moral standards upheld in the 1890 penal code. Hungria, however nostalgically, expressed the consensus among jurists of the 1930s that the 1890 code must be repealed because its moral concepts were antiquated. In 1939 he led a juridical commission that wrote the final draft of Brazil's new penal code of 1940, which dramatically redefined family honor and sexual crimes.

The ways that witnesses, victims, and defendants described honest, dishonest, and commonplace behavior in the cases that came before both Viveiros de Castro's and Hungria's courts suggest that working-class young women of the post–World War I period were not, in fact, radically different from women of preceding generations. To a great extent, their values and attitudes were compatible with longstanding popular social practices such as premarital sexual relations, consensual unions, and female-headed households. But although their lifestyles and morals were not so very different from those of their mothers or grandmothers, the context in which their behavior was interpreted *had* changed radically, in ways that explain why jurists such as Hungria were even more uncertain than their predecessors about how the courts should defend sexual honor.

The city of Rio de Janeiro underwent more than political transformation when the Brazilian emperor was overthrown and a republic established in 1889. The abolition of slavery one year earlier, which precipitated the crisis of the empire, also helped to accelerate long-term demographic, social, and cultural changes. In particular, migration from the countryside, European immigration, the resulting population boom, and the intense economic fluctuations of the early decades of the twentieth century contributed to greater individual autonomy and mobility in the city, and to a general sense of instability. Contemporaries frequently blamed this instability on the dissolution of the family and traditional morals.

As Cristiana Schettini Pereira demonstrates in this volume, a massive urban renewal project begun in 1902 did little to abate elite preoccupation with social mixing and moral decay, as poor residents, including prostitutes and pimps, continued to occupy the noble areas of down-town Rio for work and leisure. Downtown commerce and services ex-panded after the renovation, and women from increasingly varied socio-economic strata joined the wage-labor force and mixed in the streets all over the city, filling not just the factory floors of Viveiros de Castro's era but also the shops and offices that Hungria mentions.[5]

The broad social and economic changes that preoccupied Viveiros de Castro and Hungria were uneven and took place over several de-cades, which might explain why the two men held similar impressions of modern women. In the immediate post–World War I period, how-ever, fashion, leisure, the labor market, and the communications media were swiftly and dramatically transformed, leading Hungria and his con-temporaries all over the Western world to perceive their era as one of unprecedented changes in gender norms.[6] The term "modern woman" in the 1920s connoted not just a factory hand or shop clerk but a flap-per—a racy, flirtatious, assertive, androgynous figure that emerged as part of an irreverent Western youth culture. She arrived as part of a new flood of foreign films, music, and other consumer goods that washed over the Brazilian market after the First World War. Her first appearance was on the movie screens; later, she populated jazz clubs and *dancings*, as the new U.S.-style popular dance halls were called, then public beaches, and then downtown shops and offices. Much of the concern about her in Brazil echoed a similar discourse in Europe and the United States: she symbolized the technological and cultural transformations of the new century and, most important, defied the male dominance and bour-geois family values that had seemed to cement an earlier social order.[7] Brazilian versions of this discourse, however, reflected broader conflicts over the nation's cultural identity and political and economic future. Was this modern woman a welcome symbol of Brazil's youthful and cosmo-politan modernity? Or did she represent Brazil's lamentable mimicry of European decadence? Did she incarnate a uniquely Brazilian blending of the cultures of different social and racial groups or the degeneration of Brazil's traditional family values, contaminated by the nation's lowest elements?

Although "modern women" occupied a large space in the public imagi-nation, both Viveiros de Castro's turn-of-the-century factory workers and the "office girls" of Hungria's times were a small, privileged minority of the female labor force. Most workingwomen continued to perform low-paid informal and domestic labor throughout the twentieth century, and it was these women who were most likely to go to the police with complaints of sexual offenses. Yet those who appeared in Rio's courtrooms took advantage of the new meanings that could be attached to women's employment, leisure activities, and independence in order to position themselves advantageously in conflicts of various kinds. In this sense, both jurists were correct when they complained that the women they observed played a major role in transforming popular and even legal notions of virginity and honor.

Sexual Conflicts in Rio de Janeiro Courts

Although Hungria and his colleagues believed that modern women's "excessive liberty" in the nation's capital had subverted traditional notions of virginity, they could not deny that popular recourse to the law in cases of its loss remained extremely important. Far from a remnant of the past, deflowering complaints poured into local police stations at a higher rate than complaints of any other sexual crime up until the 1970s. They were, in fact, among the most frequent criminal complaints of any type through the 1940s, outnumbered only by physical assault and robbery.[8]

This study is based on records of 450 police investigations and trials of sexual crimes in Rio de Janeiro from 1918 to 1940, most of which began with a deflowering complaint. The young women who appeared in these cases interpreted their relationships with boyfriends and with their own families in ways that reflected a variety of new images of appropriate female comportment. Nonetheless, the general characteristics of records of sexual crimes had remained the same since at least the turn of the century.[9] Deflowering a woman between the ages of fifteen and twenty-one was a crime if the man employed "seduction, deceit, or fraud." If the girl was younger than fifteen or if the man used force, the crime was considered rape. Very few cases involving simple force were reported, and almost none involved rape by a stranger. Instead, relationships between the offended parties and the men they accused ranged from casual acquaintance to formal engagement. Their personal conflicts ended up at the police stations for various reasons: the man abandoned the young woman after deflowering her; gossip about the deflowering began to circulate in the neighborhood; the young woman's parent or employer found out about the deed; the couple ran away together; the young woman became pregnant. Virtually all the families that appealed to the police to resolve conflicts over young women's loss of virginity were of humble means; most were headed by mothers. The proposed resolution of most of these predicaments was marriage, which almost all the deflowered young women, whether spontaneously or after prompting by the police, claimed their deflowerers had promised them.

The mothers and daughters who testified in these cases did indeed challenge the notions of virginity and family honor that jurists such as Hungria considered "traditional." At the same time, however, they preserved or recast traditions that made these notions meaningful in their own lives. Jurists responded to the women they encountered in their courtrooms, as well as those they saw on the streets, at the movies, and presumably in their own homes, as they debated how to redefine the legal defense of female honor.

The Disputed Boundaries of Female Honor and Male Obligation

Men accused of deflowering consistently recognized and used the notion, well supported in Federal District jurisprudence, that independent, modern women were not honest and did not deserve men's respect or the protection of the court. Many defendants admitted having had sex with their accusers, and all seemed to agree that a man who took an honest girl's virginity had a responsibility to "repair the damage" through marriage. They refused to do so, however, on the grounds that the young women had either lost their virginity previously or misbehaved in ways that relieved the men from this responsibility: frequenting dance halls and clubs in their absence or attending parties or Carnival festivities without their permission.[10]

In several cases, young men admitted to a sexual relationship but insisted that they had believed that the young women in question were "liberated" or free of the close supervision that honest families maintained over virgin daughters. In 1923, for example, thirty-two-year-old textile worker Sebastião Almeida, claiming his relationship with Deolinda da Glória Nunes was purely sexual and involved no commitments of any kind, explained that he had believed Deolinda was "entirely liberated," for although she was frequently out with him in the evening, "he never heard of any complaints from her family, whose duty it would be to forbid these outings if she were, in fact, a minor and a virgin."[11] Similarly, in 1936 Severino de Souza Ferreira claimed that he had assumed that his girlfriend was not honest because "he always had total liberty with Maria, whether to go to the movies . . . or to Carnival festivities."[12]

These cases make clear that a single man was expected to be free to enjoy leisure activities that marked a woman as dishonest. More significant, when witnesses said that a young man "enjoyed a great deal of freedom in the young woman's home," or that a girl's parents gave him "liberty to go out with her," it meant that the man was considered honorable and deserving of the parents' trust. Statements of this kind were often made by witnesses for the prosecution, who condemned the man for betraying this trust.[13] Thus, whereas a young woman's honesty was contingent on her submission to the vigilance of her family, a man's honor was recognized when he was no longer subject to such vigilance, but imposed it himself.

While some men defined their responsibility to their partners as contingent on the women's obedience or deferential public conduct, deflowering cases demonstrate that men were also preoccupied with what jurists disparagingly referred to as "material virginity"—that is, an intact hymen—as opposed to "moral virginity," or a virtuous character.[14] Deflowered young women frequently claimed that they had consented to sex because their fiancés had demanded "proof of virginity" as a condition for marriage, and sometimes the men confirmed these claims. In a typical scenario, Theonilia Maria Vieira's fiancé took her to a dark alleyway in 1935 and "proposed that she let him deflower her, with the allegation that only thus would he marry her, because he wanted to be certain that she was a virgin." Apparently unsure of his commitment, Theonilia filed a deflowering complaint at the local police station the next morning. Her boyfriend, arrested and interrogated on the same day, confirmed her account and then proceeded to marry her, thus putting an end to the case.[15]

Of course, harmonious accounts and happy endings are not common characteristics of conflicts narrated in criminal records. More frequently, the woman claimed she gave her fiancé the proof he demanded, but the man countered that he "verified that she was not a virgin" by having sex with her. Most men appeared quite confident of their verification techniques. The defendant in a 1921 case, for example, declared that he would marry the offended woman if the medical examination confirmed recent defloration, "but he knew it would not because he found her quite wide [*bastante larga*]."[16] Twenty-year-old Severino de Oliveira, on the other hand, seemed less certain. There was "something strange" about his sexual encounter with his eighteen-year-old girlfriend that made him think she was no longer a virgin.[17] Her mother's police complaint apparently helped him overcome his doubt, for the couple married before the case went to court.

Working-class women acknowledged the importance of virginity in determining their marriage prospects. This was expressed clearly in the case against Antonio Ramos, a thirty-year-old textile worker accused of deflowering his cousin, twenty-one-year-old Olívia Ramos, in 1927. Olívia's mother, Elvira Rosa Ramos, explained the situation: "Her daughter had been courted for the past year by Luiz Sinhorelli, who recently wanted to marry Olívia; . . . only then was Olívia obliged to confess to the declarant that she couldn't marry Sinhorelli because her cousin and the declarant's nephew Antonio Ramos, one year ago, had deflowered Olívia."[18]

Seventeen-year-old Jandyra Marinho also found a suitor after she was deflowered but "did not take him seriously, as she knew she could not marry him since she had already been deflowered." In all three cases, the suitors rescinded their marriage proposals when they heard their fiancées' confessions and appeared in court only as witnesses against the accused deflowerers.[19]

Upon the discovery that their fiancées had been deflowered by another, a number of men took the attitude that although they intended to remain in the relationship indefinitely, formal marriage was no longer necessary. In 1922, for instance, twenty-eight-year-old Euzebio da Cunha "made a home" in which to live with fifteen-year-old Marietta Salles, with whom he later had two children. Two years later, when Marietta's father instigated a deflowering case against him, because "he hadn't fulfilled his promise to marry Marietta," Euzebio defended himself with the following story: "The first time he had sex with her he noted she was not a virgin, and on his severe interrogation, Marietta informed him that she had taken her own virginity by inserting a candle into her vagina; . . . he therefore resolved not to marry her but instead to live with her."[20] Similarly, in 1928, Almir Serra Cardosa declared that he decided not to marry his fiancée but to "live maritally" with her instead when he discovered that she had already been deflowered by her brother-in-law. His involvement with the police was limited to his testimony as a witness in the case against the brother-in-law.[21]

Even if their girlfriends were virgins, men frequently explained that they could not afford to marry and proposed to their girlfriends that they "live maritally" until they could. The civil marriage ceremony was free, but it could be difficult and expensive to obtain the necessary documents, such as notarized birth certificates and proof of age, residence, and the absence of impediments—not to mention the expense of a wedding party.[22] A more critical obstacle was the man's previous marriage, since divorce was not legal until 1977. Some deflowering victims claimed that the man lied to her about his marital status and deflowered her "under a promise of marriage," only later proposing a consensual union.[23] Other men told the truth from the start, but ended up at the police station because they failed to fulfill a promise to live together.[24]

As would be expected in records of this type, most of the young women involved expressed not only a desire for formal marriage but also the feeling that they were entitled to it in exchange for their virginity. Yet like the Puerto Rican victims of *rapto* (abduction and deflowering) analyzed by Eileen Findlay in this volume, many accepted consensual unions instead. In a letter to Rodrigo Noronha Filho, Jacy de Abreu Olinda—a nineteen-year-old domestic servant who claimed she was pregnant by Rodrigo—begged him not to abandon her because of the deflowering case her mother opened against him. "Don't blame me . . . the police made me sign the accusation. I don't want to marry you by force, and I know you didn't promise to marry me," she wrote. "I went to your room because I wanted to. Because I want to live with you. . . . I love you and I want to live with you." Jacy told the judge the same story, and Rodrigo was acquitted. The couple did not move in together, at least not by the time of the trial in 1936, one year after Jacy wrote the letter. This is not surprising, since Rodrigo insisted that although he had been having sex with Jacy every Sunday for several months, he "always assumed she was a woman without commitments, because she went to night clubs by herself."[25]

Eighteen-year-old Isabel de Oliveira, also a domestic servant, seems to have had a happier experience. She explained to police that she had allowed her boyfriend, a railroad conductor, to deflower her because he promised to marry her but that after she moved in with him, "the hardships of life" kept him from keeping the promise. After five months, her mother grew impatient and filed a deflowering complaint, but Isabel told the judge that "she resigned herself to this explanation and continues living with the defendant and even prefers this situation to marriage."[26] There were also cases in which the young woman moved in with the defendant after filing the initial police complaint and was no longer interested in prosecuting when the case came to trial, sometimes many months or even years later.[27]

Since young women often accepted consensual unions in lieu of marriage, or while waiting for marriage, it is not surprising that several deflowering complainants stated that they had "given in" sexually because the defendant had promised to "live maritally" with them, apparently considering this contract binding.[28] Judges and prosecutors were especially unsympathetic to these grievances. Yet in accepting both consensual unions and the idea that sexual relations and cohabitation were justified by a promise of formal or informal marriage, the people who testified in deflowering cases were following patterns prevalent in Brazil as well as in most other Latin American nations since the colonial period.[29]

Laws regarding marriage and sexual crimes aimed precisely at curbing informal conjugal relationships. Parents also preferred legal marriage to informal unions for their daughters. But although parents protested when their daughters consented to informal arrangements or when the man dallied in collecting the paperwork to formalize them, they generally seemed to accept the situation once it was in place. Indeed, many of the parents and witnesses who testified that the offended girl was honest and therefore deserving of marriage were themselves living in consensual unions. In several cases couples "lived maritally" in the woman's family's home after her defloration, usually with the understanding that marriage would follow. Generally, the cases of consensual unions reached the police not because of problems inherent in this arrangement but because of a crisis in the relationship: the man abandoned the woman, became engaged to another, or argued with his "mother-in-law."

In these cases, as in *rapto* trials in Puerto Rico, parents generally demanded marriage in an attempt to guarantee their daughter's and grandchildren's economic stability. Yet if consensual unions could be transient or stable, the same was true of formal marriage. Despite state attempts to mandate the indissolubility of marriage—including a constitutional provision upholding indissoluble marriage after 1934—spouses commonly separated, formally or informally, and lived with subsequent partners. According to the attorney general of the state of Rio de Janeiro in 1942, fraudulent marriage annulments were also commonly granted in the 1930s, and presumably earlier, resulting in "a truly unique situation: the common practice of *divorce by mutual consent*—something that does not exist in any civilized nation."[30] Moreover, the notion that virginity was required of women for marriage, but not consensual union, was belied by the fact that innumerable women married someone other than the man they publicly accused of deflowering them, provoking a prolonged legal debate over whether prosecution should proceed nonetheless.[31]

The distance, then, between formal and informal marriage was not as great as lawmakers assumed. Nonetheless, there is no question that deflowered girls, and especially their mothers, were aware that formal marriage brought distinct advantages, and that virginity was an important resource. Teenaged girls mobilized this resource toward a variety of ends.

"Desires Similar to Those of the Man": Sensuality and Struggles for Authority in the Testimony of Deflowered Girls

Like defendants and their lawyers, offended women and their families linked women's liberty to their sexual experience, frequently insisting that the young women were strictly supervised and "not permitted any liberty" as evidence of their virginity.[32] What liberty meant, however, was not always clear. For example, when a lawyer tried to establish the victim's lack of moral guidance in a 1940 case by asking whether she was given "liberty" to go out alone, her grandmother answered in puzzlement, "that of course Maria had permission to go out alone because she had to work."[33] This lawyer's strategy was unsuccessful. In a city in which women were increasingly absorbed into the urban labor force, few still held the nineteenth-century notion that a virgin girl would never venture out onto the street unaccompanied.

Women's participation in public leisure was more problematic. Some young women were apparently not aware that unchaperoned excursions to dance halls, movie houses, or Carnival festivities, or rides on streetcars or even automobiles with girlfriends or boyfriends were signs of excessive liberties that put their family's morality and their own virginity into question, for their testimony is full of such excursions. Frequently, the excursions were made possible by attracting a young man who could pay the way. The young women, and their witnesses, countered accusations of "excessive liberty" with alternative interpretations of the women's actions, and often of common working- and middle-class leisure. "Esther's Carnival costume did not demonstrate a lack of honesty," one witness protested, "but merely a lack of good judgment, childishness," and the Carnival "block" she danced with "did not practice excesses that would blemish the honor of the young ladies."[34] A distraught father justified his daughter's unchaperoned outings with her deflowerer by explaining that "he was intimate with [the boy's] family."[35] A mother explained that her daughter "amused herself by going to the movies, like the other girls from the neighborhood."[36]

But although deflowering victims did not hide the ways that their daily lives provided a wide margin for independence and even assertiveness, they were especially careful to downplay their own sexual freedom, describing their role as submissive and often explaining that they had "given in" to their deflowerers only under coercion—he would marry her only on this condition; if she refused, it was because she didn't truly love or trust him; or, most commonly, he would marry her only after "verifying that she was a virgin." Although few cases of simple rape are recorded, many young women complained that their deflowerers had used physical force, combined with a marriage promise or other means of seduction, to overcome their resistance. Indeed, from the way sex is frequently described by young women in these cases, male aggressiveness, and even violence, must have been widely considered to be a common, or at least potential, feature of heterosexual relations. But if one reads beyond the young women's reiterated descriptions of themselves as passive victims of male passion and their own incredulity, it is possible to detect varied and complex motives for their actions.

Increasingly over the course of the 1920s and 1930s, offended women's testimony contained a new language of sexual arousal—descriptions of caresses and words that excited them physically as well as emotionally—in addition to the older references to passivity or violence. This, together with descriptions of unconventional positions (young women seated atop or standing in front of their partners, for instance) contradicted the images of passivity that were constructed in the same testimony.[37] Yet sexual desire rarely seemed to be the sole factor that influenced their decision to give up their virginity.

In 5 percent of the cases consulted, the women had sex with their boyfriends in order to force their parents to accept a forbidden relationship, a strategy common in the Puerto Rican *rapto* cases Findlay studies and in colonial litigation throughout Latin America.[38] Although by law parental consent was required for marriage of those younger than twenty-one regardless of virginal status, conventional wisdom was that parents lost authority over their daughters upon the girls' defloration. In fact, all of these cases were resolved by the marriage of the victim to the accused.

The symbolic sexual "possession" of a woman by a man took a concrete form in these cases, as men who "possessed" a virgin woman sexually took authority over her away from her parents. "To possess" in the sexual sense was an explicitly gendered verb: men "possessed" women, never vice versa. Brazilian law legitimized this "possession." Legally women remained under the tutelage of their fathers, who represented them in all legal or business matters, until the age of twenty-one; when a woman married, this authority passed to her husband, regardless of her age. But while in theory those contending for authority were always male, the cases consulted suggest that in practice conflicts of authority involving a girl's loss of virginity usually involved female protagonists on both sides. The mother was the major authority figure for most of the young women involved. Fathers appeared to file charges, often accompanied by mothers, in only 27 percent of the cases.

Single mothers were a favorite target for lawyers seeking to denigrate deflowering victims by arguing that they lived free of the constraints that honest families placed on their women. When Magdalena Teixeira Alves brought the soldier Urbano Rodrigues to court over the deflowering of her seventeen-year-old daughter Arlette in 1936, for example, Rodrigues's lawyer argued that Arlette's downfall was entirely her mother's fault. By separating from her husband and relocating her family from a small town to Rio de Janeiro, Magdalena Alves had both broken the law and thrown her daughter into "a life of dangerous liberty."[39] Indeed, it was preposterous for her to defend her daughter's honor "as if the greater honor, that of the family, were not already destroyed to its foundations by the irregular situation [of the mother]." To proceed with the case, the lawyer argued, would set "a dangerous precedent, disrespecting the explicit imperatives of the law, and would also take from the man, head of the family, the traditional prerogatives that are attributed to him in Society, from remote times."[40] The judge in this case agreed that Magdalena Alves was "an amorphous entity," a nonperson who was legally incapable of defending herself or her family, and he declared her complaint invalid.

This was a perfectly sound decision; in fact, civil law mandated that husbands represent their wives and children in commercial and legal transactions. Yet invalidation of deflowering cases on the grounds that the mother was not the legitimate legal representative of her daughter was rare. In one case, police officials sent a mother home to get her spouse so as to avoid an outcome like that of Magdalena Alves's, but in sixteen others, women who were married to and living with their daughters' fathers successfully filed complaints.[41] The same was true of eleven of the eighteen mothers who declared that they were married to but separated from their daughters' fathers.[42] These women were evidently not aware that their marriages made them "amorphous entities." To the contrary: regardless of their marital status, mothers commonly acted as heads of their families and guardians of their daughters' honor both in and out of court. At least in the cases recorded in criminal records, mothers rarely depended on male protectors but took action themselves—interrogating their daughters' deflowerers, demanding some sort of settlement (usually a marriage promise), and going to the police to seal the agreement or when the promise was not kept.

We might suspect that the prevalence of female-headed families in these cases reflects men's preference to defend their family's honor personally, through violence or suasion, rather than rely on public authorities.[43] Yet evidence of direct action by fathers is sparse. Stories of fathers' violence against deflowerers appeared in the press but only occasionally, and the scenario was seldom pondered in the juridical literature. Deflowering records suggest instead that mothers were protagonists even when men were present. Magdalena Alves's son, for example, reported that his mother sent him out to look for his sister's deflowerer and question him about his intentions. Even the fathers who filed police complaints often testified that their wives or partners had learned of the deflowering and advised them on how to proceed.

Adolescent daughters sometimes used the ideology that demanded their submission to family vigilance in rebellions against authority—often that of their mothers. Since much of the discipline imposed on young women was justified as the defense of their sexual honor, which required the preservation of virginity, many came to view the rupture of their hymens as liberating.

The complaint filed in 1929 by Honorina da Silva Gonçalves, mother of Esmarina Maria Gonçalves, an eighteen-year-old black factory worker, is revealing:

> on the morning of March 5, the declarant was at home, as was her daughter Esmarina, [who] for a trifling reason responded rudely to a comment made by the declarant; . . . the declarant therefore said to her daughter that she was obliged to obey her until she got married; . . . Esmarina responded that all she had to do was leave with Urbano, because "she was already his"; . . . the declarant, suspicious of these phrases from Esmarina, submitted her to a rigorous interrogation, obtaining the confession from her that she had been deflowered by Urbano.[44]

In this and many other cases, the major conflict was not between "victim" and "accused" but rather between parents or guardians and daughters. After "rigorous interrogation," sometimes accompanied by beatings, many parents went to the police and filed complaints that seem to be retaliation as much against their daughter as against her deflowerer. In several cases, angry parents accused their daughters of sexual misconduct when family conflicts flared, often over daughters' courtship choices.[45]

When the need to protect virginity was eliminated, many of the restrictions imposed on young women were no longer justified. Nineteen-year-old Georgina Medeiros was clear on this point. In 1935 Georgina ran away from home, only to be found later in the afternoon by her father. According to her father's testimony, Georgina told him "that she had left home because she considered herself to be entirely free, because she had been deflowered by an individual by the name of Amaro Cavalcanti."[46] In her own testimony, Georgina explained further that "desiring to get away from her mother . . . she informed her mother of her state as a deflowered woman [*seu estado de mulher deflorada*], because her mother refused to allow a single girl to live far from her."[47]

Thus deflowering victims did not necessarily present themselves as subjugated or enslaved once "possessed" by a man. Rather, this "possession" might symbolize liberation and a breaking of bonds of dependence. This is not to idealize sexual freedom or to claim that independence, particularly economic independence, always resulted from liberated sexual behavior. Contraceptive use was limited (though mentioned in three cases), and it was extremely difficult for a young woman to support a family alone. Many lost their jobs when they became pregnant and continued living with their parents, with or without the fathers of their children. The difficulties of single parenthood were all too familiar for many of the girls' mothers, which explains in large part the urgency of mothers' attempts to force the deflowerers to marry their daughters. Nonetheless, by giving up her virginity, a young woman did increase her power to choose her survival strategy. This strategy might include marriage against her parents' or her partner's will or new status as a relatively autonomous adult within an extended family.

There is no evidence that Medeiros, Gonçalves, or other young deflowering victims were interested in jurists' debates about the relation between "modern life" and women's "excessive liberty." Their actions and choices were inspired by personal concerns. In making and explaining these choices, however, the girls responded to both historical precedents and new ideas about the freedom of "modern women" in ways that placed them at the center of public debates. Most significant, they cast themselves as independent and assertive women without accepting the dishonor that was supposed to accompany women's liberation.

More common than explicit demands for liberty, made by a few, was the less explicit insistence by most of the offended women that their daily activities were not dishonorable. They felt entitled to the respect of the men who accompanied them on the streets, in streetcars, and in the workplace; or who invited them to movies, dance halls, or for rides in taxicabs; or who convinced them to enter into sexual relationships and even consensual unions. In their behavior and in their sense of honor, these young women at once replicated the lives of their mothers and grandmothers and responded to new ways of occupying a rapidly changing city. They sought out new spaces of public leisure, appropriated some of the images about the "modern woman" they found there, and introduced a new language of liberty and desire into their affective and sexual relationships. At the same time, they continued traditional patterns of premarital sexual relations, consensual unions, and matrifocal family formation, as well as survival strategies and community networks centered on poor women's occupation of public space.

Given the generational conflict that is a central drama in many of the deflowering stories, it is ironic that the girls modeled themselves after their mothers and grandmothers in another way. The terms *moça* and *donzela*, literally "girl" or "young woman," both signified virgin in popular usage and implied puerility and dependence. In contrast, *mulher desvirginada* (non-virgin woman) signified an independent adult, with responsibilities and liberties not permitted a young virgin. This status, of course, could bring stigma and certain disadvantages. It was not, however, necessarily equated with the status of prostitute. In fact, it could be equated with their antithesis: mothers. Many young women, even if subconsciously, followed in their mothers' footsteps and chose the relative independence this status brought over the protection they could earn by preserving their virginity.

Like many of the mothers who defended their daughters' honor in court, these young women deviated from prescribed gender norms and attitudes, performing roles and expressing values that helped stretch the boundaries of what it meant to be a mother, an honest girl, and a free woman. By the late 1930s, jurists found themselves increasingly obliged to respond to these new boundaries in individual cases, as well as in their proposals for revising the provisions for the defense of family honor in the 1890 penal code.

The Marriage Promise or the Art of Don Juan?
The Adaptation of Legal Theory to Modern Women

Judges' decisions in cases of sexual crimes formed part of a vigorous legal debate on whether and how criminal law should defend female honesty and virginity, a debate that began with the very first juridical studies of the republican penal code of 1890. It intensified in the 1920s and 1930s as a result of changes in both gender norms and national politics. Over the course of these decades, countless individual judges and appeals court justices passed judgments that pushed jurisprudence in several directions, in many instances challenging the letter of the law. With the overthrow of the republican regime in 1930 by a loose coalition of progressive and conservative forces united in their opposition to what they saw as rule by a backward and self-serving regional oligarchy, the need for legal reform seemed especially critical. The new penal code of 1940 responded to jurists' demands to integrate "modern" legal concepts into criminal laws, especially those regarding honor and morality, while reaching something of a compromise on several points that jurists had debated during the previous decades.

Among the most important issues jurists debated was how to define virginity and "honest" female behavior and whether the law should defend the "minimal ethical standard" of any civilized society or the "average morality" of Brazil's population. None ever doubted, however, that lost virginity greatly reduced a single woman's chances of marriage and decent family life and that unmarried sexually active women threatened social order. These beliefs justified, among other measures, the criminalization of deflowering. The law punished deflowering, according to a frequently cited 1921 appeals decision, because loss of virginity obstructed a woman's "social function . . . in the legally and morally constituted family," leading her inevitably to prostitution.[48]

Jurists thus justified their intervention in the realm of morality by condemning sexual crimes as offenses against larger social institutions, not as physical assaults against individual citizens. The 1890 penal code, a conservative document according to contemporary jurists, had defined all sexual offenses as "crimes against the honor and honesty of the family." When progressive jurists who saw "family honor" as a symbol of antiliberal oligarchical power succeeded in eliminating the concept from the 1940 code, they redefined sexual offenses as crimes against social customs or morality (*costumes*). "Criminal law does not protect individual rights *per se*," wrote Hungria, explaining the organization of crimes under the new code, "but rather because and when they coincide with social and public interest."[49]

It remained in the public interest, according to the viewpoint that prevailed in the 1940 penal code, to protect women's physiological virginity. The question of how to define virginity, however—another issue that had provoked voluminous jurisprudential and scholarly tracts over the previous twenty years—remained murky. A virtual one-man campaign launched by a prominent legal-medical specialist, Afrânio Peixoto, in the 1920s had educated jurists on hymen morphology, showing that the absence of a rupture did not always reveal whether a woman had engaged in sexual intercourse. Peixoto also convinced most jurists, at least in theory, that "material virginity" was of negligible value in determining moral purity.[50] In recognition of this advance in scientific knowledge, the crime of "deflowering" was renamed "seduction" in the 1940 code.

Yet while ridiculing what they saw as the popular obsession with the hymen, and repeating that an intact membrane was not a foolproof sign of purity, jurists after 1940 still insisted that one ruptured outside marriage provided an entryway for moral corruption. The crime of seduction was thus defined as having sex with an underage virgin, and the courts continued to respond to popular complaints of stolen virginity that still flooded in through the next thirty years.

Not all sex with underage virgins was punishable. While judges generally agreed that physiological virginity was an important social and moral value, they disagreed on how to judge which girls deserved state protection when their virginity was lost. Should a judge dismiss a complaint by a young woman who displayed a physical desire for sex or who seemed to have enjoyed it? Was a promise of marriage the only possible means of deflowering an honest young woman? Did modern girls give up their "moral virginity"—even if they maintained intact hymens—by asserting independence, frequenting disreputable places of leisure, or dancing samba?

In a celebrated 1926 verdict, Judge Eurico Cruz answered these questions with a resounding "yes." Ruling against a young woman because she apparently felt sexual desire and sat atop her boyfriend on the occasion of her deflowering, Cruz explained that "it is inadmissible . . . that the woman . . . deny the normal passivity of her own sex . . . especially since, in the first sexual union, it is suffering, rather than pleasure, that she is due." He blamed the "modern social environment," particularly dance halls that played African-influenced music, for producing emancipated women whose virginity was worth little.[51]

Ten years later another Federal District judge passed a similar judgment regarding sensual modern girls in his acquittal of Fligialdo Gerson Lyrio, accused of seducing Antoinetta Gomes by promising to marry her. Finding the promise insufficiently "solemn," the judge argued: "Excepting . . . the case of a serious promise, of unquestionable commitment, the presumption that should be made from the fact [of the deflowering] is that, as long as normal people are involved, the woman gave in to the impulses of her instinct, to her sensuality, accepting all risks inherent in the sacrifice of her virginity."[52]

Though unsympathetic to Gomes's complaint, the judge expressed a new, significantly more benevolent attitude toward women's sexuality than had existed in earlier jurisprudence. Whereas turn-of-the-century jurists had denied that women possessed sexual desires, and judges such as Cruz in the 1920s had labeled such desires aberrant, this 1936 verdict described them as an instinctual impulse of "normal people."[53] The judge nonetheless upheld the precedent that women who "gave in" to that instinct should not be protected by law. He based his verdict on the understanding of criminal seduction as defined by the nineteenth-century Italian legal scholar Francesco Carrara: it was a crime to seduce a minor with a formal, public promise of marriage and then to break this promise after deflowering her, but girls who gave in to other, "vulgar" forms of seduction had none but themselves to blame. Some of the nation's most progressive jurists, including those who were called to draft two successive proposals for a new penal code after the overthrow of the First Republic, were promoting precisely this interpretation.[54]

A different jurisprudential tendency was cited by the appeals court justices who overturned Lyrio's acquittal: "The seduction that is required to influence the spirit of the minor, convincing her to give in, is not . . . a marriage promise . . . but rather vulgar and generic seduction; it is any seduction capable of deceiving a virgin woman and make her accept the carnal contact."[55]

This new understanding of seduction supported the increasingly popular juridical view that the law had to adapt to the times not by denying modern women the right to defend their honor but by expanding its definition of seduction. Judges were urged to draw from "sociological and psychological intuition" in order to integrate modern understandings of female sexuality and to counter new kinds of dangers young women faced. Elaborating on an important 1925 decision by Judge Galdino Siqueira, Hungria described the definition of seduction current among his contemporaries ten years later: "It is the enticement of the fragile will of the woman exclusively through suggestion. It is the persistent pleading, the enveloping blandishment, the reiterated protest of love, the madrigalesque phrase, the hot language of unsatisfied desire, the persuasive caress, the exciting prelude of kisses, of increasingly indiscreet touching. In a word: it is the refined art of Don Juan."[56]

Like those judges less sympathetic to modern women, Hungria feared that women's sexual arousal outside marriage resulted in their degradation and represented a threat to public morality. Rather than ostracize these women, however, he argued for increased judicial intervention. To fail to punish seducers who "knew how to arouse the sexual instinct," Hungria argued, "is to encourage crimes against the honesty of families, indirectly favor prostitution, augment this wind of lasciviousness that seems to be subverting women's most precious and cherished virtues."[57]

Already firmly established in jurisprudence of the 1930s, Hungria's position on seduction was written into the 1940 code. Neither the marriage promise nor the honesty of the victim was mentioned in the new law. Instead, seduction of a virgin was a crime if achieved by "taking advantage of her inexperience or justifiable trust." Against Hungria's recommendation, the maximum age for victims was lowered from twenty-one to eighteen. Together, these changes shifted the focus of the law away from the concern with mature women's virtue and toward protection of minors.

The new penal code also incorporated other changes that jurists had championed in legal treatises and in their judgments for decades. At the turn of the century, a prominent group had waged a campaign to disseminate tenets of the "positive school" in law, which held that the law should not focus on objectively defined criminal acts but on the moral, physical, sociological, and psychological characteristics of individual criminals and victims. As a new generation trained in modern criminology in the 1920s and 1930s integrated positivist notions into penal law, they unabashedly enhanced their own authority. Even conservatives such as Nelson Hungria, who considered himself an opponent of positivist legal doctrine, proclaimed that judges had a moral and professional obligation to mold the law to changing moral norms through creative interpretations.[58] Judges should take into account not only changing norms and scientific advances but the characteristics of the individuals involved in each case. Criminal law, Hungria insisted, was not simply punitive but normative; it was up to judges to apply the law in ways that fulfilled its "tutelary function of social discipline."[59] In many cases, this meant accepting changing gender norms and protecting young girls whose attitudes and stories deviated from the older model of female virtue and innocence. It also meant that jurists abandoned the same paternalistic posture for deflowered women between eighteen and twenty-one years old, eliminating for them not only a means to defend their honor, but one of the only legal means available to demand child support from the fathers of their children. Finally, although flexible legal principles and the claims of modern girls led jurists to broaden the legal conception of female honesty, their jurisprudence established a wide range of criteria with which to defend or condemn specific individuals. This meant that in practice, jurists could use their new interpretive powers in ways that continued to reflect traditional social prejudices.[60]

Notes

This chapter is an abridged and modified version of Sueann Caulfield, *In Defense of Honor: Morality, Modernity, and Nation in Early-Twentieth-Century Brazil* (Durham, NC: Duke University Press, 2000), esp. chap. 4. I am grateful to Lara Putnam for her comments and editing assistance on this version.

1 Francisco Viveiros de Castro, *Os delitos contra a honra da mulher*, 2d ed. (Rio de Janeiro: Freitas Bastos, 1932 [1898]), 21.

2 Nelson Hungria, "Crimes sexuais," *Revista forense* 70 (1937): 216–227, esp. 220.

3 Ibid., 220.

4 Ibid.

5 The literature on urbanization and Rio's urban reform is too extensive to cite here. See Pereira, this volume, nn. 4, 5, and 20; Caulfield, *In Defense of Honor: Modernity, Morality, and Nation in Early-Twentieth-Century Brazil* (Durham: Duke University Press, 1999), chap. 2.

6 See Nicolau Sevcenko, "A capital irradiante: Técnica, ritmos e ritos do Rio," in *História da vida privada no Brasil*, ed. Fernando A. Novais (São Paulo: Companhia das Letras, 1998), 3:513–620.

7 See Caulfield, *In Defense of Honor*, chaps. 2 and 3; and Susan K. Besse, *Restructuring Patriarchy: The Modernization of Gender Inequality in Brazil, 1914–1940* (Chapel Hill: University of North Carolina Press, 1996), 19–37.

8 According to Judge Atugasmin Medici Filho, deflowering remained "one of the most common crimes" after 1940. Medici Filho, "O crime de sedução no novo Código penal," *Revista dos tribunais* 134 (1941): 399–416, 416. For a detailed discussion of changing definitions of sexual crimes and the prevalence of complaints of sexual offenses in Rio de Janeiro courts in the first half of the twentieth century, see Caulfield, *In Defense of Honor*, chaps. 1, 3, and appendix A.

9   For analysis of turn-of-the-century cases, see Martha de Abreu Esteves, *Meninas per-didas: Os populares e o cotidiano do amor no Rio de Janeiro da belle époque* (Rio de Janeiro: Paz e Terra, 1989). For an early comparison of Esteves's and my data, based on a sub-set of the cases I consulted, see Sueann Caulfield and Martha de Abreu Esteves, "Fifty Years of Virginity in Rio de Janeiro: Sexual Politics and Gender Roles in Juridical and Popular Discourse, 1890–1940," *Luso-Brazilian Review* 30.1 (1993): 47–74.

10 See, e.g., Arquivo Nacional (hereafter AN), division 1, box 1776, n. 419 (1918); box 312, n. 7029 (1920); box 1926, n. 493 (1923) and n. 537 (1923); box 1813, n. 8 (1927) and n. 2082 (1939); box 1769, n. 1976 (1927); box 1776, n. 205 (1929); box 1837, n. 1575 (1937); box 1770, n. 1182 (1935); box 1779, n. 1723 (1937); box 1771, n. 2053 (1938); divi-sion 5, box 1728, n. 165 (1919); box 10817, n. 340 (1921); box 1776, n. 262 (1930); box 1731, n. 1057 (1935); division 7, box 10869, n. 77 (1931); division 8, box 2770, n. 1726 (1936); box 2815, n. 1838 (1938).

11 AN, division 1, box 1926, n. 493 (1923). I use pseudonyms for all parties in crimi-nal cases.

12 AN, division 1, box 1770, n. 1214 (1936).

13 AN, division 1, box 1807, n. 83 (1929); box 1772, n. 240 (1930); division 5, box 1728, n. 165 (1919); box 1776, n. 262 (1930); division 8, box 2770, n. 1276 (1936); box 2730, n. 2174 (1939).

14 It is highly likely that legal-medical and other professional men placed a high pre-mium on the virginity of women of their own class, even if they ridiculed working-class "hymenolatry." Retired Institute of Legal Medicine official Carlos Henrique de Andrade Gomide and two former colleagues, all of whom were at the institute in the 1940s, chuckled at the absurdity of their predominantly working-class patients' concern with virginity, but admitted that they, too, had demanded virginity of their brides. Interview with the author, Feb. 20, 1992.

15 AN, division 1, box 1813, n. 1077 (1935).

16 AN, division 7, box 10817, n. 265 (1921). See also AN division 1, box 1772, n. 1252 (1925) and n. 240 (1930); box 1738, n. 2240 (1927); box 1773, n. 159 (1930); box 1735, n. 259 (1932); box 1813, n. 2082 (1939); box 1841, n. 150 (1922); box 1838, n. 1593 (1923); divi-sion 7, box 10811, n. 50 (1919) and n. 234 (1920); box 10817, n. 265 (1921); box 10806, n. 113 (1924); division 8, box 2667, n. 161 (1923); box 2822, n. 1617 (1937).

17 AN, division 8, box 2730, n. 2174 (1939).

18 AN, division 1, box 1807, n. 1936 (1927).

19 AN, division 8, box 2770, n. 1276 (1936); division 1, box 1926, n. 326 (1922).

20 AN, division 7, box 10806, n. 113 (1924).

21 AN, division 1, box 1807, n. 301 (1928).

22 See Edgard de Moura Bitencourt, *O concubinato no direito*, 2d ed. (Rio de Janeiro: Biblioteca Jurídica, 1969), 1:39.

23 See, e.g., AN, division 7, box 10817, n. 347 (1921); division 1, box 1926, n. 537 (1923).

24 See AN, division 1, box 1737, n. 2333 (1927); box 1772, n. 1155 (1935); division 5, box 1731, n. 542 (1933).

25 AN, division 8, box 2734, n. 1183 (1935).

26 AN, division 8, box 2738, n. 1212 (1936).

27 Cf. AN, division 7, box 10811, n. 50 (1919); box 10842, n. 40 (1930).

28 See cases AN, division 1, box 1807, n. 1439 (1925) and n. 1436 (1927); box 1737, n. 93

(1928); box 1776, n. 406 (1933); box 1731, n. 542 (1933); box 1772, n. 1155 (1935); box 1733, n. 2079 (1939); box 10817, n. 347 (1921); division 8, box 2708, n. 372 (1933).

29 Asunción Lavrin, "Introduction: The Scenario, the Actors, and the Issues," in *Sexuality and Marriage in Colonial Latin America*, ed. Asunción Lavrin (Lincoln: University of Nebraska Press, 1989), 1–43, esp. 5–6; Lyman L. Johnson and Sonya Lipsett-Rivera, eds., *The Faces of Honor: Sex, Shame, and Violence in Colonial Latin America* (Albuquerque: University of New Mexico Press, 1998); Elizabeth Anne Kuznesof, "Sexual Politics, Race, and Bastard-Bearing in Nineteenth-Century Brazil: A Question of Culture or Power?" *Journal of Family History* 16.3 (1991): 241–260, esp. 243. For discussion of consensual unions and female-headed households in twentieth-century Rio de Janeiro, see Décio Parreiras, *Atividades de higiene pública no Rio de Janeiro, 1939–1940* (Rio de Janeiro: Imprensa Nacional, 1941), 28–29; Instituto Brasileiro de Geografia e Estatística, *Estudo sobre a fecundidade da mulher no Brasil, segundo o estado conjugal* (Rio de Janeiro: Instituto Brasileiro de Geografia e Estatística, 1949), 33. According to self-declarations recorded in the 1940 census, 13% of households were headed by couples living in "free unions"; another 22% by couples who were married only by a religious ceremony. Giorgio Montara, "As mães solteiras no Brasil," *Revista brasileira de estatística* 85 (1961): 1–32, esp. 2. See also Ovídio de Andrade Júnior, "Classificação da população brasileira segundo o estado conjugal," *Revista brasileira de estatística* 14.57 (1954), 172–176; Germano Gonçalves Jardim, "Os recenseamentos e a estatística do estado conjugal," *Revista brasileira de estatística* 15.57 (1954): 166–167.

30 Paulino José Soares de Souza Neto, "Repressão à fraude nas anulações de casamento," in *Anais do Primeiro Congresso Nacional do Ministério Público* (Rio de Janeiro: Imprensa Nacional, 1942), 9:123–132, esp. 126.

31 Vicente Piragibe, *Dicionário de jurisprudência penal do Brasil* (Rio de Janeiro: Freitas Bastos, 1938), 1:226–230.

32 Examples include AN, division 1, box 1807, n. 746 (1923); box 1843, n. 380 (1933); box 1813, n. 746 (1939); and box 1813, n. 1113 (1929).

33 AN, division 1, box 1813, n. 2410 (1940).

34 Apelação crime n. 7.087, Acórdão, in *Revista do Supremo Tribunal* (Rio de Janeiro) 76 (1924): 49–54.

35 AN, division 1, box 1772, n. 1155 (1935).

36 AN, division 8, box 2770, n. 1936 (1936). For similar statements about young girls seeing movies, see AN, division 1, box 1926, n. 1409 (1925); box 1743, n. 249 (1927); division 7, box 10869, n. 59 (1932).

37 See AN, division 1, box 1767, n. 2143 (1927); box 1733, n. 28 (1932); box 1770, n. 1182 (1935); box 1837, n. 1454 (1936); box 1813, n. 2410 (1940); box 312, n. 7019 (1940); box 312, n. 7063 (1940); division 7, box 10613, n. 168 (1922); box 10806, n. 124 (1924); division 8, box 2708, n. 11a (1932).

38 See Findlay's essay in this volume.

39 AN, division 1, box 1837, n. 1459 (1936).

40 Ibid.

41 AN, division 1, box 1771, n. 2140 (1939). The sixteen cases are AN, division 1, box 1946, n. 1252 (1921); box 7139, n. 2972 (1940); division 5, box 1940, n. 97 (1919); box 1849, n. 243 (1919); box 1728, n. 165 (1919); box 9144, n. 166 (1920); box 1730, n. 134 (1920); division 8, box 2666, n. 158 (1922); box 2673, n. 519 (1928); box 2670, n. 21 (1928);

box 2708, n. 478 (1933); box 2997, n. 985 (1935); box 2730, n. 1431 (1936); box 2733, n. 16216 (1937); box 2772, n. 1463 (1937); box 2975, n. 195 (1941). In another ten, it was unclear whether the mother's husband was the girl's father; of these, seven mothers filed the complaints: division 1, box 1841, n. 1194 (1925); box 1737, n. 2333 (1927); box 1772, n. 240 (1930); box 1795, n. 893 (1934); division 8, box 2666, n. 854 (1925), n. 829 (1926), and n. 25 (1926).

42 AN, division 1, box 1926, n. 1409 (1925); box 1737, n. 2145 (1927) and n. 2276 (1927); box 1735, n. 715 (1934); box 1837, n. 1459 (1936); box 1772, n. 1921 (1938); division 7, box 10806, n. 455 (1924); division 8, box 2664, n. 656 (1925); box 2679 no.73-A (1932); box 2822, n. 1122 (1935); box 2774, n. 1460 (1937).

43 Deflowering victims' families were not unusual. In the 1940 census, a third of the city's mothers declared themselves single (10%) or widowed (23%), proportions only slightly lower than those found among the mothers in the criminal records (12% single and 29% widowed). Instituto Brasileiro de Geografia e Estatística, *Estudo sobre a fecundidade*, 66.

44 Cf. AN, division 1, box 1807, n. 83 (1929).

45 Examples of particularly severe conflicts of this type are AN, division 1, box 1737, n. 2216 (1927); box 1770, n. 1214 (1936); and box 1831, n. 2159 (1939).

46 AN, division 1, box 1733, n. 1117 (1935).

47 Ibid. In the ensuing trial, Cavalcanti was acquitted at the lower court on the grounds that Georgina's "desire to be free" disqualified her as an "honest woman."

48 Piragibe, *Dicionário*, 1:229.

49 Nelson Hungria, "Em torno do ante-projeto," *Revista forense* 77 (1939): 423; cited in Medici Filho, "O crime de sedução," 412.

50 See especially Afrânio Peixoto, *Sexologia Forense* (Rio de Janeiro: Guanabara, 1934).

51 Eurico Cruz, "Sentença do juiz da 2a vara criminal, de 8 de setembro de 1926," in Piragibe, *Dicionário*, 1:234–235.

52 "Jurisprudência: Defloramento—Conceito de sedução (Acórdão da 1a Câmara da Corte de Apelação do Distrito Federal e Comentário de C. A. Lúcio Bitencourt)," *Revista de direito penal* 12 (1936): 103–114, esp. 103.

53 For analysis of turn-of-the-century juridical attitudes, see Esteves, *Meninas perdidas*.

54 Virgílio de Sá Pereira, Evaristo de Morais, and Mário Bulhões Pedreira, *Projeto do código criminal* (Rio de Janeiro: Imprensa Nacional, 1933), 66; Tiago Ribeiro Pontes, *Código penal brasileiro comentado* (Rio de Janeiro: Freitas Bastos, 1977), 341.

55 "Jurisprudência: Defloramento."

56 Nelson Hungria, "Em torno de um parecer," in *Revista de crítica judiciária* 21.2–3 (1935): 81–84, quote on 82.

57 Ibid., 83.

58 Hungria, "Crimes sexuais," 220.

59 Cited in Nelson Hungria and Romão Côrtes de Lacerda, *Comentários ao código penal* (Rio de Janeiro: Revista Forense, 1947), 8:321 n. 2.

60 For a discussion of how racial prejudice affected decisions in sexual crime cases, for instance, see Sueann Caulfield, "Interracial Courtship in the Rio de Janeiro Courts," in *Race and Nation in Modern Latin America*, ed. Nancy P. Appelbaum, Anne S. Macpherson, and Karin Alejandra Rosemblatt (Chapel Hill: University of North Carolina Press, 2003) and *In Defense of Honor*, chap. 5.

III

THE

POLICING

OF PUBLIC

SPACE

The *plena*'s dissonant melodies: leisure, racial policing,
and nation in Puerto Rico, 1900–1930s
José Amador de Jesús

The beating of the *panderos* (large tambourines) filled the nights of La
Joya del Castillo in the early years of the twentieth century. When Catherine George and John Clark played their lively rhythm of being, a
crowd gathered to listen to their improvised instrumentation and call-
and-response vocal cadences. Under the light of the narrow street's only
existing lamppost, men and women of all colors sang and danced to a
new musical genre: the *plena*.[1] The Clark-George's *plena* was a display of
imagination and spontaneity, a creative amalgam of the African-derived
bomba, a troubadour's chronicling composition, and syncopated body
movements. But what was especially novel about the *plena* was that its
subtext brought the unspeakable African presence to the center of the seigniorial city of Ponce, whose splendid port and booming sugar economy
won it the epithet of Puerto Rico's "Southern Pearl."

Over the years, however, the *plena*'s audience was transformed. Imbued with nationalist meanings, the local *plena* became *puertorriqueña*, a
sign of a national identity that appropriated traditions, constructed historical continuities, and presumed shared values to represent a "natural"
sense of Puerto Rican community.[2] Although by the late 1930s most of
Puerto Rico's middle class could dance to the popular *plena*, underlying
every note and every verbal inflection were histories of racial prejudice,
sexual regulation, and municipal policing. These are the stories of the
plena's unspeakable past, which, in the context of the early twentieth century, were necessarily about dynamics between popular expressions of
shared experiences and projects by the elite to incorporate them into the
volatile core of national culture.[3] The *plena* and its attendant social relations provide a window on how this cultural production shaped and

was in turn shaped by conflicting spatial, gendered, and racialized ideas linked to the city and the nation. They also demonstrate that it is difficult, if not impossible, to chart this history without considering how it overlapped with other ideological conceptions about municipal policing, sexual morality, and colonial authority. Before these stories conclude, we will encounter a multiracial neighborhood on the fringes of Ponce's residential center, a ferocious battle against dances, a talented musician with an onomatopoeic name, and an anxious intellectual concerned with defining the boundaries of the island's national culture.

This plot unfolds on a moving landscape, where struggles erupted over social order, leisure practices, and claims to honor and where local and national community identifications changed over time. If by the early twentieth century Ponce's popular classes sang both to claim and to challenge the racial and class exclusions within the arena of the civic space, by the mid-1930s nationalist intellectuals sang to extend the borders of national community. Examining the relationship between this form of popular culture—understood as the meanings of day-to-day practices of subordinate groups—and its discursive transformation by the elite provides a dynamic understanding of how each group created a sense of identity through turbulent, provisional, and open-ended encounters. As Stuart Hall has noted, popular culture is neither an autonomous and authentic domain nor a folklorization of dominant culture, but rather both cultures are produced in relation to each other through a "dialectic cultural struggle."[4] The shifting meanings of the *plena* orchestrate the relations between individual assertions and community affirmations and between local struggles and national politics. It is to this moving landscape that we now turn.

La Joya del Castillo: A Space in Motion

At the turn of the century the idea that certain spaces and times of day, and therefore certain people and activities within them, were safe and respectable—that is, inherently moral—was diffused throughout the city of Ponce.[5] The use of central sidewalks, streets, parks, and other public spaces by popular sectors sometimes led to condemnation of their activities as an affront to the decorum of a privileged middle class. Ponce's spatial inequalities made many activities of the popular classes more visible because their lack of private facilities made their work and leisure more ubiquitous. While middle-class people of all colors naturalized their class and status privileges, they often spoke of the inability of plebeian men and women to observe more restrictive conventions as evidence of lack of a work ethic and sexual morality, ignoring factors of time, space, and money. Middle-class Ponceños, for example, immediately equated rowdy, boisterous, and promiscuous behavior with specific *arrabales* (shantytowns), such as La Joya del Castillo.

By the early twentieth century, with the proletarization of agricultural work, the outlines of Ponce's physical development had shifted as *arrabales* proliferated on the urban periphery. From the paternalistic space of the coffee *hacienda* on the highlands, many peasants migrated to *arrabales* located between the seigniorial city and the sugar corporations. This process accelerated following the 1898 Spanish-Cuban-American War, when Puerto Rico faced an uneven integration within the juridico-political and economic structure of the United States, becoming an increasingly wage-based site of cheap colonized labor generating sugar products for export.[6] These economic transformations set the stage for conflicts over the political, sexual, and racial boundaries of the city space. As the popular desire for leisure confronted the authorities' desire for public order, the *plena* represented not only the dangers related to public dances but the more pressing affront to the national culture presented by its display of internal distinctions on Puerto Rico's cultural terrain.

It is easy to imagine the nighttime atmosphere of La Joya del Castillo during the period when the *plena* emerged. Even the name of this neighborhood reflects its inhabitants' cunning sense of irony. La Joya (the gem) was in reality nothing more than an *arrabal* located at the bottom, or *hoyo*, of the castle belonging to the Seralles, one of Ponce's famous rum-producing families. The visitor who entered from Virtue Street would encounter only two commercial establishments: Pepe Ortiz's small market and, in the center, a legendary brothel (*ranchón*) divided into cubicles. Coexisting with twenty other working-class family houses loosely arranged in a gridiron pattern, both establishments might have provided space for contention and open conflict. As the night unraveled, we can imagine strolling couples wandering through La Joya's scattered lights, occasional screaming followed by violence, and a chorus of voices following the beating of the *panderos*. It was a site where other social groups went looking for the obscure pleasure produced when morbid desires are accentuated by danger, where close proximity of different social classes could lead to powerful alliances as well as fierce disputes.

It is more difficult, however, to imagine the geography of La Joya during the daytime. Although the population of La Joya was mostly nonwhite (almost 70% black and mulatto), its visibility in the city core must have varied greatly.[7] While most black and mulatto men worked as craftsmen and agricultural laborers, the vast majority of black and mulatto women worked as laundresses or domestic servants. By virtue of their employment, men were confined to the plantation or workshop; women, however, had to traverse the city and were seen in a wide range of urban spaces. For example, Catherine George, the *plenera* with whom we began this story, crossed the town to work for the prestigious Ferré-Aguayo family as a domestic servant.[8] She may have also been required to go to the market and perform other duties that would take her to different parts of the city. This is not to suggest any privileged positioning of black and mulatto women in the Ponce's urban landscape; on the contrary, their ubiquitous presence in the city, their use of the streets, and their need to travel to their homes at night after a day's work were viewed by many Ponceños as evidence of their immorality. At the same time, these women's use of the streets and familiarity with large areas of the city suggest that the notion of the city as a male terrain does not adequately illustrate the daily landscape of Ponce.

As the culturally diverse residents of La Joya came into direct association, both in the workplace and in their neighborhood, their life experiences converged in the *plena* lyrics. Through improvisation, early *pleneros* chronicled and interpreted day-to-day events relevant to their neighborhood, challenging the privileged conception of writing as the preeminent expression of human consciousness. It is important to remember that during this period literacy was extremely limited in Puerto Rico, and for people living on the fringes of society, such as the residents of La Joya, it was almost nonexistent.[9] *Plena* music therefore became vital in fostering a coherent (if not always stable) sense of self and community. The racial diversity of La Joya meant that lingering effects of racism within the community were less obvious than they would be in the central streets of Ponce. And although there were distinct clusters of black immigrants from the English-speaking Caribbean, their daily interaction with poor Puerto Ricans may have worked to create a sense of community among a widespread and disparate people with similar socioeconomic needs and interests. Whatever this sense of community meant, it was the outcome of practical activity and social networks. In the end, much of it was the result of common pain and suffering, of job instability and racial disavowal, and of alternative practices of survival such as street vending, gambling, and prostitution. These community identifications tell the story not so much of the victory of the weak over the strong but of disproportionate hierarchical powers that found creative outlet through the *plena*'s lyrics.[10]

In the 1910s, Carola George, Catherine's daughter, brought the *plena* into Ponce's urban center. Carola and Catherine's role in the *plena*'s diffusion challenges the gendered imagery of the *plena* as a male-defined musical genre. Mounted on a melodious stagecoach, Carola and her husband, Julio Mora, paraded through the city's streets gathering audiences for their rhythm. At the same time, they publicly set forth their own ideas of everyday life and history. Middle-class Ponceños heard stories foreign to them, stories of economic vulnerability, of working hardships, and of places where sexuality stepped outside the bounds of propriety. These unfamiliar stories roamed freely through the city's streets, publicly constructing another historical memory. Typically, *plena* lyrics dealt with quotidian history, identifying specific neighborhoods or locales—such as Bélgica, La Calzada, Buyones, and Machuelito—to develop themes such as family relations, working conditions, love, death, and the local demimonde. One of the earliest *plenas* clearly illustrates the explicit use of African language and plebeian gender mores that could scandalize middle-class sensibilities and unleash racial phantasms of moral decay:

> Atabó, Atabó, mira como era Paula . . .
> Ella salio de Buyones:
> Se fue para La Calzada
> Atabó, Atabó, mira como era Paula.
>
> [Atabó, Atabó, look how Paula was . . .
> She left Buyones:
> Going to La Calzada
> Atabó, Atabó, look how Paula was.]

Not surprisingly, interactions between Ponce's middle class and *plena* music were not neutral. Racialized perceptions of its "cultural value" encouraged not only a physical but also an ideological distance between the middle class and the popular class's leisure practices. At most, the *plena*'s "exoticism" could lure some bohemian middle-class men to the places where it was danced, which suggests not necessarily that their perception of its cultural value increased but rather that they were attracted to its "primitivized" musicality. But because the *plena*'s origins and satirical overtone so conspicuously darkened Ponce, local officials considered it an affront to white, middle-class prestige and a menace to public order and private property. While popular classes described their world through the *plena* lyrics, white middle-class families expressed their concern to protect women and children from what they perceived as a dangerous source of blackness equated with moral degeneration. Questions about Ponce's cultural space were thus projected as questions of blackness and respectability.

Forbidden Dances and Spaces

Many of Ponce's middle- and upper-class residents expected the city to showcase the beginning of a new era. Following the turbulent 1898 imperial transition, these elites thought they were once more progressing, in a natural evolution, toward modernity and a civilized social order. If Ponce was to maintain its "seigniorial" splendor, it needed to conform to the elites' norms of propriety and decorum rather than succumb to the increasing degeneracy of the popular classes. Yet by the turn of the century it was impossible to demarcate clearly the opposing social meanings of respectability. According to historian Eileen Suárez Findlay, an alternative popular respectability emerged that "did not conform to elite norms." And although it partially challenged dominant honor codes by including "public concubinage, interracial partnership, and serial monogamy," it still "drew rigid lines between 'moral' and 'immoral.'"[11] Both discourses associated specific gendered practices like not dancing in public with respectability, and the more African those practices were, the more licentious the behavior. To accept the dances where the *plena* reverberated was to respond like a black person, a degenerate, or a wayward woman—that is, like a racial, moral, and cultural inferior.

In some of the *cafetines* where the *plena* was played and danced the boundary between bar and brothel was fluid, for there were spaces where strict bourgeois morality was impossible. These establishments provided alcoholic beverages and dancing but also served as inexpensive clubs where the increasing number of male laborers could solicit sexual favors.[12] As the leisure landscape changed and as more *cafetines* became available, municipal authorities found it necessary to distinguish between moral and immoral spaces. The racial, class, and gender dimensions of the urban space became a matter of serious debate.[13] Seigniorial (white) Ponceños believed respectability could be maintained when dancing was confined to private parties, where one's partners would all be acquaintances admitted by invitation. The difference between a formal and an informal gathering reinforced even more the class and racial dimension of these two dance spaces. Elite men and women met at stylish casinos, private clubs, and houses, where social debuts, extravagant balls, and patio dances were held.[14] From their perspective respectability was easily compromised if they were seen at a public dance or, worse, at a *cafetín*. However, the criteria for prosecuting those who engaged in these public dances were neither fixed nor rigid. On the one hand, municipal authorities and law enforcement had to respond to the pressure exercised by Ponce's "respectable" families, but, on the other, the city relied on dance licenses as a source of revenue.[15]

On October 18, 1909, Ponce's municipal council received a letter that initiated the intense debates about dances that followed in the next decade. Antonio Arbona and six other "distinguished" Ponceños protested against the "bailes de gente alegre" held on Aurora Street in the downtown area. They argued that these dances represented an "unedifying spectacle detrimental to morality and prejudicial to the tranquility of the residents who live there" and concluded by exhorting the municipal council "to end the vortex of evil."[16] By November a special municipal commission had recommended not only the prohibition of Aurora's street dances but also a "study to circumscribe and to determine a sector of the town for the women of ill repute who today are disseminated throughout all the city's neighborhoods."[17] In an attempt to make prostitutes less visible—and hence the *plena* less audible—municipal efforts concentrated on their containment and relocation away from central residential areas. Interestingly, both Arbona's letter and the municipality were principally concerned with the dance's public nature and the obvious moral repercussions of the indiscriminate mixing of lifestyles, not with the criminalization of prostitution per se. Nevertheless, the identification of these *cafetines* allowed police to make immediate associations between acceptable space and moral reputation and between public display of blackness and respectable behavior. Despite the moralizing and segregating efforts of the self-declared "respectable" Ponceños, alternative uses of public space by those not confined to the norms of decency continued to develop, as the migration and proletarianization of peasant men and women increased.[18]

In its early years, the *plena*'s lyrics were imbued with the world of public leisure. Its verses frequently dealt with the everyday life of prostitutes, dancers, and drinkers. This evocation of the quotidian is evidenced in what may be the genre's most famous song, "Cortaron a Elena." According to Felix Echevarría, Elena Sánchez was a woman of "la vida alegre" (the merry life) who was attacked by a jealous woman at a dance near Ponce's port.[19] "Cortaron a Elena," however, not only depicts the dangerous conditions of this prostitute's livelihood, it also expresses plebeian parameters of proper sexuality, motherhood, and familial relations:

Cortaron a Elena,
Cortaron a Elena
Cortaron a Elena
y se la llevaron al hospital.

Su madre lloraba,
¡Cómo no iba a llorar!
Si era su hijita querida
Y se la llevaron al hospital.

[Elena was slashed,
Elena was slashed,
Elena was slashed,
and they took her to the hospital.

Her mother cried,
How could she not cry!
If it was her beloved daughter
And they took her to the hospital.]

The narrator defines Elena's morality through the destructive malevolence of Ponce's nightlife. The first verse, "Elena was slashed," develops as a repetitive motif suggesting that her licentious sexual behavior found its natural and violent outcome. In the second stanza, however, the narrator envisages a return to the forms of love associated with traditional family roles. Elena was not only a prostitute but also a "beloved daughter," whose pain is worth crying about—and worth singing about! Maternal love is thus exalted and closely associated with familial suffering, unselfishness, and fidelity. In fact, for Elena's loving mother there is no place for dishonor. She is a source of boundless love and sacrifice. And because the mother figure is separated from street life and leisure, Elena is redeemed from a completely disreputable ending.

Ponce's respectable residents deemed these *cafetines* corrupt because of their lower-class clientele, which allowed for interracial socializing and sexual encounters. To the extent that interclass and black/white relationships were possible and conflicts within these relationships made public, the distinctions between the family-centered neighborhood and the immoral commercialized leisure space could be dangerously obscured. One such conflict occurred when Victoria Vegas and Concha Roberts were arrested for public disorder on a downtown street. The policeman noted that these "unruly women's" dispute was caused by "race: white against black."[20] If the fight actually resulted from racism, it reveals something about the instigators but more about how public displays of interracial confrontation could "darken" downtown Ponce. Police vigilance was more intense in the poor neighborhoods to prevent men and women of dubious sexual reputation from entering the restricted spaces of bourgeois family life. To make matters worse, if the streetwalkers—exceedingly public, flagrant, and noisy—were black, the urban landscape could change classification from respectable to its anathema: disreputable and black. For instance, many of the neighborhoods where these *cafetines* were located came to be known as either "de vida alegre" or "de negros."

The dissemination of the *plena*, indicated by the popularity of its dancing, should not be interpreted as a natural progression. Rather, it was facilitated by the increased number of men and women who entered the wage labor force.[21] During the first two decades of the twentieth century, men and women workers organized vigorously. Male cane workers, typographers, and dockworkers and female tobacco strippers, seamstresses, and hatmakers, among others, held significant strikes demanding better wages and work security. Proletarianization in turn led to an increased consumer demand for public leisure. However, municipal officials concerned with workers' productivity believed the public craze had to be brought under control. Committed to making these centers of vice less attractive to workers by attacking the problem at its "source," Ponce's police chief, Miguel Hurtado, requested an increase in the license fee for public dances. On October 4, 1916, he complained that at the *cafetín* Nueva Bélgica, "Saturdays, Sundays, and sometimes Mondays, there are around three hundred people, principally people of color from the plantations and immoral women from town, and with *panderos*, a *timbale*, and a *sinfonía*, or other analogous instruments, they produce such a noise that is impossible to bear."[22] It would be virtually impossible to separate Hurtado's race- and class-based conceptions of respectability from his anxieties about possible threats to white male superiority. In his perception, the critical mass of these vicious groups rendered invisible the significant presence of white males of all classes. If the fears that "people of color" and "immoral women" could produce a social upheaval impossible to control haunted Ponce's police, a more material specter was the possibility of the loss of an efficient labor force. As Kelvin Santiago-Valle has demonstrated, during the first half of the twentieth century the number of arrests for minor offenses reached its height during moments of increased labor mobilization.[23] Nonetheless, Hurtado's rationale for restricting the concession of dance licenses was further complicated by the lack of sufficient police personnel to control the masses and by the possible high medical cost of potential altercations. This was hardly the first occasion, nor would it be the last, that municipal officials managed to distort a complex aspect of the popular classes' life and culture. Rather than being a possible site of danger, the *cafetines* provided poor men and women a space free from the constraints of an overseer, where they could dance to a music known to them and claim their own making of history.

Underlying these written concerns was an even greater threat posed by the *plena*. The genre's satirical overtones publicly ridiculed people of wealth and caricatured working institutions. This compensatory retelling of history made authorities aware of the popular classes' (especially black) discontent about their minimal participation in official public institutions—this is, in city councils, public offices, newspaper rooms, and political leadership. At least provisionally, passionate listeners gained empowerment by using parody to mask their anger against the material conditions in which they lived. For instance, in "La rompedora" [The grinding mill], written by the black composer Jacinto Salomón, music and lyrics reproduce the sarcastic voice of an exploited worker by ridiculing the senselessness of the employer's work pressures:

> Oliver, Oliver,
> Mi amigo Oliver:
> Si la hamaca no tiene caña
> La rompedora no pue' romper
> Pregúntale al mayordomo,
> Y pregúntale al francés,
> Que si la hamaca no tiene caña
> La rompedora no pue' romper

> [Oliver, Oliver
> my friend Oliver:
> if the feeder does not have cane
> the grinding mill can't grind

Ask the overseer,
and ask the Frenchman,
if the feeder does not have cane
the grinding mill can't grind]

In the first stanza the narrator cynically addresses his "friend" Oliver, whose English name alludes to U.S. capitalist interest in the island, to complain about unjust working pressures. The singing subject deconstructs his own exploitation by repeating the obvious: "if the feeder does not have any cane the grinding mill can't grind." By poking fun at Oliver's ignorance, the speaker deprives his oppressor of any ethical superiority; in fact, his "friend" is reduced to an unthinking production machine. Even the "overseer" and the "Frenchman" refrain from such unreasonable demands. The brilliance of this *plena* lies in the subtlety of its critique, as the angry speaker humorously transforms memories of labor exploitation into a sense of self-respect. The reiteration of the last two verses allows the listener to construct Oliver's image as a derided plunderer and to support the narrator's rightful complaints.

No wonder in Hurtado's view the public transgressions of this popular genre presented both disciplinary and economic problems for Ponce. After denouncing the "denigrating" effects of these dances on the city's image, Ponce's police chief listed several other vices that the city council should control.[24] He insisted that *cafetín* dances should be prohibited rather than fined because "they are costing the municipality more . . . than what we collect from them in revenues."[25] Hurtado went further, requesting that the police be empowered to end the dances held not only in *cafetines* but in any place where alcohol was available.

Middle-class residents cared little whether or not municipal revenues would be diminished; they were more concerned with the indignities their families supposedly suffered in neighborhoods traversed by moral and racial inferiors. Thus the preoccupation of these residents had everything to do with the preservation of a respectable urban space. Control over urban space was contested after dark with music, alcohol, and sex, as the *plena*'s syncopated cadences echoed through Ponce's central streets. "La noche," by an anonymous composer, alludes to the transgressive attractions of nightlife:

Me gusta la noche
No me gusta el día
La noche es la alcahueta
De las fechorías.

Para el casado es un dios,
Porque obliga a la mujer
Para que vaya a dormir,
Mientras él se va a beber

También para el parrandero
Es la noche muy divina
Porque oculta con su manto
Y él se roba las gallinas

[I like the night
I don't like the day
It is the night that aids
mischief.

For the married man it is a god,
because it forces the woman
to go to sleep,
while he goes drinking.

Also for the carouser
the night is quite divine
because it hides with its mantle
And he steals the hens.]

In this *plena* the male narrative voice highlights how nighttime leisure forges homosocial bonding through drinking and sexual liaisons. More important, however, it reveals how men of the popular classes engage with and react to dominant discourses of women's respectability. Rather than imposing an artificial binary between popular and elite discourses, "La noche" exemplifies how the control of women's sexuality was central in maintaining a male-centered sexual order in both groups. Within the intoxicated space of the *cafetín*, the male singer/narrator can celebrate his "mischief." Conversely, the night demarcates two distinct spaces for women: one framed by the home in which they participate as cloistered wives, another by marginal hypersexuality in which women become passive bait (hens) that can be stolen. To fully achieve masculine respectability, the "parrandero" objectifies his female counterpart either into a loyal gatekeeper of the domestic space or into nonthreatening sexual prey. An amplified masculinity thus becomes the boastful centerpiece of a culture whose honor is asserted only through the control exerted over women's sexuality.

Because the speaker cannot even imagine the possibility of women's agency in determining their own sexual encounters, this *plena* may be a response to a masculinity threatened by the unstable gender order of the period. Working-class women's demands for sexual pleasure and struggles for control over their bodies increased through their significant participation in Puerto Rico's early labor movements.[26] Significantly, this *plena* was probably composed during this period, when men seem to affirm their power by legitimating notions of popular patriarchy.

For different reasons, of course, these male-centered affirmations have their corollary in the actual fears of elite white men. In order to confirm their place in a socioeconomic system experiencing crisis, many of Ponce's elite residents relied heavily on honor discourses to espouse an ethos within which they felt increasingly obliged to act as the privileged agents of respectability within the declining morality of the city. By policing city space, elites hoped to overcome both their own subordination within the new colonial government and the challenges posed by the increased mobilization of the popular classes. In short, they showed their preoccupation with demonstrating their moral standing as well as their own entitlement in the "seigniorial" city of Ponce.

Not surprisingly, within one month of Hurtado's 1916 complaints, twenty-four angry residents protested against a dance that was going to take place in the Gran Vía. Their aim was to push nocturnal dances to the city's periphery. Calling themselves "heads of honest families," these men requested, "in the name of our wives, daughters, and the refined city of Ponce," the expulsion of prostitutes from the downtown area.[27] Precisely because the complainants' economic status was threatened, conventions and appearances had to be protected from the "stain" of the licentious and scandalous; wives and daughters needed to remain chaste in manners, customs, and public perception. Retaining males' honor meant safeguarding "their" women and city from degenerate dances. Also, as when asserting control over women's sexuality, men's control over the feminized landscape was central in advancing restrictions about who could claim legitimacy in Ponce's public space. Corrupting forces had to be eradicated or, at the very least, relocated away from urban space the complainants saw as belonging to them.

One year later, Ponce's municipal council proposed a resolution prohibiting all "commercial dances attended by dissolute women [*mesalinas*], in the city's urban precinct, or in the beach village, or in any other place where families reside."[28] Trying to safeguard the funds produced by the dance licenses, Ponce's mayor initially opposed the resolution because it "affects the [economic] interests of the Municipality, without any guarantee that its objective will be accomplished."[29] The mayor doubted that these moralizing efforts worked to Ponce's benefit, since the popular classes defined morality in their own terms and acted upon them. Precisely because the municipality relied on dance licenses as a source of revenue, police measures against prostitution remained arbitrary during the first two decades of the century. After weeks of intense debate, the pressures exerted by the council and the police chief turned the balance in their favor. On December 22, 1917, the mayor passed an ordinance with a significant conciliatory alteration: while dances could not take place in the entire downtown area or near the beach villages, they were allowed in areas outside city limits.[30] Surveillance of these dances, however, was left to investigators, police officials, neighborhood commissaries, and the common citizen; that is, they remained a matter of local control. The plan to stamp out commercial dances from the heart of the city might appear to have been a victory for the moralizing forces, but it also testifies to their weakened position in the face of changing forms of gender mores and public leisure.

Prostitution, Politics, and Colonial Interventions

Up until this moment, negotiations over space in Ponce reflected local, although often conflicting, interactions between popular and elite discourses about the behavioral meanings of culture, gender, and race. Shifts in policies transcended the local level when the United States increased its regulatory role in the island's bodily matters. Not only did the possibility of sending Puerto Rican soldiers to World War I lead the United States strategically to grant American citizenship to Puerto Ricans, but, as Eileen Suárez Findlay has correctly noted, it led to the increased intrusion of the colonial state into the private homes and lives of its subjects. Fearing the infection of its soldiers, the state launched a ferocious antivenereal campaign targeting "disreputable" women across the island. One year after Ponce's municipal council passed the ordinance relocating the dances to the city's periphery, municipal authorities shifted focus, arresting any woman suspected of prostitution and obliging her to undergo excruciating medical examinations.[31] If the arrests were a pragmatic approach to safeguarding soldiers' health, they also marked these women physically and culturally. On the one hand, forcing them to un-

262   José Amador de Jesús

dergo involuntary vaginal exams marked them as disempowered objects of the colonial state; on the other hand, parading them in trucks from the small towns to the district jails of Ponce and Arecibo marked them as the embodied antithesis of national well-being.

During the seven months of the 1918 antiprostitution campaign, Ponce's landscape became a battlefield over sexual and citizenship rights, but for hundreds of arrested women (guilty or not) it meant curtailing their livelihood by sending them to distant jail cells. The debates unleashed over the antiprostitution campaign reflected the significant transformations Puerto Rican society underwent after 1898 regarding notions of citizenship and sexuality. In this climate of intense political antagonism, "seigniorial" forces such as the city council, clergymen, and elite feminists hailed the antiprostitution campaign as crucial to the security of the nation. In contrast, an increasing number of progressive professionals, radical reformers, working-class men and women, and Afro–Puerto Ricans alleged that the antiprostitution campaign posed a threat to the promise of democracy and individual liberties delivered by the United States.[32] By making prostitutes the emblem of the detrimental forces of colonialism, this constituency organized with considerable success. Using the colonizer's language of liberty and citizenship, the opposition successfully challenged the colonial judicial system, forcing an abrupt end to the statewide repression of prostitution. In short, this coalition used colonial and legal discourses of citizenship to validate their own ideas about the extent and limits of state intervention.

Nationalizing the Plena

Although in 1918 the prostitutes' cause was argued in all parts of Puerto Rico, raising issues about the boundaries of the colonial state, it would take the *plena* another decade to resonate across the island's racial and cultural boundaries. Yet as Puerto Ricans' attitudes about race became incorporated into the national imaginary, the essentializing discourse of cultural identity that followed responded both to the emerging militancy of the popular classes as well as to the corrosive effects of "Americanization."

With the transformation of the casual and spontaneous form of street performance into *conjuntos* (music groups), the *plena* started to gain public acclaim and visibility. The process began with Joselino "Bumbúm" Oppenheimer during the early 1920s.[33] After returning from a long day's work in the cane fields of Hacienda Estrella, Bumbúm, whose nickname echoed the beating of the *panderos*, sang to an enthusiastic audience willing to surrender to the pleasure of his music. In fact, his popularity increased to the point that he was able to set down the plow forever and take up the *pandero* full time in a formal *conjunto*. Before long, other *conjuntos* emerged to disseminate the *plena* across the island's racial and class divides.

Yet from the very introduction of the *plena* into Ponce's "seigniorial" residences, it was commodified and marketed in very specific forms. Middle- and upper-class Ponceños made the *plena* more "palatable" in their own way. First of all, they made it less threatening by moving it out of the corrupting space of the *cafetín*. In 1922 the residence of the García family, centrally located along Virtue Street, was one of the first "decent" households to hire Bumbúm's *conjunto*. A descendant of one of Ponce's "respectable" families described "Bumbúm" as a *"negrito de caché"* (well-mannered little black).[34] Although such patronizing remarks are meant to hide racial prejudice, they are in fact an assertion of white superiority that projects an otherness that is simultaneously exclusive and inclusive. By calling the singer a *negrito*, the speaker calls attention to Bumbúm's inferior racial origin, while by granting him *caché* or refinement he helps the musician to escape cultural marginalization. This was an embryonic formulation of what later became a commonplace in the elite's national imagination: a collective need to conceal class and racial anxieties and the elite's own colonial subordination by the objectification of a bound, suppressed, and repressed darkness.

While granting the style a wider public, the commodification process inevitably rested in cultural ambivalence. Bumbúm's crossover from poor black man to "showman" transformed the popular stereotype of the aggressive and degenerate *plenero* into a comforting entertainment figure.[35] Bumbúm's relation with Ponce's elite depended on a fundamental paradox: the crucial means through which popular classes expressed their collective aspirations became, for white listeners, merely an entertaining spectacle. This contradiction, however, gave Bumbúm access to a space previously denied. In fact, he set a precedent that other *conjuntos* followed.[36] For "respectable" Ponceños, listening to the *plena* in their homes became an acceptable family activity. Public celebrations, organized by local neighborhoods or the municipality, allowed men and women to sing and dance the *plena* without being morally tainted. For many *conjuntos* the *plena* was a vehicle both for insertion into a restricted space and for contestation once inside it. As we have seen, the beauty of the *plena* lies in concealing, behind momentary laughter, an acerbic social commentary.

What the elite did not understand was that these musical codes are a different communication system understandable to those who live them, a dialogue unrecognizable to those who do not inhabit the spaces that inspire its lyrics. *Plena* music speaks of street philosophy, characterizing neighborhoods and their habitants, and the beating of its *panderos* signals particular engagements. "Cortaron a Elena" is an example of street philosophy. "La noche" describes the carouser's quest for pleasure. And when the *panderos* suddenly cease beating, a call for competing improvisations begins. In this act of bonding, audience, dancers, musicians, and singers all come together as a community of *pleneros*.

But the *plena*'s greater acceptance should not be read as an absolute transgression or inscription. On the contrary, the *plena* became a complex cultural product subjected to particular temporal and social interpretations, one whose meanings stem from the practical language, gestures, and desire that produce specific mechanisms of community identification. In this process the *plena* was redefined by a wider segment of society, especially after modern technologies of dissemination developed in the 1930s. By this decade, the radio and record industries had made the *plena* accessible to all. If modern technologies facilitated the dissemination of new rhythms, it was the figure of Manuel "Canario" Jiménez, the first musician to record *plenas*, who brought the genre to the zenith of its popularity.[37] As the *plena* achieved commercial prominence, the 1930s fad represented a tentative valorization of musical influences long suppressed.

During this decade the *plena* also became more "palatable" as a Puerto Rican intellectual discursively transformed its context in defiance of the United States' "imperialistic pretexts."[38] The *plena* became a "genuine folkloric gesture," transcending local antagonisms by functioning as an iconic vehicle for conflating popular expressive forms with a nationalist agenda.[39] This hegemonic refashioning of national culture resulted from the concerns of Puerto Rico's intellectual elite regarding how to define Puerto Rican culture. Writing in 1935, Tomás Blanco addressed this concern by linking the *plena* to "Hispanic" cultural styles in his pathbreaking essay "Elogio a 'la plena.'" A journalist, historian, physician, and defender of civil rights, Blanco was perceived by his contemporaries as one of the foremost representatives of Puerto Rico's intellectual elite. Through selective memory, Blanco displaced conflictual aspects of the music's historical origin, effacing the histories of La Joya's residents like Catherine, Elena, and Bumbúm and their contentions over Ponce's spatial and sexual geography. Blanco's hispanophilic discourse responded on one level to cultural imperialism and on another to a whitening ideology. In both cases, however, music became the most effective trope for representing the nation.

The formation of a national imagination advocating racial inclusiveness was a long and contested debate that developed in Puerto Rico during this period. The two most persistent questions that troubled Blanco's generation were "Who are we?" and "What are we like?"[40] Paradoxically, Blanco's response connected conflicting conceptions of Puerto Rico's colonial status by emphasizing that the cultural lineage of the *plena* was in the "white vein"[41] while admitting that most Puerto Ricans were of "mixed blood."[42] Stated differently, cultural miscegenation did not occur in Puerto Rico although (and contradictorily) racial miscegenation characterized its population. That it was possible to highlight cultural whitening while pledging allegiance to the ideology of racial fraternity exemplifies the complexities of Puerto Rico's racial ideology. Blanco's foundational discourse recognized the existence of different races but included them within an encompassing notion of "Puerto Ricanness" that was supposed to supersede racial identities. His version of harmonious race relations had at least two important implications. First, it assumed that no racial divide existed in Puerto Rico, but to the extent that one did exist, it was "apologetic, bashful, and of lower degree." Second, to the degree that some prejudice persisted, it was to be explained as a "defensive echo of foreign [U.S.] aberrations."[43]

Blanco's observations emerged from the first generation of intellectuals concerned with the cultural implications of U.S. colonialism. Yet there are few references in Blanco's writings to the growing sense of crisis during that decade. The 1930s saw the Great Depression, the highest incidence of labor mobilization, and the emergence of a strong nationalistic revolutionary movement.[44] Fears and anxieties about the instability of traditional class composition and the Americanization of culture led this generation to propose a new understanding of "Puerto Ricanness." This privileged interpretation of what was Puerto Rican inaugurated many of the myths that proclaimed the island as a culturally homogeneous nation.[45]

Blanco's construction of the *plena* acquires special relevance when we consider its connection with the *plena*'s historical development as a popular form of local culture in Ponce. In an appeal to create a "typical homogenous diversity"[46]—an oxymoron in itself—the *plena* symbolized Puerto Rico's harmonious and nonviolent miscegenation process. Nonetheless, Blanco warned that in its form and content the *plena* "comments, like the Spanish romance."[47] By whitening the foundation of the *plena*'s acerbic social commentary, Blanco not only depoliticized the genre's local specificity, but he gave it a cultural value that showcased Puerto Rico's "refined" tropical musicality. Through this paternalistic transformation, Blanco silenced histories of racial and sexual confrontation with an insistent Spanish cultural affirmation fashioned in response to U.S. imperialism. In his social imagination, the United States interrupted Puerto Rico's teleological progression toward national sovereignty. Blanco developed a conception of Puerto Rican culture based on a hispanophilic interpretation of nationhood in support of what he considered traditional cultural traits.

Confronted with the predicament of the *plena*'s histories, "Elogio" claims to have transcended its problematic birthplace, a space darkened by degeneration. Hence, the *plena* needed to "overcome the *burundanga* [a badly cooked mixture] of its environment."[48] Blanco believed that the only way to make the *plena* truly Puerto Rican was to detach it from its historical origins. His image of Puerto Rican cultural identity—a well-cooked homogenous blend—required that the *plena* not remain a manifestation of difference. On the contrary, in order to preserve his cultural project for the nation, Blanco subsumed the *plena*'s conflicting claims regarding racial, sexual, and class relations into the concealing fiction of the "great Puerto Rican family."

Yet the kinds of communities to which the *plena* appealed did not constitute a family. The *plena*'s unspoken histories reveal complex racial, sexual, and class discourses of both the local and national landscape. Recast, these discourses shed light on how cultural boundaries had to be daily negotiated and how clearly marked social divides cannot explain the arbitrary logic by which these boundaries are delimited. Whether the occupants of these discrete spaces were black, working-class men and women, or prostitutes, each fought his or her way into the public from a position of political marginality. By singing and dancing to the *plena*, they could simultaneously create and contest cultural frontiers. The language of the *plena* invoked people who feel, maintain, and articulate a common sense of history. Ironically, Blanco also recognized this potential when he transformed the genre into an emblem of Puerto Rican national identity. He understood how the *plena* could mobilize collective identification to define new cultural boundaries of what the Puerto Rican community meant. Because the genre destabilized middle-class family order and racial hierarchies in the island, Blanco tried to affix the *plena* to a national character that partially closed down those possibilities. Ultimately, he fabricated a broadly appealing cultural icon to resist the "Americanization" process during the early twentieth century.

Something about Blanco's fetishized *plena* seems to touch all of the complex relations that it subsumed. He was concerned with creating a counterculture to the United States out of what was actually a counterculture in Ponce's urban landscape. Blanco's *plena* demonstrated how the achievement of national unity was signaled by the nationalization of local forms of popular expression. It centered on the work of intellectual elites whose self-legitimization was a successful replication of the style and achievements of the *pleneros* in community building. It proposed the attainment of a homogenous Puerto Rican identity, which was really an appropriation of racially mixed cultural manifestations.

Over the early decades of the twentieth century, the different communities that defined the *plena*'s meanings operated through active displacement of social dynamics, as music operates through the active displacement of airwaves. Taken together, the *plena*'s shifting meanings reveal the relationship of blacks, men and women of the popular classes, prostitutes, and the intellectual elite in all their complexity of overlapping social networks. By mapping this moving landscape, we can hear in the *plena*'s dissonant melodies a polyphony of conflicts over the use of popular culture as a system of representation from which communal and national identifications are derived and acted out.

Notes

I would like to thank Sueann Caulfield, Sarah Chambers, and Lara Putnam for their thoughtful editing suggestions. I also offer my thanks to Rebecca Scott, Pablo Ramírez, Nicole Stanton, and Wanda Rivera for their careful reading of an earlier version of this essay.

1   On the origin of the *plena*, see Felix Echevarría Alvarado, *La plena: Origen, sentido y desarollo en el folklore puertorriqueno* (Santurce, PR: F. Echevarría Alvarado, 1985). See also Juan Flores, "Bumbum and the Beginning of the *La Plena*," in *Salsiology: Afro-Cuban Music and the Evolution of the Salsa in New York City*, ed. Vernon W. Boggs (New York: Excelsior Music, 1992), 59–68; Edgardo Rodríguez Juliá, "La plena," *El nuevo día*, 9 April 1989, 1; Ruth Glasser, *My Music Is My Flag: Puerto Rican Musicians and*

Their New York Communities, 1917–1940 (Berkeley: University of California Press, 1995), 169–190; and Frances Aparicio, *Listening to Salsa: Gender, Latin Popular Music, and Puerto Rican Cultures* (Middletown, CT: Wesleyan University Press, 1998), 27–44.

2 For Benedict Anderson the nation is an "imagined community" in which local forms, cultural objects, and particular practices are imbued with nationalist meaning through the homogenizing force of repetition, simultaneity, and ritual. See Anderson, *Imagined Communities: Reflections on the Origin and Spread of Nationalism* (London: Verso, 1983), 16. See also Eric Hobsbawm, *The Invention of Tradition* (Cambridge: Cambridge University Press, 1992); and Partha Chatterjee, *The Nation and Its Fragments: Colonial and Postcolonial Histories* (Princeton, NJ: Princeton University Press, 1993). On race in the nationalist imagination, see Robin Moore, *Nationalizing Blackness: Afrocubanismo and Artistic Revolution in Havana, 1920–1940* (Pittsburgh, PA: University of Pittsburgh Press, 1997); and Ada Ferrer, *Insurgent Cuba: Race, Nation, and Revolution, 1868–1898* (Chapel Hill: University of North Carolina Press, 1999).

3 For an analysis of popular culture in Latin America, see Tom Salman, "Introduction," in *The Legacy of the Disinherited Popular Culture in Latin America: Modernity, Globalization, Hybridity, and Authenticity* (Amsterdam: CEDLA, 1996); Néstor García Canclini, *Culturas híbridas: Estrategias para entrar y salir de la modernidad* (Mexico City: Grijalbo, 1990); and Gilbert Joseph and Daniel Nugent, eds., *Everyday Forms of State Formation: Revolution and the Negotiation of Rule in Mexico* (Durham, NC: Duke University Press, 1994). For Puerto Rico, see Lillian Guerra, *Popular Expression and National Identity in Puerto Rico: The Struggle for the Self, Community, and Nation* (Gainesville: University Press of Florida, 1998). On popular music and the national imagination, see Simon Frith, *Performing Rites: On the Value of Popular Music* (Cambridge: Harvard University Press, 1996).

4 Stuart Hall, "Notes on Deconstructing the Popular," in *People's History and Socialist Theory*, ed. Rafael Samuel (London: Routledge, 1981), 442–453.

5 My discussion of Ponce's respectability is informed by the work of Eileen Suárez Findlay's *Imposing Decency: The Politics of Sexuality and Race in Puerto Rico, 1870–1920* (Durham, NC: Duke University Press, 1999). See also Angel Quintero Rivera, *Patricios y plebeyos: Burgueses, hacendados y obreros* (Río Piedras, PR: Huracán, 1988); and Ivonne Acosta, *Santa Juana y Mano Manca: Auge y decadencia del azúcar en el valle del Turabo en el siglo XX* (San Juan, PR: Cultural, 1995).

6 See Acosta, *Santa Juana y Mano Manca*; Andrés Ramos Mattei, "The Growth of the Puerto Rican Sugar Industry under North American Domination, 1899–1910," in *Crisis and Change in the International Sugar Economy, 1860–1914*, ed. Bill Albert and Adrián Graves (Norwich, UK: ISC, 1984), 121–131; and Quintero Rivera, *Patricios y plebeyos*, 32–41. See also Kelvin Santiago-Valle, *"Subject People" and Colonial Discourses: Economic Transformation and Social Disorder in Puerto Rico, 1898–1947* (Albany: State University of New York Press, 1994), 35–48.

7 According to Ponce's manuscript census, by 1910, of the total population living in La Joya, 31% were white, 42% black, and 27% mulatto; of the blacks and mulattos, 14% were from other Caribbean islands. Of the active working population, 48% were males and 52% were females. While 72% of the black and mulatto men of working age were agricultural laborers (35%) or craftsmen (37%), only 10% of the white men were agricultural laborers and 7% were craftsmen. Of all women laborers, 82% were black and

The *Plena*'s Dissonant Melodies   269

mulatta, and of this group 78% were domestic laborers. In contrast, only 18% of the total female work force was white, and of this group 39% were domestic laborers. This information is taken from *1910 Population Census* (Washington, DC: National Archives Trust Fund Board, 1982), microfilms schedules T624, rolls 1774, 412–442.

8 Echevarría, *La plena*, 78.

9 Although the public school system installed by the United States, to Americanize as well as educate Puerto Ricans, reduced the level of illiteracy, in 1910 it was still 66.5%. See Negrón de Montilla, *Americanization of Puerto Rico and the Public School System, 1900–1930* (Río Piedras, PR: Universitaria, 1975).

10 The *plena* reveals the transformation of the African-derived *bomba* through the influence of musical styles from the Dominican Republic and Barbados.

11 Findlay, *Imposing Decency*, 105–106.

12 On prostitution in Latin America, see Donna J. Guy, *Sex and Danger in Buenos Aires: Prostitution, Family, and Nation in Argentina* (Lincoln: University of Nebraska Press, 1991); Katherine Bliss, *Compromised Positions: Prostitution, Public Health, and Gender Politics in Revolutionary Mexico City* (University Park: Penn State University Press, 2001); and Sueann Caulfield, "Birth of Mangue: Race, Nation, and the Politics of Prostitution in Rio de Janeiro, 1850–1942," in *Sex and Sexuality in Latin America*, ed. Daniel Balderston and Donna J. Guy (New York: New York University Press, 1997), 86–100. For Puerto Rico, see Findlay, *Imposing Decency*.

13 On the relationship of day-to-day practices and the public sphere, see Jürgen Habermas, *The Structural Transformation of the Public Sphere: An Inquiry into a Category of Bourgeois Society* (Cambridge: MIT Press, 1962); Michel de Certeau, *The Practice of Everyday Life* (Berkeley: University of California Press, 1984); and Elsa Barkley Brown and Greg Kimball, "Mapping the Terrain of Black Richmond," *Journal of Urban History* 21 (1995): 296–346.

14 Displays of the pomp of these dances appeared frequently in Ponce's newspapers. For example, in an article about a dance that took place in the Spanish Center, *El águila* noted: "Everyone of Ponce's society was there. The center of the saloon had a truly regal décor. An overwhelming sense of luxury filled the ample rooms . . . while the perfumes emanating from the elegant ladies, with their elegance and beauty, complemented the magnificence of the event." "El baile de anoche," *El águila*, Jan. 7, 1910.

15 Letters from Ponce's police chief to its mayor addressing this ambivalence can be found in the Ayuntamiento section of the Archivo Histórico del Municipio de Ponce (hereafter AHP).

16 "Expediente sobre escrito de A. Arbona y otros pidiendo que se vo[t]e una ordenanza para prohibir la celebración de bailes atentatorios a la moral pública, Oct. 1909," in AHP, leg. S-113, exp. 18. Emphasis in the original text. The signers of the letter were Antonio Arbona Oliver, Justo C. Algarín, Felix Caro León, Jorge Fernández, Julio Gautier, José Bioscochéa, and Pedro González.

17 "El secretario del municipio de Ponce que suscribe, noviembre 1909," in AHP, leg. G-218, exp. 22.

18 The police records used are Ponce's *Libros diarios de novedades de Ponce* (hereafter NP) in the Archivo General de Puerto Rico (hereafter AGPR). This record provides offender's name, color, and birthplace, as well as the reason and place of the arrest. Information is also given about the victims and, in some cases, the penalty imposed.

19 Echevarría, *La plena*, 115–120.

20 AGPR, NP, Dec. 1917–Feb. 1918, 57.

21 See Gervacio L. García and Angel Quintero Rivera, *Desafío y solidaridad: Breve historia del movimiento obrero puertorriqueño* (Río Piedras, PR: Huracán, 1982).

22 "Letter to the Mayor," in AHP, leg. G-27, exp. 6.

23 See Santiago-Valle, *"Subject People."*

24 "Letter to the Mayor," in AHP, leg. G-27, exp. 6. The public vices that he referred to were speeding bicycles on the sidewalks, gambling in the plaza, screaming vendors, children playing in the street late at night, the exposure of naked children, and immoral acts not specified by the penal code.

25 Ibid.

26 Findlay, *Imposing Decency*, 135–166.

27 AHP, leg. G-27, exp. 15b, "Señor Capitan de la Policía Insular," Nov. 1916. The letter was signed by: Carlos Rodríguez Vázquez, Tomás Peralez, Moncerrate González, Miguel Ruiz, Luis Rigau, and Fidel Rivera. The other eighteen signatures were not available in the file, but in a previous letter police chief Hurtado made reference to twenty-four signatures.

28 AHP, leg. G-280, exp. 2, "Expedientes sobre ordenanza prohibiendo los bailes de empresas donde concurran mesalinas," Dec. 1917.

29 AHP, leg. G-28, exp. 2, "Al honorable consejo," Dec. 2, 1917.

30 Ibid.

31 Findlay, *Imposing Decency*, 167–201.

32 Ibid., 180–189.

33 See Echevarría, *La plena*, 127–143; Flores, "Bumbum," 59–67.

34 Felix Echevarría Alvarado, interview with the author, Ponce, PR, 6 Nov. 1997.

35 Ibid. Echevarría used the English word *showman*.

36 Echevarría, *La plena*, 131. Some of the most famous *conjuntos* that emerged in other neighborhoods were the Aranzamendi Brothers in Tenerías; Chivo Román in La Torre; and Mario Rivera in Bélgica.

37 Glasser, *My Music Is My Flag*.

38 Tomás Blanco, "Elogio a 'la plena,'" *Revista del ateneo puertorriqueño* 1.1 (1935): 100.

39 Ibid., 106. On Blanco's racial ideology, see Arcadio Díaz Quiñones, "Racismo, historia y esclavitud," in *El prejuicio racial en Puerto Rico* (Río Piedras, PR: Huracán, 1985), 15–91.

40 *Indice* (1929–1931), the principal literary journal of the period, carried on an intense debate concerning the Puerto Rican national identity. In its issues from April to November 1929, under the title of "Who Are We? How Are We?," the journal posited three questions to the country's most prominent intellectuals: "(1) Do you think our personality as a nation is completely defined?; (2) Is there a way of being unmistakable and genuinely Puerto Rican?; (3) What are the definite signs of our collective character?"

41 Blanco, "Elogio," 101–102.

42 Ibid., 100.

43 Ibid., 99.

44 On strikes, see Taller de Formación Política, *¡Huelga en la caña!* (Río Piedras, PR: Huracán, 1982). On massacres of members of the Nationalist Party in Río Piedras in

1935 and Ponce in 1937, see Manuel Maldonado Denis, *La conciencia nacional puertorriqueña: Pedro Albizu Campos* (Mexico City: Siglo XXI, 1972).

45 On the nationalist imagination during this decade, see José Luis González, "Literatura e identidad nacional en Puerto Rico," in *Puerto Rico: Identidad y clases sociales*, ed. Angel Quintero Rivera, José Luis González, Ricardo Campos, and Juan Flores (Río Piedras, PR: Huracán, 1981), 45–80; and María Elena Rodríguez Castro, "Las casas del porvenir: Nación y narración en el ensayo puertorriqueño," in *Revista iberoamericana* 59 (1993): 33–54.

46 Blanco, "Elogio," 102.

47 Ibid., 101.

48 Ibid., 101.

Prostitutes and the law: the uses of court
cases over pandering in Rio de Janeiro at the
beginning of the twentieth century
Cristiana Schettini Pereira

At the end of the nineteenth century debates over prostitution intensified in Brazil's capital city, Rio de Janeiro. Regulation of "prostitution zones" was a major law enforcement priority, which the police believed demanded drastic measures. Yet there was no consensus among
the police, much less among other urban authorities, regarding the kind
of danger prostitution presented and what public authorities should do
about it. Newspapers ran sensationalist stories about the traffic in European women who were brought as slaves to Rio de Janeiro or Buenos
Aires, where they were forced into prostitution. Jurists and physicians
debated state regulation of prostitution, but, faced with widespread opposition to such regulation, they focused instead on defining laws regarding pimping or pandering (*lenocínio*), which became a crime for the
first time in the new penal code of 1890. Beginning in 1902, the republican government began to send official representatives to international
conferences organized to fight the traffic in women. Its major objective
was to differentiate the Brazilian capital from its Argentine neighbor,
which, by regulating prostitution, had earned a reputation as a haven for
traffickers.[1]

This chapter will analyze a selection of criminal trials involving pandering from the early years of Brazil's republic to reveal how the people
involved—police officers, jurists, the accused, and witnesses—made use
of the law in particular ways at different times. The trial records reveal
changes in police strategies for controlling prostitutes and other groups
of people who occupied the city's downtown. By justifying police intervention as a moral imperative, the new law created a new instrument that
police and jurists used in their attempt to reorganize republican urban

space. Yet pandering trials also document some of the strategies prostitutes and madams developed in response to police attempts to control how they occupied urban space. Finally, these trials sometimes provided prostitutes official backing in their attempts to confront landlords who charged exorbitant rents or even to work out conflicts in a troublesome love affair.

The prostitutes who became the topic of public debate at the end of the nineteenth century had been living in the city's downtown for more than a decade. Their visibility suddenly became an urgent problem in part because of the changes Brazilian society as a whole was undergoing. Formal abolition of slavery in 1888, together with the proclamation of the republic the following year, coincided with the strengthening of political alliances that made possible the implementation of dramatic, violent measures that transformed urban space in the nation's capital city.[2] Scientific and technical justifications for racist, classist, and sexist political decisions fueled the processes of urban renovation, in a manner analogous to that of other Latin American cities.[3] Many contemporaries believed that these changes would "civilize" the capital. Although there was little agreement about what that meant, there was a general consensus among elite Cariocas (Rio de Janeiro residents) about the urgent need to free the city of any sign of the colonial past by modeling the urban landscape and lifestyle after those of Paris.[4] Key sectors of the national elite, insecure in the face of the apparent demise of seigneurial dominion, increasingly relied on biological theories of racial difference to justify social hierarchies and maintain their own positions of privilege. At the same time, the belief that the population would gradually become whiter as a result of natural selection and European immigration nurtured the dream of a European civilization in the tropics.[5]

Police concerns with the visibility of prostitution in the city's downtown and with the mixture of newly arrived white European prostitutes with those of African descent resonated with more general social fears about what was seen as unprecedented social instability. Alarmist discourses about the immoral presence of prostitutes of different classes and origins revealed an underlying belief that the proper organization of urban space would create the republican social order of which many elite Cariocas dreamed.[6] Stories of the traffic in white women, which mobilized xenophobic and racist fears, were a favorite genre.[7] With protagonists—victims as well as their kidnappers—from distant European cities, these stories created the impression that the new Brazilian republic shared Europe's social problems. "White slavery," with its images of sexualized, deceived, and victimized women unable to control their own lives, carried political implications that were more convenient for Rio's "civilizers" than the old, discomforting problems of African slavery and the visibility of black Brazilian prostitutes. These latter were historical realities they preferred to forget.[8]

The content of criminal trials for pandering in turn-of-the-century Rio de Janeiro would certainly surprise a reader informed only by daily newspapers or literature of the period. In contrast to the romantic stories of sophisticated French prostitutes and pimps and white slaves from far-off lands that inhabited the popular imagination, the trials record quotidian conflicts among owners, managers, and tenants of boardinghouses, pensions, and tenements—many of them native-born Brazilians. The high number of acquittals and cases dismissed before trial seems to be explained less by the machinations of mysterious criminal operations— another popular idea at the time—than by the constant disagreements among police authorities, public prosecutors, lawyers, and judges about how to define "exploitation," about the parameters of state intervention into private lives, and about the legal status of prostitutes in a society that did not formally recognize prostitution but considered it a necessary activity. Even more important, the trials uncover prostitutes who did not fit the stereotype of the white slave. Finally, the trials demonstrate that the courts were one among many arenas where prostitutes participated in struggles over the meaning and uses of public space in the new regime.

The 1890 Penal Code defined pandering in three ways. Under article 277, to pander was to "incite, favor, or facilitate the prostitution of one person to satisfy the dishonest desires or lewd passions of another," that is, to act as a "go-between." Article 278 aimed to punish pimping, described as "to induce women through violence or threat to work in prostitution traffic and to share the profits of prostitution." The same article also criminalized the provision of "lodging, aid, and abetment to the industry of prostitution, for direct or indirect profit," which was meant to punish hotel and brothel owners.[9]

The cases analyzed here reveal how police and justice officials used this legislation in neighborhoods that underwent urban renewal in the early years of the twentieth century. Two moments stand out. The first is 1896, when the police precinct chief, Luiz Bartholomeu de Souza e Silva, targeted women who rented rooms to prostitutes. He used the laws on pandering to launch the republic's first large-scale police "moral sanitation campaign." By arresting landladies who rented to prostitutes, he sought to force them out of certain downtown areas. The second moment came almost twenty years later, in 1915, when police precinct chief Silvestre Machado opened twelve investigations of hotels that rented rooms to couples by the hour. This precinct chief used the laws on pandering to police and control establishments characterized by the rapid circulation of people, in which the differences between prostitutes and other women could become ambiguous in the eyes of the authorities. To a great extent, Machado was dealing with the consequences of his predecessors' campaigns: the strategy of evicting the residents of downtown brothels had led to the growth of another type of sexual commerce, which had permitted prostitutes to avoid police vigilance and to continue working the same streets as before.

These investigations of hotels, which took place during the first six months of 1915, marked a significant change in the focus of police vigilance and anticipated a change in the laws regarding prostitution. In September of the same year Congress would significantly broaden the parameters of the crime of pandering, formally acquiescing to the resolutions of successive international congresses against the traffic in women. The new law made it a crime to provide "any assistance or aid to the trade of prostitution," a phrase that replaced the expression "providing lodging, aid, and abetment." With this wording, legislators hoped to put an end to the ambiguous interpretations that had justified many acquittals.[10]

Yet the ambiguity reappeared in another section of the new law, with the introduction of the term "house of tolerance." Borrowed from the French regulamentarist system, the term was already being used by different authorities to mean various things: places for quick encounters, hotels that rented rooms by the hour, buildings where prostitutes rented rooms, or any place where prostitution was practiced. The new law did not help define the term but rather transformed it into the subject of a heated dispute among jurists that would last well into the 1920s. Their debates over the meaning of "house of tolerance" expressed different conceptions about how the police and the criminal justice system should deal with prostitution. While some judges tolerated brothels on specifically delimited streets under strict police vigilance, others condemned any relationship that they saw as exploitation of prostitutes, regardless of the consequences for the police policy of restricting prostitution to specific streets. In practice, the change in the law, which made it a crime to "maintain or exploit houses of tolerance; permit entrance in a residence to persons of different sexes, or of the same sex, who meet for libidinous purposes," resulted in a broad application of the law, as much by police precinct chiefs as by judges.[11]

The trials examined here resulted from the two police campaigns mentioned above (one in 1896, the other in 1915), which took place in the same central region of the city. The two groups of trials illustrate the complicated relationship between police and judicial authorities, as well as changes in the strategies and lives of prostitutes who insisted on occupying the downtown in spite of police attempts to "moralize" that space.[12] Police campaigns were never restricted to the application of criminal law. In fact, police authorities struggled to gain social legitimacy and judicial support for their actions and for the notion that the police should be free to resolve certain problems, such as public prostitution, themselves. In great part, this freedom was granted in the regulations governing the police force. A 1903 regulation established one of the police's fundamental prerogatives by guaranteeing precinct chiefs the right to repress prostitutes "without prejudice to the appropriate judicial process, as [the police] deem best for the well-being of the population and public morality." This gave the civil police a written license for arbitrary enforcement.[13]

Newspapers in these years show that even before the ambiguous regulations of 1903 and 1907 were passed, precinct chiefs habitually employed unorthodox methods of repressing prostitutes: they evicted prostitutes from their homes, ordered them to shut their windows after ten at night, prohibited them from using hats under certain circumstances, and even prohibited all women from walking on the streets alone at night.[14] These measures, together with the campaigns analyzed below, indicate that instead of following a general plan, the policing of prostitution in Rio de Janeiro varied from precinct chief to precinct chief and consisted basically of negotiations between the neighborhood police and local residents. The various police actions also demonstrate that police found it increasingly difficult to differentiate prostitutes from other women who moved throughout the city, as became especially clear in the 1915 trials.

Throughout the first part of the twentieth century, localized and decentralized police actions converged in two ways. The first was an increasing interest in guaranteeing legal support for police autonomy in dealing with prostitutes and other groups. The second was a progressive movement toward segregating prostitutes spatially.[15] In the campaign launched by the precinct chief Bartholomeu in 1896, the goal was simply to oblige prostitutes who lived downtown to move, without any concern as to where they would relocate. By the time the precinct chief Silvestre took over in 1915, it was already common practice for the police to designate certain streets bordering the downtown as "tolerance zones," where women evicted from central streets could reestablish their businesses.

The period was marked by divergent positions among jurists. Judge Francisco José Viveiros de Castro, who adjudicated the very first pandering trials, continued to insist on a broad interpretation of the law. He considered any assistance given to prostitution, including renting rooms to prostitutes, a crime. His position, however, was contested through numerous acquittals in the appeals court, which attempted to delimit more precisely the scope of the crime. Cases from 1915 on, in which taverns and hotels were targeted, also routinely ended in acquittals, even when judges were sympathetic to the police moralization campaigns. By the 1920s a new trend emerged. Despite the persistent disagreement over what a "house of tolerance" was, many judges decided to convict only those responsible for houses located outside of areas where the police tolerated prostitution. Judicial recognition of these areas of "tolerated prostitution" suggests that police measures were gaining legitimacy in the eyes of judges and that police zoning policies had become more effective.[16] Effectively granting police the autonomy they sought to deal with prostitutes, jurists helped disseminate the idea that because these women did not possess honor, they did not deserve the same legal treatment as honorable women. They thus reproduced the logic prevailing in many other Latin American judicial systems, reinforcing the importance of sexual honor as one of the defining aspects of women's legal status.[17]

Judge Viveiros de Castro elaborated this idea explicitly in one of the republic's first pandering trials. The case of Mariana Gother, a thirty-five-year-old from the "backlands of [the northeastern state of] Bahia" who rented rooms to prostitutes in downtown Rio, began with the testimony of two of her tenants.[18] Each of the women, young migrants from the rural interior of Rio de Janeiro state, stated that she periodically rented a room from Mariana at 12,000 reis per day, not including food or furnishings. The accused stated that she did not own the house but herself rented it for 250,000 reis per month and that she did in fact sublet rooms to prostitutes.

Ten days later, two other residents, young migrants from the northeastern backlands, declared that they were currently each paying 10,000 reis per day to the accused. The precinct chief concluded that the accused received nine hundred thousand reis per month for the three rooms, creating a net profit of 650,000 reis. It was evident to Luiz Bartholomeu that "Mariana Gother is a harlot and, according to the evidence, benefits from the prostitution of her tenants." The public prosecutor accepted Bartholomeu's report, and the investigation became a criminal trial. Unlike in most pimping trials, in which witnesses disappeared after their initial testimony at the police station, police were able to round up the same witnesses when it came time to take testimony before the judge. These "backland" women, hailing from impoverished regions where the bulk of the population was of mixed or African descent, represented a mode of prostitution often ignored in the public discourse in which French and Polish prostitutes took center stage. Despite their disadvantageous national and regional origins, however, it appeared that they each earned enough to pay at least three hundred thousand reis per month in rent, more than Gother paid for the whole house.

According to defense attorneys, Mariana Gother was "an elderly woman" who had no other source of income than to sublet "to her colleagues." Without denying that Mariana was also a prostitute, her lawyers reminded the judge that subletting was a "common practice nowadays." In fact, subletting was a common livelihood at a time of economic crisis, especially considering the housing shortage, aggravated by the continual influx of migrants.[19] Gother's lawyers also suggested that having prostitutes as tenants was a particularly profitable undertaking.[20] In an attempt to avoid having her character judged on the basis of her sexual behavior, her lawyers emphasized that she had a reputation as a person of good public conduct, confirmed by her clean police record and a document signed by neighboring merchants. The willingness of these men to support Mariana publicly suggests that they saw beyond her sexual activities to other aspects of her day-to-day comportment and her value as a neighbor.

Not surprisingly, the judge in the case, Viveiros de Castro, refused to accept these criteria and indicted the defendant. Brazilian law, he wrote, "decided the issue in clear and explicit terms," and since it had been proven that Mariana Gother "provided rooms in her house . . . for women to exercise prostitution" and that she profited from it, she was guilty. "The offense of pandering is not an attack against honor, as in rape, but rather includes acts that tend to incite, favor, facilitate moral corruption. The prostitute is thus included."[21] With this verdict, Viveiros de Castro initiated a long juridical debate on the definition of pandering.

In distinguishing crimes against honor from crimes against morality, he contributed to a juridical tendency that sought to broaden control over various groups that would not be granted full citizenship in the new republican order. Honor, as Viveiros de Castro understood it (and unlike the way Mariana Gother's lawyers and neighbors presented it), would guarantee or deny access to the judicial system to people like Mariana.

Viveiros de Castro's logic left no room for doubt regarding the position of the tenants in the case. As prostitutes, women without honor, they were not deserving of legal protection: although they were the most affected by the crime of pandering, they were never considered to be victims but merely witnesses. As Sueann Caulfield has shown with regard to the crime of deflowering, Brazilian legislation privileged the defense of family honor over the individual rights of the victim. Even in crimes involving victims who might be considered "honest," the law did not seek to protect their physical integrity or their individual rights but rather "larger social institutions," that is, "the family" or "social customs."[22] When dealing with women notoriously devoid of honor in the eyes of jurists such as Viveiros de Castro, the idea that the law might serve the interests of the victims was not even contemplated. By locating pandering as a crime against custom, the judge stood in favor of police campaigns against the interests and individual rights of landlords.

Yet Viveiros de Castro's view on the matter was just one among many. Mariana's lawyers appealed his decision, presenting another list of merchants who attested that she lived in a state of poverty and comported herself decently, as well as a declaration from the police precinct stating that she had sold her rent contract on the house to another woman, who was a prostitute, as were her new tenants. Eventually the appeals court absolved her on the grounds that there was no proof that she had induced anyone to prostitution or that she had profited from such dealings.

Evidently, if Chief Luiz Bartholomeu really intended to put an end to the houses of prostitution in his district, criminal trials for pandering were a slow, labor-intensive, and ultimately ineffective way to do so. However, pandering cases were just one of the police's strategies for controlling prostitutes. Many others, involving extralegal measures, were only sporadically reported.[23] Indeed, the incriminating testimony of Mariana's tenants might well have resulted from blackmail or other pressure by the police. After all, the end result of their testimony was to legitimize a police action that worked against them by penalizing their landladies and forcing all of them to move out. These trials allow us to begin to understand how police precinct chiefs such as Luiz Bartholomeu took advantage of preexisting conflicts between tenants and landladies and widespread perceptions of exploitation as they pursued their own agenda.

This aspect reappears even more clearly in the trial of Pepa Sinai, once again presided over by Judge Viveiros de Castro. Pepa, a fifty-two-year-old Austrian, was accused of subletting rooms to prostitutes in three houses, all located in the same region.[24] Her tenants were Russian, German, and Austrian women, a little older than Mariana's tenants. These women paid monthly rents of one hundred thousand reis for a furnished room, board not included, while Mariana's tenants paid daily sums for rooms they occupied. Pepa herself declared that she paid two hundred thousand reis for each house. She emphasized that she made little profit from subletting the houses since each held only two tenants.

This argument did not convince the prosecutor. In testimony before the judge, a police inspector stated that the residents of one of Pepa's houses had filed a complaint that she exploited them by charging excessive rent. In their court testimony, Pepa's tenants continued to complain that their rent was too high but avoided suggesting that they were dependent in any way on their landlady, denying that she intervened in their choice of clients, lent them money, or provided meals. These prostitutes sought to take advantage of police crackdowns in order to resolve their own conflicts and control exorbitant rents.[25] For them, being an "exploited prostitute" bore no relation to stereotypes involving personal relations and dependency. This stance frustrated the prosecutor and the judge, who fished for evidence that Pepa Sinai had "aided and abetted" their prostitution. Yet the tenants stubbornly insisted that all they wanted was lower rent.

For their part, Pepa and her lawyers attempted to argue that both high rents and accepting prostitutes as tenants were unavoidable in the section of the city where the houses were located. Thus, they attempted to prove that the houses were already inhabited by prostitutes before being rented out by the defendant. And, just as Mariana's lawyers had done, Pepa's defense called three witnesses—a Brazilian salesman, a German carpenter, and a Portuguese businessman—who had known the defendant for four, three, and fourteen years, respectively, through her previous professional activities, such as catering and owning another boardinghouse. Her lawyers thus tried to establish her good reputation among her neighbors as evidenced by her honest business practices and her long-term personal ties. The lawyers attempted to create standards of feminine honor—including the capacity to support oneself and long-term acquaintance with neighbors—that countered the standards predominant in the courts.[26]

None of these strategies, however, was enough to change the convictions of Viveiros de Castro, who said in his final sentence that the defendant "divided her houses into cubicles and rented those cubicles at an exorbitant price to prostitutes." The judge convicted Pepa based on an image of promiscuity and lack of hygiene, which was immediately contested by Pepa's attorney when he appealed. It was during this phase of the trial that her lawyer laid bare the logic that inspired the police campaign. In Chief Bartholomeu's eyes, the lawyer argued, it would be enough to have inherited a building on the streets Bartholomeu had condemned to be accused of pandering. Even he, a lawyer who defended "harlots' causes" in court, could be accused of abetting prostitution. Viveiros de Castro's broad interpretation of the pandering law potentially implicated anyone who associated in any way with prostitutes. Challenging this interpretation, lawyers such as the one who represented Pepa defended the landlords' individual rights.

Although Mariana Gother and Pepa Sinai's convictions were overturned by higher courts, Judge Viveiros de Castro's attitude toward prostitution was widely shared by jurists, as was evident in the law itself. Since prostitution was not formally recognized, a person could not be convicted for merely exercising it. Therefore, the police strategy was to criminalize prostitutes through existing laws, such as those prohibiting indecent exposure or vagrancy. The legislation against pandering was another instrument for indirect repression. It helped establish some degree of control over not only locales of prostitution but collective housing in general. Although most of the deponents in pandering cases were prostitutes, certain ways of interpreting the law, such as that sustained by Viveiros de Castro, could affect people who lived near prostitutes, just as Pepa Sinai's lawyer warned.

Yet for many prostitutes, accusations of pandering could be an opportunity to show up at precincts and courts as victims rather than suspects. Beyond disagreements between lawyers and judges as to the location of prostitution and the individual rights of landlords, many women used police campaigns and the law to defend their interests and what they considered their rights, such as the right to a "fair rent." Mariana Gother, Pepa Sinai, and their tenants did not seem to live in an underworld: they shared with other urban workers everyday problems, like the high cost of living. Their lawyers highlighted this, emphasizing that these women's survival strategies included common working-class practices such as subletting, and that they established long-term ties with their neighbors. Most significantly, these women's persecution by police seems to have been part of a broader republican effort to intervene in downtown working-class housing, resulting in the forced relocation of many residents.

The case of a woman who appeared twice in pandering trials, first as a victim and later as the accused, offers a glimpse of the mechanisms by which police attempted to establish moral control over downtown residents. Twenty-six-year-old Adelia Visel, an Austrian, went to the police to denounce Gabriel Sckimilovitz, a forty-four-year-old shoemaker, as her pimp.[27] Adelia said she had lived with Gabriel for two years and, because of his threats, gave him money and jewelry. Preparing for a trip to Buenos Aires, Gabriel threatened to kill her if she did not give him more money, forcing her to move to another house to get away from him. The precinct chief organized a face-to-face confrontation between Gabriel and Adelia and then arrested him aboard a ship that would have taken him to Buenos Aires.

Adelia's testimony sounds like a classic tale of pimping, complete with foreigners with "tongue-twisting names" and a poor prostitute victim who after endless suffering finds the courage to denounce her oppressor.[28] The story convinced the precinct chief and the prosecutor. Neither, however, was interested in proving that Adelia had been exploited. They were more excited about arresting a suspicious Russian in transit to Buenos Aires. Neither of them asked Adelia about the fact that she had been Gabriel's lover since they lived together in Europe, where she was already engaged in prostitution. Nor did they attempt to explain the logic of arresting a man on his way to Buenos Aires when it was common practice for police to pay the passage of suspected pimps to that city.[29] They also ignored Gabriel's testimony that he had lived with Adelia for many years in both Europe and Brazil and had never exploited her.

However, Adelia's story was challenged by the testimony of her colleague Paulina Lopes, a twenty-four-year-old Pole. Paulina confirmed that Adelia lived for a time with Gabriel and that he did in fact receive money from her, but she also said she did not know whether he forced her into prostitution. Paulina, while perhaps intending to help her friend Adelia, nonetheless acknowledged that, for her, living with a man and giving him money were different from being forced into prostitution and exploited by him. Paulina also said that during a stay in Buenos Aires sometime earlier, Adelia had told her that she wanted to break up with Gabriel when she returned to Rio. Finally, Paulina stated that Adelia was currently living with a bar owner on Rua Sete de Setembro. Adelia did not appear to testify at the arraignment, and the case was dropped.

This outcome did not mean that all expectations of those involved in the case were frustrated. At least for the police precinct chief, the glory of imprisoning a foreign pimp may have been sufficient. If Adelia's intention was to scare her ex-lover, for revenge or to keep him away, the course of the trial may have been enough to achieve her aim. In this trial, as in others that began with a denunciation by a woman, the prostitutes themselves reinforced the stereotypes of victimized prostitute and exploitative pimp in order to use the trial to solve their own problems with their men.[30] Other evidence, such as Paulina's perception of the couple's relationship, reveals that these stereotypes might be masking quite contradictory dynamics.

Adelia lived for some time with the bar owner whom Paulina mentioned, Frederico (a thirty-two-year-old native of Portugal). We encounter them again in a lawsuit six years later, when they were accused of subletting rooms to prostitutes in a house on Rua Sete de Setembro owned by Frederico.[31] This trial gives further indications that women identified as prostitutes or former prostitutes maintained long-term love relationships. After living for a while as a prostitute, Adelia was now presented as Frederico's companion and as the go-between for rental agreements with other prostitutes. The house had three alcoves, three bedrooms, and a sitting room, in addition to a small outhouse. According to Frederico's testimony, Adelia gave him three hundred thousand reis per month from the alcoves' rent, "keeping the rest as pin money, since in his capacity as her lover, the deponent consents to this." He seemed to treat her as his spouse, publicly taking responsibility for her. There is no indication whether Adelia continued to work as a prostitute, but clearly she was using her previous connections to help her companion in his business.

Through these two moments in Adelia's life we can see the changes in one prostitute's identity in the courts. In six years she had gone from victim to villain, which meant that she moved from a position that permitted her to mobilize the law in her favor to one in which she was the target of the same law. Ironically, the shift reflected her upward mobility. Social ties established during her early years in Brazil allowed Adelia to trade her forty-four-year-old "Russian" for a more financially successful thirty-two-year-old Portuguese man who offered new opportunities for her to make a living. Social ties also helped her find tenants—Spanish and Portuguese—willing to pay very high rents.

Frederico's lawyer insisted on the absurdity of a law punishing someone for renting a house to prostitutes, arguing that by the same logic it should also punish anyone who sold them clothes or food. Like other lawyers representing landlords, he argued that his client had no other option than renting the front house to prostitutes because "there are no family people who wish to rent it, much less live in it, since none of the houses or stores facing the street in this neighborhood are inhabited by families." To prove this, he presented as defense witnesses several merchants living on that street who housed their families and wives in the backs of the buildings where they worked. The witnesses considered it normal for families to live in places such as the inn in the back of the house rented out by Frederico and Adelia, in boardinghouses, or inside commercial buildings, but never facing the street. The one witness who admitted that she rented out rooms on Rua Sete de Setembro was careful to note that only single young men lived in the rooms facing the street. She made a point of emphasizing that she herself lived in the back of the building. A young man who rented from her confirmed that on that street families lived only "in rooms facing the interior patios or behind commercial spaces."

The press constantly denounced the "promiscuous" mixing of poor families, single men, and disreputable women in downtown housing, and police chiefs used the same image to justify moralization campaigns. But in fact, the internal spaces of downtown buildings seem to have maintained a tacit moral segregation. Violent police actions often worked to destroy this moral organization of space, which was not only long-standing, but indeed may have inspired the original layout of these very old houses.[32] At the start of the twentieth century the buildings were condemned as unhealthy and inadequate, and soon many of them would be demolished. Decades earlier, however, the long, narrow hallways denounced by public health inspectors as insalubrious seem to have been constructed to separate the street from the residential area.[33]

Meanwhile, the buildings' residents seemed to accept the fact that, because they exercised a form of trade, the prostitutes could occupy the front of these houses, alongside the stores and shops. Families would occupy other parts of the buildings. Interestingly, trials such as that of

Frederico and Adelia were based on complaints not by other tenants or neighbors but only by tenants who were prostitutes. Engaged in a very specific kind of commerce, prostitutes found it difficult to restrict their activities solely to the space designated for them. For example, when they needed to use the sanitary or bathing facilities located at the back of the buildings, they circulated through other residential parts of the houses, not just the storefronts.[34]

The first group of pandering trials thus demonstrates various dimensions of police initiatives regarding prostitution. Prostitutes' living quarters were spatially delimited, separating them from other residents. When landlords were penalized for renting to prostitutes, these tenants were forced to change their addresses and the terms of their leases. Thus not only prostitutes but also people who associated with them were stigmatized. When precinct chief Bartholomeu began his "moral sanitation" campaign on the downtown streets, he was initiating a process whose effects reached beyond the relocation of prostitutes, strengthening a tendency to deny basic rights—such as the inviolability of the home, the right to move throughout the city, and the right to legal protection—to those lacking the imprimatur of honor. Yet, ironically, the same judges who refused to consider the interests of the people most affected by their judgments could not prevent the trials from establishing prostitutes' claims to certain rights or from using the trials to legitimate various kinds of arrangements that were customary among downtown residents.

The massive reconstruction of Rio's downtown, which reached its peak at the beginning of the twentieth century, aimed principally to destroy collective living quarters and evict their residents in the name of physical and moral hygiene. Yet when the dust settled, these people were still there. At first glance, prostitutes seemed to have followed the trend identified by the lawyer Evaristo de Moraes, a prominent critic of police measures, who noted that prostitutes had dispersed to points throughout the city, now primarily occupying small hotels. As they solicited clients on the streets, rather than from the doorways and windows of their previous residences, they became more visible than ever. By the mid-1910s, pandering trials no longer recorded prostitutes' complaints of high rents and irresponsible landlords. Instead, they demonstrate how police and judicial authorities reacted to these changes by shifting their attention to new places and social networks. They also reveal some of the ways different groups of workers, including prostitutes, escaped police vigilance.

Beginning in the 1910s, police changed the focus of their investigations of pandering to the small hotels and, later, to rooming houses that survived the demolitions: particularly those located outside the areas designated by the police for prostitutes. The objective of precinct chief Silvestre Machado in his 1915 campaign, as well as others who opened similar investigations in subsequent years, was to find direct proof that the couples found in the rooms of those places were there for "libidinous purposes." Such a discovery would permit police to accuse the proprietors of running a "house of tolerance" and prosecute them for pandering.

One of the reasons that precinct chief Silvestre attacked hotels with accusations of pandering was that, in fact, these hotels were among the few options left for women who insisted on engaging in prostitution downtown. Certain proprietors and managers established agreements with local prostitutes. The prostitutes would find clients at a nearby bar (*botequim*) and take them to a hotel. In some cases, both establishments belonged to the same individual, as was the case of Adelia Visel's companion, Frederico. In exchange, the women received a meal and a place to sleep. We also find references to groups of prostitutes loitering in the hotels themselves, which justified police surveillance of their management, now suspected panderers.

The Spaniard Ramón Paradella, owner of an inn where Laura da Silva lived, had no idea of the problems this tenant would cause him.[35] When precinct chief Silvestre began his first investigation in 1915, Laura, identified as a "skinny little Brazilian mulatto," provided tremendous assistance by accusing the Spaniard of prohibiting her from entering his establishment. The Spaniard defended himself by declaring that he had simply made an agreement with Laura that she would sleep at the hotel for five thousand reis a day. He later refused her a room simply because she was behind in her payment. Laura's death from illness before the case came to trial saved Ramón from a conviction. If Laura seemed not to have many options in the final months of her life, two other young Brazilian women decided to leave Petrópolis to try to earn "a barrel of money" in Rio de Janeiro, making a deal with an owner of an inn, who would bring clients to them.[36] Some years later, in a trial against a Portuguese owner of a *hospedaria*, three Brazilian women confirmed that they practiced prostitution in his hotel but denied that he had induced them to do so.[37]

Inns and other hotels became an alternative workplace for prostitutes, most of whom were Brazilian, but they were also a cheap shelter in which many more poor women and men crowded together to spend the night, often on cots. For this reason, they had been the target of police surveillance and persecution for some time. The pandering investigations offered a new moral justification for this long-standing police intervention. Managers, most of whom were Portuguese, were frequently held in custody for several months, without the faintest idea of what crime they had commited by renting rooms to couples, while lawyers, prosecutors, and judges debated whether the couples found in the hotel's rooms were there for "libidinous purposes." In many cases, the debate only ended when the women detained and identified in police precincts as prostitutes proved later, in court, that they were actually factory workers, cooks, or laundresses who habitually met their boyfriends at the hotel in their spare time.[38]

Another impediment to police efforts against inns was the conflict between police and municipal authorities. Inns were generally licensed by the city, and their owners paid taxes. As an indignant lawyer protested, a justice system that let the city charge hotel owners "elevated taxes" and at the same time demand that the innkeepers practice "an internal policing that no employee could possibly achieve" was "the epitome of exploitation." The prosecutor agreed with the lawyer, recommending that the case be dismissed.[39] This was the reason why inns were so difficult to control. Not only did they contribute substantially to the public coffers, but they were frequented by a great variety of people, which made it difficult for police, and often even for the management of the establishments, to distinguish among different kinds of sexual encounters.

Yet it was precisely "internal policing" that judges increasingly demanded. The notion of moral contamination gained prominence as the focus of pandering trials moved from houses of prostitutes to places of quick encounters. In the end, hotel and boardinghouse employees would indeed be responsible for the sexual behavior of their tenants and guests if they wanted to avoid arrest. The introduction of the term "house of tolerance" in the 1915 legislation points to this change, as Judge Eurico Cruz explained in a 1927 sentence. "The great evil, which should be attacked at all costs . . . [consists of] the houses of tolerance that have been secretly making their way into family neighborhoods, at first almost without scandal, because of the dissimulation of the couples who go in and out, out and in. Rape and deflowering in these places are frequent."[40]

The characterization of places of prostitution as places of adultery, deflowering, and rape—places where honest women were led astray—reveals a fear of social mixture and lack of control over the guests and residents of hotels, a fear already articulated in 1915. Judges' rising concern over "clandestine prostitution" confirms the confusion and horror that the unconventional behavior of "modern women" provoked in judges such as Eurico Cruz.[41] "Notorious prostitutes," such common figures in criminal trials at the end of the nineteenth century, were replaced in the 1920s by women whose identities were less clearly defined, who both intrigued and unsettled judges.

All of this suggests that Police Chief Aurelino Leal's 1917 proposal to grant police the right to intervene autonomously in cases of "suspect" activity had important repercussions in the courts. Even without total consensus among magistrates in the city, sentences in the 1920s helped support police prerogatives to intervene in a broad range of relationships that could be characterized as pandering. In addition to stigmatizing various kinds of activities that went beyond commercial sex, this new judicial tendency also aided police efforts to separate, by whatever means they chose, notorious prostitutes from other groups of workers.

The dangers of the promiscuity represented by the "houses of tolerance" in the eyes of many legal authorities helped to strengthen a segregationist position, which held that the best solution for prostitution was to confine it to a specific region and intensify state intervention in the organization of public spaces. Neoregulationist postures influenced many sentences.[42] The reduction in the number of prostitutes whose complaints resulted in criminal trials seems to suggest that judges were now leaving these issues to the discretion of the police. When trials involving establishments housing prostitutes reappeared in the 1920s, many judges acquitted the defendants as soon as they proved their houses were located on streets known for prostitution. In these cases, police action, referred to as "preventative," had apparently been sufficient for the goal at hand.

Antipandering legislation was thus used to various ends in the early years of the republic. Police actions, as well as the 1915 amendments of the pandering laws, were justified through a discourse that emphasized the international, and particularly European, dimension of the crime of pandering and therefore reinforced persistent turn-of-the-century images of the "commerce of pleasure." Patterns of enforcement, however, highlight local issues, mostly related to the creation of republican public space. The defense of individual rights was frequently eclipsed by the need to defend "customs." This led to a significant reduction, in the first decades of the twentieth century, of the legal opening that during the early years of the republic had permitted landlords and tenants to make use of the law, in different ways, to defend their rights to live, work, and have some protection from police intervention.

Many aspects of prostitutes' lives and the ways they used legal mechanisms reveal precisely the opposite of the widely held segregationist view of a mafia-run, low-life underworld. These women's problems were the same as those faced by much of Rio de Janeiro's working population, particularly those who shared the downtown area for residence, work, or leisure. The difference was that their social experiences as "public women" made them more vulnerable to a variety of actions by public authorities. The pandering trials were just one of these actions. As we have seen, these trials can be read in ways that reveal some changes in the organization of prostitution, in strategies of police vigilance over collective housing, and in the relationship between police and judicial authorities in the early decades of the republican regime. But they also allow for a different reading. While police officials, judges, and doctors used accusations of pandering and prostitution to restrict prostitutes to a one-dimensional identity as sex vendors, the same trials reveal these women as tenants, landlords, consumers, clients, rivals, and lovers—in short, multifaceted individuals who acted in defense of their own rights.

Notes

This chapter presents results from my doctoral research, funded by Fundação de Amparo à Pesquisa do Estado de São Paulo from 1997 to 2001. I am grateful to Maria Clementina Pereira Cunha, Donna Guy, and Lara Putnam for their comments on earlier versions. I am especially in debt to Sueann Caulfield for her careful readings and the work of final translation.

1   These are themes discussed in Pereira, *Que tenhas teu corpo: Uma história social da prostituição no Rio de Janeiro das primeiras décadas republicanas* (Rio de Janeiro: Arquivo Nacional, 2005). On prostitution in Buenos Aires during this period, see Donna J. Guy, *Sex and Danger in Buenos Aires: Prostitution, Family, and Nation in Argentina* (Lincoln: University of Nebraska Press, 1991), and *White Slavery and Mothers Alive and Dead: The Troubled Meeting of Sex, Gender, Public Health, and Progress in Latin America* (Lincoln: University of Nebraska Press, 2000). Regarding the "white slave traffic," see also Edward Bristow, *Prostitution and Prejudice: The Jewish Fight against White Slavery, 1870–1939* (New York: Shocken, 1982). For a recent account of a Jewish prostitute's experience in Buenos Aires, see Nora Glickman, *The Jewish White Slave Trade and the Untold Story of Raquel Liberman* (New York: Garland, 1999).

2   Américo Freire, *Uma capital para a República: Poder federal e forças políticas locais no Rio*

de Janeiro na virada para o século XX (Rio de Janeiro: Revan, 2000); Sidney Chalhoub, *Cidade febril: Cortiços e epidemias na corte imperial* (São Paulo: Companhia das Letras, 1996), chap. 1.

3   Several authors characterize the urban renovation policies in Rio de Janeiro as racist and classist; see Chalhoub, *Cidade febril*; Jaime Larry Benchimol, *Pereira Passos: Um Haussman tropical—A renovação urbana do Rio de Janeiro no início do século XX* (Rio de Janeiro: Secretaria Municipal de Cultura, Turismo e Esportes, 1992); and Robert Pechman and Lilian Fritsch, "A reforma urbana e seu avesso: Algumas considerações a propósito da modernização do Distrito Federal na virada do século," *Revista brasileira de história* 5.8–9 (1985): 139–195. Sueann Caulfield demonstrates that these policies are also sexist in "Getting into Trouble: Dishonest Women, Modern Girls, and Women-Men in the Conceptual Language of Vida Policial, 1925–1927," *Signs* 19.1 (1993): 146–176, and *In Defense of Honor: Sexual Morality, Modernity, and Nation in Early-Twentieth-Century Brazil* (Durham, NC: Duke University Press, 1999), esp. chap. 2.

4   Nicolau Sevcenko, *Literatura como missão: Tensões sociais e criação cultural na Primeira República* (São Paulo: Brasiliense, 1985); Jeffrey Needell, *A Tropical Belle Epoque: Elite Culture and Society in Turn-of-the-Century Rio de Janeiro* (Cambridge: Cambridge University Press, 1987). Needell argues that the valorization of French prostitutes in this period was directly related to the Carioca elite's internalization of Francophile values and taste.

5   See the introduction to this volume. Regarding the "politics of seignorial dominion," see Sidney Chalhoub's essay in this volume and his "What Are Noses For? Paternalism, Social Darwinism, and Race Science in Machado de Assis," *Journal of Latin American Cultural Studies* 10.2 (2001): 171–191. See also Lilia Schwarcz, *O espetáculo das raças: Cientistas, instituições e questão racial no Brasil* (São Paulo: Companhia das Letras, 1993); and Nancy Stepan, *The Hour of Eugenics: Race, Gender, and Nation in Latin America* (Ithaca, NY: Cornell University Press, 1991).

6   See José Amador de Jesús's essay in this volume for an analysis of social concern with the occupation and signification of urban space in Ponce, Puerto Rico, in the same period. Amador finds that there, as in Rio de Janeiro, these concerns were expressed through discourses of respectability and morality that were informed by race, class, and gender.

7   See Alain Corbin, *Women for Hire: Prostitution and Sexuality in France after 1850* (Cambridge: Harvard University Press, 1996); and Judith Walkowitz, *Prostitution and Victorian Society: Women, Class, and the State* (Cambridge: Cambridge University Press, 1980), which discuss the uses of these narratives in France and among British feminists. See also Guy, *White Slavery*. Narratives of the traffic in Brazil are discussed in Margareth Rago, *Os prazeres da noite: Prostituição e códigos de sexualidade feminina em São Paulo (1890–1930)* (Rio de Janeiro: Paz e Terra, 1991); Lená Medeiros de Menezes, *Os estrangeiros e o comércio do prazer nas ruas do Rio (1890–1930)* (Rio de Janeiro: Arquivo Nacional, 1992); and Beatriz Kushnir, *Baile de máscaras: Mulheres judias e prostituição— As polacas e suas associações de ajuda mútua* (Rio de Janeiro: Imago, 1996). I discuss the interpretations of these authors in Pereira, *Que tenhas teu corpo*, chap. 2.

8   In her contribution to this volume, Keila Grinberg highlights this tendency to ignore the recent and persistent past of slavery, analyzing the silence regarding slavery on the

part of Brazilian legislators and jurists who wrote about the history of the civil code after 1871. She argues that, in part, this silence results from a particular project for a liberal nation that was incompatible with the memory of slavery.

9   See José Viveiros de Castro, *Jurisprudência criminal: Casos julgados—Jurisprudência estrangeira—Doutrina jurídica* (Rio de Janeiro: Garnier, 1900), 46–47.

10 Alberto Sarmento, *Tráfico de mulheres (lenocínio): Parecer sobre o projeto de modificação dos artigos 266, 277 e 278 do Código penal do Brasil, definindo os crimes de que trata a conferência nacional de Paris* (São Paulo: Typografia Brasil, 1911).

11 Regarding the original meaning of the expression in the French context, see Alain Corbin, *Women for Hire*; Jill Harsin, *Policing Prostitution in Nineteenth-Century France* (Princeton, NJ: Princeton University Press, 1985). For a contemporary critique of European prostitution regulation, see Abraham Flexner, *Prostitution in Europe* (New York: Century, 1914). The different position of Brazilian judges in the 1920s is analyzed in Pereira, "Que tenhas teu corpo," chap. 3.

12 The cases analyzed here are part of a group of seventy-eight trials and police investigations from 1890 to 1930, which constitute the totality of pandering trials originating in Rio de Janeiro's Sixth Criminal Division that are held by the National Archive. Most of the trials prior to 1920 originated in the fourth and fifth police districts.

13 Aurelino Leal, *Polícia e poder de polícia* (Rio de Janeiro: Imprensa Nacional, 1918), 125–126; Marcos Luiz Bretas, *Ordem na cidade: O exercício cotidiano da autoridade policial no Rio de Janeiro, 1907–1930* (Rio de Janeiro: Rocco, 1997).

14 See "Assalto ao direito," *O paiz*, Jan. 24, 1901, in which the newspaper denounces arbitrary police action regarding prostitutes. In *Fon-fon*, May 11, 1907, there are commentaries about the prohibition of women's presence on the streets after 10 p.m.; cited in Bretas, *Ordem na cidade*, 72. Before that, *O malho*, Dec. 13, 1902, criticized the police chief for restricting women's circulation through the city at night. The strange regulation on the use of hats was an initiative of the Fifth District precinct chief in 1912, against which a group of women protested through a habeas corpus suit: Maria Rainin e outras, unnumbered case, box 1799, Sixth Criminal Division, 1912. All trials cited henceforth are located in the National Archive, Rio de Janeiro.

15 Both tendencies are presented in Leal, *Polícia e poder de polícia*. On prostitution segregation in the twentieth century, see Sueann Caulfield, "The Birth of Mangue: Race, Nation, and the Politics of Prostitution in Rio de Janeiro, 1850–1942," in *Sex and Sexuality in Latin America*, ed. Daniel Balderston and Donna J. Guy (New York: New York University Press, 1997), 86–100.

16 Some of the major rulings of the period can be found in Vicente Piragibe, *Dicionário de jurisprudência penal do Brasil*, vol. 2 (Rio de Janeiro: Freitas Bastos, 1938); and Anésio Frota Aguiar, *O lenocínio como problema social no Brasil* (n.p., 1940).

17 See Martha de Abreu Esteves, *Meninas perdidas: Os populares e o cotidiano do amor no Rio de Janeiro da belle époque* (Rio de Janeiro: Paz e Terra, 1989); and Caulfield, *In Defense of Honor*.

18 Mariana Gother, n. 121, bundle 2517, Sixth Criminal Division, 1896 (Corte de Apelação).

19 The rising value of real estate in the area brought about by the urban reforms aggravated the long-standing housing deficit. Oswaldo Porto Rocha, *A era das demolições: Cidade do Rio de Janeiro, 1870–1920* (Rio de Janeiro: Secretaria Municipal de Cultura,

1995). On the cost of living, Sylvia Damazio, *Retrato social do Rio de Janeiro* (Rio de Janeiro: EDUERJ, 1996); Teresa Meade, *"Civilizing" Rio: Reform and Resistance in a Brazilian City, 1889–1930* (University Park: Penn State University Press, 1997).

20 Lilian Fessler Vaz records the enormous hikes in rents at the turn of the century. She reports that in 1905 the rent for a room in a rooming house could be from twenty thousand to twenty-five thousand reis and that a little house in a shantytown could go for between fifty thousand to sixty thousand reis, much less than a prostitute paid in 1896 to share a room with another woman downtown. Lilian Fessler Vaz, "Contribuição ao estudo da produção e transformação do espaço da habitação popular: As habitações coletivas no Rio antigo" (MA diss., Pontifícia Universidade Católica/Universidade Federal do Rio de Janeiro, 1985), 197.

21 Viveiros de Castro's position becomes even clearer in his discussion of the rape of prostitutes. For him, even when they were rape victims, prostitutes did not deserve legal protection, since "abusing [a prostitute] against her will does not prejudice her future, does not stain her name, her reputation." He suggests that this crime be treated as a misdemeanor. José Viveiros de Castro, *Os delitos contra a honra da mulher* (Rio de Janeiro: Freitas Bastos, 1936), 123–124.

22 See Sueann Caulfield's essay in this volume and her *In Defense of Honor*, chap. 1.

23 In the case of the precinct chief Bartholomeu, other practices, as well as his strategy for gaining notoriety through the campaign against prostitutes, were reported in the press by a journalist who always accompanied him during these campaigns. His newspaper reports were later published as a book: Ferreira da Rosa, *O lupanar: Estudo sobre o caftismo e a prostituição no Rio de Janeiro* (Rio de Janeiro: n.p., 1896).

24 Pepa Sinai, n. 485, box 1983, Corte de Apelação, 1897.

25 For more on uses of the police by people involved in personal conflicts, see Bretas, *Ordem na cidade*.

26 See Brodwyn Fischer's essay in this volume, which discusses how certain aspects of personal honor could be associated with access to citizenship.

27 Gabriel Sckimilovitz, case 23, box 1971, Sixth Criminal Division, 1891.

28 For police, a "tongue-twisting name" (*nome arrevesado*) was enough to make someone a suspected pimp. This prejudice on the part of the police was noted by the turn-of-the-century writer Lima Barreto, cited in Chalhoub, *Cidade febril*, 23.

29 Cristiana Schettini Pereira, "Que tenhas teu corpo," chap. 2; Marcos Bretas, *A guerra das ruas: Povo e polícia na cidade do Rio de Janeiro* (Rio de Janeiro: Arquivo Nacional, 1997).

30 Additional cases are discussed in Pereira, " 'Que tenhas teu corpo,' " chap. 2. The accusation of pimping seems to have been a relatively common personal insult, as Brodwyn Fischer suggests in her contribution to this volume.

31 Adelia Visel e Frederico Casemiro da Silva, n. 532, box 1862, Sixth Criminal Division, 1897.

32 This was what lawyer Evaristo de Moraes argued in 1920, during the relocation of prostitutes from downtown in advance of the visit to Brazil by King Albert of Belgium. Evaristo de Moraes, *Ensaios de patologia social: Vagabundagem—Alcoolismo—Prostituição—Lenocínio* (Rio de Janeiro: Leite Ribeiro and Maurillio, 1921), 282–283. On the preparations for the visit of King Albert, see Caulfield, *In Defense of Honor*, chap. 2.

33 Vaz, "Contribuição ao estudo da produção," 32–34.
34 This was the case for the prostitute Ernestina Grinberg, who sublet a house belonging to the Brazilian Manoel Bastos Soares, who also owned a paint store near the house. One of the complaints of Ernestina and her colleagues against Manoel was that it was impossible to use the house's interior patio (where a washing area and sanitary facilities were located), since there were other tenants living at the back of the house. Manoel Bastos Soares, n. 508, box 1970, Sixth Criminal Division, 1897.
35 Ramón Paradella, n. 893, box 1768, Sixth Criminal Division, 1915.
36 Manoel Rodrigues Maia, n. 445, box 1797, Sixth Criminal Division, 1915.
37 Antônio Alves da Silva, n.7 27, box 1978, Sixth Criminal Division, 1921.
38 Francisco Jerpe Blanco, n. 1452, box 1837, Sixth Criminal Division, 1921, in which the couple was a typesetter and his girlfriend; in the trial against José de Oliveira, n. 1193, box 1880, Sixth Criminal Division, 1925, the two women found in the hotel were a cook who lived on the Vintém Hill and a worker at a bag factory.
39 Manoel de Castro e Francisco Moura, n. 213, box 1837, Sixth Criminal Division, 1920.
40 Acquittal sentence for Rosita Gerstler, transcribed in *Revista criminal* 1 (July 1927): 13.
41 On Eurico Cruz's position on the behavior of "modern girls" in the 1920s, see Sueann Caulfield's essay in this volume.
42 Judge Nelson Hungria was one of the most famous defenders of this position. See his lecture given at the Brazilian Social Hygiene Council (CBHS), transcribed in *Revista criminal* 3 (Aug. 1927): 19–23. On the CBHS, see Sueann Caulfield, *In Defense of Honor*, chap. 3.

The stigmas of dishonor: criminal records, civil rights, and forensic identification in Rio de Janeiro, 1903–1940
Olívia Maria Gomes da Cunha

Outraged at police agencies' unscrupulous use of criminal identification methods based on the description of "body parts," Senator Barata Ribeiro took the floor on October 10, 1906, to demand clarification from law enforcement authorities. Ribeiro noted that individuals were taken into custody and subjected to a humiliating process of "anthropometric identification," often only to be released by the judge without charges. "By what right do suspects' photographs and fingerprints remain on file?" the senator asked indignantly. "Society is guided by its legal institutions, and these same institutions deem it fit to preserve forever the stigmas of dishonor, the results of the anthropometric identification of an innocent man: records that should only serve to keep track of repeat offenders. Can you think of any greater absurdity? Or more illogical cruelty?"[1]

The examples Ribeiro cited—stories of innocent victims of obstinate police persecution—inspired little sympathy in his listeners. Instead, he collided head-on with law enforcement authorities' zeal for "scientific" means of identifying those who frequented their precincts. Aggravating the procedure that Ribeiro considered a "disgraceful" source of discomfort and shame—in which prisoners were forced to remove shoes and socks and "clothing above the belt" so that anthropometric measurements could be taken—this "shameful experience" was itself documented visually in photographs of prisoners facing forward and in profile. These photographs, of faces painfully ill at ease, eyes cast downward in humiliation, soon decorated the crime reports of the city's major newspapers. All this occurred despite the law mandating that identification procedures be undertaken in strict secrecy.[2]

For Ribeiro, criminal identification records were markers of public degradation: "stamps of suspicion" and "stigmas of dishonor." His metaphors suggest an instant and indelible alteration of the social status of individuals in custody. Taking as given that passage through a police precinct was a painful and degrading experience, Ribeiro questioned the notion of recidivism that inspired this strategy of prevention, and he asked whether imprisonment without conviction was a violation of detainees' civil rights. In response, fellow senator Oliveira Figueiredo insisted that the identification of prisoners had no broader implications for the citizenry at large, and that prisoners' legal rights were only altered after they were sentenced, since it was "the conviction [that] turned white to black."[3]

Unswayed, Senator Ribeiro called his colleagues' attention to a scene that he was apparently convinced would rouse their fears. An item that had recently appeared in the newspaper *Jornal do commércio* had described the visit of a group of forensic medicine students to the Office of Identification. As a "demonstration," two women in custody for unspecified crimes were used as subjects to show off the utility of the miraculous new fingerprinting technology. Surely, Ribeiro argued, this publication revealed the perils that "respectable women" might suffer at the mercy of the new identification methods. In addition to having parts of their bodies exposed, women would be vulnerable to public shame and humiliation: "Who knows if sometime in the future we might not demand a record in the form of a part of the buttocks or even, when the insatiability of shameless research has exhausted its sources of obscenity, a woman's breasts."[4]

Were the senator's concerns, his rejection of scientific progress, merely the last gasp of an outdated morality? It seems not. Nearly thirty years later the same issue excited similar anxieties, this time in an experienced district police chief in the federal capital of Rio de Janeiro. Complaining to the nation's president in 1932, Olyntho Nogueira railed at what he termed the "chaotic interference of anthropology and ethnology" in a reform project for the civil police. In response to procedures aimed at detailing the different "physical characteristics of the human races," Nogueira felt obliged to remind the president that "undressing prisoners" was prohibited by law. The dangers that came with making criminal identification universal and obligatory worried Nogueira: the entire citizenry could be subject to profound shame. Like Senator Ribeiro, Nogueira depicted a hypothetical female victim to underline the moral offense of identification procedures: a "wife" who through the "instinct for self-defense" wounds a burglar must "be submitted to an ethnologic examination" before the judge can proclaim her innocence.[5] Nogueira also worried that the privacy of the exam might not be respected, and he envisioned terrible procedures in which parts of the body might be fondled, pinched, squeezed, and scratched.

In contrast, most early-twentieth-century writings on criminal identification techniques are dominated not by concern for the inviolability of the body but rather concern for the inviolability of the state, insisting on the need for sophisticated scientific, legal, and law enforcement devices to protect society from potential criminals.[6] Acclaimed for not only its functionality but also its "symbolic effect," the identification registry soon spread to all of Brazil's state capitals. A U.S. consular employee, impressed by the efficiency of the identification system adopted by São Paulo police in 1921, described for his superiors the ease with which it kept track of "strangers" arriving in the city. Apparently police were also successfully exploiting the new method's preventive potential. According to this observer, "a person who has his identification recorded with the police is less liable to commit a crime under sudden excitement or abnormal conditions than one who is not so recorded."[7] The supposed practicality and powerful symbolism of civil and criminal identification systems spurred their adoption in many Latin American countries in the same era.[8]

The senator and the police chief used shocking examples—naked female bodies suffering minute examinations—to highlight the way identification procedures publicly linked physical attributes to social and moral values. For precisely this reason I have chosen to call attention to the criticism identification methods inspired before explaining why they were incorporated into the institutions fundamental to Brazilian state formation. Ribeiro's and Nogueira's apprehensions should encourage us to imagine the sinister undertones of science rather than take its usefulness for granted.

Criminal Identification in Practice

In the pages that follow, I analyze identification procedures through a close reading of vagrancy trials from early-twentieth-century Rio de Janeiro. It was in those years that police identification became central to "preventive criminal policy" toward minor crimes and misdemeanors such as gambling and vagrancy. Vagrancy laws codified moral judgments regarding labor patterns, judgments that were then applied to many who may not have shared those assumptions. Police in Brazilian cities targeted as vagrants immigrants and nonwhites temporarily unemployed or employed in certain kinds of informal work. While elsewhere in the world increasing numbers of poor, jobless migrants in major cities prompted the adoption of the first social welfare policies, in Brazil vagrancy continued to be treated as a law enforcement issue: studied through the lens of forensic medicine, denounced as a threat to public security, controlled through urban regulation and marginalization.[9] As the image of the dangerous vagrant gained prominence, legislative proposals and police reports could summon a presumption of danger with simple tag phrases: "wandering aimlessly," "loitering in a state of idleness," "lives in an illicit manner," "without employment or domicile," or "unoccupied." Yet vagrancy remained an amorphous concept, easily manipulated and ready to be used in diverse situations.

The presumption of danger was grounds enough for countless people to be taken to the precincts, interrogated, identified, fingerprinted, imprisoned in "correctional colonies," and, eventually, freed without ever having been convicted. The circuitous routine was not aimed at conviction: the ritual itself fulfilled police goals. The entire process was documented in a permanent file (*ficha*) held by the precinct, and the former "suspect" was now permanently marked as *fichado*. Paradoxically, given the lionization of science in this setting, identification was most effective in labeling people *socially*—for at the technical level, as we shall see, the procedures were often nearly useless. To understand identification procedures we must see them as part of the narrative creation of potentially "criminal individuals," a characterization crafted through the fusion of physical, moral, and behavioral descriptions.

Officials repeatedly praised the system's success at differentiating among individuals and thus distinguishing "citizens" from "criminals." Identification procedures enabled the state to link people's "civil" names to physical-anatomical descriptions of their bodies, thus imbuing the purely moral "personification" of patronymic description with attributes of organic "individuality."[10] A number of scholars have noted that the turn-of-the-century Brazilian state drew a sharp distinction between "individuals" (objects of scientific study, subject to the rule of law, and potential targets of legal and disciplinary action) and "persons" (those who possessed family and personal connections that freed them from the disciplinary action of laws and legal institutions while guaranteeing their honor). Anthropologist Roberto da Matta emphasizes the *extralegality* of the social privileges enjoyed by "persons," who, in his view, considered their status superior to that of "citizens."[11] My analysis of the theory and practice of civil and forensic identification, however, suggests that it was precisely the differential recognition of "personality" and citizenship *by law enforcement agents* that guaranteed civil rights and legal protection for some—and justified their denial to others.

The court cases analyzed below provide a window onto the actual social processes through which the language of forensic medicine consolidated distinct representations of the individual and the person. The semantic and bureaucratic routines of identification branded men and women indelibly. At the same time, identification perpetuated social representations of the nonperson that would prove tragically enduring in Brazilian society.

Women were a minority among vagrancy detainees during the 1930s in Rio de Janeiro's *pretorias* (lower courts), where most cases involved unemployed young men of color.[12] But the narratives produced by cases involving women are particularly revealing of the prescriptive role of judicial procedures in characterizing "antisocial" behavior. These narratives reveal that techniques supposedly designed to prevent criminality were performed instead as rituals of social branding—as Barata Ribeiro would have it, "stigmas of dishonor."[13] Female suspects became criminalized through identification practices employed less as technical-scientific aids to police work than as mechanisms for the production of specific social identities.

Reckless Bodies: Classification, Subjectivity, and Criminal Narratives of Women

The police who picked up Elza that afternoon in January 1932 seem never to have considered the possibility of her already having been through the system. Two policemen found her "wandering aimlessly" through the city's streets and forced her to accompany them to headquarters. Neither the witnesses nor the court clerk specified the circumstances surrounding Elza's arrest. Instead, they produced an *auto de flagrante* (the "eyewitness account," a text that opens judicial proceedings, supposedly describing the events that led to police intervention) that is identical to those for numerous cases of the same sort from the same era. The language used in describing the "suspect," the authoritative tone of statements that claim to attest to her behavior but mention only unspecified "knowledge" about her, and the indirect responses to interrogations elided from the clerk's report all imbue this type of record with an implacable sense of repetition and routine.[14] These formalities concluded, Elza was taken to the Office of Criminal Identification and Statistics (*Gabinete de Identificação e Estatística*, or GIE) to undergo identification procedures, and from there to the Forensic Institute for a disability examination, before entering the detention center (*casa de detenção*) to await judgment.

At the GIE, an agent pressed Elza's fingers onto an inkpad and then rolled each one on a paper form. Almost thirty years after Senator Ribeiro voiced his concerns, police identification no longer relied on anthropometric measurements. No longer were men and women in custody forced to pose naked for photographers. Criminal identification methods had changed years earlier at the initiative of a man still directing the GIE at the time of Elza's arrest, Félix Pacheco. The new system—depersonalized and pragmatic, or so it seemed—used numerical systems to catalogue the singular arcs and crevices of fingerprints. Defending the decision to adopt dactyloscopy as the definitive identification method, Pacheco called attention to the intimate nature of "individual images" and the "humiliating" character of criminal photography. "Everyone is the rightful owner of his own physiognomic expression. My countenance, the expression of my eyes, the particular lines of my semblance, my look of sadness or joy or the smiles that dance across my lips are exclusively mine . . . and belong to no one else. . . . Skin hides the physiology of our organism, the sacred inheritance of each and every one of us. It is equally certain that there exists an external moral region, which is guarded and protected by the clothing with which we cover ourselves."[15] According to Pacheco, photography did much more than record the physical aspect of an individual. Semblance and physiognomy, feeling and honor made up the private domain or "moral region," which both characterized and belonged to the individual, and these could be violated by photographic technology. For Pacheco, only an efficient and scientific method like fingerprinting could put an end to these images of public humiliation. Still, as we shall see, the shift in technology seems to have done little to alter the larger social implications of identification.[16]

Thus when the doctors came to examine her in prison, a card upon which police identifiers had noted her "criminal identity" now accompanied Elza. She was described as a thirty-year-old woman, *preta* (black), born in Minas Gerais, and currently employed as a "domestic." The doctors uncovered no physical disability or illness that might hinder her from working and concluded their evaluation by labeling her a woman of "solid constitution."[17] Interrogated several days later by the judge of the Fifth Criminal Court, Elza was unable to explain why she had left her last job, in the house of an "Italian gentleman," after only two months. Since there was no prior registry of Elza in the archives of the GIE, the judge demanded to know why she had remained unemployed since then. "Fraudulent" or "thieving domestics" were frequent characters in crime reports of the era, which may explain some of the judge's concern. Press coverage of the "domestics" associated feminine labor with ideals of subservience and submission, remnants of the recent slave past. Like prostitutes, the "domestics" provoked a moral panic that spurred doctors and police to institute mechanisms to monitor their movements constantly.[18]

In Elza's case, the judicial inquiry was never concluded. Two days after the judge had requested more information about Elza's last job, the director of the detention center asked that she be sent to the Hospital de Assistência aos Psicopatos (Hospital for the Insane) because she evidenced "symptoms of mental alienation." No mention is made of what behavior provoked such suspicions. We know only that Elza was transferred to the hospital and remained there for eight months, during which legal authorities received no word whatsoever on her status or diagnosis.

After insistent demands from her court-appointed attorney, hospital officials finally sent a report to the judge confirming her sanity, so that he might issue her sentence. In the report, the doctor, W. Pires, explained the hospital's delayed diagnosis as the result of doubts as to the real "identity" of the "patient Elza." The doctors' suspicions stemmed from medical records, which they apparently judged more reliable than the police identification documents that had accompanied Elza to the hospital. Pires claimed that Elza was actually Honorina, a patient who had already been committed three times before, brought in by officers of various precincts for the same offense of vagrancy. The evidence that had made them suspect her "real" identity consisted of "clinical psychiatric observation" reports issued after her (supposed) first internment in 1931.

When Honorina entered the hospital on that occasion, her police identification card described her as a domestic servant, "mulatto," thirty-four years old, who during the exam appeared "calm, depressed, apprehensive, in good humor, and alert," with no "experience of venereal disease." According to the medical intake report, Honorina declared that when taken into custody as "disturbed" (police had described it as "wandering aimlessly"), she was simply suffering a "crisis." During later interviews with the hospital's doctors, this and other stories about her life were interrupted by fits of crying every time she mentioned the loss she felt at being separated from her daughter. Although Honorina denied any use of alcohol, her habit of frequenting environments considered likely to provoke "delirious states" and other mental disturbances in "individuals of a weak constitution" was cited as the cause of her depression. "She attended many spiritualist sessions and practiced *macumba* [religious rites generally associated with Afro-Brazilian cults]—she hears voices that tell her that her daughter has died and sees apparitions—for the past six years she has been the victim of attacks in which she nearly loses her senses . . . and adds that these same events are preceded by an initial scream that arises from a lump in her throat." Along with other details noted down after a series of observations, such symptoms led the famous psychiatrist Henrique Roxo to diagnose Honorina's problem as episodic delirium.[19]

If Pires's suspicions as to Honorina/Elza's actual identity were indeed correct, all the information on Elza's identification records was false. Contrary to the identity police had attributed to Elza, Honorina was a native of the state of Bahia, which she had left four months earlier to work in the home of a well-known family. Honorina later left that job, citing "disagreements with family members" as the principal cause. It was some time afterward, while walking down the street, that she suddenly became aware that the people around her were "different, as if they were dead, and that they wanted to kill her" together with "her daughter." Suddenly she "began to speak and to gesticulate, at which time a gentleman brought her in to the police station." According to the doctors, Honorina attributed much of her "disturbed" behavior to her "weak state," "because for the past several days she has not eaten well and has been out doing a great deal of walking looking for work." If Elza was indeed Honorina, both the identifiers and the forensic physicians who had deemed Elza fit to work had been in error. More striking still, if either police or medical authorities had believed in the efficacy of comparing fingerprints, there should have been no further confusion about the identity of Honorina/Elza. The dilemma could have been resolved immediately with a pronouncement by the GIE. Strangely, no one seems to have thought of doing any such thing.

The second time Honorina was taken into custody she remained two months in the hospital before being released. The police claimed to have found her "disturbing the peace" and "uttering words that morality forbids repeating." While the doctors had repeatedly claimed that Hono-rina/Elza did not use alcohol, alcoholism was one of the reasons used to justify her detention on this occasion. Upon entering the hospital as Elza in January 1932, she exhibited behavior and reactions similar to those recorded in the earlier psychiatric observations. The clinical report generated during this internment noted that her state of mind was sometimes altered by mild episodes of "expressive physiognomy, gesticulation, and mimicry." She claimed to have gone on an outing and "since she did not know how to return home, began to wander the streets, eventually being taken in to the police station." The clinical observations of Honorina/Elza did not stop the judge from ruling her a "vagrant" on the grounds that her physical and mental state did not hinder her from working. Nonetheless, just as she was about to be returned to the detention center, Elza was sent back to the Hospital for the Insane "because of a failure to connect ideas or have any notion of what is happening to her." One month after this sudden internment, the judge ordered that she be freed to care for herself as soon as "her liberty poses no threat to society." Apparently none of this made him reconsider his judgment of vagrancy.

While the confusion surrounding Honorina/Elza's identity was unusual, in other respects her case was quite typical of vagrancy cases directed at women, structured by the counterpoint between the accused's disruptive public behavior and the authorities' attempts to comprehend that behavior within forensic or psychiatric schema. Vagrancy accusations against men were inevitably accompanied by suspicions that the "vagrancy" was linked to crimes like robbery, theft, or murderous intent. The "vagrant" was by definition an individual whose illicit activities could not be proven but were suspected in association with his general idleness. In contrast, "vagrant" women, like those accused of prostitution or public obscenity, were characters whose sick or out-of-control bodies threatened to trespass the boundaries of modesty and silence. As in Elza/Honorina's case, the politics of identification were responsible for the translation of a narrative language rich in moral judgments (including the "patient's" declarations as well as others' judgments of her) into a narrow repertoire of legal-medical terms.

Unlike the inconsistent diagnoses that marked Honorina/Elza's time in custody, a police investigator identified Lara as a "habitual inebriate" the moment he came across her downtown. He warned her to "go look for work" and stop hanging around the bars; she ignored him and continued drinking and "causing disturbances" in the streets.[20]

Known as *mãozinha* (little hand), the laundress Lara lived on the

Morro da Favella (a hillside shantytown), was twenty-seven years old, and worked as a domestic servant. At the time of her arrest in 1932, Lara claimed she was unemployed because she suffered from "paralysis" on her right side and was prone to "epileptic attacks."[21] But the GIE presented evidence taken to confirm police accusations: since 1924 Lara had been taken into custody innumerable times as a "vagrant." (Only once had she been convicted.)[22] Doctors examining the "morena" (dark-skinned) Lara diagnosed congenital atrophy of her right forearm, a problem that severely reduced her ability to perform "more general or common work, even in the crudest fashion." As for her claims of epilepsy, while doctors never witnessed an attack, information gleaned from the prison warden and the fact that the patient presented what they termed an "epileptic character" authorized them to take her word. The doctors saw in Lara symptoms of mental deficiency, and one noted that "judging by her weak mental state and her history, including the testimony of the prison warden who reports that her imprisonments are frequent and constant, there is manifest evidence of both instability of character and, most likely, 'ambulatory mania,' consistent with her mental deficiency and epilepsy." Here and elsewhere, the rhetorical construction of women's identities attributed their vagrancy to their weak nature rather than to criminal intent. Images of insanity, physical disability, and vulnerability to moral degeneration erased intentionality even as they confirmed culpability.

Implicit or explicit accusations of prostitution invariably appear in the documents such cases generated. Sometimes these accusations became central to evidence against the accused; other times, they were completely incidental to the case. Like Honorina/Elza, Almerinda was taken into custody for "wandering aimlessly" and "in a state of total idleness." The precinct's *policiais-identificadores* (identification police) categorized her as a "black" woman ("de cor preta") and as a "prostitute." All the witnesses listed on the *auto de flagrante* agreed that she was a "habitual vagrant." But Almerinda herself declared that she was a "cook" and that, when taken into custody, she was on her way to learn to dye "by order of her employer." This fact was later confirmed by the employer himself, who described Almerinda as "dedicated and a hard worker." Even though Almerinda had found herself in this situation previously, and in fact had once been interned in the Division of Psychopaths of the Hospital for the Insane, the judge took her employer's testimony as proof of her capacity for "rehabilitation through work" and acquitted her.[23]

Supporting testimony from men—employers or companions—generally carried great weight when women stood accused of vagrancy. Léa, a thirty-nine-year-old widow, was taken into custody in 1935 and accused of falling back into vagrancy. Her Record of Previous Criminal Activity contained multiple accusations of the same sort; the doctors examining her concluded that she presented no "functional disturbance" and was therefore fit to work. In a defense plea written in her name, Léa insisted that after enduring multiple unjust arrests with only one conviction, she "had had the pleasure of enjoying her liberty . . . and of finding Pedro . . . an employee of Lloyd Brasileiro who brought her to reside with him, where they have been living as if married ever since . . . with whom the accused is quite satisfied and her aforementioned companion is satisfied with her as well." As Pedro "does not permit this domestic servant to seek employment, she occupies herself with household tasks. . . . The accused hopes that your honor will hear the testimony of her companion . . . [who will confirm] that the accused was and still is rehabilitated." Finding Léa to be "supported by her husband," the judge acquitted her.[24]

It should be clear by now that the performative aspects of the sup-posed crime mattered far less than the "physical-moral" characteristics of the accused woman, which were assumed to indicate her disposition toward a given type of criminality.[25] Thus the mind-numbing repetition within each case of the attributes, aspects, and qualities that identify the accused as vagrant were essential to the process of judgment, not symptoms of judicial redundancy. Physical descriptions—of skin color in particular—were fundamental components of each accused individual's "criminal profile." The diverse color categories employed crafted differential images of the criminal individual. A "black woman" "wandering aimlessly"? She must be a prostitute or a deceitful domestic: the forensic taxonomy held no other options for her.

The case files of Elza/Honorina, Lara, Almerinda, and Léa help us understand how identification procedures criminalized socially margin-alized individuals, be they single women, domestic servants, or pros-titutes. In spite of the belief in the infallibility of fingerprints, only a few specialists were actually capable of reading information from them, and even those specialists might discount their probatory value. Rather than seeing fingerprinting as a functional tool, we thus come to see it as one element of a ritual complex, performed in a legal-scientific lan-guage, aimed at revealing to society a single physical-moral image of each individual. Within this ritual complex, the repeated inscription of the ac-cused individual's occupation, age, sex, race, civil status, and physical, mental, and moral diagnoses was just as important as the taking of her fingerprints. The descriptive labels located her socially; the fingerprinting stamped her bodily uniqueness onto that social configuration.

From the inaugural moment—the police accusation—when the initial "identification" of those in custody was enunciated by eyewitnesses and mediated by court clerks, through forensic identification at the GIE and the medical examination in the Forensic Institute, accused persons were assigned not a single identity but rather an overlapping and sometimes contradictory set of them. There are numerous cases of people who entered precincts as "incorrigible vagrants" and left as stevedores or salesmen, "prostitutes" who left as domestic servants, adults who left as minors, and needless to say *negros* who left as *pardos* (brown-skinned) or *pardos* who left as whites. Each suit was made up of a continuous and never entirely coherent barrage of verbal images. All these interventions worked together to perform the function theoretically assigned exclusively to criminal identification techniques: they created a criminal identity.

Marking Race: Anthropometry, Ethnology, and the Difficult Art of Description

Judgments about racial difference permeated police practice in Brazil, yet perceptions of race were never simple. To illustrate this, let us study the identification forms used in Rio de Janeiro, before and after the transition from anthropometry to fingerprinting around 1907, and track the conflictive persistence of race in identification documents in the decades that followed. Known in Brazil as *bertillonage*, the "anthropometric method" devised by Alphonse Bertillon in the late nineteenth century relied on three categories of bodily descriptions followed by specific combinations of body-part measurements. In the scheme proposed by the French anthropologist there was no single category reserved for the description of either skin color or "race," and the first records adopted in Brazil reflect this.[26] French anthropometry assessed "chromatic," "morphologic," and "complementary" characteristic features; on the rare occasions when "excessive" values in these areas were understood to be linked to the ethnic or racial origin of the subject, this information was prominently noted.[27]

In the various types of anthropometric records found in the GIE's files we can see the original influence of the French model as well as the way it was reinterpreted after adoption in Brazil.[28] The primary difference between the two models lies in the organization of facts. Looking at one of the older forms, used by the Judicial Identification Service in Rio de Janeiro in the last decade of the nineteenth century, we see that under the rubric "individual characteristics" there is a mixture of both civil data and what Bertillon called "descriptive information." This reclassification suggests that, rather than faithfully copying the European model, the Rio police already had their own referential logic and descriptive style. The particularities of the Brazilian police's descriptive habits would become even more apparent over the following decades, as anthropometry was superseded—at least in theory—by the supposedly less subjective dactyloscopy.

Law professor Edgar Simões Corrêa, who assumed leadership of the GIE in Rio in 1914, was both fascinated and delighted with the possibilities of fingerprinting, defining it as a "great weapon in defense of society."[29] Yet he insisted, "I do not consider the taking of fingerprints to be a basis of systematic identification but rather merely a means of revealing the identity of the criminal."[30] For the former use, he believed, "the admirable Bertillon system" remained essential. Elysio de Carvalho similarly advocated the use of all available identification methods, including both anthropometry and dactyloscopy. Only by endowing each member of society with an individual identity, unique and unmistakable, could the state guarantee the full enjoyment of civil liberties and at the same time preserve the public order. According to Elysio, "As identification is a measure that both guarantees individual liberty and serves to defend society, the great problem of identity will be resolved with the obligatory identification of all people who make up the society."[31] Universal identification, according to Elysio and other proponents, would fulfill two complementary purposes. It would enable police to keep a continuous watch over individuals they recognized as "suspects," and it would create a great archive of "identities," which could provide a basis for future research regarding the "ethnic and racial composition of nationality."[32] It was with this latter goal in mind that the 1932 reform of the Civil Police of Rio de Janeiro created the Laboratory of Criminal Anthropology, a division dedicated to "ethnologic and anthropologic research" located within the Institute of Identification.

Comparing these identification procedures with the original method proposed by Bertillon reveals the priorities and assumptions, most notably about race, of Brazilian doctors and officials. Examining fingerprint forms used in the early decades of the GIE, we find a continuous process of simplification and a parallel movement toward the elimination of some identifying attributes, perhaps in response to the debates over "obligatory identification" in the press and among politicians. Still, one element of physical description consistently remained relevant to criminal identification: skin color. A remnant of the anthropometric system, the reference to skin color not only remained on forms but became one of the primary concerns of identifiers as well as police and court clerks, who always insisted on noting this "characteristic" of suspects. Particularly striking is the habit of some police identifiers of noting the prisoner's race on records where such information was not required. One identifier in particular made such action routine: not insignificantly, he noted the prisoner's race in the space marked "motive for imprisonment."

Did skin color remain on forms because it was a relatively easy attribute to describe? Hardly. Brazilian identification manuals published in those years contain a vast and unwieldy variety of taxonomies and categories of skin color. And if the guidelines for marking race were incoherent, their application was even more so. Some officials rejected data that raised any doubts, such as "racial subcategories" and "idiosyncratic terms," in favor of more generic categories. Others insisted that no official classification scheme would work: not only was the "race" of any individual impossible to pin down, but the effort to do so was humiliating for all involved. Aurélio Domingues, a doctor and director of the GIE of Recife, wrote in 1929 of the embarrassment that surrounded the obligation to assign a race to persons undergoing identification.

> In the branch I direct, I have been witness to and sometimes acted as judge in scenes straight out of Molière, when controversy has arisen from the color of an individual's epidermis, and, what is even more embarrassing, when it is inscribed on his identity card. . . . One man says he doesn't want to be a black, another man says he's white, another doubts that he's a *pardo*. . . . There are actually cases, even aside from those misunderstandings resulting from vanity, in which it is really difficult to satisfy a person's wishes and at the same time not abandon the ethics of the labor at hand. What does one do? Certain designations regarding skin color, for example *moreno* [dark], have little meaning ethnographically. It would be better to say *trigueiro* [swarthy]. I think this sort of difficulty might be lessened, even altogether eliminated, in the following way: if we cease listing the color of one's epidermis on identification documents.[33]

Domingues described not only the difficulty but the discomfort inherent in selecting the color terminology that would be used to constitute a determined identity. His commentary helps us to understand why the listing of "race" disappeared from some official documents. It should not be seen in isolation. The eugenic theories that invaded certain scientific circles in Brazil were never uncontroversial, and investigations at the Laboratory of Criminal Anthropology led researchers to criticize certain anthropological theories of race and skin color as having no scientific value.[34] The degree of internal police dispute over race marking, coupled with the insistence of certain employees on taking note of color, indicate that commonsense notions of race were no less conflicted than their scientific counterparts.

In essence, the "science of identification" was a hybrid domain that mediated between the *private*—the body, systematically scrutinized and classified—and the *public*—the social, grouped into categories and entered into records. The identified body was made both singular and social at the same time. Its marks, aspects, tendencies, movements, and actions entered into a realm of public knowledge geared toward a social end.[35] For this very reason, any discussion of the issues involved in identification inevitably overstepped the narrow boundaries of crime prevention. To label the "color of one's epidermis" obliged one to address the racial identity of Brazilian social structure itself.[36] The process of creating official knowledge might confront state agents with truths they preferred not to acknowledge.

Civil Names and Civil Rights: Differentiating Individuals within the Nation

Benedict Anderson has argued that geopolitical, ethnic, racial, and administrative classification systems are essential to state building and nation formation because they provide the mechanisms through which individual subjects are included in or excluded from national communities. His arguments illuminate the intense debates over identification procedures in early twentieth-century Brazil. The obsessions of Brazilian state policy at the time were much the same as those Anderson describes for Southeast Asia: a dual preoccupation with frontiers and with the human/territorial image of the nation.[37] In the Brazilian case, urban policing became a key arena for mechanisms of categorization and control that dictated which individuals and populations would be excluded from the national project.

Leonídio Ribeiro, a doctor responsible for the criminal identification policy adopted in the Federal District in 1932, believed that modern social life demanded the rationalization and control of naming as well as identification practices: "In order to recognize the individual through this means of identification, in practice, it is necessary for everyone to have the right to his own name, without others also being in the position to use it."[38] All citizens should have the right to choose their "civil name" but not to alter it, just as it was impossible to modify certain characteristics of one's physical constitution. Cuban anthropologist Fernando Ortiz put forth similar arguments in an analysis of modern identification techniques for Havana legal authorities in 1916. Ortiz linked the *right* to choose one's name with society's *obligation*, through the state, to safeguard it. Both Ribeiro and Ortiz saw the significance of the civil name as connected to a particular notion of "personality." As Ortiz explained, "Certainly there will be some who will cherish and promote their own personalities while others will systematically try to lose theirs. It is society's duty to guarantee the desire of the former and impede the fraud of the later, while permanently solidifying the personality of each one."[39]

Legal handbooks and dictionaries published in Brazil in the first decades of the twentieth century categorically separate definitions of civil and criminal identity and restrict the physiological dimension of identity to penal/criminal identification. Thus, while civil identity results from "a group of qualities and activities that create the individual as a distinct social being, legally considered a person," criminal identity is analogous to "physical identity" and consists of "an individual's particular somatic characteristics."[40] Note how moral qualities are attributable to *persons* while physical qualities are attributable to *individuals*. Returning to the first law regulating obligatory criminal identification in Brazil, we see that those accused of "political crimes," "crimes against the free exercise of political rights," "administrative offenses," commercial infractions, adultery, slander, insults, and, finally, "crimes that are not exactly criminal," were exempted from the process of criminal identification.[41] In other words, some persons could break the law and still not merit a criminal identity.

Civil identity was a civil *right*; criminal identity a legal *obligation*. The distinction affected civil law as well as criminal anthropology and forensics. In order to obtain an identity card—a requirement for business activities, providing state recognition to new entrepreneurs—citizens were asked to place a request at the police precinct, including their date of birth, parentage, place of residence, occupation, and civil status.[42] Citizens whose civil rights were not fully recognized were denied the legal right to an identity card: thus, women and children could only request a card with the authorization of their husband, father, or guardian.[43] In contrast, to receive a criminal identity one needed only to have been the object of one policeman's suspicions—for, as we have seen, that was enough to earn passage through a precinct. Police authorities had the right not only to assign identities but to do so through a lengthy incarceration (no conviction necessary) over the course of which those in custody were located in a forensic taxonomy via "physical-moral" evaluations, which then formed part of their permanent "record of previous criminal activity."

The process used to identify Honorina, Almerinda, and others had changed from the anthropometric method that so offended Senator Barata Ribeiro in 1906. Nevertheless, the refusal of some accused "vagrants" to sign the eyewitness declarations against them, and the sense of distrust that led many others to refuse to have their fingerprints taken, suggest that the shamefulness of identification had nothing to do with the technology employed. Rather the "stigmas of dishonor" resulted from the transformation of "suspected" illicit activities into a permanent record. The element of social branding inherent in this process ensured that whatever techniques police identifiers used would become synonymous with public humiliation. Body and personality—inscribed, combined, classified, and assembled into police archives—became complementary aspects of a single social mark, the *identity*, that protected esteemed persons and stigmatized common individuals.

Notes

The careful readings and criticisms by Sarah Chambers, Sueann Caulfield, and Lara Putnam, as well as suggestions and comments from Jasmine Alinder and Peter Fry, were very important during the preparation of this text. I am grateful to all of these scholars.

1   Session of Oct. 10, 1906, *Anais do Senado Federal* (Rio de Janeiro: Imprensa Nacional, 1906), 3:398. For a full examination of the early twentieth-century debate over identification in Brazil, see Olívia Maria Gomes da Cunha, *Intenção e gesto: Pessoa, cor e a produção cotidiana da (in)diferença no Rio de Janeiro, 1927–1942* (Rio de Janeiro: Arquivo Nacional, 2003).

2   Chap. 20, arts. 149–159, decree 3640, April 14, 1900, in *Coleção das leis do Brasil* (Rio de Janeiro: Imprensa Nacional, 1900), 342.

3   Oct. 10, 1906, *Anais do Senado Federal*, 3:397.

4   Ibid., 3:390.

5   Olyntho Nogueira, "O projeto de reforma da polícia está errado" (manuscript, Rio de Janeiro, 1932), National Archive of Brazil (henceforth AN), Secretaria da Presidência da República, box 527.

6   For comparative material see Michel Foucault, *Discipline and Punish: The Birth of the Prison* (London: Macmillan, 1985), and "About the Concept of the 'Dangerous Individual' in Nineteenth-Century Legal Psychiatry," *International Journal of Law and Psychiatry* 1 (1978): 1–18; Robert A. Nye, "Crime in Modern Societies: Some Research Strategies for Historians," *Journal of Social History* 11 (1978): 490–507, and *Crime, Madness, and Politics in Modern France* (Princeton, NJ: Princeton University Press, 1984); and Nancy Leys Stepan, *"The Hour of Eugenics": Race, Gender, and Nation in Latin America* (Ithaca, NY: Cornell University Press, 1991). On the combination of fingerprinting and anthropometric procedures with criminal photography, see Allan Sekula, "The Body and the Archive," in *The Contest of Meaning: Critical Histories of Photography*, ed. Richard Bolton (Cambridge: MIT Press, 1989), 343–389.

7   Report by E. M. Lawton, American Consulate, São Paulo, Oct. 15, 1921, U.S. National Archives Collection held at the Brazilian National Library, microfilm roll 15, 519.

8   Juan Vucetith, "Insuficiência do sistema anthropométrico," *Boletim policial* 3 (1907): 23–32; Astolpho Rezende, *A luta técnica contra o crime* (Rio de Janeiro: Imprensa Nacional, 1914).

9   On vagrancy cases in early twentieth-century Rio de Janeiro, see Sidney Chalhoub, *Trabalho, lar e botequim: O cotidiano dos trabalhadores no Rio de Janeiro da belle époque* (São Paulo: Brasiliense, 1986); Marcelo B. Mattos, *Vadios, jogadores, mendigos e bêbados na cidade do Rio de Janeiro no início do século* (MA thesis, Universidade Federal Fluminense, 1991); and Adriana de R. B. Vianna, *O mal que se adivinha: Polícia e menoridade no Rio de Janeiro, 1910–1920* (Rio de Janeiro: Arquivo Nacional, 1999). For comparative material, see Christian Topalov, *La naissance du chômeur, 1880–1910* (Paris: Albin Michel, 1994).

10 For a discussion of the notions of "antinatural name" and "natural name," see Gumbleton R. Daunt, "Da identidade das pessoas naturais," *Arquivos de medicina legal e do Gabinete de Identificação* 4.10 (1934): 167–171.

11 Sérgio Carrara, "A ciência e a doutrina da identificação no Brasil, ou o controle do Eu no templo da técnica," *Boletim do Museu Nacional* 49 (1984): 61–84; Sérgio Carrara, *Crime e loucura: O aparecimento do manicômio judiciário na passagem do século* (Rio de Janeiro: Editora da Universidade do Estado do Rio de Janeiro, 1998); Sérgio Henrique Abranches, "Nem cidadãos, nem seres livres: O dilema político do indivíduo na ordem liberal-democrática," *Dados* 28 (1985): 5–25; and Roberto da Matta, " 'Do You Know Who You're Talking To?!' The Distinction between Individual and Person in Brazil," in *Carnivals, Rogues, and Heroes: An Interpretation of the Brazilian Dilemma*, trans. John Drury (Notre Dame, IN: University of Notre Dame Press, 1991), 137–197.

12 Cases involving women made up only 13.85% of those studied. Cunha, *Intenção e gesto*, 428.

13 On the notion of social contamination, see Mary Douglas, *Purity and Danger: An Analysis of Concepts of Pollution and Taboo* (New York: Praeger, 1966).

14 After this first phase of the process, a formal accusation was allowed for the obligatory

312   Olívia Maria Gomes da Cunha

identification as well as for "preventative custody." Elsewhere I have analyzed these issues in a review of close to four hundred cases of vagrancy involving men and women taken into custody in the same period on the streets of Rio de Janeiro. See Cunha, *Intenção e gesto*.

15 Félix Pacheco, "O Sr. Renato Carmil e o retrato na polícia," *Jornal do commércio*, Rio de Janeiro, Oct. 18, 1906, 3.

16 While the regulations in regard to the administration and functioning of the Gabinete de Identificação e Estatística (henceforth GIE) had been altered numerous times between 1903 and 1940, instructions as to identification procedures remained relatively unaltered and poorly defined. See decree 6440, "Regulamento do Gabinete de Identificação e Estatística," March 30, 1907, *Coleção das leis do Brasil* (Rio de Janeiro: Imprensa Nacional, 1907), 523.

17 AN, Seção da Justiça (henceforth SDJ), Quinta Pretoria Criminal do Rio de Janeiro (henceforth 5° PCRJ) 13167 (Jan. 4, 1932), 11.

18 The decree that reformed the police in 1907 instituted a document specifically designed to resolve this: the Identification Card for Domestic Service. Since this identification was voluntary (unlike the standard identification card), such registries were never abundant. AN, Documentação não identificada (henceforth GIFI), series 6j 1 to 75, 90, and 92. The differential treatment of "domestic servants" was maintained in the 1932 reform project for the Federal District civil police. Under the new regulations, cooks, waiters, maids, gardeners, laundresses, and wet nurses were to be identified by the GIE before and after leaving the residence in which they had been employed. See *Projeto de lei orgânica da polícia civil do Distrito Federal, 13 de maio de 1932* (Rio de Janeiro: Imprensa Nacional, 1932), 329.

19 For statistics on the most common psychiatric ailments among "patients" interned in psychiatric hospitals as a result of police intervention, see Henrique Roxo, *Anais de assistência aos psicopatas do Distrito Federal, 1931* (Rio de Janeiro: Imprensa Nacional, 1932). On internment and treatment policies for the mentally ill in the early twentieth century and their relation to public security concerns, see Magali Gouveia Engel, "A loucura na cidade do Rio de Janeiro: Ideias e vivências" (PhD diss., Universidade de Campinas, 1995).

20 AN-SDJ, 5° PCRJ–70.13364-1932.

21 Ibid., 13.

22 The one time Lara was convicted she was sentenced to three months in the Dois Rios Correctional Colony, founded in 1893 to shelter "vagrants" and "beggars." See decree 145, July 11, 1893, *Coleção das leis do Brasil* (Rio de Janeiro: Imprensa Nacional, 1896); and decree 4753, "Aprova o regulamento da colônia correcional de Dois Rios," Jan. 28, 1903, *Coleção das leis do Brasil* (Rio de Janeiro: Imprensa Nacional, 1907).

23 AN-SDJ, 5° PCRJ–70.13318-1932.

24 AN-SDJ 5° PCRJ–70. Dec. 21, 1935. It was common for "letters of defense" presented by illiterate defendants to be written by guardians or cellmates. Cunha, *Intenção e gesto*, 38.

25 Luiz Fernando D. Duarte, *Da vida nervosa nas classes trabalhadores urbanas* (Rio de Janeiro: Jorge Zahar/CNP, 1986).

26 On the justifications given for its reappropriation in Brazil, see Archibald Rudolph Reiss, "Os métodos científicos nos inquéritos judiciários e policiais," *Boletim policial* 2 (1907): 16; Aurelino Vianna, *Guia prático do identificador eleitoral* (São Paulo: Pira-

tininga, 1933), 33; and Elysio Carvalho, "A identificação como fundamento da vida jurídica," *Boletim policial* 5.15, 16, 17 (1911).

27 Bertillon included as "chromatic" characteristics: eye color, the "nuances of the hair," and "facial coloration." Bertillon at no time used categories in reference to chromatic tonality; rather his categories indicated the quantity of blood and pigment: the *blush* revealed in criminal countenances. Initially, it is clear that any reference to racial or ethnic origin was cited only as an excess or anomaly. However, once in evidence, such information preceded and stood out from the rest. Alphonse Bertillon, *Album d'identification anthropométrique et instructions signalétiques* (Melun: Imprimerie Administrative, 1893), plate 61.

28 AN-GIFE 6J92–GIE.

29 Edgar Simões Correa, "Dedos que acusam," in *A luta técnica contra o crime: Conferências jurídico-policiais*, ed. Astolpho Rezende et al. (Rio de Janeiro: Imprensa Nacional, 1915), 245–56; quote on 246.

30 Correa, "Dedos que acusam," 253.

31 Elysio Carvalho, "A identificação como fundamento da vida jurídica," *Boletim policial* 5 (1914): 14–25; quote on 19. On the spread of the theory of social defense among doctors and lawyers in Brazil at the turn of the century, see Marcos César Alvarez, "Bacharéis, criminologistas e juristas: Saber jurídico e a nova escola penal no Brasil (1889–1930)" (PhD diss., Universidade de São Paulo, 1996).

32 Leonídio Ribeiro, "O Instituto de Identificação," *Revista de direito penal* 1–2 (1933): 337–341; quote on 340.

33 Aurélio Domingues, *Manual prático de identificação (sistema vucetich)* (Recife: Editorial do Autor, 1929), 81–83.

34 For discussions of the "scientific value" of racial classifications, see Bastos de Avila, *Questões de antropologia* (Rio de Janeiro: Brasileira, 1935); and Alvaro Fróes da Fonseca, "Os grandes problemas da antropologia," in *Primeiro Congresso Brasileiro de Eugenia: Atos e trabalhos* (Rio de Janeiro: Sociedade Brasileira de Eugenia, 1929), 63–86.

35 The distinction between public and private is expounded on by Leonídio Ribeiro in *Medicina jurídica* (Rio de Janeiro: São José, 1945).

36 Giralda Seyferth, "A invenção da raça e o poder discricionário dos esterótipos," *Anuário antropológico* 93 (1995): 175–200.

37 Benedict Anderson, *Imagined Communities: Reflections on the Origin and Spread of Nationalism* (New York: Verso, 1983), 170. This argument is not new. In *The Birth of the Clinic: An Archaeology of Medical Perception*, trans. A. M. Sheridan Smith (New York: Pantheon, 1973), Michel Foucault mentions the territorialization of bodies through the description and production of a body of knowledge as a specific strategy of domination. See also John Comaroff and Jean Comaroff, *Ethnography and the Historical Imagination* (Boulder, CO: Westview, 1992), 41.

38 Leonídio Ribeiro, "Prova de identidade," in *Criminologia* (Rio de Janeiro: Sul Americana, 1957), 375.

39 Fernando Ortiz, *La identificación dactyloscópica* (Madrid: Daniel Jorro, 1916), 4.

40 Pedro Nunes, *Dicionário de tecnologia jurídica*, 6th ed. (Rio de Janeiro: Freitas Bastos, 1965), 66.

41 See decree 6440, "Regulamento do Gabinete de Identificação e Estatística," March 30, 1907, *Coleção das leis do Brasil* (Rio de Janeiro: Imprensa Nacional, 1907), 154. "Pros-

titutes and women taken into custody for infractions of public morality" were also exempted from the criminal identification process—yet as we have seen, women suspected of prostitution and accused of vagrancy were not.

42 In the earliest attempts to institute these documents, physical attributes such as skin color, eye color, facial hair, and fingerprints were also included.

43 Decree 14078, Dec. 25, 1920, *Coleção das leis do Brasil* (Rio de Janeiro: Imprensa Nacional, 1920), 2:629.

CONTRIBUTORS

José Amador de Jesús is a PhD candidate at the University of Michigan. He is the coeditor
(with Fernando Coronil) of *Historia y memoria: Sociedad, cultura y vida cotidiana en Cuba,
1878–1917* (2004). His dissertation examines how the flow of medical theories shaped the
construction of national identities in early-twentieth-century Cuba, Puerto Rico, and
Brazil.

Rossana Barragán received her doctorate in history from the Ecole des Hautes Etudes en
Sciences Sociales in Paris and is currently professor at the Universidad Mayor de San
Andrés in Bolivia. The editor of *Tinkazos* (a Bolivian social sciences journal), she focuses
her research on women, family, and ethnic identity in the nineteenth and twentieth centuries. Among her publications are *Espacio urbano y dinámica étnica: La Paz en el siglo XIX*
(1990) and *Indios, mujeres y ciudadanos: Legislación y ejercicio de la ciudadanía en Bolivia
(siglo XIX)* (1999).

Sueann Caulfield is an associate professor of history at the University of Michigan. She is
the author of *In Defense of Honor: Morality, Modernity, and Nation in Early-Twentieth-
Century Brazil* (Duke University Press, 2000); "The History of Gender in Latin American Historiography," *Hispanic American Historical Review* 81.3–4; and a number of
articles on gender, race, and honor. Her current research explores illegitimacy and family
structures in twentieth-century Brazil.

Sidney Chalhoub is a professor of history at the Universidade Estadual de Campinas, Brazil. He has published three books on the social history of Rio de Janeiro: *Trabalho, lar e
botequim: O cotidiano dos trabalhadores no Rio de Janeiro da belle époque* (1986), on working-
class culture in the early twentieth century; *Visões da liberdade: Uma história das últimas
décadas da escravidão na Corte* (1990), on the last decades of slavery in the city; and *Cidade
febril: Cortiços e epidemias na corte imperial* (1996), on tenements and public health in the
second half of the nineteenth century. His most recent book is *Machado de Assis, historiador* (2003), about the literature and political ideas of the most important nineteenth-
century Brazilian novelist. His current research interests include Machado's essays, illegal
enslavement, and public policies regarding land tenure in nineteenth-century Brazil.

Sarah C. Chambers is an associate professor of history at the University of Minnesota. She
is the author of *From Subjects to Citizens: Honor, Gender, and Politics in Arequipa, Peru,*

1780–1854 (1999) and articles on criminal law, domestic violence, and female epistolary in nineteenth-century South America. Her current research focuses on the family, politics, and the state during Chile's struggle for independence from Spain.

Olívia Maria Gomes da Cunha is an associate professor of cultural anthropology at the Universidade Federal do Estado do Rio de Janeiro (UNIRIO). She is the author of *Intenção e gesto: Pessoa, cor e a produção cotidiana da (in)diferença no Rio de Janeiro, 1927–1942* (winner of the 1999 Arquivo Nacional Award, published in 2003) as well as an edited volume with Flávio Gomes, *Quase-Cidadão: histórias e antropologias do pós-emancipação no Brasil* (Editora da Fundação Getúlio Vargas, forthcoming). She is currently working on ethnicity and nationalism in Cuba and Brazil.

Eileen J. Findlay is an associate professor of Latin American history at American University. She has published *Imposing Decency: Sexuality and Race in Puerto Rico, 1870–1920* (Duke University Press, 2000). Both of her current research projects focus on historical memory, social movements, and emigration. The first explores recent Cuban émigrés' memories of the Cuban Revolution. The second analyzes the stories told about the diaspora by Puerto Ricans throughout the twentieth century.

Brodwyn Fischer is an assistant professor of history at Northwestern University. She received her PhD in history from Harvard in 1999, and has since written articles on issues of law, poverty, race, and urban history in Brazil. She is completing work on a book entitled "The Poverty of Rights: Law, Citizenship, and Inequality in Rio de Janeiro, 1930–1964," to be published by Stanford University Press.

Laura Gotkowitz is an assistant professor of history at the University of Iowa. Her work on race and gender in twentieth-century Bolivia has appeared in collections published in Bolivia and the United States. She is the author of the forthcoming book *Within the Boundaries of Equality: Citizenship, Race, and Nation—Bolivia, 1880–1952*.

Keila Grinberg is an assistant professor of history at the Universidade Federal do Estado do Rio de Janeiro (UNIRIO) and the Instituto de Humanidades da Universidade Cândido Mendes (UCAM). She is the author of *Liberata, a lei da ambigüidade: As ações de liberdade da Corte de Apelação do Rio de Janeiro no século XIX* (1994); *O fiador dos brasileiros: Cidadania, escravidão e direito civil no tempo de Antonio Pereira Rebouças* (2002); and *Slavery, Freedom, and the Law in the Atlantic World* (with Sue Peabody; forthcoming, Bedford). She has published a number of articles on slavery, law, and social history in Brazil. Her current research focuses on the practices of reenslavement in nineteenth-century Brazil.

Peter Guardino is an associate professor of history at Indiana University. He is the author of *Peasants, Politics and the Formation of Mexico's National State: Guerrero, 1800–1857* (1996) and *The Time of Liberty: Popular Political Culture in Oaxaca, 1750–1850* (Duke University Press, 2005) as well as a number of articles on nineteenth-century Mexican history. His current research interests focus on the issue of identity during Mexico's 1846–88 war with the United States.

Cristiana Schettini Pereira is a research affiliate of PAGU—Núcleo de Estudos de Gênero at the Universidade Estadual de Campinas (UNICAMP), São Paulo, Brazil; and of the Centro de Estudios Latino americanos of the Universidad Nacional de San Martín, Argentina. Her doctoral dissertation, "Que tenhas teu corpo: Uma história das políticas da prostituição no Rio de Janeiro das primeiras décadas republicanas," won prizes from the Centro de Pesquisa em História Social da Cultura (CECULT-UNICAMP) and the Brazilian National Archive, which will publish it in 2004. She is now studying prostitutes who moved between Rio de Janeiro and Buenos Aires at the end of the nineteenth century, a project supported by a fellowship from the South-South Exchange Program for Research on the History of Development (SEPHIS).

Lara Putnam is an assistant professor of history at the University of Pittsburgh. She is the author of *The Company They Kept: Migrants and the Politics of Gender in Caribbean Costa Rica, 1870–1960* (2002). Her current research explores the lives of migrants' children in and around the Caribbean over the course of the twentieth century, with special attention to the changing roles of labor, sexuality, and education in the transition to adulthood.

nal identification, 295–297, 311; defense of, 148–149, 171–172, 181, 290; documents signifying, 192–193; and employment, 32–33, 36, 147, 191; family, 73, 234–238; and *favela* residents, 189–191; and gender norms, 16–17, 177, 202; and insult suits, 131–135, 145–149, 156–172; and Latin America, 7–19; and law, 27–33, 68–78, 180–183, 278–282, 286; and marital status, 146, 188, 206–207; and men, 169–171; and military service, 32–33, 36–37; modern, 16–19; and patriarchy, 42–44; in Peru, 27–33; and privacy, 40–42; and prostitutes, 164, 278–280, 286; and race, 188; and *rapto* suits, 202, 206–208, 210–211; and sexual control of women, 1, 4, 157, 259–261; and sexual virtue, 34, 131, 168, 171, 182; and slander suits, 177–196; and virginity, 202, 204–211, 226–227; and women, 167, 183–188, 278–282, 296–297

Honorable citizenship, 12; in Bolivia, 71–73, 79; in Brazil, 109, 179–180, 192–196; of indigenous peoples, 71, 76–80; and infamy, 79; and men, 29–33, 40–42; and morality, 30; and patriarchy, 41; in Peru, 28–37, 41–44; and public sphere, 30–33; and recognition by law enforcement, 299; and sexual virtue, 34; and sexuality, 262–263; and women, 10, 29–40, 43–44, 71, 74

Honorina, 301–305, 311. *See also* Elza

Hungria, Nelson, 223–227, 239, 241

Hurtado, Miguel, 257–259, 261

Iaiá Garcia, 96, 100

Icarahy, Eugénie Juliette Carneiro Leão de Barros de, 183–185

"Ideas of a Canary," 9, 19, 87–94

Identity. *See* Citizenship

Illegitimate children, and infamy, 74–75

India, and insult suits, 139–140, 142–143

Indigenous communities: birthright in, 8, 52–53, 57–59, 62; cargo system in, 7, 50–63; community service in, 54–55, 59, 62–63; custom and liberal law in, 50–51, 56–63; legal systems of, 52; and patriarchy, 52–53; riots in, 55; women's role in, 54–55

Indigenous peoples, and legal status, 71, 75–80

Infamy, 70, 73; and citizenship, 71–73, 79; and illegitimate children, 74–75; as punishment, 70; and women, 74–75

Injurias (insults), 39, 150

Insult suits, 11, 12, 131–135, 143–144, 156; and *alcahuetas*, 142–145; in Bolivia, 131–149, 150; in Brazilian legal code, 182; and *cabrão*, 190; and cantina owners, 163; and *chola*, 135, 139–143, 149; and class formation, 132–135, 139–140, 148–149; in Costa Rica, 156–172; as defense of honor, 148–149, 171–172; elites and, 168–169; and honor, 131–135, 145–149, 156–172; and *india*, 139–140, 142–143; and men, 157, 159–160, 170–171; and migrant workers, 144, 156–157; and national origin of participants, 157–158, 162; between neighbors, 161–162, 186; and prostitutes, 164, 190; and public space, 168; and racial slurs, 132–135, 139–140, 142; and sexual virtue, 132–134, 139–149, 156–159; and sexuality, 142–145; and slanging

Library of Congress Cataloging-in-Publication Data
Honor, status, and law in modern Latin America / edited by
Sueann Caulfield, Sarah C. Chambers, and Lara Putnam.
p. cm.
Includes bibliographical references and index.
ISBN 0-8223-3575-1 (cloth : alk. paper)
ISBN 0-8223-3587-5 (pbk. : alk. paper)
1. Law—Social aspects—Latin America. 2. Social status—Latin
America. 3. Honor—Latin America. I. Caulfield, Sueann.
II. Chambers, Sarah C. III. Putnam, Lara.
KG99.H66 2005
340'.115'098—dc22   2004029836